PANGS OF PARTITION

PANGS OF PARTITION

VOLUME II

The Human Dimension

Edited by

S. SETTAR
INDIRA BAPTISTA GUPTA

INDIAN COUNCIL OF HISTORICAL RESEARCH

MANOHAR
2002

First published 2002

ISBN 81-7304-305-1 (Set)
ISBN 81-7304-307-8 (Vol. II)

Published by
Ajay Kumar Jain for
Manohar Publishers & Distributors
4753/23 Ansari Road, Daryaganj
New Delhi 110002

Typeset by
A J Software Publishing Co. Pvt. Ltd.
New Delhi 110005

Printed at
Lordson Publishers Pvt. Ltd.
Delhi 110007

Contents

Introduction

The Partition of India is a much debated issue in the history of South Asia. One will never know exactly how many people died in the riots which accompanied it, but around seventeen million people had to relocate themselves across the newly drawn boundaries. The magnitude of such an uprootment is unprecedented in recorded history. In 1997, fifty years after the event, the Indian Council of Historical Research felt that it was time to review some of the established theories concerning Partition, focus attention on a wide array of individual and collective experiences of migration, trauma and the intense nostalgia of the displaced for the undivided past. The result was the present collection of essays representing various disciplines and showing the multiple strands of the historical evidence available on Partition.

The factors which led to Partition apart, the roles of individual leaders (and parties) who by their acts of omission and commission made it a *fait accompli*, have been discussed extensively. It is common knowledge that this complex issue has been made somewhat more complicated by the conflicting approaches of historians. At least three familiar pictures are before us: the imperialist (British); the Pakistani (Muslim); and the Indian (Hindu). However, some common issues have been raised by all these three advocates, such as: What led to Partition? Could it have been avoided? What is the share of the colonial power (divide and rule), India (Hindu domination and Congress authoritarianism) and Pakistan (Jinnah's intransigence and Muslim separatism)? Besides these, the role of individual leaders, 'accidental' factors and 'chances' that came by and other such issues, have also engaged all of them.

The imperialists regarded Partition as a natural consequence of the communal divide, the history of which could be taken back either to the Arab invasion of Sind or to the annexation of the Punjab by Mahmud Ghazni; what Indians and Pakistanis got in 1947 was only a generous hand out from them—a mere transfer of power. To the Indians and Pakistanis, on the other hand, independence was a hard won fruit, an outcome of a long and bitter struggle involving prolonged suffering and painful sacrifice. Perhaps, here ends the agreement between the two—they part ways to reiterate their individual compulsions and convictions to justify, condone and also to question the necessity of Partition as well as its consequences.

To a section of Muslims, partitioning the country was the only way out, if they were to escape the grip of the Hindu majority. They needed nothing less than 'double deliverance'—from the majority Hindus and from colonial authorities. To the majority of Indians (were they only Hindus?), the fears of the Muslims were unfounded. They held that the millennium old history of coexistence bears a testimony to this, and if there were occasional frictions between Hindus and Muslims, they were no different from frictions found in the history of any two communities or any two sects. The question of Muslim integration was never in doubt, for Indian culture was never claimed to have been created by Hindus alone. Also the Muslim share either in the national movement or in the National Congress was never questioned. In any case, the fear of the Muslims was proved unfounded in the end as a substantial section of this community found a secure home in India and are thriving as freely as any other community in independent India.

The present two volumes are organized on the principle of a certain complementarity. If the first volume, *Parting of Ways: History, Politics, Economics* can be termed to be a historian's history, the second, *Human Dimension: Culture, Society, Literature*, is a people's history. If the first maps the grand narrative of Partition with new perspectives on contemporary events and the leaders who played a prominent part in them, the second listens to the marginal voices and focuses on the popular culture of the period. If the first volume takes a scholarly view of the complex interplay of historical events during the closing years of the British Raj, the second takes off from where the first ends and reconstructs, with equal profundity, a microscopic view of the fall-out of Partition. Both volumes, however, supplement and sustain each other and offer an exciting range of discussion.

The seventeen papers, which constitute Volume I, deal with some familiar and some not so familiar problems. With a fresh perspective and new sources, they add, alter, strengthen and modify the prevalent arguments. The imperialist stand is questioned and reviewed by Bishwa Mohan Pandey. This issue also surfaces in some other papers. Lal Bahadur Varma, for example, reminds us of the two divergent approaches to Partition and of its impact on the writings of history books in India as well as in Pakistan. Partha Sarathi Gupta highlights the importance of documents as a corrective to stereotyped accounts.

The major concerns of about half a dozen papers relate to the role of personalities. V.N. Datta examines the acrimonious controversy surrounding the role of Lord Mountbatten in the Radcliffe Award, in the backdrop of the working of the Boundary Commission, the claims of political parties, and the Radcliffe Award itself. B.R. Nanda brings to light Gandhi's deep concern for the restoration of peace during the winter months of 1946-7, when the recrudescence of violence spread across the country. Gandhi remarked in June 1947: 'I find myself all alone.... Everybody is today impatient for independence. Therefore there is no alternative.' Chittabrata Palit goes into the positive aspects of Gandhi's satyagraha, his efforts to reconcile the warring communities and his final stand on Partition. When independence came, he reminds us, Gandhi was a broken man. 'Leave me alone to shed my tears', was all that he asked for.

Sucheta Mahajan goes into various aspects of the national movement and points out how it succeeded in building up a national consciousness sufficient to wrest independence and how the Congress party failed to keep the country united. Khwaja A. Khalique feels that the 'demand for Pakistan made in 1940 was a logical culmination of a long standing communal divide'.

Crucial contemporary issues, such as the role of the Constituent Assembly of India and the coalition politics in UP during 1937, which precipitated Partition, are discussed at length by S.K. Chaube and Salil Mishra. Kanchanmoy Mojumdar goes into the majority-minority syndrome and the widening of the Hindu-Muslim divide which was exploited by the local elements to their advantage in CP and Berar. The complex scenario in the North-West Frontier Province and the events that led to the worsening of the communal situation are brought out boldly by Parshotam Mehra. The happenings in the Oriya princely states, the role of some prominent tribal leaders and tribal politics in Central India as well as the North East, the role of the Akalis in Punjab, are the other issues which have engaged the attention of Jayanta Sengupta, K.S. Singh and Bir Good Gill, respectively.

The two papers of Dwijendra Tripathi and Shri Prakash take us to the politics of economics. The role and reactions of the capitalist class, both Hindu and Muslim, in the backdrop of contemporary political developments are analysed by Tripathi. The irrationality underlying the division of the country and the economic hardships it caused, both to India and Pakistan, are outlined by Shri Prakash.

The twenty-three contributions that constitute Volume II dwell on the consequences of Partition, captured by creative writers from non-conventional sources, but professional historians are not completely excluded from it. These papers fall broadly into four groups: personal reminiscences; recollections by contemporaries; impressions mirrored in creative literature; and events and incidents which inspired the visual media (in particular, films and paintings), narratives and popular culture. The rich mosaic of material spread out before us, should add a new dimension to our understanding of the saga and supplement our knowledge of it derived from archival sources. Personal narratives expose and enrich the hidden currents of history. Though an act of remembrance is always piecemeal, such bits and pieces could be effectively used to knit an interesting quilt of varied memories and emotions. Creative writers, poets and artists, who experienced Partition either personally or through others, have articulated with greater sensitivity, and have captured the multi-dimensionality of human suffering more realistically than some of the conventional historians. They do not get obsessed with the specifics of causes and results, they do not attempt at quantifying evidence, they do not believe it necessary to decorate their statements with quotes and notes, but the kind of stark reality that emerges from their works is hard to come by in conventional historical accounts.

Volume II begins with an essay by Krishna Kumar on the portrayal of Partition in school books of India and Pakistan. He observes that writers of both countries broadly share the state sponsored ideological biases in representing the events, which are then imprinted on young minds. R.K. Agnihotri doubts whether this 'Partition' could be regarded as final or complete, because unlike a mass of land an integrated psyche, characteristic of the northern parts of the subcontinent from the times of the Bhaktikal, cannot be fully or permanently fractured. As one of the victims of Partition who suffered the demographic dislocation Satish Gujral recalls, without any trace of malice or rancour, some significant moments from his experiences and traces the impact of riots, murder, brutality, indignity, abduction, rape and dislocation suffered by the innocent during and after Partition.

Three papers introduce us to different genres of creativity that deal with Partition. Though Partition does not form the main theme of Ritwick Ghatak's films, Partha Chatterjee finds its recurrent presence as a riveting memory image of that cataclysmic event. Badri Narain Tiwari discovers its multiple strands in the *nach* drama, folk songs and proverbs of the

Bhojpuri region. Keshav Malik shows how Satish Gujral, the painter, handled the difficult and painful subject of Partition with conviction.

Bhisham Sahni, one of the most notable creative writers on Partition, has revealed his childhood experiences to Alok Bhalla. His recollections of the social milieu of the pre-Partition days, emphasize the harmony in which the religious affairs of different communities could be conducted in an atmosphere of tolerance. Reviewing the life, literature and politics of the two countries, Mrinal Pande observes that neither of them has recovered fully from the deep hurt suffered during Partition. Urvashi Butalia and Monmayee Basu, both from refugee families, draw from women and their experiences to weave moving tapestries of violence and indignity suffered by them. They explore history through the memories of the unknown and the anonymous to emphasize the rich benefits of placing the oral alongside the conventional evidence.

In the backdrop of a spate of literary activities in Punjab, K.S. Duggal situates himself amidst other creative writers to show how Partition was handled with commanding resilience and sensitivity by them. A recurring sentiment noticed by him is the wistful longing of the uprooted Punjabi to revisit his home and play fields. In what has been published in newspapers, magazines and journals during the fiftieth year of independence, Mushirul Hasan detects a common refrain, both in popular as well as in scholarly writings, that Partition was a colossal tragedy brought about by hot-headed and cynical politicians, who failed to grasp the implications of the division made along religious lines. Yet, he asserts, it is still possible for the people rather than the governments to make sense of the poignant writings of creative writers and poets. Nandi Bhatia also points out how literary works store the collective consciousness of the people and provide alternative sources of history. These 'marginal' experiences, though an intrinsic part of the Partition saga, would remain outside our reach, if the historian were to stick only to the official records.

Though Partition does not figure as the main theme in the plays and stories of Sharadindu Bandopadhyaya, Anindita Mukhopadhyay sees it as a grim backdrop in at least five of his stories. Sukrita Paul Kumar highlights the effective manner in which short stories captured the poignant moments of the Partition drama. Sadaat Hasan Manto's unique technique of telling stories has received wide acclaim. He mirrors what he sees. He does not attempt to seek solutions. Critically examining the English translations of some of his work by Khalid Hasan, Alok Bhalla sees several of these unique qualities sacrificed and he also raises some questions relating to the ethics of a translator.

An interesting aspect of Bengali literature is its total indifference to Partition, as virtually no short stories or novels of significance dealt with it. However, in contrast to this, its poetry was overwhelmingly preoccupied with this event. Total absence of it in one genre of literature and its dominant presence in another have confounded the historians of Bengali literature. Tapati Chakravarty makes an attempt to unravel this paradox. Holding Attia Hosain's novel *Sunlight on a Broken Column*, an 'aesthetically satisfying' work which 'presents the tragedy of partition with great objectivity', Naresh Jain highlights the changing Muslim attitude captured in this novel through the consciousness of a young Muslim girl of a *taluqdari* family, during the tumultuous decades of the 1930s and 1940s. Ameena K. Ansari takes up the tragic tale of Munshi Chitram or Dauji, a Hindu conversant with the Muslim idiom and a dedicated scholar of Persian. He refuses to give up his ancestral home in Pakistan and thus becomes a stranger, a 'metaphorical outsider', who faces the harsh realities of Partition in his own hometown.

Jayanti Chattopadhyay picks up two plays written and staged in the first decade after Partition and draws attention to the problems faced by the playwrights. Presenting pictures of Partition from different perspectives is Alok Bhalla's stories collected in three volumes. M. Asaduddin puts these volumes under scrutiny to show how these stories provide us with competing versions of truth and multiple points of view that lead to a richer and a more nuanced understanding of Partition. Kamlesh Mohan deals with a story that is based on a real incident of a mother looking for her lost son and in the process experiences the gory and dehumanizing conditions of a refugee camp. Taking up Khushwant Singh's *Train to Pakistan*, Shikoh Mohsin Mirza exposes the event that led to the transformation of a sleepy village 'into a cauldron of conflicting loyalties' on one August night of 1947, when a train load of massacred men, women and children arrives in the village.

Preparation of these two volumes was a great experience for both of us. What little we have achieved in these two volumes was made possible only by the cooperation of the contributors. Some of them sympathetically considered our suggestions and met our requirements unstinctingly, others infused fresh insights into our project to enhance its importance. We are grateful to all of them. We are beholden to Mrs Nirmala Parashar for allowing us to look into the portfolio of S.L. Parashar (1904-90) and borrow his sketches for the jacket design. Our appreciation to the publishers for the immense pain they have taken and for the patience they have shown in producing these volumes. We thank the authorities of the ICHR for encouraging this venture.

Needless to say the views expressed in these volumes are those of the contributors and not of either the editors or the ICHR.

4 February 2000

S. Settar
Indira Baptista Gupta

Partition in School Textbooks: A Comparative Look at India and Pakistan

KRISHNA KUMAR

On 15 August 1947 India became independent. Unfortunately, the victory of the glorious struggle of the Indian people for independence was tainted by ugly happenings immediately before and after the achievement of independence. Millions lost their homes, several thousand persons were killed.

The Story of Civilization, Vol. II, *History Textbook for Class X*, by Arjun Dev (NCERT, New Delhi), p. 163

After the establishment of Pakistan, the entire subcontinent was engulfed in the communal riots. The riots were widespread in Punjab, Delhi, Bengal and Bihar in which 15 lacs people were murdered, 50 thousand women were abducted and more than one crore people had to migrate.

Pakistan Studies for Secondary Classes (IX-X), by H.A. Rizvi, J. Iqbal, G.A. Khan and Q. Abbas (Punjab Textbook Board, Lahore), p. 46

This essay makes a brief attempt to examine the treatment given to Partition in school textbooks of history used in India and Pakistan. Far from being an exhaustive study, the essay aims at identifying and interpreting certain prominent tendencies that characterize the portrayal of Partition in school textbooks of the two countries. The essay is divided into three parts. The first section presents certain theoretical issues and a discussion of certain common characteristics of the systems of education in India and Pakistan, which have a bearing on the teaching of history at school. Following this somewhat theoretical discussion, the essay proceeds to note in the second section the major differences and commonalities identifiable in the portrayal of Partition in the school history textbooks of the two countries.

* This essay is based on the author's ongoing study on the portrayal of the freedom struggle in school textbooks in India and Pakistan for which he has been awarded the Jawaharlal Nehru Fellowship.

An attempt to explain these characteristics comprises the third, concluding part of the essay.

I

School textbooks of history represent a genre of history which, despite its individuality and importance, hardly ever get scholarly attention. Neither Carr nor Collingwood[1] discuss the peculiar problems that the writing of history for a school textbook presents. The recent book by Evans, which presents an elaborate defence of history as a discipline against the assaults of post-modernist critics, makes no mention of the historian-child relationship implicit in textbook writing even though some of the problems arising from this relationship are similar to the ones raised by certain post-modernist critics.[2] These problems have to do with the difficulties inherent in sharing evidence with an audience which is generally assumed, on account of age, to be intellectually incapable of making sense of the historical method. Children's lack of intellectual maturity empowers school historians to omit from their accounts any indication of the basis on which a claim or interpretation has been made, and also of how—that is, by what methodological procedures—the account derives its claim to certainty. School texts of history, thus, take on the character of an authoritative story, totally undisturbed by acknowledgement of uncertainty or doubt, conflict of opinion or difficulty of judgement on account of inadequacy of evidence.[3]

This character of school textbooks of history contrasts sharply with the character of school textbooks of other subjects. Textbooks of science, for instance, may not always meet the explicit norm of arousing curiosity or the desire to conduct an experiment, but they do, as a matter of routine, cite an experiment as a basis for the point being made. Language texts actively ask the child-reader to think what an author or poet might have meant and how that intended meaning gets conveyed. Other subjects, too, have certain inbuilt features which allow, even in a system of education not known for its child-centred character, the young readers to negotiate their relationship with the text, so that they can establish the text's credibility or truth-value within the parameters of a discipline, which they are supposed to learn. School history stands alone in this respect inasmuch as it does not exhibit any expectation that the child-reader of history should learn something *about* the discipline of history and not just about its product—that is, the historical account given in the textbook. Indeed, we can say that the verb *learn*, when it is applied to history, as it does in the previous sentences, takes on a meaning peculiar to history as a school subject. It means becoming familiar with history, that is, its narration, without developing any tools of learning, which the term *learning* implies, at least in rudimentary ways, in every other subject.

This peculiarity of history as a school subject and of history textbooks, gets magnified by a dominant and common characteristic of the system of education both in India and Pakistan. On account of a set of factors related to the colonial legacy, which cannot be discussed here in detail without causing serious digression,[4] the system of education in both India and Pakistan is deeply influenced by a 'textbook culture'. Briefly, this culture is characterized by a policy of 'prescribing' a textbook, as opposed to 'recommending' it, and by several pedagogical features arising out of this policy. One of these features is that the text assumes an incontrovertible authority, as contrasted with a functional value, as a tool for teaching. The text becomes symbolic of an authorized version of the subject matter; the authorizing power being, of course, the state officials and other relevant state functionaries who prepare, publish or select the textbook. In history, as we can easily imagine, the authorized version means an officially approved representation of the past.

It is possible to argue, as Rennie does, that all modern nations 'use history to build a sense of national identity by structuring an image of a common past'.[5] School textbooks in every country, we can indeed say, present perceptions of the past which resonate, if not always directly reflect, the view generally accepted by the state. British textbooks which might record the plundering of British colonies are non-existent. American textbooks documenting the destruction of native Indian tribes are rare.[6] However, in systems of education such as the British and the American, the possibility exists, at least in principle, that a teacher might use a variety of resources to permit children to learn about the fate of colonized or native people.[7] The 'textbook culture' of colonial educational systems, such as those prevailing in India and Pakistan, leaves no room for the use of resources other than the prescribed textbook. Indeed, there may be a social consensus that teacher-autonomy in this matter could be misused. Daily teaching as well as the final examination are based on the single prescribed textbook, hence the truth-value attached to the narration it contains is beyond contestation, at least by the teacher.

Together, the 'textbook culture' and the peculiar nature of history as a school subject, discussed above, have decisively influenced the major characteristics of textbook writing in history in India and Pakistan. One characteristic is that textbook writing is perceived in both countries as a politically significant activity. In fact, history textbooks have occupied centre-stage among the different kinds of hegemonic contests for which education, as a social institution, provides room and facility.[8] Another characteristic is that textbooks in both countries are uniformly narrative in style, offering no space for an argumentative treatment arising from an acknowledgement of contending perspectives on an event. Also, the narrative remains continuously sketchy, tied up as it is with specific names, dates and places, and emphatically indifferent towards details of a less certain or less specific character. For reasons we will presently notice, the sketchy nature of the narrative is more glaring in Pakistani textbooks than in their Indian counterparts.

In both India and Pakistan, policy makers of the period following independence recommended the amalgamation of history into a new, interdisciplinary subject, named 'social studies'. This amalgamation was recommended as a step towards modernization.[9] It entailed a rational reorganization of history, geography and civics into an interdisciplinary body of knowledge. The decision was implemented in a half-hearted manner by nominally clubbing the three subjects under one textbook cover, showing no interconnections or reorganization. The clubbing did, however, reduce the number of pages in which the syllabus of each subject could be treated, so that the overall size of the textbook would not become unduly large. Thus, the inclusion of history in social studies forced the writers to be as sketchy as possible, a tendency which already existed but now got worse, especially because the syllabus did not get any briefer. In Pakistan, social studies was further transformed into 'Pakistan Studies' under the imperative to use education as a means to socialize the young into state ideology.[10] In this new incarnation, history became even less important as a subject of study, sharing the highly limited space of a textbook with not just geography and civics, but also with a descriptive knowledge of Pakistan's ideology, its international relations and its place among Muslim countries.

It should now be self-evident that the school textbooks used for the teaching of history in both India and Pakistan have rather limited space for *any* single topic, even if that topic is as significant as Partition. It is just another topic to be covered in the general narrative of the freedom struggle, which figures generally in the textbooks prescribed for grades VIII and X.[11] The mode of coverage is a seriatim of the major events that led to Partition. These major events are quite differently chosen in the two countries, and their number in Pakistani books is far smaller. The treatment given to these events, although brief and superficial in both countries, is contrastingly different in terms of perspective, tone and judgement.[12]

II

The most obvious difference between the textbooks of India and Pakistan in their portrayal of Partition is that for Indian textbook writers Partition marks a tragedy, both human and political, which India had to suffer in her moment of freedom, while for the Pakistani writer Partition is synonymous with freedom, denoting birth and success. Although the text writers of both countries portray Partition as the 'price' of freedom, the price is interpreted differently. In the Indian texts Partition is presented as the only option, that was available to the Congress leaders, for achieving their goal of independence under the circumstances prevailing in mid-1947. In Pakistani texts, the price associated with Partition is cited as the 'unjust' handing over of certain parts of the erstwhile united India to the new India rather than to Pakistan. The human suffering associated with Partition is mentioned in both sets of texts, but merely as a matter of secondary importance. The fundamental difference noted above, distinguishing the Indian text writer's view of Partition as a sad episode marring the joy of freedom from the Pakistani text writer's view that Partition was a great achievement, pervades the knowledge and the awareness that the textbooks attempt, or at least intend, to impart to their young readers.

We are looking at two separate orbits of knowledge and awareness, drawn out of a single body of data. Perhaps this is unnecessary tautology, given the fact that the Partition of India and Pakistan was brought about by, and indeed constituted, a situation in which the two major contending participants claimed to perceive mutually exclusive scenarios. The demand for the Partition was based on the two-nation theory of the Muslim League, which the Congress perceived to be a false theory. The post-independence courses of history that the two countries have followed can be legitimately seen as a symbolic extension of the original difference of perception. This longer view of history would also render the opening sentence of this paragraph tautological. However, tautology is a minor risk quite worthy of being undertaken when the awareness we are talking about is crucially linked with the hostile relationship between the two countries. Indeed, the two orbits of awareness, which Indian and Pakistan textbooks draw out of a single body of historical data, provide fine and rather startling evidence of a perfect symmetry in the role of education, in general, and the role of history teaching, in particular, in the two countries.

Let us look at this symmetry a little closely. In both India and Pakistan, curriculum policy has evolved within the larger framework of 'nation building', a concept highly relevant to the post-colonial nations of the Third World. In the context of educational and, particularly, curricular policy, the term nation building stands for the ideological foundations of the nation state. For reasons not very difficult to probe, these foundations have been rather more visible in Pakistan than in India. It may be valid to argue that India does not have an explicitly ideological state in the sense in which it is there in Pakistan. Such an argument must depend heavily on the differentiation we might concede in the meanings of the term 'ideology'. We may regard nation building as a programme of socialization or initiation into a set of political values, and not necessarily an organized ideology. In Indian textbooks, nation building has meant belief in 'secularism'—a rather flabby concept in itself, often used as a nominalist instrument—as a value-perspective to design the narrative of the freedom struggle, especially its final phase in which the 'secular' and the 'communal' strategies of public mobilizations are said to have come face to face with each other. From this perspective, the birth of Pakistan implied a denial of secularism by those who demanded Pakistan and those who encouraged and assisted the demand by their allegedly manipulative tactics. In Pakistani textbooks, on the other hand, it is the two-nation theory which supplies the nation-building perspective for shaping the narrative of freedom. From this perspective, free India was a Hindu state even if a substantial part of its population was Muslim. It is customary to call Pakistani school historiography ideological in a derisive sense of the term, which connotes deliberate misrepresentation to suit a purpose. The use of a secular perspective, by the same token, is treated as a guarantee for objectivity.

It is useful to ask why, despite such a contrast in perspective, both Indian and Pakistani textbooks treat Partition so cursorily and briefly. Typically, the trauma of uprootment and the violence suffered by millions of people is mentioned in a few lines exemplified by the quotations used as epigrams at the start of this essay. These lines refer to the riots as 'ugly' and 'communal', and leave it at that. Both Indian and Pakistani authors use such adjectives to label the riots apparently implying that the riots were a setback to the 'nation' that was coming into being in the two countries. What the riots meant to the people who lived through them is not even brought to the attention of the young reader, let alone delineated or discussed in any detail. Displacement, violence and resettlement remain unelaborated words. Gandhi's assassination receives equally short and superficial mention, opening up no possibility of reflection on its larger context.[13] In Pakistani texts, even this nominal mention is denied to Gandhi. In some Pakistani textbooks of freedom, Partition is transmuted into an occasion of celebration so completely that violent riots get no acknowledgement whatsoever. In the ones where the riots are mentioned, it is pointed out that Muslims reacted to Hindu attacks.

III

For a plausible explanation of this cursory treatment of Partition in both Indian and Pakistani textbooks, we can look in three directions. The first is the direction leading to considerations of a technical or pedagogical nature. One can justify the extreme brevity of the reference to Partition by saying, for example, that Partition is merely one of the hundreds of events that have to be covered in the narrative of India's history from ancient times to independence in classes VI to VIII, or again in class IX and X, or yet again, this time for those who choose to study history as an elective subject, in classes XI and XII. Unless history as a school subject is conceptualized differently, allowing for prioritization of events for an in-depth discussion, this technical ground for justifying a cursory treatment of Partition will continue to have some validity. Another ground of a similar kind relates to assumptions about children's capacity to learn. School historians are not always known to have formal knowledge of educational psychology, yet a generalized impression of how much detail children can cope with seems common among historians who write school textbooks. The perception implicit in Indian textbooks is that children cannot enjoy and comprehend deep or sustained analysis of any single event. Such a perception does not deter writers like Arjun Dev or Bipan Chandra[14] from stuffing their history textbooks with 'facts', with a density as high as ten facts in one paragraph, nor from using long winding sentences; but it seems to suffice as a ground for avoiding details on matters like the violence associated with Partition or the causes of Gandhi's assassination. The Pakistani school historian can as well be said to have a similar case, indeed a stronger case, along this direction. The 'happy' aspect of Partition—the fact that it gave Pakistan its birth—is so supremely important, the Pakistani school historian seems to imply, that its juxtaposition with the tragic aspects of Partition will make the discussion too confusing to be comprehended by young readers.

A second direction leads to the recognition of the intellectual constraints or compulsions, which impel both Indian and Pakistani historians to dispose of Partition as a topic with a brief mention. For remarkably similar reasons, we would say if we adopted this hypothesis, that both Indian and Pakistani historians wish to sanitize the narrative of the freedom struggle by avoiding a detailed discussion of the traumatic incidents that marked Partition. A major rationale for such avoidance might be the desire to preserve the celebratory character of independence. Elaborate enquiry into the politics of Partition and the massacre could mar, in the Indian case, the stature of at least some of the leaders of the nationalist struggle in its final phase. School historians typically delineate this final phase of the struggle as a time of vicious manipulation by the British and Muslim communalists. The mid-1940s get projected in nearly all school histories used in India, including the much-celebrated NCERT series, as a period when the horses of nationalism suddenly lost both the drive and direction, which they had supposedly maintained since the 1920s. A cursory mention of the Partition riots helps to keep Partition in the series of manipulative steps taken by the British to keep India subjugated. It also helps to maintain the theory that Partition was mainly caused by the obstinate and manoeuvring style of Jinnah, that it was not necessarily an outcome of the socio-political conditions, which had been gathering momentum for a considerable length of time, quite visibly since the 1920s. If Partition were to be portrayed from the perspective of socio-political conditions leading to it, the purposiveness associated with history teaching at school would have to be defined quite liberally. And any liberalization of the goals of history-teaching at school would pose a considerable threat to the pantheon, as well as the canon, of the freedom struggle assiduously composed since the 1960s. For one thing, the ideology of Hindu majoritarianism will have to receive a much deeper scrutiny than it does at present, even at the hands of avowedly Leftist historians.

In the Pakistani case, an elaborate discussion of the Partition could be seen as involving the serious risk of arousing doubts about the validity of the idea of Pakistan itself, particularly the idea of Pakistan as a nation, which was unjustly treated at the time of its birth and which remains perpetually hostile to India. The huge migration of people, which took place as a result of Partition, was necessitated by the specific nature of the demand for Pakistan and by the geography that the carving out of the new nation implied. Portrayal of Partition-related events at any length could well mean the possibility of young students and their teachers feeling impelled to probe the rationality of the two-nation theory, which gave birth to the idea of Pakistan. Even though such probing would be addressed to decisions made long ago and to leaders long dead, it would hardly be consistent with the policy of using education to transmit a tailored picture of the past and the present. Far easier and more consistent with this policy is to treat the token teaching of history as an opportunity to tell a one-sided story, malign India and to socialize the young into an inheritance of rancour.

A third direction for seeking an explanation for the evasive portrayal of Partition in school history can be traced along the line inherent in recent post-modernist criticism of history as a discipline.[15] The criticism is that history, in its present construction as a discipline, is poorly equipped to represent the horror of events like the holocaust. Following this line, Pandey[16] has questioned the ability of Indian historians to do justice to the violence and suffering inherent in several incidents and processes of modern India's past. The language available to the historian and the discourse in which historiography functions, do not permit the experience of ordinary people, who live through traumatic events like Partition, to be recognized Pandey argues. This is why, he feels, recent history writing appears 'singularly uninterested' in exploring the meaning of Partition for those who lived through it. Following this line of reasoning, we can say that if history as a discipline is so poorly equipped to deal with violence and suffering, school textbooks of history, which are required to be sketchy on account of the manner in which the history curriculum is conceptualized, can only make things worse. Pandey's concern is with the general problems of history as an area of knowledge, and with how it is presently constituted, particularly in contrast to literature. His critique of historiography raises interesting issues for those of us who may be especially worried about the quality of history writing for the young. For one thing, it presents a case for the introduction of literature as a source of support material for the study of history in schools. It also suggests that designers of the school history curriculum need not feel that they must work within the sacred, untouchable parameters set by the discipline of history. Some measure of freedom among future curriculum designers may be necessary to transcend the constraints imposed by the discipline on the portrayal of events, like the Partition of India and Pakistan.

Before we close this essay, it may be useful to consider an argument one often hears in favour of avoiding conflict-ridden topics. The argument is that events of a complicated, conflict-ridden nature are best avoided or dealt with briefly, because justice cannot be done to them in the limited space available in a school textbook written for young readers. Implying this compulsion, the class VIII textbook of the Eklavya series—rightly appreciated for its generally imaginative rendering of history—says after a brief write-up on the events leading to the Partition: 'Why and how India's Partition occurred is a tragic and difficult story which you will study in later classes' (translation from Hindi is mine).[17] The quote used at the beginning of this essay also illustrate the school historian's remarkable attempt to compress the enormity of an incident like the Partition in two or three sentences! Can it be that the school historian does not have the freedom, apart from the space, to explore and unravel a complex event like the Partition in an objective manner? Ideological compulsions are one constraint; the balance of political forces at the time of writing is another. These constraints need to be looked at separately in the cases of Pakistan and India.

It may be argued that following the dismemberment of Pakistan in 1971, its rulers confronted the crisis of national identity by phasing out history from the school curriculum. History and identity are deeply related; having suffered a serious injury in its post-1947 self-image, Pakistan tried to forge a new one by crafting a new history—an adjunct of 'Pakistan Studies'—for its children. This new history was designed to be simplistic, even false, because it was meant to serve as an instrument for overcoming a political and emotional crisis, not merely as a portrait of Pakistan's heritage. Minimizing the trauma of Partition was a part of this design.

The Indian case is apparently more complex. All school histories, including the NCERT series, were designed to contribute to the nation building agenda of the early decades of independence. Nation building implied the construction of a pantheon and a canon, both of which demand a considerable degree of simplification and design. Partition was a particularly difficult topic to handle in the context of nation building because it provided a brutal proof of the Hindu-Muslim conflict, which the system of education—a major instrument of nation building—was not supposed to recognize as a historical reality. The canon of nation building continues to deem any acknowledgement of Hindu-Muslim conflict as a symptom of communalism even if such an acknowledgement may be required for a scientific, and in that sense secular, study of society and its history. The school historian, in his role as a nation builder, is required to treat in a furtive manner any event that can be seen as a consequence of Hindu-Muslim conflict. The riots that followed the Partition or the assassination of Mahatma Gandhi are two such events. Phrases like 'millions lost their homes' and 'several thousand persons were killed' (which is not true; the number of people killed was in lakhs, not thousands) are the necessary shorthand in which the horror suffered by ordinary men and women has to be covered for the desirable development of the young generation's collective personality. Fifty years after independence, when the nation has hopefully been built, there is every reason to question the validity of a pantheon, which has no room for ordinary men and women. True, the battle of secularism has not been won yet but that news itself should inspire us to question the ethical and intellectual appropriateness of a mode of school historiography, which is based on rather inadequate, if not obsolete, concepts of curriculum, teaching and psychological development of the young.

NOTES

1. E.H. Carr, *What is History*? (London, 1961); and R.G. Collingwood, *The Idea of History* (Oxford, 1946).
2. R.J. Evans, *In Defence of History* (London, 1997).
3. This may not be necessarily true of all countries, but as a general statement it indicates a universal trend. See Ruth Rennie, 'History as Policy Making', in *International Social Science Journal*, Vol. CLVI (1998), pp. 289-301; also see idem, 'Nations and their Past: the Uses and Abuses of History', *The Economist* (21 December 1996), pp. 73-6.
4. Krishna Kumar, 'Origins of India's Textbook Culture', in idem, *What is Worth Teaching?* (Hyderabad, 1992).
5. Rennie, 'History as Policy Making', op.cit.
6. Idem, 'Nations and their Past', op.cit.
7. This autonomy has come under some pressure under the recent reforms brought about as part of the 'national curriculum' policy.
8. See *Seminar*, Vol. CD (1992), on 'Education and Ideology' for the debate in India, and A. Khan, ed., *Islam, Politics and the State* (London, 1985) for the debate in Pakistan. Also see Ayesha Jalal, 'Conjuring Pakistan: History as Official Imagining', in *International Journal of Middle East Studies*, Vol. XXVII (1995), pp. 73-89.
9. For the ups and downs faced by the idea of 'social studies' in India, see V.K. Raina and H. Dhand, 'History and History Teaching in a Third World Country', in V. D'Oyley, A. Blunt and R. Barnhardt, eds, *Education and Development* (Calgary, 1994). For the background on Pakistan in this context, see K.K. Aziz, *The Murder of History* (Lahore, 1992).
10. For a discussion justifying the ideological role of textbooks in the context of 'Pakistan Studies', see I.H. Qureshi, *Miraj to Domes* (Karachi, 1986).
11. In Pakistani textbooks, the narrative appears in other classes too, in varying lengths.
12. See A. Powell, 'Perceptions of the South Asian Past : Ideology, Nationalism and School History Textbooks', in N. Crook, ed., *The Transmission of Knowledge in South Asia* (Delhi, 1996), pp. 190-228. Another comparative essay on this subject is N.C. Beheras, 'Perpetuating the Divide: Political Abuse of History in South Asia', in *Contemporary South Asia*, Vol. V, No. 2 (1996), pp. 191-205.
13. See Krishna Kumar, *Learning from Conflict* (Hyderabad, 1996), for an analysis of the treatment given to Gandhi's assassination in an NCERT textbook.
14. These are the authors of, respectively, *The Story of Civilization* (Vol. II covers the

Indian freedom struggle) and *Modern India,* published by NCERT for classes X and XII.

15. For a compendium of recent debates on the nature of history, covering the post-modernist criticisms of history as a discipline, see B. Fay, P. Pomper and R.T. Vanh, ed., *History and Theory* (Oxford, 1998).
16. Gyanendra Pandey, 'The Prose of Otherness', in D. Arnold and D. Hardiman, eds, *Subaltern Studies VIII* (Delhi, 1994).
17. *Samajik Adhyayan* (in Hindi), Class VIII (Bhopal, 1994), p. 125.

On a Pre-Partition Partition: The Question of Hindi-Urdu

R. K. AGNIHOTRI

The irreparable damage that the Partition of the Indian subcontinent inflicted on the people of India and Pakistan, makes one shiver even today. Thousands of lives were lost; women were raped and humiliated; the loss of property could hardly be estimated; and millions were rendered homeless. Never in the history of mankind had such a large-scale migration taken place in such a short time. What is worse is that this nightmarish experience of Partition left such deep scars on the minds of Hindus and Muslims that they are nowhere close to healing even after 50 years. The trauma of mass migration, mayhem and murder resurfaces whenever there is an attempt at reconciliation. At least some of this violence could have been avoided if the British were not in such a hurry to leave, as if to prove the point: 'We told you so, you are incapable of ruling your country.' As M.J. Akbar points out,[1] despite all the propaganda and provocation, Hindus, Sikhs and Muslims alike were at a loss to understand why they had to leave the villages of their birth. The August of 1947 saw:

> Blood colour the fields of Punjab. The refugees, only a trickle before August 1947, now crossed over in waves . . . those trains and caravans and truck convoys carried so much fresh poison in them that it seeped across the subcontinent and is still powerful enough to destroy life.[2]

One innocent victim of this ruthless and brutal Partition was the shared language and literature of the people of pre-Partition India. The

* Thanks are due to S.K. Das, Harish Trivedi, Aditya Mukherjee, Bodh, N.N.Tewari, Mridula Mukherjee and Sucheta Mahajan. I am particularly grateful to S.K.Das who discussed some of the issues raised in this paper with me. Aditi Mukherjee read through an earlier draft of this paper and made several useful suggestions most of which have been incorporated. The usual disclaimers apply.

Unless otherwise specified, translations are my own. In the transcription capital letters, for example, T and D indicate retroflex sound (Hindi *Tavarg*) and the use of '-n' indicates nasalization of the preceding vowel sounds.

grandparents and parents of today's Hindu and Muslim children spoke the same language, wrote in the same script, read the same newspapers, sang the same songs and shared their joys and sorrows through a common set of narratives, rituals and festivals, even though both maintained distinct religious and ethnic identities. The processes of linguistic and cultural partition had started much before the actual Partition in 1947. And yet this partition could never be complete because, unlike a mass of land, it is difficult to divide a social mind.

Let me start with an autobiographical note and some empirical studies.

AN AUTOBIOGRAPHICAL NOTE

As a young boy in the 1950s and 1960s, I witnessed an older generation of Hindu and Muslim relatives and friends, sharing a language and a culture (probably today I should say a variety of languages and cultures), and noticed with a sense of sadness the foundations of that sharing gradually disintegrating among my friends and juniors. All my education was in the *nagari*, or from the middle school onwards in the Roman script. Yet the so-called Urdu speakers and writers were a very active and meaningful part of my world. From a generation, which could share in normal conversation Kabir, Premchand, Ghalib, Faiz, Nirala and Keats, among several others, and have a sustained discourse on them, irrespective of whether they read these authors in the *nagari* or the Perso-Arabic script or both, I felt we were moving towards a world of increasing polarization and the focusing of social, cultural and linguistic norms. In the small sleepy town of Nahan, in the Sirmaur district of Himachal Pradesh, my parents, very liberal otherwise, forbade me to associate any longer with two of my very dear schoolmates, Shaheed and Anwar. That was the time when I think I lost touch with the idiom of the street and could never return to flying kites and making fire-crackers. My father constantly told me that Muslims have been great friends, always sincere and honest, but 'you know . . .', etc. He was also convinced that in the interest of national unity all of us should speak 'pure Hindi' and write in the *nagari* script, though he could never do either himself.

I studied in Mandi, Himachal Pradesh, for my middle and high school and college. I grew up learning Hindi/Urdu, Punjabi and Mandyali as my native languages, like several of my friends. We also learnt Sanskrit and English. A fluid multilingual repertoire was the norm rather than an aberration. For a word like 'boy', I knew *laRkaa*, *baalak*, *shishu*, *munDaa*, *baal*, *maThThaa*, *bhaau*, *launDaa*, *chokraa* and *choruu*. Such richness spread across the lexicon and was shared by the whole community. This multiplicity of languages in a small town was never seen as a problem.

Later, when I came to Delhi, I made more friends speaking different languages. Very often some of us would get together in the evening on the lawns of India Gate, recite poems and critically evaluate them and in the end almost always return to discuss the increasing separation between the language of the people and the new 'pure Hindi' of All India Radio, nascent Doordarshan, Hindi newspapers and magazines and, most of all, of Hindi literature. Though literature from the other side of the border was not easily available, I at that time, assumed that comparable developments must be taking place there as well. Of course, I subsequently realized that Urdu/Hindi was the native language of a very small group in Pakistan, even though Partition was considerably predicated on the association of Muslims with Urdu. In 1970, I found a copy of the poems of Faiz (1969) in the *nagari* script. I was simply overwhelmed by the simplicity and power of some of his poems and asked my friends and myself, whether he was simply not still the greatest Hindi/Urdu poet. I think it is in Faiz, Kaifi Azmi, Dhumil and other similar poets, in both India and Pakistan, that we may trace the natural descendants of Kabir or Tulsi.

I can only invite readers to share the joy I have felt in reading *Shiishon Kaa Masiihaa*. I reproduce one short poem here (I know some readers would want glosses and translations. But the paper would become completely unwieldly if I provide them. I can only assure you that the effort you put in to find their meanings, if you do not understand Hindi/ Urdu, will be worth your while). Are poems like 'ham jo taariik raahon men maare gaye', 'yah fasl umiido kii hamdam', 'shaam', 'kab Thahregaa dard', 'paas raho', etc., Hindi or Urdu poems ? Decide for yourself:

Jab terii samandar aankhon men

yah dhuup kinaaraa, shaam Dhale
milte hain dono vaqt jahaan
jo raat na din, jo aaj na kal
pal bhar ko amar, pal bhar me dhuaan
is dhuup kinaare, pal do pal
honTon kii lapak
baahon kii chanak
yah mel hamaaraa, jhuuTh na sac
kyon raar karo, kyon dosh dharo
kis kaaraN jhuuThii baat karo
jab terii samandar aankhon men
is shaam kaa suraj Duubegaa
sukh soyenge ghar-dar vaale
aur raahii apnii raah legaa

(This verge of light where at sunset, night and day meet; it is neither night nor day; neither today nor tomorrow; immortal for a moment and ever transient; at this threshold of light, for a moment or two, there is that sensuous movement of lips and clinking of bangles; this union of ours is neither true nor false; why complain then and why blame anybody; why lie; when this evening's sun descends in your ocean eyes, men of the world will sleep peacefully and the traveller will be on his way.)

EMPIRICAL STUDIES

For a variety of reasons, I started studying Linguistics in 1971 and in 1973 it was time to write a dissertation for my M.Litt. The time, I thought, was ripe to examine in some detail Chatterji's remark,[3] that though in spirit Hindustani might be considered the most liberal and reasonable language, a very influential school had recently checked this natural trend and decided to fill Hindi with Sanskrit words to saturation. Even after 15 years of Partition, Chatterji thought of India and Pakistan as one linguistic and cultural zone: 'India single and undivided of January 1947, which still lives in the consciousness of the World.'[4] According to him, Urdu is but the Muslim style of the great Hindi speech and 'Hindi Literature' would include not only the Khari-Boli, Braj and Bundeli writings, but also those of Awadhi, Rajasthani, Bhojpuri, Maithili, Magadhi, mixed Punjabi and Dakkhini. About Urdu literature, which he decides to treat separately, he says:

> Urdu literature, which had an independent history, would gladly be claimed as part of Hindi literature, as the grammars of Urdu and Khari-Boli Hindi are almost identical. 'Hindi' and 'Urdu' from this point of view are looked upon as but two different 'Styles' of the same language, Urdu being specially dubbed as 'Musalmani Hindi'. However correct the position might be linguistically, Muslim as well as many Hindu writers and users of Urdu will not accept it.[5]

Why Chatterji or linguists since did not think of writing a history of north Indian (including Dakkhini) literature, which would include Urdu literature is, I think, a question all of us need to ask ourselves. There must be some socio-political and historical reasons behind not accepting the obvious and creating a divide where none actually existed. The separatist tendencies in linguistic engineering did not stop at creating the 'Muslim-Urdu' and 'Hindu-Hindi' equations, but set into motion forces of Sanskritization within the secular Hindu world. In my 1973 work, I examined the oral, written, normative and attitudinal behaviour of native speakers of Hindi.[6] I took 50 teachers of the University of Delhi as my sample. Of these, 25 were lecturers of Hindi and 25 of other subjects in humanities and social sciences. There were striking differences between the two groups in all aspects of linguistic behaviour, namely, oral, written and normative. It was clear from the personal interviews I conducted that the lecturers of Hindi preferred a Sanskritized style even in informal conversation. For them, the model for future Hindi would come from a Sanskritized version of the variety of the language spoken in Allahabad and Benaras; the other lecturers felt that the language of Delhi and Lucknow should constitute the basis for future Hindi without any conscious linguistic engineering.

In order to examine the written behaviour of my informants, I translated a text from Premchand's *Karmbhuumi*[7] into English and asked my informants to translate it back into Hindi. Of the seven words on which colloquial and Sanskritic alternants were possible, the Hindi lecturers used Sanskrit words over 61 per cent times, while the corresponding figure for the other lecturers was only 33 per cent. Not only that, the general style of writing was significantly different; expressions such as *aarakshiya vibhaag* for 'police', *aarakshak* for 'policeman' and *ashvaarohii* for 'horseman' were found only in the translations of Hindi lecturers. It was clear that the new 'pure and standardized Hindi' would disown considerable part of its lexical heritage; that commonly used words with recognizable linguistic antecedents in Persian, Arabic, Turkish, English, etc., would be discarded and replaced by their Sanskrit equivalents and that all new words technical or otherwise would be taken or crafted from Sanskrit.

The investigation of the Hindi news media by Singh[8] and Srivastava and Kalra[9] showed that though Hindi was creating linguistic resources through a variety of means to meet the new functional roles it was expected to fulfil in society, its increasing Sanskritization was creating barriers in comprehensibility. By the 1990s, the linguistic consequences of these primarily political moves were becoming increasingly transparent. A new generation had grown up: unfamiliar not only with Ghalib and Faiz but also with Kabir and Premchand; nor could they understand Prasad or Nirala. It was only with some difficulty that one could explain Dhumil or Nagarjun to them; the staple diet was Bombay film Hindi. The damage that inevitably accompanies the loss of literary sensitivity in a community is there for everyone to see.

Ahmad set out to examine[10] the mutual comprehensibility of the Hindi and Urdu news bulletins among 'Urdu' (Muslim) and 'Hindi' (Hindu) speakers, respectively. He found that the comprehensibility of the former was only 49 per cent as against 77 per cent of the latter. He concluded:

It is clear that the process of sanskritization of Hindi has resulted in a substantial loss of population that hitherto understood and participated in the life of Hindustani. It appears that Urdu has not closed its doors to the outside influence. It has not only retained the native Hindustani words but has also borrowed freely from English. Not surprisingly, Hindi speakers find the Urdu news bulletin well within their range of comprehension. Hindi on the contrary is increasingly closing its doors to outside influence. Even words and constructions that are a part of the heritage of the common man are being replaced by unfamiliar words. It is therefore not surprising that Urdu speaking informants, though living in a predominantly 'Hindi World', find the Hindi news bulletin beyond their comprehension.[11]

HINDI/URDU OR HINDI AND URDU

It is widely accepted (see, for example, Chatterji,[12] Beams,[13] Sharma,[14] Rai,[15] Rahman,[16] among others) that Hindi and Urdu are but two names of the same language. It is called Urdu when written in the Perso-Arabic script (associated with Muslims) and Hindi when written in the *nagari* script (associated with Hindus); at best there are some lexical and phrasal differences. The basic phonological inventory, lexical stock, including pronouns, postpositions, roots, number system, parts of the body, etc., and the syntactic structures are shared across the board. Two scripts can never on their own constitute the basis of establishing two different languages; in fact, several Hindus regularly wrote in the Perso-Arabic script just as several Muslims wrote in the *nagari* script.[17] In fact when towards the end of the nineteenth century, Premchand switched from writing in the Perso-Arabic script to the *nagari* script, he did not switch suddenly from 'Urdu' to 'Hindi'. He realized that the *nagari* script was far more extensively used in the rural areas, by both the Hindus and the Muslims. He simply wanted to reach a wider audience and, of course, make a better living. Trivedi argues[18] that Premchand noticed that Urdu was regarded as the language of the Muslims and switched to 'Hindi' to reach the Hindus. Sharma emphatically argues[19] that Premchand thought of language in a democratic and nationalist way; he could never think of dividing languages on the basis of religion. Perhaps readers of Premchand would agree that he was a Hindi/Urdu writer rather than a writer of Hindi and Urdu.

And yet the two names are regularly used for the same language and its literature segmented into two parts largely on the basis of script and religion. Do Kabir, Rahim, Premchand, Nazeer Akbarabadi, Mir, Ghalib and Faiz, among scores of others, belong to Urdu or Hindi literature? Am I a native speaker of Hindi or Urdu or neither or both? In order to examine these questions, it is important that we understand the nature of language and literature as it is particularly accentuated in multilingual societies. It is also important that we begin to appreciate the nature of relationship between linguistic identity, ethnic membership, social organization, religious sectarianism and political power.

NATURE OF LANGUAGE

Formal linguistics has imposed on us a view of language, that is essentially systemic and monolithic. The concept of 'a language' that in some fundamental sense precedes its speakers is necessary for a linguist and, in the process of describing that language, he reinforces that concept. A language is seen as a system in which a set of rules is paired with a lexicon. In this view it is always possible to say that a given rule or a given word belongs to language X. It also implies that the literature of a language can only be written in that language. It is a bit circular: we first define what that language is and then find it in a given piece of literature. Whenever linguists come across expressions or constructions that do not fit their conception of a language design, they treat them as abnormalities, for example, code-mixing, borrowing, pidginization, etc. Words and linguistic rules fortunately do not require any passports to cross linguistic boundaries set up by linguists. In fact, the constant and often effortless traffic between words and structures of different languages is the rule, rather than the exception. The history of human linguistic and literary behaviour actually runs contrary to the standard view of language as a homogeneous system. What linguists delight in separating as languages, varieties, dialects, etc., actually flow into each other effortlessly, constantly creating new expressions in both formal and informal domains. If we wish to understand the Hindi-Urdu question in a historical perspective, it is important to internalize this fluid view of language, where people exist before languages do, even if they are endowed with an innate Universal Grammar. Linguistic behaviour is essentially characterized by variability; there are no sharp boundaries that separate one community or one speech variety from another, with the result that the range of shared literary and cultural behaviour is indeed very large. It is not the case that comprehensibility levels suddenly decline because you have just crossed a state boundary.

THE BHAKTIKAL

Such linguistic and cultural fluidity was the most striking feature of the Indian subcontinent till its Partition in 1947 and later in the division of India into linguistic states. This fluidity exists even today but it has been considerably tampered with by linguistic engineering under political pressures. The rich literature of about 300 years (AD 1350 to AD 1650, approximately) of the Bhaktikal of undivided India is indeed a classic example of this fluidity. Poets like Kabir, Surdas, Jayasi, Mirabai, Tulsidas and Rahim were not writing in 'a language'; even today they are an active part of the consciousness of several 'states', where different languages are supposed to be spoken. The poetic sensitivity, language and philosophy of these poets knew no geographical, linguistic or religious boundaries. Rai quoting extensively[20] from the works of the Sufis, Nathpanthis and Kabirpanthis, among others, has shown how Khari-Boli developed out of an interaction between local languages, Sanskrit, Prakrit, Apabhransha and Persian. As Chaturvedi points out,[21] the linguistic range of Kabir extended from Bhojpuri in the east to Rajasthani in the west. In Kabir's poetry, one finds not only isolated words but also whole phrases, expressions and idioms from what today may be characterized as Awadhi, Braj, Khari-Boli, Rajasthani, eastern Hindi, Urdu, Punjabi, Apabhransha and Bengali. He was probably the first people's poet, writing about them in their languages. Similarly, the contribution of Tulsidas to both Awadhi and Braj, and eventually to 'Hindi', is widely recognized. Mirabai, as is well known, is claimed not only by Rajasthan but also by the Hindi heartland, Gujarat and Punjab. Rahim, perhaps a friend of Tulsidas, was well-versed not only in the local languages of the people but also in Arabic, Persian, Turkish and Sanskrit. As if anticipating the later 'Urdu' poets (with whom it was a common practice to jointly create couplets), folklore has it that Tulsidas sent the following line of an incomplete couplet to Rahim:

surtiya nartiya naagtiya, as chaahat sab koya

and Rahim is supposed to have completed the couplet as follows:

god liye hulsii phiraii, tulsii so sut hoya

(All women whether of divine or earthly origin wish to have a son like Tulsi)

Consider, for example, the following couplet from Kabir:

kabiir kautig diiThaa deh bin, rabi sasi binaa ujaas
saahib sevaa maahii hai, beparvaahii daas[22]

(Kabir has experienced the miracle of having seen the Formless, and, of light without the sun or the moon; he is completely devoted to the service of the Lord and is free from all worries)

What linguistic labels shall we attach to *kautig*, *diiThaa*, *ujaas* or *beparvaahii*? Is the couplet Hindi, Urdu, Hindu or Muslim? *Kautig* is said to be related to Sanskrit *kautuk*, *diiThaa* to Sanskrit *drshTi* or Prakrit *diTThi*, *ujaas* to Sanskrit *udyati* or Prakrit *ujjaua* or to Sanskrit *udbhaas* and Prakrit *ujjhaas* and *beparvaahii* is, of course, of Persian origin. Notice that Kabir uses *diiThaa* as a verb; its historical antecedents are all nouns. Where does all this lead us? Are we any wiser as to determining the language of this couplet ? Or for that matter the language of all the Bhakti poets? Examine the following Mirabai citations from Mishr:

saam mhaa baahRiyaa gahyau (Rajasthani)

man ko mail hiya te na chuuTii (Brajbhasha)

mane laagii kaTaarii premnii (Gujarati)

laagii sohii jaaNai lagan dii piir (Punjabi)[23]

Comparable citations may be seen in Chaturvedi.[24] Such a classification, of course, assumes that it is possible to classify Mirabai's poetry into different languages but the fact is that even today her songs are widely understood from Himachal to Madhya Pradesh and from Gujarat to Bihar. Although Chaturvedi, in general, subscribes to standard linguistic classification, he is forced to acknowledge that 'Mira has not written her poetry in separate dialect-forms; several languages have been mixed in her basic language, principally Braj and Rajasthani'.[25] Such literary traditions are possible only in extremely rich and fluid lexical contexts of the verbal repertoire of people and poets. Surdas, for example, uses *murlii*, *benu*, *bansii*, *baansurii* and *murlikaa* for 'flute'.[26]

THE POLITICS OF 'HINDI' AND 'URDU'

It should be clear that the Bhaktikal is not an exception but the rule for normal linguistic and literary activity. The kind of fluid multilingual repertoire that characterized my childhood must have been a normal societal feature of the Bhaktikal. It is so even today. It is just that the language of literature and mass media has moved far away from the language of the people. Linguistic engineering, leading to focused and reified varieties, is an inevitable consequence of social exploitation in which a premium is placed on the language of a select élite. It becomes imperative for the ruling élite to restrict its access to the masses and make high levels of proficiency in it a necessary requirement for all important social positions. This was true of Sanskrit in ancient times, of Persian in the Mughal period, of English during the British Raj and it is true in contemporary India of English, in general, and in some areas of High Hindi or standardized regional languages. The ways in which vernacular education and languages of the people were marginalized in colonial India may be seen in the work of Bhokta[27] and Jha.[28] Ethnic, religious and geographical divisions had very little to do with sharing languages and literatures in moments of togetherness that cut across these boundaries. As Ramvilas Sharma says,[29] those who wrote in Urdu included both Hindus and Muslims. A considerable amount of Hindu religious literature has been written in the Perso-Arabic script. The division of the shared linguistic heritage of central India into Hindi and Urdu resulted from the intrigues of feudal and imperial powers to keep the common people divided and keep themselves in power. Today insistence on High Hindi is associated with majority communalism. According to Sharma:

> Those who in their enthusiasm for Hindutva wish to make Sanskrit the national language of India or wish to saturate Hindi and other Indian languages with Sanskrit words, neither understand the development of Sanskrit nor do they recognize how Indian languages can best develop.[30]

According to Rai[31] and King,[32] two events which contributed significantly towards the separation of Khari-Boli into Hindi and Urdu were its Persianization in the eighteenth century and its Sanskritization, since the nineteenth century. And both these events had political rather than linguistic motivations; they were designed to keep a select élite in power, particularly in moments of high insecurity. The first event was accompanied by the decline of the Mughal Empire; the second with the decline of the British Empire, formation of linguistic states and the rise of the importance of English. Rai is convinced that the responsibility for snapping the natural development of Hindavi, and its subsequent split into Hindi and Urdu, lies squarely with those who attempted to eliminate Sanskrit words from it. He says:

> Therefore I am convinced that Urdu now is not just a dialect of Hindi but a language. However, what I must stoutly contest is Urdu's claim to being a common language of the Hindus and the Muslims, *that* modern Urdu is not—and old Urdu . . . most certainly was.[33]

On what basis is it decided that Urdu was a dialect of Hindi? Do some lexical differences constitute enough linguistic grounds for giving two names to the same language? What is wrong with saying that language X when spoken by ordinary Muslims is called Urdu and when spoken by ordinary Hindus is called Hindi? Why is recent and persistent and far more radical relexification of Hindi not regarded equally responsible for the twin names? And, in the face of all this, how is it that Faiz, Parveen Shakir, Nida Fazli, Pash, Ada Zafri and Ibne Insha, among scores of others, are avidly read on both sides of the border, as well as inside and outside the walls of old Delhi? Why do we have more and more *nagari* editions of the 'Urdu' poets? Why are Hindi films so popular in Pakistan? Why are Pakistani plays so popular in India? Why do we still have Muslim friends? It should be clear that Rai's book is really a part of the problem. Ahmad has effectively shown[34] that the eighteenth century Persianization movement involved much more than just elimination of Sanskrit words. According to Rai,[35] Nasikh took the Persianization trend to its farthest extreme. But Nasikh's *matrukat* (discarded words) and the changes made by other scholars went much beyond vocabulary; in fact some of the structural changes introduced attempted to eliminate the imitation of Persian structures from Hindi. The following formulations and examples are from Ahmad.[36] The structure of the Noun Phrase (NP) and the Pre/post-positional Phrase (PP) in the pre-eighteenth century Urdu was based on Persian:

NP—Determiner - Noun - Adjective
PP—Preposition - Noun Phrase

The eighteenth century changes freed these structures from Persian influence and we have the contemporary Hindi-Urdu structure:

NP—Determiner - Adjective - Noun
PP—Noun Phrase - Postposition

Thus a structure such as:

ek ustaad daanaa kar-azmudaah

(one teacher wise experienced)

is now rewritten as:

ek daanaa aur kar-azmudaah ustaad

(one wise and experienced teacher)

As Ahmad points out,[37] what Rai further ignores is the fact that in the eighteenth century itself there were several poets who revolted against the purification agenda both in theory and practice. Poets like Insha-allah Khan Insha, Nazeer Akbarabadi, Mir Taqi Mir, Zauq and Zafar were among those who wrote in the language of the common man and formed important links in the unbroken chain, that still sustains the shared heritage of the language and literature of Hindi/Urdu. It is important to remember, as Sharma reminds us repeatedly,[38] that Persian was not anybody's native language in India, be he a Hindu or a Muslim. For both it was a foreign language as the Muslim invaders were Turks, Pathans or Mughals. These were small warrior tribes, who must have retained their ethnic identities in spite of being united by a common religion and local languages. It is true that significant changes had taken place during the 200 years that separate Kabir and Rahim from say Mir (1723-1810) and Nazeer (1740-1830). For one thing, the language of central India was back after a long sojourn in the Deccan, enriched further by languages such as Telugu and Kannada. But poets like Mir and Nazeer, like Kabir and Rahim earlier, knew the importance of writing in the language of the people. Mir is supposed to have said that only those familiar with the language spoken on the stairs of Jama Masjid can understand his poetry. Here are some couplets from Mir:

ulTii ho gayii sab tadbiren kuch na davaa ne kaam kiyaa
dekhaa is bimaariye-dil ne aakhir kaam tamaam kiyaa

(All plans have gone amiss, all recipes have failed; this ailing heart, you see, has undone me at last)[39]

On what basis should we say that this is not the best of Hindi/Urdu poetry? Does *bimaariye-dil* disqualify it from being a Hindi couplet? What about the Persian words in the Bhakti poets? Here is another one:

ashk aankhon men kab nahiin aataa
lahuu aataa hai jab nahiin aataa

(Eyes are always filled with tears. And when that does not happen, blood oozes from them)

Or consider some of Ghalib's well-known couplets:

ye na thii hamaarii kismat ke visaale-yaar hotaa
agar aaur jiite rahte yehii intzaar hotaa

(To have met my friend was not my fate; a longer life would have entailed a longer wait)[40]

aashqii sabr talab aur tamannaa betaab
dil kaa kyaa rang karun khuune jigar hone tak

(Love demands patience but desire will not wait; what hues should my heart reflect till it bleeds to death)[41]

Nazeer, of course, was a people's poet *par excellence*. His poems such as 'holii', 'aagre kii tairaakii', 'riich kaa baccaa', 'bacpan', 'koraa bartan', 'til ke laDDoo', etc., were very popular and are easily understood even today 'koraa bartan' begins as follows:

kore bartan hai kyaarii gulshan kii
jisse khiltii hai har kali tan kii
buund paanii kii unme jab khankii
kyaa vo pyaarii sadaa hai san-san kii

taazgii jii kii aur tarii tan kii
vaah kyaa baat kore bartan kii

(New utensils are like flowerbeds in a garden; they make everybody happy; when a drop of water slides down a new utensil, it produces the most beautiful *san-san* sound; it refreshes the mind and body)

Most of the words and expressions used by these poets are easily understood even today. Poets, who continue writing in this style, are still around. Guess whether the following modern poems or couplets are in Hindi or Urdu:

(1) bas itnaa yaad hai

duaa to jaane kaun-sii thii
zehan me nahiin
bas itnaa yaad hai
ki do hatheliyaan milii huii thiin
jinme ek merii thii
aur ek tumhaarii

(I do not recollect what I prayed for; I only remember that a pair of palms was held together one of which was mine and the other yours)

(2) *sau baar umr paaun to sau baar jaan duun*
sadqe huun apnii maut pe kaafir nahiin huun main

(I am not a sinner; I love death; if I receive life a hundred times then I will die a hundred times)

(3) jiivan saathii se

dhuup me baarish hote dekh ke
hairat karne vaale
shaayad tuune merii hasiin ko
chuukar
kabhii nahiin dekhaa!

(Why do you look so surprised to see it raining in sunshine; perhaps you have never felt my laughter!)

(4) *ujaale apnii yaadon ke hamaare saath rahne do*
na jaane kis galii men jindagii kii shaam ho jaaye

(Leave the light of your memories with me; who knows where in my life it will get dark)

It is possible that your guess is right in terms of whether the poet is a Hindu or a Muslim or whether the poem was originally written in the *nagari* or Perso-Arabic script; the question is what reasons would you give to classify these poems into different categories. As Brass points out,[42] there were enough similarities and dissimilarties among Hindus and Muslims to create a composite culture or create two separate nations. Language obviously belonged to the former category though it was extensively used to justify the latter.

DOCUMENTATION BIAS

As we noticed above, Chatterji treats Hindi and Urdu literatures separately, without giving any substantial reasons. Traditionally, histories of Hindi and Urdu literature have generally been written separately. In fact, historians of Hindi literature, assumed to be associated with the majority Hindu community, either do not mention Urdu literature at all or take special pains to explain why Urdu literature does not form part of the mainstream Hindi literature in spite of the fact that writers of both not only spoke the same language but also belonged to the same society and cultural milieu. Chaturvedi compares[43] the 'Hindi' poets Dev, Ghananand and Padmakar, with their contemporary 'Urdu' poets, Mir and Ghalib. He says:

Though there are differences in their poetic style and tradition, these poets belong to the same linguistic area. The interesting thing is that as a means of day to day communication, Hindi and Urdu are the same. So far pronunciation and grammar are concerned, modern Khari-Boli Hindi is much closer to Urdu than to Braj,

Awadhi, Bhojpuri or Malvi. But when it comes to the language of poetry, the two become different.[44]

Chaturvedi then quotes a well-known couplet from Ghalib:

na thaa kuch, to khudaa thaa, kuch na hotaa, to khudaa hotaa
Duboyaa mujhko hone ne, na hotaa main to kyaa hotaa!

(God was there even when nothing else was; He would have been there even if there were nothing; beinghood has destroyed me; if I were not there, nothing else would be there)

He raises the legitimate questions: Why is this not regarded as a part of Hindi literature? Why are those who are eager to appropriate Braj, Awadhi, Bhojpuri and Maithali literatures as Hindi literature desperately trying to keep Urdu literature out of this rich tradition? Chaturvedi's answers are as expected, unconvincing. Urdu literature does not consist only of ghazals; *nazm*, *masnavi*, *marsia*, *qasida*, *rubai* and *giit,* and a variety of other forms are as much a part of it. It is also suggested that Urdu poetry is simple and straightforward and does not work in terms of images and music, which are the hallmark of Hindi poetry. The fact is that around the middle of the eighteenth century, there was a decline in the quality of Hindi poetry and the best of Hindi/Urdu poetry was written by some Muslim poets. The sense of joy one experiences in reading Kabir or Tulsi is witnessed again only in Ghalib and Mir. Nobody would dream of keeping Tulsi or Kabir out of Hindi literature even though they used a variety of different languages because of their disarming simplicity, balanced rhythm, linguistic precision and philosophical depth—the very same features that characterize Ghalib and Mir, who were writing along with a large number of other poets, Hindu and Muslim, in a language that was so much a part of 'Indian' culture. It is only in such poets that the joy of gaining an insight into the nature of life is coupled with the sadness of its transience.

POLITICAL CONTEXT OF PURE HINDI

The pursuit of the Sanskritization of Hindi has continued unabated since the nineteenth century, with the result that several of the well-known Hindi poets are not at all comprehensible, even to the more serious native speakers of Hindi/Urdu. When a majority community reasserts itself after centuries of slavery, the first thing it does is to talk in terms of 'us' and 'them'. When the struggle for the freedom of India began to take shape, the search for symbols was directed not towards the composite culture of the medieval period but to the ancient Hindu glory; others could only be accommodated now in the Hindu fold. As Pandey has so effectively shown,[45] the constitution of local communities on the basis of caste, sect, region, occupation, etc., changed dramatically with the colonial rule, which brought about administrative integration, new communication systems and a single urban market. The boundaries between different communities began to be defined more sharply. The Hindu community consolidated itself through a variety of means, including the Arya Samaj Movement, Hindu Mahasabha, Cow Protection Movement, etc.

The linguistic issue should not be treated in isolation from these socio-political developments. New places of power had been created and new strategies had to be forged to acquire them. As Krishna Kumar points out,[46] the battle over script became significant because the Persian script was a reminder to Hindus of the former power of the Muslim aristocracy. The Devanagari Pracharini Sabha of Meerut was founded in 1882, Nagari Pracharini Sabha of Benaras in 1893 and Hindi Sahitya Sammelan in 1910. The rest is well-known history. Shukl,[47] the famous historian of Hindi literature, congratulates Lallu Lal for successfully eliminating a large number of Perso-Arabic words from Hindi, particularly those which had become difficult to be so identified. We need to ask ourselves why Bhartendu, Prasad, Pant, Agyeya or Muktibodh are not a part of the common Indian consciousness or why those who listen to Pash, Dhumil, Dushyant or Nida, with pleasure, refuse to read anything by some of the modern Sanskritized poets. There is, I think, enough evidence in history to tell us that whenever the language of literature has moved too far away from the language of people, literature has degenerated. We are now beginning to feel that as these processes enter into mass media, democratic institutions also degenerate.

CONCLUSION

This paper has tried to cover a large area both in terms of historical time and in terms of the linguistic and political issues addressed. A certain amount of diffusion is, therefore, inevitable. The main point is that linguistic engineering is often undertaken at the behest of a select élite trying either to appropriate political power or to maintain the status quo. Such interventions, whether of Persianization or Sanskritization, are disastrous both for mass participation in the process of social change and for literary excellence. The common man, on the other hand, shows a remarkable resilience to rise above these maneouvers and even today there is a 'social mind', that enjoys Hindi/Urdu speech and literature; and this in spite of a pre-Partition partition and everything that has been done since to Sanskritize Hindi.

NOTES

* References that are not used specifically in the notes but were useful for the article are E. Annamalai, ed., *Language Movements in India* (Mysore, 1979); H. Bahari, 'Hindi Bhaashaa kaa Vikaas', in *Hindi Sāhitya*, Vol. I (Allahabad, 1962); S.K Chatterji, *India: A Polyglot Nation and its Linguistic Problems vis-a-vis National Integration* (Bombay, 1973); J. Das Gupta, *Language Conflict and National Development* (Berkeley, 1970); H.R. Dua, *Language Planning in India* (New Delhi, 1985); J. Fishman, C.A. Ferguson and J. Das Gupta, eds, *Language Problems of Developing Nations* (New York, 1968); S.S. Harrison, *India: The Most Dangerous Decades* (Princeton, 1960); E. Haugen, *Language Conflict and Language Planning* (Cambridge, 1966); A.R. Kelkar, *Studies in Hindi-Urdu* (Poona, 1968); S.H.A. Kellogg, *A Grammar of the Hindi Language* (London, 1876, 3rd edn, 1938); Robert D. King, *Nehru and the Language Politics of India* (Delhi, 1997); B. Krishnamurti and A. Mukherjee, eds, *Modernization of Indian Languages in News Media* (Hyderabad, 1984); W.E. O'Barr and Jean F. O'Barr, eds, *Language and Politics* (The Hague, 1976); Ram Gopal, *Linguistic Affairs of India* (Bombay, 1966); M. Sadiq, *A History of Urdu Literature* (Delhi, 1964); B.R. Saxena, *Dakkhini Hindi* (Allahabad, 1952); 'Urdu: A Symposium in the Shadow of Linguistic Genocide', *Seminar* (monthly), No. 332 (1987); C. Shakle and R. Snell, *Hindi and Urdu since 1800: A Common Reader* (London, 1990); R. Singh, *Linguistic Theory, Language Contact and Modern Hindustani* (New York, 1995); idem, ed., *The Yearbook of South Asian Languages and Linguistics* (New Delhi, 1998); G. Viswanathan, *Masks of Conquest: Literary Study and British Rule in India* (Delhi, 1989); P. Wallace, ed., *Region and Nation in India* (New Delhi, 1985); and S. Zaheer, *Urdu, Hindi, Hindustani* (Bombay, 1947).

1. M.J. Akbar, *India: The Siege Within* (Delhi, 1985), p. 150.
2. Ibid., p. 151.
3. S.K. Chatterji, *Indo-Aryan and Hindi* (Calcutta, 1960, repr. 1969).
4. Idem, *Languages and Literatures of Modern India* (Calcutta, 1963), p. 2.
5. Ibid., p. 110.
6. R.K. Agnihotri, *Choice of Styles in Hindi, Papers in Linguistic Analysis*, Vol. 2 (1977), pp. 43-52.
7. Premchand, *Karmbhuumi* (Premchand Rachnavali 10) (Delhi, 2nd edn 1987), p. 271.
8. A.B. Singh, in B. Krishnamurti and A. Mukherjee, eds, *Modernization of Hindi in News Media* (Delhi, 1984), pp. 29-40.
9. R.N. Srivastava and A. Kalra, in ibid., pp. 41-53.
10. R. Ahmad, 'News Bulletins in Hindi and Urdu: A Study in Mutual Comprehensibility' (M.Phil dissertation, University of Delhi, 1997).
11. Ibid., p. 47.
12. Chatterji, *Languages and Literature of Modern India*, op.cit.
13. J. Beams, *A Comparative Grammar of the Modern Aryan Languages of India* (New Delhi, repr. 1966).
14. Ramvilas Sharma, *Bhashaa aur Samaj* (New Delhi, 1977).

15. A. Rai, *A House Divided: The Origin and Development of Hindi/Hindavi* (Delhi, 1984).
16. T. Rahman, *Language and Politics in Pakistan* (New York and Delhi, 1996).
17. Sharma, op.cit, p. 312.
18. Harish Trivedi, 'The Urdu Premchand, The Hindi Premchand', *Jadavpur Journal of Comparative Literature*, Vol. XXII (Jadavpur, 1984), pp. 104-18.
19. Sharma, op.cit., p. 318.
20. Rai, op.cit.
21. R. Chaturvedi, *Hindi Sahitya aur Samvedna ka Vikas* (Allahabad, 1986), p. 40.
22. M. Gupt, *Kabir-Granthavali* (Agra, 1969), p. 23.
23. R. Mishr, ed., *Madhyakaaliin Kaavy Sangrah* (New Delhi, 1991), p. 49.
24. Chaturvedi, op.cit., p. 51.
25. Ibid., p. 52.
26. N. Saxena, *Sursagar Shabdavali* (Allahabad, 1962), p. 360.
27. N.P. Bhokta, 'Marginalisation of Popular Languages and Growth of Sectarian Education in Colonial India', in S. Bhattacharya, ed., *The Contested Terrain: Perspectives on Education in India* (New Delhi, 1998), pp. 201-17.
28. H. Jha, 'Decline of Vernacular Education in Bihar in the Nineteenth Century', in ibid., pp. 218-28.
29. Sharma, op.cit., p. 312.
30. Ibid., pp. 3-7.
31. Rai, op.cit.
32. C.R. King, *One Language, Two Scripts* (Bombay, 1994).
33. Rai, op.cit., p. 288.
34. Ahmad, op.cit.
35. Rai, op.cit., p. 252.
36. Ahmad, op.cit.
37. Ibid.
38. Sharma, op.cit.
39. K.C. Kanda, *Masterpieces of Urdu Ghazal from 17th to 20th Century* (New Delhi, 1992), p. 79.
40. Ibid., p. 119.
41. Ibid., p. 129.
42. P. Brass, *Language, Religion and Politics in North India* (London, 1974).
43. Chaturvedi, op.cit., pp. 58-60.
44. Ibid., p. 59.
45. Gyanendra Pandey, *The Construction of Communalism in Colonial North India* (Delhi, 1990).
46. Krishna Kumar, 'Quest for Self-Identity', in *Economic and Political Weekly*, Vol. XXV, No. 23 (1990), pp. 1247-55.
47. R. Shukl, *Hindi Sahitya ka Itihasa* (Varanasi, 1940).

Crossing the Jhelum

SATISH GUJRAL

Partition was yet to arrive on the 15 August 1947, but the air started to thicken right with the declaration of 'Direct Action' by the Muslim League. From Calcutta, the winds blew to Noakhali and then the fury was unleased at Lahore, where I also lived. Even before it reached Lahore we had a foretaste of it in my home town, Jhelum, a hundred miles midway between Lahore and Rawalpindi. The city itself was spared, but the villages around it were totally divested. My father Avtar Narain, a Congress leader, was not a man easily ruffled, yet he was so shaken when he visited me in Lahore in the aftermath of this that the feeling of despair and outrage seemed too much for him to hide.

Still nobody believed that the Partition was inevitable, in spite of the fact that an Interim Government had been already formed in New Delhi to work out the modalities of dividing the country.

My father who was a member of the Constituent Assembly of Pakistan seemed to have reconciled with the Partition as a *fait accompli*. Though the region was torn between killing and arson, day in and day out, most of the inhabitants lived under the illusion that all this would come to an end on the 15 August, once Jinnah's dream was fulfilled. It was this that made me stay put in Lahore right up to the doomsday. I had taken refuge for more than a fortnight in the house of my family friend Lala Achint Ram, father of Krishan Kant, our present Vice-President. This portion of Lajpat Rai Bhavan had become a sort of subsidiary refugee camp because of its proximity to the DAV College Hostel, wherein was housed the main refugee camp of the town.

Prior to 1 August, I had laughed at those who were fleeing Lahore to protect themselves and their valuables in places outside the future boundaries of Pakistan. Those who stayed back believed that the chances of Lahore going to Pakistan was no more than 50 per cent. Finally, on 13 August, Radcliffe gave his Award leaving us in no more doubt as to the fate of that city. Curiously, the news of such magnitude was conveyed to us not by newspapers (which had ceased publication) but by posters pasted on the walls of our camp. These posters proclaimed: 'Do not burn now. It is Pakistan's property.'

I spent a fortnight in Lajpat Rai Bhavan where Lala Achint Ram also lived. The Bhavan was overflowing with refugees so much so that there was no space left between it and the adjoining camp in the hostel of DAV College. Each new arrival had a new tale to tell, each ghastlier than the one we had heard earlier. Children would come minus parents and parents minus children. Survivors who were not physically maimed were so gravely wounded emotionally, that survival seemed a torture.

My parents, along with my younger sister, had gone to Karachi where my father was to take the oath as one of the two Hindu members of Pakistan's Constituent Assembly. My elder brother Inder was already there, as he had settled in Karachi a few years earlier. There had been no contact between my parents and me as all modes of communication were dead. However, on 17 August, my father flew in and found me at Lajpat Rai Bhavan. He had flown courtesy the Pakistan government, on the plea that he should be with his flock at Jhelum in their hour of crisis. But flying 800 miles was easier than driving 100 miles from Lahore to Jhelum. It was at this hour that Jawaharlal Nehru also flew in, accompanied by Lady Mountbatten.

When Nehru and Lady Mountbatten together faced the sea of refugees in the camp, the encounter visibly shattered Nehru, as he had to be rescued from the fury of his audience. Fifty years have passed by since the event took place on that humid evening, but the scene has remained frozen in my imagination. A hero worshipped till only yesterday, Nehru was turned into a villain; he was held responsible for all the misery unleashed on the refugees. He had betrayed their trust, they felt.

Taken to Lajpat Rai Bhavan, Nehru sat surrounded by some leaders, including my father, Lala Achint Ram and Bhimsen Sacher. It was supposed to be a high power meeting to charter the future course of action to ensure the security of those who were to live in Pakistan. As the others waited silently, Nehru simply gazed towards the ceiling holding his chin in the cup of his hands. Then, looking at my father, he blurted: 'What do you think? Is peace possible?' How he could address this question to my father with whom he had only a nodding acquaintance, was a mystery. My father, of course, understood. Nehru, as became apparent in a moment, was addressing the question to himself. Prior to his departure from New Delhi, both the Indian and Pakistani governments had given up the possibility of peace and had reconciled to the exchange of populations as the only solution. Yet, Nehru did not wish to swallow the bitter pill; hence kept the news to himself. But the encounter at the refugee camp, a few minutes earlier, had numbed his resolve. Without looking at anyone in particular he disclosed the Cabinet decision to those who had assembled in Lajpat Rai Bhavan. Before the fall of night, the modalities for evacuation had been put into shape. My father was given the responsibility of evacuating all non-Muslims from the Jhelum district. It was by noon of the next day that the army, which was still undivided, provided us with a car and an escort, comprising a small contingent of Dogra military personnel. I was worried for my father because by all counts the journey was a death trap. This was also endorsed by the army men who had come to deliver the car and the jawans.

It was at this juncture that Raja Gaznafer Ali walked in. He was a native of Jhelum and now a Minister in the Pakistan government. In spite of their political differences, my father's friendship with the Raja had remained constant. Their attachment to each other was rather odd considering the contrasts in their personalities and predilections. My father was a recluse, the Raja was an extrovert. My father was a sort of puritan, the Raja was an unabashed pleasure hunter. The Raja informed my father that he was also bound for Jhelum but not to help evacuation. His mission was quite the opposite. He wanted my father to persuade non-Muslims to stay back, promising to secure a guarantee from his own community for the safety of those who stayed back. My father did not seem to take the Raja's argument with any seriousness, surrounded as he was by the devastation that undermined the Raja's assurance. The Raja, however, succeeded in persuading my father to travel in his car to Jhelum. Whether he did this to save my father from possible attack or for furthering his argument *en route* could not be made out. I had earlier begged my father to take me along to which he had not conceded. The Raja's offer made him agree to take me, as he now saw less immediate danger to both his and my life.

The journey from Lahore to Jhelum turned out to be a nightmare. In spite of the Raja's escort clearing the route, it remained hazardous. The mob on the way was uncontrollable and made little exception even to those claiming official protection. The devastation spread out on either side of the road did much to dampen the Raja's enthusiasm. He soon maintained a glum silence. The journey that usually took three hours to complete, took eight hours. But just as we reached Sarai Alamgir, a small village located near the Jhelum river before you cross over the bridge to reach the town, the Raja regained his old enthusiasm. Putting his hand on my father's shoulder he said, 'Well, Lalaji, let us try.' Sitting on the front seat next to the driver I watched my father in the rear-view mirror. He did not answer, and the Raja seemed to have taken my father's silence for consent. He seemed relieved.

My father had not spoken during the entire journey. But knowing him as I did, I could read him clearly. Ever since the beginning of his adult life he had fought for the independence of his country. He had sacrificed a thriving law practice and spent long spells in prisons. He had made his son, wife and foster son follow his footsteps. As a culmination of all this struggle, he had seen the fruit of independence. The land was free of the foreign yoke. But it had disowned him as one of its sons, depriving him of the right to live where he was born. And this, when he was past his prime and with little to begin afresh in another land where he had no roots. He was a lawyer by profession, but he had given up his career when Gandhiji declared it an immoral profession. That was years before this. He had no desire to resume it, even if left with no alternative. Torn with all these forebodings, he seemed to succumb to the Raja's suggestion. Soon after reaching our home both friends began in earnest to convince their respective communities to give their proposal a chance and stay back. But before their arguments could sink into the sceptics all around them, events overtook them.

Their efforts to convince the people not to panic and stay back, however, received wide acclaim on both sides of the border. Both Jinnah and Gandhi sent them telegrams of congratulation on their efforts. The adulation, however, became meaningless as ugly events began to unfold in Kashmir and defeat their grand efforts.

It was Kashmir that sealed the destiny of the people of my small district. While the Raja and my father were busy reassuring safety for those who stayed back, Pakistan's first raid on Kashmir was announced. The border of Kashmir state was less than 30 miles from Jhelum, making the latter a convenient staging point for Pakistani armies. Had it been only this military operation, the effect may have been less drastic on our town. But what made the matter worse was the use of Kablis as the front men in the aggression by Pakistan. These tribals belonged to the no-man's land that lay between the borders of Pakistan and Afghanistan. For centuries, they had thrived on obeying no law and recognizing no government. The Hindus of Pathohar, the area that is spread between river Jhelum and Sind had lived with an inherent dread of these Kablis, whose favourite occupation was kidnapping for ransom or bullying the locals with muscle power. The descent of these tribes dislocated the little faith that the local Hindus and

Sikhs had in the reassurances of my father and the Raja. When the first batch of Kablis began to project their presence in rabid ways, the little hope of safe living was wiped out, even in my father.

These tribals who were bound for Kashmir had been lured by the Pakistani army with promises of loot and women; their sentiments were further fired with zeal for *jihad* against infidels. The presence of Hindus and Sikhs, camped around our house, was too tempting for them to resist. They besieged our house, which was almost like a border post of the camp. The night of the siege was a nightmare that still haunts me repeatedly. The wild dance staged by the Kablis, accompanied by barbaric gun shots into the air all night, served as a prelude to the attack. Had it not been for the persistent pressure from the Raja on the Pakistani police and timely intervention of the latter, none of us would have survived to tell this tale of death and horror. The dawn, however, added another chapter to this epic story.

Next morning, a handful of evacuees arrived from the nearby village called Rohtas. One of them was Heera Singh, a long-standing client of my father in his law business. He was the *sahukar* (moneylender) and landlord in his village. A hefty sardar, though he was, he was only a shadow of his former self when he stood before my father that morning. He did not or could not speak; but the agony suffered by him was clearly imprinted on his pale face. Heera Singh told us that though he had prepared himself to join our camp three days earlier, he had stayed back in his village because of his faith in the reassurance given by the Raja and my father. Overjoyed by the prospect of safe living, he had even invited several of his neighbours belonging to both communities for a feast, infecting the invitees with his own brand of optimism. The feast was hardly over and the daylight had hardly faded when a gang of Kablis arrived and besieged his house. They had been on a killing and raping spree all over the village. They could not easily invade Heera Singh's *haveli* as it was strongly fortified. It was the house built by Sher Shah Suri, the Afghan ruler of Hindustan, during the time of Emperor Babar, the founder of the Mughal Empire.

Heera Singh was armed with a modest stock of ammunition. As the siege began, he positioned himself and his two sons at the *mumti* of the *haveli*, placing his three daughters, wife and an aged mother in the inner confines of the house. Besides the stock of ammunition mounted on the *mumti*, he also piled up a generous quantity of whiskey bottles to rejuvenate himself in this hour of crisis. The *mumti* provided him and his sons a panoramic view of the surroundings of their *haveli*, making it no cakewalk for the tribals to reach its doors. As the siege progressed, Heera Singh reinforced himself from the bottle before returning every round of fire; but he knew well that it was a losing battle as his limited quantity of ammunition was bound to be exhausted sooner or later. While he struggled with his attackers, the rest of the villagers (Hindus and Sikhs, who had survived, and the Muslims who remained untouched) were silently huddled in their houses. By the morning, Heera Singh had been left with only a few bullets and he had lost both his sons in the dark of the night. They had died fighting to their last breath against the tribals. He was alone and he had less than half a dozen bullets left with him. Seeing the end staring in his face, he climbed down to reach his family, hearing the thunderous shouts of 'Allah ho Akbar' and the sound of breaking of the gate of his *haveli* by the attackers. He had no time left. He shot each one of his family members in the head, but found no more cartridge left to end his own life.

But just at this juncture before the Kablis had completed their attack on his *haveli*, the army had arrived on the spot after hearing about the attack from his good Muslim neighbour, who had made a dash for reporting it in the dead of night. No doubt Heera Singh had 'survived', but it was this very sordid story of survival that destroyed my father's resolve. We decided to evacuate immediately. The Raja also left for Karachi.

My father was an introvert. He rarely allowed his emotions to surface. But listening to these tales, day in and day out, he also found it difficult to suppress his inner pangs. There were moments, when the tension built up within him seemed to burst out and ooze through his pores. He was a God-fearing man, but seeing what God had allowed his creatures to do to each other, he wondered whether there was any other power to beseech for help.

The transportation of the evacuees only added to the tales of horror spread all around us. Often, I accompanied the convoys consisting of about half a dozen trucks. For many, the journey to the promised land turned out to be the last one. In spite of the armed contingent we had been provided with, the ambushes on the way could not be avoided, for the attackers outnumbered the guards manifold. There was no set pattern in their assaults, nor would they come from known spots. As such, no protection could be expected even from the advance patrolling contingent. All we could do was to advise the refugees not to offer any resistance and when it was demanded they should part with their belongings. Any kind of resistance led to outright slaughter, accompanied by brutalities too ghastly to endure. On occasions, the attack would turn into genocide sparing only females who were either raped on the spot and then killed with sadistic pleasure, or carried away. These severities were interspersed with wild *bhangra* dances and the brutal beat of drums. One such dance was performed around impaled infants, struck on spikes.

The genocides, however, were not confined to any one side of the border. The performance on one side was equally matched by that on the other. If it were Hindus and Sikhs that were targeted on one side, the Muslims bore the brunt on the other.

Jullundhur, having become the capital of East Punjab, necessitated my frequent visit to it, especially to give assistance to my father. The same necessity often took me to New Delhi, too. This made me an unwilling witness to scenes of slaughter on the Indian side also. The worst among them was the attack on the Muslim Girls' Hostel at Amritsar. The inmates of this hostel were stripped and forced to march in a procession through the city up to the main market called Hall Bazar. There they were openly gang-raped, subjected to the most perverse treatment that the worst sadistic imagination could conceive, and finally murdered. Our car was forced to a halt at this spot on our way back to Jhelum from one of our visits to Jullundhur. The site was packed with a dense and wild crowd, which had gathered to watch the ghastly *tamasha* staged at the Hall Bazar. From the window of my car, I tried to search for signs of horror or compassion on the faces of those who stood around me, I could find none.

Over a period of time, witnessing such horrors frequently, I too had probably hardened up. Such incidents ceased to create in me the intensity of revulsion that I had experienced in the beginning. No calamity appeared to affect my numbed perceptions, which had frozen into stone. The agonies of Partition had left their permanent impact on all those who like me were witnesses to such orgies.

Yet, there were some redeeming elements in this Partition epic. It was evident in the way the unfortunate refugees, who formed convoys that travelled on foot and bullock carts, treated each other during such encounters. Of course, more often than not, such encounters ended in massacres, resulting in the total annihilation of those who happened to be on the wrong side of the border. Yet instances were not lacking when both sides sympathized with each other and extended help in whatever manner they could. This assistance would at times be hardly more than offering a cup of water and other such minor things. But what mattered more than these material things was the emotional understanding of the other's plight, and this concern was precious, indeed.

The month of September 1947 brought about the infamous 'Beas

Catastrophe', caused by the torrential rain, which swelled all the five rivers of Punjab at a time when the evacuation of refugees was at its chaotic climax. The convoys on foot used to be miles long. Even after the vanguard had crossed the borders, the rear would take several days to cross into the promised land. Ambushes often disintegrated these convoys, breaking the continuity of line and dissecting parts of it into separate units. The two convoys that encountered each other on that rainy day happened to be just that type of dissected parts, each going its own different way. What they shared for their temporary halt was a common stretch of land that separated the Beas river and one of its tongs that parted from it a little way upstream and rejoined it a mile or so downstream. Camping on this stretch without shelter, and constantly pounded by torrential rain, these unfortunate ones were suddenly relieved of all their suffering, as both parts of the Beas rose in spate and sucked them into its waters in the dark of the night. It took months to get the air cleared of the stench created by thousands of human and animal bodies, which lay scattered around. Nobody cared to think of burying or cremating the bodies. The concern was more for the living than the dead. So overpowering was the stench of rotting corpses, that one had to bury one's face in a towel as one drove past that road.

By March 1948, we had managed to send to India most of the families either brought by us or who had managed to reach the camp at Jhelum on their own. Yet, we could not call it a day and wind up the camp. Some inmates who had lost one or two of their family members insisted that they were still alive, and would join them sooner or later. Searching them was like the proverbial search for a needle in the haystack. There were no clues, nor had we resources to attempt it. The army had long been divided. We had only three constables belonging to the Pakistan Police as our security. As the war in Kashmir intensified, the Pakistan government grew concerned about our presence at that strategic point and wished us to vacate as early as possible.

My father, of course, felt duty-bound towards the evacuees and kept on searching for their missing relatives. How we succeeded in locating and rescuing some of them is a long story. The story of Jaswant Kaur may well be illustrative of this. This girl was recovered from Khewara, a village known for its rock salt mines and located in the hilly ranges that run along the flanks of Jhelum city. Though only 30 miles away from Jhelum, it took us quite a time to reach this village because of the unpaved road on this hilly stretch. Jaswant Kaur was 15 when she was rescued by Gulam Ishaq, a friend and neighbour of her father. Actually, she saved herself by hiding in the shed behind her house when her family was attacked by the mob and her father and two brothers were murdered. Her two sisters were abducted but her mother, Kartari and a teenage brother somehow managed to slip out and join the party, which was subsequently picked up by the rescuing army and brought to our camp.

Jaswant Kaur had remained in hiding till Gulam Ishaq found her after two days. He took her and the family's abandoned house for himself. Gulam Ishaq also presumed that the rest of the family of Jaswant Kaur had been killed. Having daughters of the same age, he felt a paternal affection for Jaswant, but being aware of the frayed tempers in the village, as a camouflage, he announced that he intended to take her as his wife. Even the *nikah* was performed but the marriage remained unconsummated. My father had served as a law consultant to the administrative authorities of the salt mines, and had also helped sort out land disputes of several families in that region. He decided to approach Gulam Ishaq, who had been one of his clients, for help in finding Kartari's daughters. When my father called on Gulam Ishaq he was not aware that the girl he was searching for was with him. While pleading ignorance about her whereabouts, Gulam, however, promised all help and also visited Kartari at Jhelum to show his concern for the family. Seeing him, Kartari fell at his feet. Though Gulam Ishaq was moved by Kartari's grief, he was no longer in a mood to part with Jaswant Kaur, for during her stay with him their courtship had developed into a bond of love between the two. Though he commiserated with Kartari, he did not confess that he knew about Jaswant.

We had no acquaintance with Jaswant's mother prior to her arrival in the camp. But the length of her stay forged a link that grew stronger with the lapse of time. However, we had no proof of the survival of her three daughters, including Jaswant. All we had was Kartari's conviction that the girls were still alive somewhere, a conviction which was commonly shared by all those with missing relatives who lived in the camp. What made her different from others was her persistence. Others gave up hope after some time, but she remained convinced of her daughters' existence and said that she would not leave the camp even if we were to abandon it.

It did not, however, take long for my father to discover that Jaswant Kaur was in the custody of Gulam Ishaq and that she was now his lawful wife. My father also became convinced that Gulam Ishaq exercized some influence in the region and could easily withstand pressures from the administration. The only way out was to let Jaswant Kaur know that her mother and brother were alive in Jhelum and that she would be able to communicate with them, if she so desired. The help to establish the link between Jaswant and her mother came from an unexpected quarter. Anwar Khan, one of the policemen in the contingent, happened to belong to Khewara. Initially, it was he who had brought the news about Jaswant to my father. Anwar Khan now managed to inform Jaswant about her mother's presence in the Jhelum camp. How he did this, we thought it prudent not to probe into.

By this time, Jaswant appeared to have gained Gulam Ishaq's confidence so much so that he let her see her mother. She had apparently promised him that she would return, and to strengthen his confidence, she had even allowed Gulam Ishaq to consummate their marriage on the night before her visit. But once reunited with her mother, Jaswant went through another trauma and found it hard to part with her mother and brother. She confessed how she was torn between the pull of her family and her love for Ishaq. Ishaq too seemed to have an inkling of Jaswant Kaur's dilemma. He visited the camp daily and stationing himself at Jhelum. Any effort on our part to shift the scale in favour of her mother was fraught with danger as she was not expected to keep it secret from Ishaq. Moreover, Ishaq was known for his uncontrollable temper and impulsive actions. All we could dare was to keep a vehicle ready to shift Jaswant the moment she showed signs of succumbing to her mother's persuasion.

When that moment arrived, my father lost no time to put the three in a station wagon and despatch them to Amritsar. This took place at the early hours of the day, after the whole night was spent by the two women in crying and cajoling each other. My father also sent me along with the trio, because he feared Gulam Ishaq's wrath may fall on any one of us. I was asked not to return until my father gave a green signal. This made the trip as hard for me as it was for Jaswant Kaur. I could not, for a moment, tear my mind off from the consequences my father may have to-face in the camp after our departure.

I later learnt that Ishaq was the first one to call on my father the next morning, hardly hours after our departure. Much to my father's surprise, Ishaq's explosive reactions on learning that Jaswant Kaur had departed did not come through as expected; on the other hand, he simply broke down and began to weep endlessly. He was a giant of a man, with the glowing pink complexion of an Afghan. The spectacle of the man of such build so reduced by grief, was hard for my father to bear. It took a long time for Gulam Ishaq to compose himself, and then to confess to my father what all he had gone through. He then pressed my father's hand, thanked him for saving him from further embarrassment and departed.

The story of Jaswant Kaur does not end with this, nor does it conclude my father's obligations to the family. With this and other similar, 'operations rescue', my father had woven a tangled web around himself. He could free neither himself nor my mother from it for the rest of their lives.

Rescuing these women and children in those chaotic times proved easier than resettling them. We discovered this when the process of rehabilitation began on the promised land. My mother informed me what was awaiting at the other end. When I went to house our first batch of evacuees in Jullundhur, I confirmed for myself my mother's suspicions. The camp indeed had been turned into a brothel. Not only was it difficult to trace the surviving kin of the evacuees but when found, it proved to be a Himalayan task to convince the kith to accept their women who bore the stigma of rape and molestation. My mother came up with an idea of how to take care of such destitutes, at least upto the time they could be rehabilitated. She opened a Home for them.

My mother had been evacuated from Karachi along with my brother Inder, his pregnant wife and my two sisters, via the sea to Rajkot and then by train to New Delhi. They had to sleep on the railway platform of Delhi Station on arrival as the city was under curfew. My mother then moved to Jullundhur with my two sisters, where she found a dilapidated dwelling in the suburb of the city called *Basti* Gazaan. The house and the *basti* had been vacated by the fleeing families of Muslim cobblers. Taking another abandoned structure in the neighbourhood, she started to house and care for the refugees, little knowing that the arrangement would outlive her and would involve my father as well. It was in this camp that we deposited Jaswant Kaur, Kartari and her son.

My mother was relieved that unlike others, Kartari showed no signs of the stigma-complex attached to her daughter, though she had lived for months in the house of Gulam Ishaq. But this was only a short-lived hope. Soon, the results of Jaswant Kaur's cohabitation with Gulam Ishaq began to show up. Initially Kartari showed no signs of panic and seemed to have accepted it as a *fait accompli*, but her teenage son, Bhagwan Singh, could not be reconciled to it. To him, the family's *izzat* had been sullied. The very thought of the taunts he would have to suffer due to his sister's sins was too much for him to bear. Finally Kartari chose to side with her son, inspite of my mother's persistent pleas and even threats. The mother and son slipped out of the camp one day, leaving Jaswant Kaur to her fate. My mother had to endure not only Jaswant Kaur, but several others who had been similarly abandoned.

With the passage of time, the inmates in my mother's camp began to grow in numbers, as did also my mother's burden. Carrying photographs and the personal details of the rescuees, she would go from camp to camp in search of their kin. Instead of reducing the burden on herself, my mother began to accumulate more load as the news of her dedication to the cause of the suffering began to attract more and more refugees. Many of those who came to her were not the victims of Muslims in Pakistan, but victims of their own countrymen.

My father who watched all these developments soon realized that this could not be handled single-handedly by my mother. For him, this posed a dilemma. His membership of the Pakistan parliament had now been shifted to the Indian parliament, necessitating his presence in New Delhi for almost half of the year. With the meagre allowance given to MPs in those days, he could not afford to keep two houses, one in Jullundhur and another in New Delhi; nor could he bear to live away from his wife at his age. He finally made his decision. He resigned his seat in Parliament and joined my mother in her work.

It was the beginning of the Nari Niketan movement in India. Both my mother and father devoted their lives to it. My father died in 1979, leaving all his assets to the Niketan. My mother continued to work in the Niketan till her demise. The citizenry of Jullundhur expressed its gratitude by naming the road that runs in front of the Nari Niketan after my father. My mother, who lived eight more years, refused to accept any honour for herself, rejoicing in the honours bestowed on her husband. It was only in 1997, that the Government of Punjab named after her the proposed Medical Institute in the city.

Nari Niketan of Jullundhur did not down its shutters with the demise of both my parents. My brother, Inder, has kept its flag flying, imparting added dimensions to its activities.

The Films of Ritwik Ghatak and the Partition

PARTHA CHATTERJEE

By the time India was partitioned in 1947, the world had already seen several devastating tragedies: the extermination of six million Jews at the hands of the Nazis for purely racial and ideological reasons; the murder of an identical number during the Stalinist purges in Communist Soviet Union in the 1930s; and before that the 'legitimization' of the use of chemical weapons in the Great War of 1914-18 perfected at the California Institute of Technology in the USA, that paved the way for the atom bombs dropped over Hiroshima and Nagasaki by the Americans to end the Second World War. An era of push-button technology for destroying the world had been ushered.

Ours has been a century where countries have been partitioned to fulfill the economic and political ambitions of formidable groups, completely ignoring the cost of human suffering, which has been enormous and continuous. Even in such callous and unpromising times the Partition of the Indian subcontinent registered as an awesome tragedy. But unlike other such historical events that spontaneously produce memorable artistic creations in literature, theatre, cinema, painting and sculpture, artistic works produced as a result of the Partition have not been adequate to the occasion. Among the exceptions are the short stories of Saadat Hasan Manto[1] in Urdu and the eight films by Ritwik Ghatak in Bengali, in six of which the political bifurcation of Bengal and by implication, India, plays a crucial role.

This article does not purport to be a comparative study of Manto and Ghatak and their respective methods of work. It would, however, be interesting to note the differences in their approach. The Partition never figures directly in Ritwik Ghatak's films; rather it is a riveting memory image of a cataclysmic event that had far reaching consequences. In Saadat Hasan Manto's short stories one becomes, through the author's astonishing narrative drive, willy-nilly a participant/observer of a given moment, set in a specific historical period.

The story 'Thanda Gosht' (Cold Flesh) is about an ordinary man so driven out of his mind, by the bestiality surrounding him during the communal riots that he goes and rapes an unconscious woman who, unknown to him, is dead and her body is turning cold. Another story 'Khol Do' (Open Up) is about a despairing Muslim father trying to locate his missing young daughter. She is finally located in an unconscious state in the attending doctor's tent in a refugee camp. Her father is greatly relieved to find her, but we know she has been gang-raped by the *razakars* (vigilantes) of her own community who were supposed to protect her. In the first story, it is suggested that a young Sikh, having taken leave of his senses, violates a dead woman, who may well be a Muslim. The second story clearly states the male desire to defile and destroy innocence and beauty and indeed the well-springs of life that transcend religious and political barriers.

There are other stories too where members of different communities, blinded by rage slaughter each other, including the one in which a man is casually stabbed to death and then his pyjamas are lowered to see if he is circumcised or not! And one of the assassins exclaims that a mistake has been committed! Similarly in 'Gurmukh Singh ki Wasiyat' (in its English translation called The Assignment) an old, ailing Muslim judge living with his beautiful young daughter, pre-teenage son and an older retainer in a Hindu quarter of Amritsar city during the carnage is visited on the day of Id by the son of Gurmukh Singh, a recently deceased Sikh, whom he had helped get justice and win a tricky case. The youth delivers *sevaiyyan* (sweet noodles) as a mark of respect like his father did earlier. As he is about to leave the locality he is accosted by a bunch of ruffians, whose leader says: 'Sardarji now that you have completed your assignment can we proceed with ours?' One can imagine the rest.

In Manto's stories the perspective is that of a profoundly compassionate witness. This is so perhaps because he had literally lived through the Partition and was at the height of his creative powers for the five or six years following the event. Ghatak too had been through the trauma of this historical moment but he was still a very young man. By the time Ghatak directed *Nagarik* (Citizen) in 1952 he was 26 years old. In artistic terms, he was a gifted child-man. The opening shot of the film with the camera travelling over the girders of Howrah Bridge in Calcutta and the as yet anonymous narrator's voice saying, '*Aami taake dekhe chhilaam. Aami taake chine chhilaam*' (I had seen him. I had recognized him), already has perceived the flow of time. History has become memory and memory history. Within minutes we are plunged into the lives of an impoverished refugee family from East Bengal living mostly on hope in Calcutta, waiting in vain, for life to turn for the better.

The film ends both on a note of despair as well as hope, as the impecunious family has to move to poorer lodgings, their potential bread-winner the young protagonist having failed to get a job. But long after the film is over, the image of Probha Debi as the all-sustaining mother stays in the mind. Her strength, compassion and vulnerability give credence to the opening images of the film and the narrator's observations. It also gives dignity to humanity, which is paupered and uprooted by history and enhances its stature.

Following the non-release of *Nagarik* (it was released in 1977, a year after his death), Ghatak, the card-carrying member of the Communist Party of India and one of the leading lights of its culture wing, Indian People's Theatre Association (IPTA), proceeded to Bombay to keep the pot boiling. He wrote for his mentor, Bimal Roy, a ghost story of enduring charm, *Madhumati*, and returned to Calcutta in 1957, to make the whimsical and poetic *Ajantrik*, about a taxi driver who drives his old rattle trap of a Chevrolet in tribal lands, touching Bengal and Bihar. The machine fails and 'dies' amidst lush nature, almost as an act of inevitability. The film bombed at the box office.

His next film *Bari Theke Paliye* (The Runaway Child), was supposedly for young children. Here a village schoolmaster's son, Kanchan, runs away from home and arrives in metropolitan Calcutta, in search of the El Dorado he has read about. During his adventures in the city, he meets Haridas a *channa chur wala* (roasted gram seller), who sports a false beard and turns out to be an unemployed schoolmaster, apart from being a refugee from East Bengal and a victim of the Partition. When Haridas learns that Kanchan has left home without informing his mother he becomes very concerned. The little boy asks him in turn about his mother and Haridas tells him that she is no more and that she died in great suffering. Here the word 'mother' acquires a dual significance: first as the giver of life to an individual and then as a symbol for the motherland that was unified Bengal. This is more so because of the opening words of the ditty that he sings to sell his wares: '*amaar naam Haridas pauthe ghuree baaro maash*' (My name is Haridas and I walk the pathways all the year around). He is not just an unemployed teacher turned itinerant gram seller, but also an eternal wanderer in search of the beacon of truth and compassion, due to the refugee status conferred on him by the politics of nationalism.

Ghatak the expelled Communist could yet effortlessly see through the masquerade of political and historical machination and perceive with poetic insight the aspirations of the common citizen. He emerged as the second truly great artist, from among the ranks of the Communists in independent India, to march forward triumphantly achieving one artistic success after another. The other great artist was Manik Bandhopadhyaya, who had really done his best work before and during the Second World War.

Meghe Dhaka Tara (The Cloud-Capped Star) was made in 1959, purely as a commercial chore to pay off bills, but what emerged was an undisputed masterpiece, set in a colony of refugees from East Bengal in suburban Calcutta. The entire place has a semi-rural atmosphere, recalling the past. The living quarters are fortified thatched huts. Everybody lives in the genteel poverty of the displaced lower, middle class with only the contentment of the past, sometimes imagined, as a succour against present-day poverty.

Nita, the sole support of a family steadily going down in the world, sacrifices herself and is consumed by tuberculosis, before the fortunes of her dear ones are finally restored. Her siblings flower, even her old school-master father paralyzed in an accident, suddenly recovers and spends his time running after his mischievous little grandson, who tends to climb onto the terrace of the newly built home, which was till then only a vulnerable impermanent structure. Her musician brother financed by her in his years of learning, finally makes good and comes to save the family but fails to save her. Life may have gone on but it would never be the same again. The dispossessed have to find their equilibrium 'standing over the bones' of those whom they have loved the most.

Komal Gandhar (E Flat), made in 1961, is a serio-comedy with lilting folk music of East Bengal and songs of revolution, composed by IPTA artists like Salil Choudhary, Hemant Kumar and Jyotirindra Nath Moitra. It includes Rabindra Sangeet, as well. It is both a celebration and an elegy. With wit and razor sharp perception it chronicles the divisive forces already at work, within the cultural movement of the Communist Party of India and inside the party itself.

There is a teasing dual movement within the structure of the film: first, there is the forward movement of the young troupe of actors entertaining ordinary people in the small towns and the countryside, in the hope of sharing their own idealism with them; and second, is the powerful, nostalgic pull of a past, which is still alive. There is the presence of the protagonist who talks of his mother, living on the other side of the river Padma, as he stands on its banks at Lalgola in West Bengal. He looks at the land on the other bank and wants his beloved to see it. This is the eastern province, which then formed part of a new country called

Pakistan. He confides that his mother practically died of starvation, implying two things at the same time, the physiological and spiritual lack of nourishment. The body and spirit or soul are wounded, on ocassion, simultaneously and fail almost at the same time, when faced with unspeakable violence, which is, in turn, interpreted as an historical inevitability by chroniclers!

There are other overt references in the film to the Partition: the shot of the camera moving forward rapidly on the railway track at Lalgola, to simulate a subjective angle, from the point of view of the engine, that comes to a halt abruptly to create a collision-like effect; and the screech of the brakes of the engine is again a cry of lament for the immediate past and the destruction of a more congenial way of life before politics and the blessings of modern civilization vitiated it. Since cinema deals largely in time and associative memory, one may suggest that in its conception this cinematic idea contains within it Fazlul Haq's dream of a federation of East and West Bengal independent of both India and Pakistan. In retrospect it does not seem such a far-fetched notion, as both East and West Bengal lost heavily on the economic, and well as the cultural, front through the Partition of the subcontinent. The East became a vassal state of Pakistan and remained so until it broke away in 1971 to form Bangladesh. The only link between East and West Pakistan was religion. In terms of culture, language and temperament they were poles apart.

The possibility of forging an independent political identity is handled with a touch of wistfulness in a sequence where the leader of the travelling players is presented with a medal by an ordinary woman, because she is deeply moved by the play they have just performed. The medal belonged to her dead son, who also took part in amateur theatricals. Fighting back her tears she exclaims, '*Tomrai to amaader Mukundo Das. Tomrai to amaader Khudiram*!' (For us you young men are like Mukundo Das and Khudiram!). In a single sentence the director links two revolutionary figures from pre-First World War Bengal, who had stood up against the might of the British. The exceptional popularity of Mukundo Das, a peripatetic folk singer, was due to the contents of his songs. They had a rousing effect on rural folk exhorting them to challenge the tyranny of the British administration, which discouraged local cottage industries in order to foist its own products instead. His lyrics had a great influence during the period of the first partition of Bengal in 1905, when Lord Curzon was the Viceroy of India. Khudiram Bose, a boy revolutionary, threw a crude home-made bomb at the carriage of Kingsford, the Sessions and District Judge, in Muzaffarpur in north Bihar and a Presidency Magistrate,

Bengal, 1904-8. Unfortunately the carriage was carrying the draconian judge and magistrate's wife and a house guest, Miss Kennedy, and not the man himself. The two ladies died in the explosion. Khudiram was mortified when he knew the truth. He was hanged later in 1908.

Ghatak achieved these artistic counterpoints and obligatos quite instinctively. His cinema for all its swift cross-currents of ideas seemed created wholly out of the moment rather than carefully pondered over a period of time. There are indeed many moments in *Komal Gandhar* where the past enhances our understanding of the present. The folk song *Ey paar padda! o paar padda moddikhane chaur tahaar moddhe boshe aachen shibbo shaudagaur* (Along this bank flows the river Padma and it flows along the other bank too, in the middle is the little island where lives Shiva the great trader), speaks of the vital composite culture that existed before the great division of the province placing the two halves, east and west, in different countries.

A traditional wedding song is played at the beginning of the film as the credit titles roll, *Aam tolaaye zoomur zaamur, kola tolaye biya, aiye lo shundoreer jaamai mukut maathaye diya* (A stirring of delight in the mango groves, a wedding in a clearing by the banana grove, see all, here comes the bridegroom wearing success' crown). This very same melody is repeated in many places throughout the story, with telling effect, as the hero Bhrigu sits with his lady love, Anusuiya, in the silence of the fern-filled landscape of the *khoai* in Shantiniketan. In retrospect, among the many interpretations of the scene proferred, one may possibly be that of a longing for a reunified Bengal, a throwback to easier and happier times. This view can be fortified by citing another sequence from the film, the staging of Kalidas' Sanskrit classic, *Shakuntala*, especially the scene with the eponymous heroine at her toilette preparing, with the assistance of the damsels in her company, to look beautiful for her beloved, King Dushyanta, who would betray her soon and, in a remarkable feat of amnesia, not recognize her or his child that she has brought into the world. It is indeed tempting to interpret this scene as a betrayal of the flowering and verdant Mother Bengal.

Komal Gandhar in artistic terms continues to astonish but its box-office failure was said to be engineered by vested political interests. Ghatak was by then physically and emotionally ravaged by the betrayal of his so-called friends in the Communist Party. His descent into alcoholic despair began and his life slowly went to pieces. But not before he had made the superb film *Subarnarekha* (The Golden Line), certainly amongst the most probing cinematic studies of homelessness in our century. His obsession with the Partition remained in his psyche, as this film was to reveal.

Subarnarekha was the product of chance. After suffering financial ruin Ghatak proceeded to Bombay at the behest of his actor-friend, Abhi Bhattacharya. An advance from a producer after a fortuitous meeting, led to the shooting of the film. It is about Ishwar Chakravarti, who arrives in a refugee camp in Calcutta from East Bengal with his little sister Sita. The place is called Navajeevan (New Life) Colony and true to form—in terms of the director's vision—it is set in semi-rural surroundings. The local landlord raids the place and has his minions kidnap some women, including Bagdi Bou. Her little son Abhiram is taken on, out of compassion by Ishwar. Ishwar is soon offered a job by an old friend Rambilas, whom he happens to meet in the street. The friend has a foundry by the river Subarnarekha. Ishwar is called a coward and a renegade by his school-master friend who runs Navajeevan Colony. Ignoring the jibes he proceeds with Sita and Abhiram to start a new life on the banks of the river, that promises so much. It is almost a foregone conclusion that such a story would end in tragedy. That it would acquire the reputation of a classic, cutting through time, space and the barriers of language and culture was probably beyond the imagination of the artist himself! The film is a product of its times, as well as of the debris of human consciousness left by the partition of Bengal and the Partition of India.

The film is full of echoes and ghosts from the past. The trajectory of the narrative is such that it prepares us for the things to come. First, on the arrival of Ishwar and his family, his bumptious new assistant tells little Sita that there are big, beautiful butterflies playing amongst the fragrant flowers, near the river Subarnarekha. Ishwar rebukes him: 'One should never lie to children, they catch on.' Then, as time passes, Abhi and Sita are seen playing at flying planes, in an abandoned World War II British airfield. Suddenly through a swift tracking shot the taxing of an aircraft before take off on the runway is simulated. Then shortly afterwards Sita points out to Abhiram the skeleton of a building and says: 'The (British) Sahibs would fly out to drop bombs on Burma and come back and enjoy themselves at the club!' In the third memorable incident, from Sita and Abhi's childhood, Sita suddenly comes face to face with a *bohurupee* (quick change artiste) made up as Ma Kali, the goddess of destruction. She is frightened and runs into the arms of the local accountant, a distraught old man, whose daughter has run away with her lover. The elder scolds the wandering actor: 'Why do you frighten little children?' 'I did not try to scare her Sir, she just ran into me!' replies the man.

Time passes. Sita and Abhiram grow up and fall in love. Ishwar wants to send him to Germany to become an engineer, probably because he thinks that the future belongs to science. Suddenly a commotion, at the small local railway station, changes the course of their lives. A dying old woman on the platform is called Bagdi Bou by her poor lady companion. Abhiram recognizes his mother. He performs her last rites and tells Ishwar of the incident. Abhiram and Sita's marriage is now violently opposed to by Ishwar, the champion of science, on grounds of caste as he is now aware that his little foster brother is really from the lower echelons of society. Abhiram and Sita elope to prevent her marriage arranged elsewhere, by her brother. Ishwar's world falls apart. The film then takes on the dimensions of a profound morality tale.

Ishwar is said by the locals to have gone mad. In his grief, at the loss of his much beloved little sister and Abhiram, he tries to hang himself. Just then his old schoolmaster friend from Navajeevan Colony appears like a ghost at the window and exclaims: '*Raat kauto holo uttor mele na*!' (How far gone is the night. There is no answer!) Suicide postponed, they go together to spend Ishwar's hard earned money in Calcutta, the city of sin. They go to the races. They go to a posh restaurant and get drunk. The broken down teacher declaims in Sanskrit: 'What you cannot touch is not real.' After a few drinks he quarrels with Ishwar on an esoteric point, while discussing mythology, and states in disgust: 'Nachiketa was a fool . . . wanted to know the secret of life.' The two friends then stagger into a cab in search of more pleasure. They come to a young singer, who is, unknown to herself, roused from deep sleep by a shrewd old crone, to make her debut, like the singing courtesans of old. An inebriated Ishwar recognizes the now widowed Sita, who picks up a *bontee* (a curved sharp blade attached to a fixed plate used for cutting vegetables and fish) and kills herself. Next morning there is an almighty scandal and headlines in the newspapers. After an exhausting trial, Ishwar is acquitted by the courts and heads home with Sita's little son in tow.

Ishwar has lost his job. The fields are full of ripe grain. He hears his little nephew singing the same Tagore song, that Sita used to sing as a child: '*Aaj dhaaner khete raudro chayaar looko churee khela re*' (Sunshine and shadow play hide and seek in the fields laden with ripe grain). The fields across the railway tracks are blessed with a bountiful harvest and there is an air of expectancy. Suddenly the little one stops singing and asks his uncle: 'Mother used to say that big, colourful butterflies play among the flowers by the Subarnarekha river. Is it true?' Ishwar Chakravarti, the man of honour, is faced with the greatest dilemma of his life, whether to lie to the young one or not? After a moment's hesitation, he nods and says 'Yes!'.

Nephew and uncle walk away through a craggy landscape towards the horizon, accompanied by a life-renewing hymn of Tagore, sung with great feeling and played on the soundtrack. The old and the young have gone on in the world, in search of a new home. They do not carry any mementos with them, other than their own meagre belongings. The idea of finding a new home, first mooted in *Nagarik*, is pursued in *Meghe Dhaka Tara* and then in *Subarnarekha*, with a poignancy and an intensity that haunts and keeps resurfacing at unexpected moments, like a melody lying asleep in the subconscious mind.

Titas Ekti Nadir Naam (A River Called Titash), Ghatak's penultimate film made in Bangladesh in 1972, does not deal directly with the Partition, but it tackles the moral, ethical and political problems connected with displacement. It is a magnificent film about the dissolution of a fishing community in the early 1920s. The river changes course and begins to shrink, the fishermen panic and disperse and their land is taken over by a community of traders. The final tragedy and the irony of this change is witnessed by a dying woman and a child, running through the paddy fields, playing with a leaf whistle.

The Partition of 1947, the War of Liberation in Bangladesh in 1971, the central character Neelkantha Bagohi's own vagabondage and the rise of the Naxalites are the sum and substance of Ghatak's last film, *Jukti Takko Aar Gappo* (Arguments and a Story), made in 1971-4. The film is full of strong autobiographical elements and the director is busy most of the time making clumsy and pompous apologies for a misspent life. The chronic alcoholic, Neelkantha (the name is deliberately chosen to liken him to the leading Hindu deity, Lord Shiva, whose throat turned blue, after he drank all the poison in the world on the churning of the ocean, *samudra manthan*), is a strong blend of a crashing bore and a visionary.

Within minutes of the start of the film, Neelkantha's wife leaves him because of his unpredictable lifestyle and unreliable character, taking with her their pre-teenage son, named Satya (Truth). Neelkantha leaves the house he has been living in and takes to the streets because he can to longer pay the rent. He begins his last journey through life with a bearded youth, who hero worships him. Soon they meet a refugee girl from East Bengal fleeing the murderous Pakistani Army. In one of the few genuinely moving sequences in the film, Neelkantha asks her: 'Who are you Mother? Are you the soul of my shattered ravaged Bengal.' The terrified girl replies: 'Yes I am Bangabala', literally meaning a woman of Bengal. Along with Bangabala and the hirsute young man, Neelkantha moves across Calcutta, picks up an old Sanskrit teacher being harried by stupid children and together they leave Calcutta for the countryside, where they run into an old *chau* (folk dance form found in West Bengal and Orissa) dance master. The stage for his dance macabre is set, when Neelkantha gets into a scrape with the local landlord and his thugs and, in the melee, his newly acquired companion the old Sanskritist is accidentally killed. Moving deeper into the countryside they come across a group of young Naxalites. Neelkantha exchanges reams of dialogue with them, almost all of it ideological ping-pong. A police attack follows and Neelkantha is killed in the crossfire, united in death with his wife, son and Mother Earth.

The Partition of India is referred to quite regularly in the film. The uprooted Neelkantha is a product of the event. His protégés are going to be victims of future divisions of land and psyche, while their self-seeking masters and rulers sell out to more powerful bidders within and without the country.

The Great Calcutta Killings of 1946, the riots in Noakhali, the wave of murderous insanity that swept undivided Bengal, the riots in Lahore, the butchery in other parts of Punjab and northern India, will all have been forgotten, while the sufferers in Ghatak's films could easily be international refugees like the Yugoslavs, Lebanese, Palestinians, Vietnamese and the people who came from those parts of Africa that were under the British, French, Belgian, Portuguese, German or Dutch rule in the last 150 years.

The scene changes. Some moments from Ghatak's films: the old accountant in *Subarnarekha* tells little Sita of how King Janaka of Mithila found his daughter Sita, while tilling the soil; a *baul* asks in song, '*Maajhee tore naam jaani naa, aami daak dimu kare*?' (O boatman I do not know your name. How shall I call out to you?); in *Meghe Dhaka Tara* and, in *Komal Gandhar*, two very small girls make chalk drawings on the floor, wipe them off, wanting to start all over again.

NOTE

1. All references in this article are to Balraj Manra and Sharad Dutt, ed., *Collected Works of Saadat Hasan Manto* (in Hindi) (Delhi, 1998); and Khalid Hasan, ed., *Kingdom's End—Short Stories of Saadat Hasan Manto* (New Delhi, 1990).

Partition Memory and Popular Culture

BADRI NARAIN TIWARI

This paper studies the multiple forms in which a single event, the Partition of India, is perceived in the popular mind in the Bhojpuri region, and how these remembrances are reflected in their cultural performances, that is, in *nach* drama, folksongs and proverbs. The Bhojpuri region of Bihar consists of districts such as Bhojpur, Rohtas, Buxar, Champaran, Muzaffarpur, etc., in which the Bhojpuri dialect is spoken. Here I propose to study three folk narratives about Partition, remembered by the folk mind, which are a part of Bhojpuri culture.

On the theoretical plane the study of memories contain rich discourses. It has attracted immense research by philosophers and scientists.[1] The psychology of memory was translated into the sociology of memory, especially by Herbert Marcuse. Whereas Freud concentrated on the individual psyche, Marcuse concentrated on the social psyche. Memory is now not only considered part of the 'psychical world' but also the domain of social investigation. The researches on the relationship between memory and history became a leading field of investigation in the 1980s. The initial studies stayed close to theoretical issues. The Maurice Harbwachs work on collective memory paved the way for historians and anthropologists to study the role of memory in the construction of national identity.[2] Other French historians like Legoff, Furet and Pierra Nora enriched the study of memory in the social and historical context.[3]

I

During rural fairs arranged around Arrah, Bikram, Sasaram and neighbouring areas, small booklets are found to be displayed on a soiled *dhoti* on the footpath. Some spectators glance at the contents and some purchase them. These booklets are based on folk tales, folk songs, folk proverbs and other popular subjects. They are printed in the small presses of Patna, Varanasi and Calcutta, on cheap paper. The cost ranges from 50 paise to 20 rupees. Some people call these folk literature, some popular literature and some others cheap literature. The circulation of these small pamphlets runs into lakhs among the semi-literate *ganwais* (rural people) and *kasbais* (people of small towns). One such booklet is entitled *Bantwara*, written by Surya Nath.[4] It tells the story of two brothers, who used to live prosperous lives in a small village. Once in a dream, a serpent, named *irshya* (jealousy), went into the ear of the younger brother. Next morning, after getting up, he was filled with jealously. Gradually this *irshya*, destroyed the peace and harmony of that house and the brothers started living separately. Both of them had to live distressed lives. The author concludes with the sentence: 'A country was divided into two lands—one India and another Pakistan because of this *irshya* only.'

In this metaphorical narrative, splitting of a family is used as the symbol illustrating the Partition of India. Family-partition is a very popular symbol in the folk psyche. This symbol has been used very effectively to show the tragedy of the Partition. Another possible explanation is that the symbolic power of the Partition of India, *Bharat vibhajan,* has been used by authors to make their narrative of personal relationships powerful. Whatever be the truth, it is evident that the Partition is viewed as a tragedy in the life of the Indian subcontinent. In addition, according to this narrative,'jealousy' is presumed to be the root cause of it.

The causes of a partition could be complex historical, political or economic factors, but the folk psyche simplifies it through popular narrative and converts it into 'a type', which imparts the elements of popularity to any narrative. If one deconstructs the metaphor of this narrative, one finds that India is the elder brother and Pakistan the younger brother or the Hindus are symbolized as elder brothers and the Muslims as their younger brothers. In this story jealousy is shown to have crept into the younger brother, that is, in the hearts of the supporters of Pakistan. Thus those who demanded a separate Pakistan are treated as irresponsible. But it is also mentioned that a serpent named 'jealousy' entered through his ears during the night, when he was asleep. Consequently, even the truant younger brother is not assumed to be a sinner; but the blame is laid on the feeling of jealousy, which has entered into him, resulting in the rift between the brothers. Since this popular booklet is written by a Hindu writer, it is possible that a common Hindu folk perception of the tragic event gets reflected in it.

II

In the Bhojpuri region, dance and *nautanki* shows are important means of folk entertainment, especially on the occasions of marriages and festivals. One such dance group is the Nagesar Dance Party, which presents plays with romantic, social and patriotic themes. *Bedesia*, *Chambal Ghati Ka Lootera*, *Reshma Chuharmal*, *Sorathi Birjabhar*, *Damad-Vadh* and *Bantwara* are favourite plays. Some of the plays staged by these dance parties are written by the eminent writers like the Bhojpuri poet and dramatist, Bhikari Thakur. Some are collected and published in the form of popular booklets and some others are only composed by the authors. According to its time and context, *sutradhaars* (narrators) of these dance parties, in their own way, construct and deconstruct the themes of dramas written by others. It is also interesting that actors and *sutradhaars* of these dance groups are mostly illiterate people from the lower castes.

Most of the dramas performed by the Nagesar Dance Party are written and directed by this group. One play describes the Hindus and Muslims living together in India. Both the communities lived in harmony and were like the two banks of a river or the two branches of a tree. The story goes something like this: one group is led by Nehru and Gandhi Baba. The English assure Jinnah, the leader of the second group, that after independence he would be made the king of the country. On the other hand, Nehru is told that only he would become the ruler of the country. This question of ruling the country becomes the cause of fighting amongst them, and India gets split into two parts. Gandhi Baba grieves, yet India gets divided.

This play has comic interventions, during which the clown in the drama makes the public laugh by a variety of his short satirical caricatures. One such comic character is the *neta* (leader) through whom the trickery, ambitions and lack of character, generally associated with the leaders of the subcontinent, are exposed. Here is an example:

Bap tabah ba beta se
Desh tabah ba neta se

(Father is in agony [destroyed] because of his son, the country is distressed because of its leader)

And again:

Are wahi neta log
Jo desh ke bant dihlas.[5]

(Oh! the same leaders who have divided our country)

Thus, in the light of the contemporary strained relations between the two communities and in reinterpreting the event of the Partition, the *neta* is treated as a 'type' and assumed to be the sinner. In illuminating the present folk psyche the play effectively reinterprets the past, in this case the Partition.

III

During festivals, like Dussehra and Diwali, the youth in the villages enact plays through the night. People of the village see these plays, which could be based on religious, social, patriotic or romantic themes. Some plays are such, which have been repeated many times in the last ten years, in the way similar to *Ramlila*, *Krishnalila*, *Veer Kunwar Singh*, *Shahid Bhagat Singh*, *Chandra Shekhar Azad*, *Gora Badan*, *Shahari Ladki*, *Dahej*, etc. These plays are usually selected from those printed in the form of popular booklets and available for sale in the *kasbas* and fairs. Actors and directors of these plays are usually young people, who are educated but unemployed, or who are studying in schools and colleges. So the performances echo the opinion and thinking of the literate and educated rural youth. The entertaining plays, with songs or comic episodes, contain one or the other social message.

On the occasion of Dussehra, during the performance of one of the plays, staged in Khutaha Bazaar, the following song was heard by this author:

Aapas mein mat lado bhai
Dhan dharm koi cheez nahin hoti
Dharm ke naam par desh ko mat banto bhai.[6]

(Brothers do not fight. Money and religion are not so important. Do not divide the country in the name of religion.)

This song shows us that in the rural literate psyche, the fragmentation going on today in the name of religion, gets linked with the past division of the country in the name of religion. In this way the Partition of India in 1947 transforms itself into a metaphor of all the partitions occurring in the name of religion.

CONCLUSION

Popular memory is not an unevocative and innocent domain.[7] It contains multiple voices. These investigations of memory and remembrance, in their own small way, have broken the myth of 'History' (that is, one history) and established the theoretical basis for multiple histories. Howard Zinn proposed many reasons in defence of the view that there could be no single representative account of any given phenomena.[8] About the process of remembering the past, it is not that the past is a contested terrain, selectively remembered or conveniently forgotten or something invented.[9] That is why Steven Rose proposes that people's memories in term of records of their own experiences must be treasured, but they are also very fragile.[10]

Thus in the contemporary folk psyche, there is no single narrative for the Partition but it has multiple narratives. These are presented here in three different ways: the first gives prime place to jealousy; the second mentions the ambitions of leaders and the role of Englishmen in the communal tangle; and in the third religion is assumed to be the cause of Partition. The second narrative is the most specific, *vis à vis* Partition. It points a finger at Englishmen as being the cause of the Partition of India. In addition, it does not exclude the ambitions of Nehru and Jinnah as being less responsible for it. The various reasons contained within these narratives point to different layers of collective memory, which in turn reflects the differences cropping up due to differing experiences of a reality in different locations. Therefore, one cannot negate the possibility of other narratives of Partition in Bhojpuri life.

In conclusion we may point out that in all the three narratives there is tendency to perceive, reinvent and reinterpret the past in the context of a present crisis.

NOTES

1. Jeffrey A. Barash, 'The Source of Memory', *Journal of the History of Ideas*, Vol. CVIII, No. 4 (October 1997), pp. 707-11.
2. See Patrick H. Hutton, 'The Role of Memory in the Historiography of the French Revolution', *History and Theory*, Vol. XXX, No. 1 (1991), pp. 57-69.
3. Ibid.
4. Surya Nath, *Bantwara* (Patna, 1978).
5. Recorded in Ojhwalia Village of Sahar Thana, Bhojpur District of Bihar, on 5 August 1996.
6. Recorded in Khutaha Bazaar, on 17 November 1998.
7. Hutton, op.cit.
8. Howard Zinn, *The Politics of Past* (Boston, 1970), p. 3.
9. Ibid., pp. 3-9.
10. Steven Rose, *The Making of Memory: From Calculus to Mind* (London, 1992).

The Unsettling—Satish Gujral and His Paintings on Partition

KESHAV MALIK

The Partition, surely, is personal history for those of us who are above 50 winters. I being one of them, my review of the cataclysmic event is likely to be less of an objective account and more that of a musing witness. After all, here was a legislated amputation from which wound the blood of life still oozes, at times only in driblets but earlier in an alarming flood. The mind of the witness wanders distressed, unable to find a satisfactory solution to what happened and why, and so his emotions fester. The whole issue appears labyrinthine.

To speak of myself, I was in Sialkot and Lahore just a few days before the fatal date—returning as I was then from Srinagar by road. There did not seem much outward sign of what was to come like an avalanche within days, but when it finally came millions upon millions were engulfed in the catastrophe. How many millions? So many were encompassed in its gruesome misery, that it was impossible to have kept a count.

The facts of history are to be coolly pondered over by scholars, but those in the thick of a maelstrom like the one of the Partition, cannot remain entirely passive, especially those gifted with such perceptual sensitivity as could capture the tragic event through an artistic media.

Satish Gujral, among others, felt the full impact of the Partition personally. Like many others his family too was uprooted from its native ground. But the talent and craft he had acquired in the Arts College in Lahore, which was subsequently enriched by his art training in Bombay, or still later and more fatefully in Mexico, enabled him to express in oil-on-canvas the pathos of the Partition. His subjects were the affected human beings—common people unable to come to terms with what had devastated their lives. The painter caught out his weeping, anguished men and women not in normal—that is, uneventful—moments, but in the throes of ruination, when all was lost, their faces contorted, their bodies writhing

* I am grateful to Satish Gujral for allowing me to publish his paintings.

and their eyes looking upwards uncomprehendingly. Blinded and with a pain beyond belief each one of them appear inconsolable.

Such visual depictions follow in line with the highly volatile and expressionistic manner of the Mexican masters. Their works too have the same alarm and flaunt the same whirlwind of brush-strokes and seem to wrap up everything in their relentless passage. Instead of the so-called beauty of style there is raw energy in this act. The works disturb the viewer's complacency and will not leave him or her at rest. And so viewing Satish Gujral or the Mexican masters, you can only wring your hands in utter despair. But this is no melodrama, rather it is a meditation in which your own personal consciousness is sought to be irrevocably involved. You too have got to despair and repent before you can be free from their hold to take the oath that you will not be forgetful in future. A pain like this you are obliged to share in and then you emerge a changed, sobered and wiser person.

Some of the art perforce has got to be discreetly sweet and brings about a state of tranquillity in our hearts. Such states are necessary moments for human life and no one looks forward to them with expectation, considering the very hazards that assail life at every turn. But a merely lulled or beguiled existence, one in which you have become oblivious of the existential contingencies, as of the wariness and caution demanded of you, would be fatal. Things like the Partition do not happen every day, and yet maybe there could well be another such. It is, perhaps, no use crying over spilt milk, and heed good advice to look only to the future. Yet you are human, only to the extent that facts—even unsavoury ones—of history are remembered from time to time. That is the necessary toll you have got to pay to earn your comfort in the present tense. Eternal vigilance they say is the price of liberty. History repeats itself or history does not repeat itself. Which of the two propositions is right? Either way, one has got to take thought, to reflect, to meditate the facts of the past and to take a leaf out of the pages of history.

The way, therefore, to enjoy Satish Gujral's works on the Partition is to remember that behind the present picnics of India's upper middle classes is a huge lesion, the slaughter of millions on both sides of the border, that behind it also has been the expression of spite, venom and untold carnage, all those cruelties beyond belief. Indeed, that is the backlog intact from the morally still unsorted out centuries. The pain that is registered in the painter's compositions is a sign that the work of healing is still not complete. The Partition was only one such upshot. Even as the centuries old rift in the culture's psyche was beginning to be healed and things were

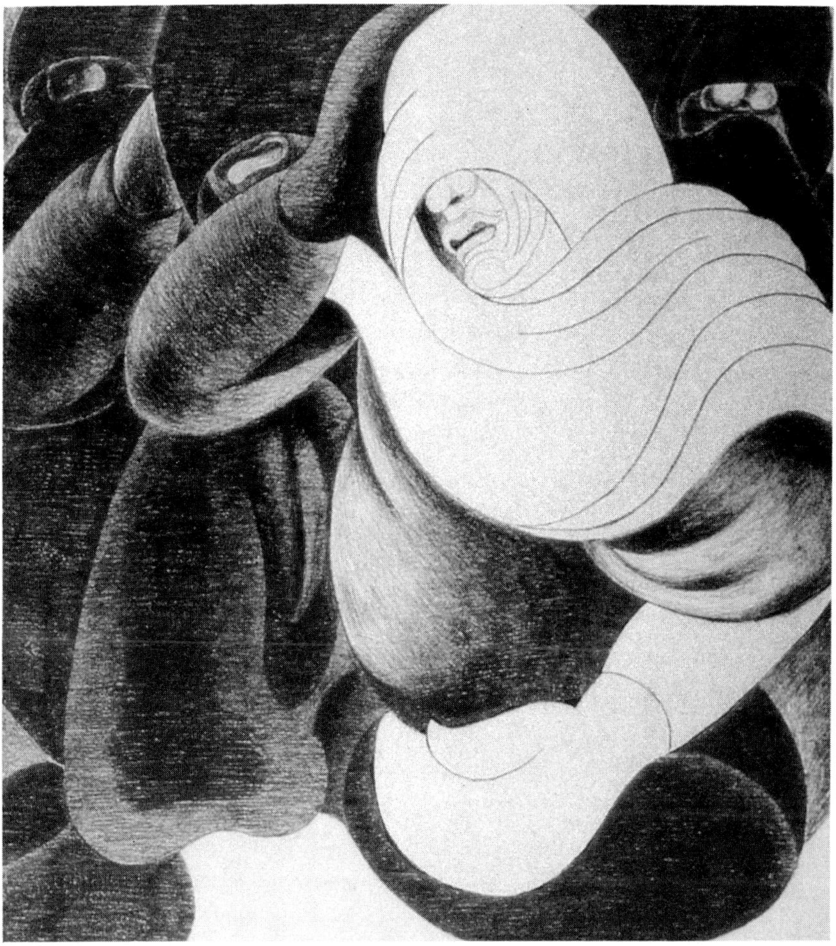

MOURNING EN-MASSE, 1947-48

SNARE OF MEMORY, 1954

THE PILGRIM, 1952

DANCE OF DESTRUCTION (2) 1950

SERMON ON THE MOUNT, 1952

MOURNIGN EN-MASSE (2), 1948

settling down to a semblance of the humane, came the great divide and once more the atavistic powers were let loose. The price of the division was that innocent bystanders—the defenceless had to pay, as always, with their lives and their life's belongings. Therefore, art such as is depicted in Satish Gujral's earliest works is meant to make you feel and react personally. And only after that you are enabled to take the appropriate oath that things like this will not come to pass again.

Whether Satish Gujral's works are 'great', is not our concern over here. What is of the moment is that they convey genuine emotion. In this sense are they vital and vitalizing. Works such as these are publicly shareable since they pertain to our common life ground. They connect us all, without smothering us in needless propoganda.

Of course, the artist in Gujral was successful in expressing such heavy uncontrollable emotions without any artistic guile, since he had by the early 1950s acquired a good grounding in his craft. He had learnt his lessons from the Mexican masters well and these were of the greatest use to him in this genre of work. The several styles that he has since pursued entail entirely different strategies. These later works are far more indiscerpt and not 'head on', being more artistic or aesthetic expressions of a form or of distanced numinous contents, rather than displaying the immediacy or the intensity of those earlier works, which were charged with sorrow. That sort of work is certainly not undertaken everyday—you do not, after all, live at the peak for more than a few moments. And yet the expression of the same becomes crucial for our own catharsis.

Among those in the visual arts of the day, Satish Gujral is almost about the only one who has tackled a difficult and painful subject with conviction. A few contemporary writers did attempt something similar for creative writing—among them are Amrita Pritam and Bhisham Sahni. Of course in the two Bengals, there were still other voices, who recreated the echoes of the wail of a forlorn humanity, in the same manner as they had given expression to the Bengal famine preceding it.

As is evident, the aftermath of the Partition is still with us in a big way, ghosts like this are not easily laid to rest. This task is to be tackled by those of the subcontinent who have a wide enough awareness and, thereby, also possess a keen conscience. Anyone of these cannot be mercenaries of the establishment on either side of the border. They have to determine their creative fields in the arts, in the broadest sense. And only then would their works really be acts of faith testifying to long memories. The whole meaning and purpose of dwelling on the Partition and other such momentous events cannot be academic alone and at least not so for the ordinary citizen. It ought to be in order to fortify personal convictions as in order to guide the conduct of our own lives. The act is, in no sense, a mere vicarious, high class intellectual entertainment or accomplishment.

Till this day, off and on, I myself still feel the tremors of that event which happened 50 years ago and especially so in the hours of the night. Then nightmares come and revisit *verboten* spaces under strange circumstances, ever so often crossing the border. Either that, or similar spectres of the de facto partition in the state of Kashmir. These are intimations from the underworld of the self, which one normally keeps down during the day time but only to have it stage a comeback in the small hours of the night. There was something 50 years ago and then something in 1965, and then in 1971, et al. There is such a huge backlog at the deep core of one's head needing solutions, crying for an airing.

I have aired this part of my buried self in poems over the years, and in this way have responded to Satish Gujral's earlier visions. I was also one of the first to write about his Partition work, in the early 1950s and to have met with these works in New York in 1953 and, then again, in London in 1954. Thus I was able to come to terms with his spirit in some small ways.

The Landscape of Memories and Writing of Tamas*: An Interview with Bhisham Sahni*

ALOK BHALLA

My interview with Bhisham Sahni was conducted in English on 18 June 1996, at the Indian Institute of Advanced Study, Shimla, where both of us were visiting fellows for a brief period. Before recording the interview we had met often and discussed our own attempts to understand the events that led to the Partition of the Indian subcontinent in 1947 and the different fictional representations of that period by a range of writers from India and Pakistan. As we talked about his childhood in Rawalpindi, and his days in Lahore, between 1915 and 1947, it seemed as if, in the process of recreating his personal, political and religious past, Bhisham Sahni was reaffirming some of the social assumptions of his life and writing, since, as if, in part at least, the point of his recollection lay in its value for the work he had done after his migration to India. Even though he had been a witness to the violence of the Partition and forced to leave behind all that he had known and cherished when he left Rawalpindi on 13 August 1947, his conversations with me were always free from rancour and vengeful memories. It was not that he had forgotten the days of riots, arson and murder. Rather, for him, they were grim aberrations, which sometimes happen when social and political reason is suspended. In some larger human sense, the years around the Partition were, he thought, empty of meaning, logic and purpose; years of *tamas*, of blank darkness. The Partition, he insisted, was a mistake; the result perhaps of the fatal idolatry of religious politics, which tempted some of us and against which we failed to guard ourselves. Writers like Saadat Hasan Manto, he said, may have in moments of despair, concluded that the violence of the Partition days was a sure sign of the degradation, which had marked every instance of the nationalist movement, and a final refutation of our capacity for decency and freedom. He was honest enough to concede that, after having witnessed the horrors of the Partition, he was sometimes willing to accept

Manto's evaluation of ourselves. His memories, however, refused to let him forget that there was also a time, prior to the Partition, when our social and experiential habitat was such that we were able to conduct our religious affairs in tolerant regard for each other and without paranoiac hatred.

His life prior to the Partition, he insisted, was dominated by anti-colonialist politics and not by communal antagonism. As he spoke, it became clear that what he remembered of his past was consciously inflected by Gandhian and Nehruvian concerns—concerns which seem to have rarely left him since. During his detour through the landscape of memories, one felt that he was reaffirming days of deep-rooted friendships, reliable acts of world-making and exemplary beliefs; that he was once again reordering for himself a historically stable world, before the Partition suddenly forced him to confront a phantasmagoric time in which more than two million people were slaughtered, more than ten million were forced to migrate and countless number abducted, raped and sold into slavery. Of course, Rawalpindi and Lahore of his memories of pre-Partition days were not idyllic communities. He was more than ready to acknowledge that life's contingencies there, as everywhere and always, offered enough chances to prejudice, bigotry, stupidity, opportunism and contradictory loyalties to make for the usual miseries of everyday life. But, still, life was stable enough to suggest that Rawalpindi and Lahore were 'home' with their own kind of claim and grace and civilizational purpose. He could not remember any compelling examples to suggest that the relations between the Hindus and the Muslims were so marked with opposition, suspicion and humiliation that the genocide of 1947 was historically foredoomed.

Inevitably, thereafter, our conversations turned to *Tamas*, which was first published in Hindi in 1974 and given the Sahitya Akademi Award in 1975. We talked about the series of communal riots in post-independence India, which had persuaded him to re-examine the violence of the Partition days, in the novel. The Partition, we agreed, was a particular historical event, the result of a singular moment and its ideological passions. The Hindu-Muslim violence had other causes and other provocations. It was important for us to make that discrimination, because our ways of dealing with many of the present conflicts in the country hinged on our understanding of the Partition either as a unique event or as merely a bloodier example of a long history of communal conflicts. Neither of us was tempted by the arguments of the ideological and religious right in India and Pakistan, that the agenda of the Partition had still to be completed. If there was nothing 'historically necessary' or 'natural' about the Partition in the first place, there was even less justification either in the campaigns to divide the nation further into smaller religious fragments or in the acts of vandalism designed to undermine the secular structure of the nation. Instances of communal riots, the destruction of Babri Masjid and the sectarian terror in Punjab or Kashmir did not point to the existence of a tragic fault-line in the identity of the country; they were instead, aberrations within the composite ethos of the nation; signs of unresolved economic and social difficulties and not examples of unredeemable antagonism between religious groups.

In order to prepare ourselves for the interview, we decided to see the film based on *Tamas*, directed by Govind Nihalini. The film was made in 1987, about 13 years after the publication of the novel. Bhisham Sahni was one of the writers of the screenplay, and hence partly responsible for the radical changes in the narrative structure of the story. He also acted as Harnam Singh, a moral centre in the filmic version. While considering the difference between the novel and the film, I wondered why he had agreed to play the role of Harnam Singh, an old Sikh who runs a tea shop in a small village. By accepting this role, was he in some way reliving the political refusal of his father, who was a reasonably prosperous businessman in Rawalpindi, to migrate in 1947? His father's historical understanding, he told me, was not very different from that of millions of Hindus and Muslims. Like countless others, his father did not believe that mere change of rulers, meant 'exile' for people like him from the land where they had their memories, genealogies and tradition. I pointed out to him that such disbelief marked nearly every fictional account I had read about the Partition, for example Intizar Hussain's *Basti* or 'Hindustan Se Ek Khat' (A Letter from India), Ashfaque Ahmed's 'Gadariya' (The Shepherd) or the last part of Krishna Sobti's *Zindaginama.*

I wondered why, in a significant departure from the novel, Harnam Singh had become a figure of moral courage in the film. In the novel, he is an emblem of uncomprehending sorrow and his suffering is a representative example of everyone who survived those genocidal times. After he reaches the refugee camp, he talks obsessively about all that he had lost and pleads inconsolably for help. In the film, however, he acquires a tragic dignity and becomes a Gandhian figure, who can set aside his own sorrow in order to help someone in greater need of solace. Instead of being a bewildered old man, whom one pities, because he has no hope of a life of meaning and purpose, he decides to adopt Nathu's pregnant wife as his daughter. He neither inquires into her past nor worries about the fact that she is the wife of a Hindu and a *chamar.* The novel is bleak, and promises neither forgiveness nor redemption. The film, however, ends with Harnam Singh's instinctive resistance to barbarism. His decision to make Nathu's wife a part of his family is not only a fine gesture of 'in-gathering' and community-making, but is also contrary to the politics of separate identities and hysterical assertions of religious difference, which led to the Partition of 1947 and which still threaten our peace. With this act, his name acquires a new resonance. Instead of being every man who suffers, he becomes an example of what any man ought to do and be ('Harnam' is an abbreviation of Hari Nam meaning God. However 'Harnam' can also be translated as 'any name').

Bhisham Sahni said that when he played the role of Harnam Singh in the film, he felt such deep empathy for him that he forgot the pathos with which the character is depicted in the novel. He added that the moral fortitude of Harnam Singh in the film was perhaps a result of his own increasing confidence in the ability of the country's composite ethos to withstand new separatist threats and, at the same time, to reach out to its neighbours in order to establish a new lease of peace in the region.

I suggested that despite some fundamental differences in the narrative thrust of the novel and the film, the primary force of both the versions of *Tamas* lay in the assertion that, even during the darkest hours of the Partition, there were a number of non-heroic and fallible people, who continued to abide by the covenant of a civil society, which always places greater value on 'well-doing' than on religious *fatwas*. Thus, Nathu intuitively knows that he has done wrong by allowing himself, out of greed and lust, to become the cause of the defilement of a mosque. He does not regard the communal frenzy that follows the discovery of a pig's carcass on the steps of the mosque as a triumph of his Hindu identity, but sees it as a sign of the ruin of his ethical self (in the film version, when he sees the dead pig before the mosque, he says to himself: *Maine paap kiya hai*—I have sinned). He feels the indignity of having been used because he is poor and draws from his error of judgement the stern moral that his misdeed is so grievous that he may have to atone for it with his life. It is this process of thought that makes him so achingly human and the subject of our profoundest sympathy and pity—emotions which one does not have for any of the other characters whose actions are merely charged with religious and sectarian enthusiasm.

Similarly, when Harnam Singh and his wife knock on Rajo's door seeking refuge and mercy, she does not forget that she is a Muslim, but finds herself facing the only elemental question that really matters: What is the human worth of the politics of religious identities being played out around her? Confronted with this human plea, she understands that, whatever her religious faith, her affective being, which has been formed within a multi-religious society, can retain its integrity only if she fulfils her responsibility towards the old couple, no matter who they are and what their religious faith is. After some hesitation, she decisively says: '*Na jao ji, ruk jao, sankal chada do . . . Ghar aaye ko nikaal dun? Allah ke dargah mein sabhi ko jana hai . . .*' (Don't go, stay. Lock the door . . . You knocked at my door with some hope in your heart. . . How can I throw you out of my house? We'll all have to stand before Allah's *dargah* someday...).

During another conversation, Bhisham Sahni agreed with my assertion that the essential subtext of almost every narrative instant in *Tamas* is that, prior to the Partition, hardly anyone would have asserted that their identities as Hindus and Muslims had been formed in contempt of each other. Indeed, if seriously questioned about the traditions within which they located themselves, they would have constructed, with the help of similar recollections, a life-world which was communally shared. It is not that they would have presented their villages and towns as utopian communities—obviously not, since utopias are merely imaginative structures against which we judge our various failings. They would, however, have affirmed that their finite human lives, their social fates, were entangled with each other, that their religious selves were not separate from the work they did, as also the friendships they formed or the language they spoke together within the same living spaces. That is why, when the Partition did finally happen, and was accompanied by such enormous violence, it left them utterly bewildered. This sense that for a majority of the Hindus and the Muslims, the Partition happened without any forewarning, is recreated with terrifying precision in *Tamas* in the scene in which Inder, a young Hindu fanatic, kills an old Muslim perfume-seller.

Inder is excited by fantasies of Hindu glory and masculine pride. In the film version, his khaki shorts, steel-rimmed glasses and lean intensity, identify him as a member of the Rashtriya Swayamsevak Sangh. One day, when everyone is at home because of riots, Inder sees the perfume-seller passing through a deserted street. Determined to prove his courage to his companions, he begins to stalk him. When the perfume-seller finds Inder walking beside him, he assumes that the boy wants the reassurance of an elderly man. He puts his hand on Inder's head, and asks: 'Son, where are you going?' The gesture and the words of affection fulfil the expectations of the culture. Together, they reaffirm kinship, instead of an egotistical identity. An old man instinctively offers help to a boy, who ought to be within doors at such an hour of danger. The perfume-seller, of course, recognizes the boy as a Hindu. It would have made no sense to him, even if the times were communally charged, to assume that Inder wanted to kill him.

As, perhaps, what I have said above indicates, our conversations about *Tamas* and the Partition were scattered, tentative and exploratory. Therefore, when we began to record the interview, we neither retraced what we had talked about earlier, nor began with a set of predetermined questions and answers. Each of us, of course, had some assumptions about the subject we wanted to discuss, but we did not want the interview to become merely a confirmation of positions we had taken earlier. Our only understanding with each other was that we would focus attention on *Tamas*, and the memories and experiences that had gone into its writing. Considering that we had talked about *Tamas* over days, it seemed to both of us that the formal interview began *in medias res*—that is, perhaps true of all dialogues. We were aware that we were retracing the paths we had travelled before. That was more true for Bhisham Sahni. He was talking about matters he had considered once before in 1974 while writing *Tamas*, and then again while working on the film.

The transcript of the interview was, by our prior agreement, first edited by me and then revised by Bhisham Sahni. The printed text, therefore, does not always coincide with what was originally recorded, but has been reshaped by after-thoughts, additions and erasures. It does, however, retain the fragmentariness and processual form of a dialogue. One could think of the text as a sort of flow-chart of thoughts, tentative conclusions and reformulations, fleeting reflections, pauses and shifts in arguments, detours through the shadowland of memories and recognition of something understood with clarity. What emerges at the end is a sense of the presence of Bhisham Sahni, a feeling of what he has become as a result of his childhood in Rawalpindi and youth in Lahore, his interactions with his family and his Muslim neighbours, his early ideological fascination with Gandhi and later involvement with the Left and his work as a writer of some of the most significant novels about our national identity.

My own understanding of him as a person and a writer is that he is someone who refuses to speak the language of hate and revenge. He still has an abiding sense of friendship towards his early days in Punjab and sorrow over its irretrievable loss. He speaks fondly of Rawalpindi and Lahore, not because of some vague nostalgia for them, but because his life memories connected with those places offer him, even now, resources for making moral and political judgements.

The interview was conducted in English.

AB : You began working on *Tamas* only in 1971. It was finally published in 1973. Why did it take you so long to write about the Partition horrors? You were, after all, a witness to all that happened in the 1940s and an active participant in some of the political events of the period. How much of the novel is based on your personal experiences?

BS : While writing, there are certain experiences which come out immediately which strike you at once, even though while you were living through those experiences they may not have struck you as very significant or very important. But somehow, later on, while you are writing they hit the eye—they sort of come back to your mind. And you use them in your writing. But if, while writing, one puts down one's pen, sits back and tries to recollect, many other details crop up. So one has to somehow dig them up with the help of one's memory. But while writing you don't do it. You are preoccupied with what you want to say. You use your experiences, therefore, many things are left out; many things that might have been significant, though of a minor nature. But, after writing *Tamas*, I did remember some things I used to recollect which had relevance, which had significance, which later on I thought I might have used, but then . . .

AB : Do you remember some of them now?

BS : (Laughs). Yes, I would, if I were to sit down again.

AB : One thing that struck me while I was reading *Tamas* was that . . . and we'll get back to *Tamas* later . . . when writers like Intizar Hussain or Qurratulain Hyder write novels about the Partition they seem to begin with their childhood. Somehow they all seem to look back to their past—particularly the past which is concerned with their childhood—nostalgically. And, there are some things which they remember with such fondness, that at times it seems as if it is those things which have made them, given them their identities. Let me give an example. When Intizar Hussain writes about his childhood and youth in pre-Partition India, he nostalgically recalls green parrots, *imli* trees, wells with their own ghosts, fields of yellow mustard flowers, etc. These are the kinds of details that are repeated again and again in his stories. Similarly, in his novel, *Basti*, he writes about stories which he had heard from village elders—both Muslims and Hindus. What he seems to suggest through these details is that before the Partition there was a sense of community—a sense of a social habitat. I was talking recently to Qurratulain Hyder. The things she remembered very distinctly about her childhood in Lucknow, and which really seemed to have defined Lucknow for her, was that a Muslim used to sing in the local *Ramlila*, and that '*malai* was made out to dew',—a beautifully sensual detail. But in *Tamas* that kind of nostalgia is absent. *Tamas* seems to begin at the point of crisis.

BS : Yes.

AB : You were born in Rawalpindi in 1915. Do you remember your childhood days? What were the relationships between Hindus and Muslims like in Rawalpindi in those days?

BS : I'll tell you . . . Although I was writing about the events that took place in 1947, here and there, I used a few things that I had noticed during my childhood to create a background for some scenes in the novel. For example, I was about 10 or 11 years old when the first communal riot took place in Rawalpindi.

AB : That was in 1926. You mention it in *Tamas*.

BS : Yes. And that was the time when I saw half the sky lit up with flames. The grain market had been set on fire. The flames rose high. I had never experienced that kind of thing earlier. We were standing on the roof of our house. I saw the fire. I was fascinated by it. Not that I was not terribly frightened by it (laughs). I had never seen such a glow. When I looked down below—towards the horizon—I saw the flames rising. I was scared. But as far as the sky and the glow were concerned they were also very attractive. I made use of my memory of that fire. Because in 1947, when the riots broke out, the entire grain market was not set on fire. It was a minor detail in the novel, but drawn from the memory of my childhood. You are right. Qurratulain Hyder might have been writing about the Lucknow of her childhood days and perhaps contrasting life at that time with the communal tensions later. She might have had that purpose in mind. But I had no such purpose in mind. I wrote the novel because when I went to Bhiwandi, I suddenly remembered the Rawalpindi riots. I happened to see the riots in Bhiwandi. Some of the things I saw there were so similar to what I had experienced at Rawalpindi that I started writing. And then one thing suggested another. . . I myself figure in my novel—in scenes where I describe the activities of the Congress. I participated in *prabhat pheries*, etc.

AB : Did you actually participate in them?

BS : Yes. yes. As a matter of fact, when the first stone throwing took place I was there . . . I mention that in my novel. . . . You know the Congress *tameeri* programme used to take us to certain localities to clean gutters. I used to go along with my comrades, the Congress people. We also used to visit predominantly Muslim areas. And we were very warmly welcomed there.

AB : I see . . .

BS : Yes, very warmly welcomed.

AB : What year was it?

BS : Just on the eve of the Partition.

AB : And you were still welcomed?

BS : Yes, yes. The riots had not yet broken out. But then...while we were cleaning and sweeping, the persons who had welcomed us earlier came and told us to go away.

AB : That is described in the novel.

BS : Yes. Tension had begun to develop. People threw stones at us. We left the place. We had to choose certain lanes that were predominantly Hindu lanes so that we were not attacked (laughs).

AB : But you had Muslim comrades with you. Did they walk with you through Hindu lanes?

BS : As a matter of fact, it was a Muslim who had invited us to clean the lanes in the area. I don't know if he was a CID man working inside the Congress (laughs). His name was Sher Khan. So, part of the novel is autobiographical. But the centre of it is not about my own experiences. It is concerned with more general experiences.

AB : Yes. But what was your world prior to 1946-7 like? Prior even to 1926? What I am really asking about is your childhood in Rawalpindi. Your father had his own business there. Did you ever feel before 1926—which may have been a turning point in many places in the north and not only in Rawalpindi—that people were beginning to define themselves as Hindus and Muslims? That there were tensions between them, and that these tensions were really irreconcilable?

BS : It's like this. We were living in a predominantly Muslim area. My father was a commission agent by profession, a businessman. Most of his clients were Muslims. He used to take orders for a French manufacturer of gold thread, lace, *gotta* and *zari*, which he used to sell in Baluchistan, Quetta, Peshawar and to a certain extent in Kashmir and Kabul. That was the market. My father had lived for 20 years in Peshawar and had developed this agency there. When he moved to Rawalpindi his clients—mostly Muslim Pathan merchants—used to come and place orders with him. He used to be very cordial with them. But they never dined at our place.

AB : Was that common to most Hindu-Muslim relationships?

BS : Yes. If they did dine at our place—or had tea or something—my mother used to scrub the utensils with pieces of burning coal.

AB : That happened in many homes.

BS : Further, my father was an Arya Samaji. Very active, very staunch. We had Muslim friends, but they never came to our house. Only one friend of mine did—when I was studying in Intermediate. He was so close to me that he used to come inside the house. But normally the Muslims did not come in. We had Muslim friends, but we were discouraged from playing with them.

AB : By your parents?

BS : Yes.

AB : What about the parents of your Muslim friends?

BS : I don't know. You see, we were middle class people. Those boys were generally lower middle class children, mostly children of *tonga* drivers, etc. The locality was like that. But the children were playful and nice. Children don't discriminate. We were, however, discouraged from mixing with them. We were sent to an Arya Samaj school. And there was a certain bias against Muslims.

AB : Were there any Muslim children in the school?

BS : Yes, there were, but only a sprinkling. An Arya Samaj school didn't normally admit them. But there were a few and some of them were very bright boys. But still, although we were not very conscious of the differences between us, yet a certain amount of reservation, a certain distance was there . . . was there, yes.

AB : You don't have memories like Intizar Hussain, Qurratulain Hyder or Rahi Masoom Reza do, of a communally shared childhood. You don't remember that Hindu and Muslim children had or shared common myths and rituals. Such a sense of a shared life doesn't form a part of your childhood, does it?

BS : It does, but not in remote childhood. Later on, yes—very closely, in fact—Altaf Hussain, for instance, was a very dear friend of mine. We used to go out almost every day. I played with him. I attended his marriage. I also had many close Muslim friends when I went to Lahore to study. I was fond of playing hockey. And the hockey teams consisted predominantly of Muslim players. We were very close to them. In college, I lived in the hostel. And in the hostel everything was commonly shared.

AB : I still want you to tell me more about your life in Rawalpindi before you moved to Lahore. I don't know much about Rawalpindi. My parents used to talk about Rawalpindi and places like Lyallpur. My question is as follows: Would you, like Intizar Hussain or Qurratulain Hyder or any number of other writers who have written about the Partition, be able to locate your childhood in Rawalpindi as a place where there was a reasonably harmonious society; a society which could function; a society which, despite the reservations you described, didn't seem to suggest that the tensions or distances between the Hindus and Muslims would ever become so antagonistic that they would sometimes lead, not only to complete separation, but also to carnage. Do you think about your past in Rawalpindi nostalgically?

BS : Now that I look back, yes. Naturally. I do think that there was a kind of coexistence among the communities. My parents and the parents of my Muslim friends did see themselves as very distinct entities. The do's and don'ts inside our homes were such that they made you conscious of the differences. But, as children, we were hardly concerned with these differences.

AB : But were the people of your parent's generation antagonistic?

BS : Not antagonistic. . . . But you see the Arya Samaj was terribly anti-Muslim.

AB : That's right. Of course. It was one of their major planks.

BS : During the congregations or the annual functions of the Arya Samaj, lecturers often came from outside and there was a clear bias against the Muslims in their lectures. They were quite outspoken about it.

AB : You are talking about a period up to 1925 ?

BS : Yes. But I still believe that the communal problem was a development of the first 15 or 20 years of the twentieth century. I don't think that Indian society was a society of communal tensions earlier. Because the quality of relationships, which Qurratulain Hyder or Intizar Hussain mention, was a reality. The kind of tensions we witnessed at Rawalpindi in say the 1920s was very different from the earlier historical prejudices, whether among Muslim rulers or amongst Rajput rulers. Of course, there were spurts of violence . . . but there were also very powerful movements in the medieval times to influence our outlook and our relationships, particularly in areas like the Punjab. Tensions between communities were aberrations.

AB : Was the Arya Samaj and its new communal consciousness, also an aberration?

BS : Yes. It was not a permanent feature either of our social life or of our culture. That's what I think. You know, in your essay on Manto, you have brought this out. You link the 1919 incidents with 1947 and say that Manto was so disillusioned that he thought bloodthirstiness was in our blood. He was happy in Bombay and had very cordial relationships with the Hindus. If you read his stories, more than half his characters are Hindus. Then he went to live in a place (Lahore, after 1948) where there were no Hindus. And what he had always regarded as an aberration, became a permanent aspect of our society after the Partition. That made him very unhappy. And then, perhaps, in a moment of dejection, he came to the conclusion that we are a bloodthirsty people. And that it was, therefore, logical that we should have killed each other.

AB : Yes. You are right. I don't disagree at all.

BS : That is how I read Manto. You see it depends upon the ruler. If Aurangzeb wanted to create tensions, he succeeded in creating them. Akbar wanted a more liberal kind of atmosphere to prevail. In feudal times, it had a lot to do with the ruler. In our times, the authorities, the British government, wanted to create tensions and succeeded.

AB : Now that you have brought up the subject of the British. . . . When I talked to Intizar Hussain, he constructed the history of a composite culture prior to the 1890s, just as you do. In fact, everybody would probably locate the beginning of communal tensions around the 1890s. We know that the first communal riots took place in that decade.

BS : Yes.

AB : Then there was a lull for a long time. Of course, there were tensions again, but there were also ways in which they were negotiated, till the major riots began around 1926.

BS : Quite right.

AB : If you look back or when Intizar Hussain looks back—he is also engaged in the reconstruction of the history of this culture—he does not worry too much about kings, but talks about the kind of popular, daily, non-political lives that people used to lead, of which the great examples would be Nizamuddin Aulia, on the one hand, and Kabir and Mira Bai, on the other. That is how he would construct his popular history of India before the Partition. How would you construct a history of communal relationships?

BS : In the same way.

AB : In the same way?

BS : Yes. I think that in the medieval times, there was a very powerful upsurge of liberal thought. In the fourteenth century particularly, Delhi became a centre of learning and culture. The Sufis came from Persia. India became a powerful centre. It is very interesting that the Bhakti movement also flourished at more or less the same time. And there was a confluence of the two. There is, no doubt, that a new perspective began to emerge. It was very conducive to harmonious life and fellow feeling. This went on for two, three or four centuries and left its impact. So that at the level of small towns, people learnt to live side by side, despite their different faiths. There was also the consciousness that most people who had become Muslims were really Hindus to begin with. There were places where, for example, the entire community of weavers had got converted to Islam. But, then, if people belonging to one religion convert to another religion there is bound to be interaction, bound to be give and take. A different kind of life, a different kind of social life begins to develop. This happened here also. Therefore, certain things were just taken for granted. Differences in faith were taken for granted. Differences in customs, ways of life, eating habits, and so on, were taken for granted. This helped in the process of accommodating one another. There was cordiality between people of different faiths. Therefore, there was no reason why people should not have learnt to live as good neighbours. So I think communal antagonism was a development that took place in the British period. The British were convinced of the differences between the Hindus and Muslims. This also suited them, as their own numerical strength was small. They had come and established their empire through all sorts of means. Making use of differences between people within a family, and so on, was a part of their game and they succeeded. Afterwards, they wanted to stabilize themselves and one of the methods they used was to support one community at one time and the other community at another time. They were not very interested in the culture of the country. So, I believe, they were responsible for the tension that developed. The pity of it is that we have not learnt from our experiences. We are still carrying on from where they left off.

AB : Let's assume that what you are saying is right. That the British were responsible for the communal division of the country. Yet that doesn't explain entirely the rise—even in your own family—of the

Arya Samaj prejudice against the Muslims. How would you explain the rise of Muslim consciousness? We know historically that the Muslim League was formed first and the Hindu Mahasabha a little later. Contrary to what we now sometimes feel, that is the case. Were there economic reasons for the rise of Muslim consciousness?

BS : I have had the occasion to read the fiction written in the closing years of the last century. When people like Bankimchandra were writing of a new kind of awareness, a new kind of consciousness had developed. There was a trend to glorify and glamorize our past and our culture in our writing.

AB : But only selectively.

BS : Yes. Side by side they began to say that while India was great in the past, it began to decline when it came into contact with an inferior culture. However, a new awareness began to develop at the beginning of the twentieth century. Along with the glorification of the Hindu past, of Aryavarta, and so on, there was a reformist trend amongst the Hindus. Later, a broader consciousness also developed . . . it is a complex thing . . . The influence of the British was very much present. Their institutions, their progress, even their love of justice, and so on. Many, many things. The British had an impact. Anyway, while the Muslims were blamed by some of our writers for the degradation or the disintegration of our culture, there were other writers who wrote in the same period, about the degradation of Hindu institutions. They were, for example, critical of what was happening in holy places of pilgrimage.

AB : Was there a similar change in the consciousness of the Muslims during the same period? Didn't the Muslims try to define themselves as distinct from the Hindus? Didn't they also reconstruct their history?

BS : Yes, quite right. But their relationship with the Hindus was different from the relationship of the British with the people they governed. The British kept themselves aloof from Indian social life. There was, however, a close interaction between the Hindus and the Muslims.

AB : Perhaps we could now move on to your days in Lahore. You joined Government College, Lahore, in 1933. As a student there, did you ever feel that there was a sense of separation between Muslim and Hindu students?

BS : So far as the student community was concerned, there was no consciousness of discrimination between the Hindus and Muslims;

my classmates were Hindu and Muslim. On the playing fields we were always together. Further, the college had certain norms of behaviour that were always observed. Even if there was any discrimination by the authorities, they never made it apparent. The college authorities did not permit the Congress to promote its agitational programme in the college. I remember that when I was in the sixth year of college, a boy in the first year who came to college wearing a Gandhi cap, was expelled within an hour. The principal of the college was an Englishman. The same could not be said of DAV College, which was a stone's throw away from Government College. Remember that Bhagat Singh was at DAV College. It was his base. Anyway, the atmosphere within Government College was apolitical. Who were the students who went to the Government College? They were the sons of Muslim zamindars, the sons of Hindu bureaucrats and the sons of the middle classes who had done well in their studies. Most of them were generally not interested in politics. If there was a sense of separation between them, it was a result of external events. Something like the Communal Award had just been passed. That affected Hindu students, especially those who were planning to sit for the civil service examinations. The general impression was that whereas a Muslim boy could walk into any office and get a job, a Hindu boy could not.

AB : Was there a lot of opposition in the student community to the Communal Award?

BS : Resentment, yes. Specially amongst Hindus. Otherwise, there was no discrimination.

AB : Was there resentment at the popular level against the Communal Award?

BS : Inside the college there was no politics. Students were not supposed to discuss politics. That was the established norm. Students were there to study, to take part in debates, go to the playing fields, etc. Let me narrate an event. I took part in a debate. I was then in the fourth year in college. I did not know much about politics then. The principal of the college, H.L.O. Garret, was an army man and a historian. The subject to be debated was 'Dictatorship versus Democracy'. I spoke against dictatorship. I didn't know much about the subject. A friend of mine, who was in the sixth year, wrote my speech. I crammed it and delivered it. My friend had equated Hitler with Stalin. The principal liked the speech immensely (laughs). At a theoretical level, one could discuss politics in the college. But students were not allowed to participate in the political activities of the country.

AB : This was also the period when the influence of the Muslim League was on the rise. What were your responses to it?

BS : When I was a student in Lahore, Nehru was very popular. But not in the Government College. When he came to Lahore, thousands of people thronged to listen to him. But nobody from our college thought of going to his meeting. We felt we were exclusive. But still, even in our college, we knew that the national upsurge was becoming very powerful.

AB : Who were the exemplary figures in the national movement for the Hindu and Muslim students in Lahore? Whom did you look up to as a student? You have already talked about Bhagat Singh and Nehru. As you know, between 1918 and the resurgence of the Muslim League, Gandhi was the exemplary figure for both the Hindus and the Muslims. For example, I have been reading the Hunter Commission Report on the massacre at Jallianwala Bagh. One of the things that emerges very clearly from it is that Gandhi was regarded as a *wali* by the Muslims and a Mahatma by the Hindus. Both the communities respected him. During the same period, there were exemplary figures amongst the Muslim leadership too—figures respected by the Hindus and the Muslims. For instance, Maulana Shaukat Ali, Maulana Mohamed Ali, Dr Ansari, Dr Kitchlew and later on, Maulana Azad. Do you remember who your exemplary figures were during those days?

BS : Yes. As far as the four years I spent in Government College are concerned, all political activity was, at least for me, blotted out. I had, of course, heard of Nehru and Gandhi. And since, DAV College was close by, I knew about people like Bhagat Singh. Let me give an example. There were two student unions in the Punjab University at that time. One was politically very active, and dominated by the Congress people. Its leader was a man who later became a legislator and a minister in the Punjab government. . . . What was his name? If your father were alive, he'd remember his name. . . . Anyway, he was the leader of the student's union controlled by the Congress. The University had set up another student's union also. It was not connected to any political party. In fact, I even became its President (laughs). It was purely academic. The Vice-Chancellor of the University was a certain Mr Woolner. He was a Sanskrit scholar; a very fine gentleman. The government had built a Woolner Hall for students. I was very active in the second, the non-political, union. I was personally never a part of the other student's union. The effort of the University administration was to keep students away from the national movement and the Congress dominated union. But during my stay in college, the political environment changed. Some students organized, what they called, 'The Renaissance Club'. People like Ramesh Chandra, a prominent political figure later, Mehmood and Mazhar, two brothers, who were the sons of Nawab Muzaffar Khan and very active later in the political life of Pakistan, became members of The Renaissance Club. It was politically more vocal. Hindu and Muslim students, together, were members of that club. I also joined it.

AB : So, The Renaissance Club, formed around 1939, was not communally divided?

BS : No, not at all.

AB : After your MA, you became an active member of the Congress party. Why did you join the Congress? Your ideological position changed later.

BS : It's a long story. . . . I did my MA in English literature. My father was a businessman. He was very keen that I join him in business. He also wanted my elder brother, Balraj, to join him. As a matter of fact, my brother did join him for sometime. . . . Well, anyway, while I was in Government College, Lahore, I became fond of the theatre and began to act in plays. After my MA, I returned to Rawalpindi to join my father. I also started teaching in a local college as an honorary member of the faculty. I used to take a few classes there, because the principal of the college told me that it would be easier for me to stage plays in the college, if I also taught there. It was during my stay there that I found myself being drawn towards the Congress party. Not actively, but the atmosphere was so charged with its political demands that I was tempted. Also, soon after my MA in 1938, I had met Gandhiji. By 1937 or 1938, my brother, who had joined my father for a while, had decided to leave him and go to Shantiniketan to teach Hindi. From Shantiniketan, he went to Sevagram Ashram in Wardha to live in Gandhiji's ashram. Since he happened to be in Wardha, I went to stay with him for about three weeks. That gave me an occasion to see Gandhiji moving about. I used to attend his prayer meetings, see him at his work, accompany him on his morning walks, etc. After that, I went to attend the

Congress session at Haripura in 1938. My father, who had come down to Bombay on a visit, also went with me. The session at Haripura was a very important one politically. Besides, the atmosphere was surcharged with anti-colonial sentiments. I continued to be drawn to the Congress after I returned to Rawalpindi, which was, then a small and a remote town.

AB : Did the Congress party at Rawalpindi have many Muslim members?

BS : No. The majority of the Congress members there were Hindus. But the Muslims were not active in the Muslim League either. In fact, I don't think that by 1938 the Muslim League had become a significant political party, at least not in Rawalpindi. It did not yet have an all India presence. Indeed Rawalpindi at that time was a major recruitment centre for the army and the Muslims from the area joined the army in large numbers. One of the biggest army cantonments was at Rawalpindi. So, whole divisions were made up of recruits from there. The army certainly didn't encourage politics. Incidentally, Muslims formed about 80 per cent of the population of the area.

AB : When you started taking an active part in the Congress, how did your Muslim friends react? Did you, for instance, talk to Altaf Hussain about your politics? You have already mentioned him as one of your best friends.

BS : Oh, yes. We stopped talking to each other (laughs). Altaf Hussain became a Muslim Leaguer. But that was later, closer to the Partition.

AB : But in 1938?

BS : There was no strain in 1938.

AB : There is a lot of fictional writing about the Partition, which deals with political divisions between families and friends. I have in mind works like Ismat Chugtai's 'Jadein' (Roots), Attia Hosain's *Sunlight on a Broken Column,* Yashpal'*s Jhoota Sach*, Rahi Masoom Reza's *Aadha Gaon*. What is striking about these works is that while they describe the antagonism generated by different members of a family supporting the Congress, the Muslim League or the Communist Party, there is never a sense that the differences are so acute as to make it impossible for people to live together—never a sense that the country is about to fall apart and plunge into a genocidal civil war.

BS : Let me tell you about a Muslim family that used to live in our neighbourhood, close to our house. It was a very enlightened family.

One of the brothers was a barrister, another was a Communist, another was very active in the Congress and yet another was a member of the Muslim League. It was, in fact, from the brother who was a barrister that we first heard that Pakistan had been formed. He stood opposite our house and started shouting, 'Pakistan Zindabad . . . Pakistan has been made.' He was an older man . . . not my friend. . . .

AB : But why did Altaf Hussain stop talking to you?

BS : Actually we moved away from each other. I became a very enthusiastic Congress worker and he became a Muslim League sympathizer. We drifted apart. Later, after 1947, we corresponded with each other and even spoke to each other on the telephone.

AB : What is interesting to note in your recollections—as well as in the recollections that inform the work of Ismat Chugtai, Manto, Kamleshwar, Yashpal, Attia Hosain or Rahi Masoom Reza—is that you still seem to think fondly of people you grew up with. It doesn't matter to you whether your friends of childhood were Hindu or Muslim. What is of importance, in what you have said, is that prior to the Partition your identity, as an individual, was formed in relationship with other individuals, with others seen as human beings, and not as Hindus and Muslims. Indeed, neither you nor Altaf Hussain seems to have defined yourselves as Hindus and Muslims before the politics of religious identities intervened to disrupt your friendship. Your experience doesn't seem to be unique. Autobiographies of people, who lived through pre-Partition India, as well as the fictional works written after the Partition, reinforce what you have said. It is as if before 1940, people scarcely thought that their primary identities were defined by the religions to which they belonged. Their identities were made, instead, through the usual complex process of debate and negotiation with each other as businessmen, workers, students, teachers, etc. The fact that they were also members of specific castes and religions seems secondary. What puzzles me, therefore, is why did these people, whose daily lives were made up of a series of diverse interactions, suddenly decide that their identities as Hindus and Muslims were of greater importance than they ever had been before, and that as Muslims and Hindus they could no longer live with each other? At what stage did they become intolerant of each other?

BS : It is important for me to insist at this stage, that even though the political demand for a partition of the country separated people, the sense of separation was only temporary. In fact, such separations are always temporary, unless, of course, one is a die-hard communalist—but people who are not politically motivated rarely ever become communalists. Even now, when I remember Altaf Hussain, I become sentimental. He was such a warm fellow. In the last letter he wrote to me he said, 'We must meet before I die' (a long pause). He rang me up one evening to invite me to his son's wedding. He also invited two or three other close friends of his in India. We called each other and decided to go to Pakistan to attend Altaf Hussain son's marriage. Unfortunately, the invitation had come so late that it was impossible for us to get visas. So, we could not go. A little later, when my daughter went to Rawalpindi, she met him. She wanted to take a photograph of him. But he refused. He said, 'I don't want Bhisham to see me as an old man.' In one of the last letters, he said, 'I have a strong desire to see my old friends. I also have a strong desire to go to Mecca. These are my strong desires. . . .' Now, there is no expression of communalism here, only a sincere expression of friendliness.

AB : Why would a man like him, who was a dear friend of yours, and whom you still recall so fondly, ask for and support the Partition?

BS : That is understandable at a political level. . . . We didn't talk about it, but I suspect that the Muslims felt that India was a predominately Hindu country and that their future lay in having a separate nation of their own. That was the main theme of Jinnah's demand also.

AB : One should remember here that the demand for Pakistan was made only in 1940. Prior to that there were only hints that it would be better if the two communities lived apart. There is nothing in the memoirs of the period or the fictional accounts to suggest that the demand for a separate Pakistan was widespread, or even voiced by many prior to 1939-40. So much for people who still go about saying that Pakistan was either 'historically inevitable' or that the demand for a separate country by the Muslims was a 'natural' corollary to their distinctive identity.

BS : Yes, but soon after the Pakistan demand was made, the polarization became rapid. The crystallization of politically antagonistic positions was very fast. In fact, once such a political process starts, people do begin to define themselves differently.

AB : They give up their family and friends?

BS : Well, family and friends become secondary.

AB : I see. Perhaps you are right. . . . We are still talking about the early

1940's. You said that you had met Gandhiji during that period. Was he one of your exemplary figures?

BS : Yes. In fact, he was a very open man. Anyone could go for a morning walk with him and talk to him. My brother, who was at Wardha with him, introduced me to him. Gandhiji asked Balraj, 'Will he also work here?' My brother replied, 'No, he has come here only for a visit.' Gandhiji laughed when he heard that. He was a cheerful kind of man, who was always ready to laugh and talk. . . . Anyway, during my stay at Wardha, I spent my time listening to him and to other leaders there. I also wanted to strike up a conversation with Gandhiji. So, during one of his walks, I said, 'Gandhiji, you came to Rawalpindi in 1926-7, after the terrible riots at Kohat. On your way back, you stopped at Rawalpindi. Do you remember?' That set his mind working. I was amazed to find out how clearly he remembered his two days in Rawalpindi. He knew where he had stayed, and asked me about a certain Mr Jan, who was a barrister, a Muslim and his host. He asked about his health. At that point, Gandhiji's private secretary, Mahadev Desai, who was walking behind us, interrupted the conversation, and started reminiscing about how they had travelled by car from Kohat, etc. I was soon sidelined (laughs).

AB : Your description of the Congress workers in the beginning of *Tamas*, struck me as a bit ironic. The novel is, of course, written many years later. Did you view them ironically even when you were working with them?

BS : You are right. In the novel, the Congress workers are viewed with a certain degree of ironic detachment. But I think I was remarking only on their attitude towards the question of violence, in that section.

AB : But you are also ironic about the kind of work they were doing . . . the street-cleaning programme, for instance. You describe it at length in the novel, and critically.

BS : The criticism of the Congress programmes was being voiced even then by the party workers themselves. Also by the Socialist wing of the Congress party. The Socialists were not adherents of Gandhi's ideology. The two groups were not above ridiculing each other.

AB : That is one aspect of the scene in the novel. The party workers, however, also ridicule national leaders. In the novel, it is Nehru, the rising star, who is mocked through the figure of Mehtaji. He is made fun of by others because he looks like Nehru, and regards himself as a man in the same mould. In the film version of the novel, Mehtaji is chided because he sees himself as Babu Rajendra Prasad. Is the scepticism towards Nehru in the novel a result of later thinking about the past, or had it begun to creep into your own attitude towards Nehru even in the early 1940s?

BS : No, it is perhaps a result of a later reflection.

AB : There is another sceptical note in the novel, which is different from memories of the work you did in the Congress at that time. The Congress workers in *Tamas* are not as idealistic or selfless as they may have appeared to you is your youth.

BS : You are right. That is because, I had all sorts of experiences during the Partition riots, which I was trying to come to grips with during the writing of *Tamas*. For example, there was a Congress worker, a prominent person, who wanted me to store cartridges in my house. By then there were riots everywhere. He said, 'I have this bundle of cartridges, can you keep them?' Maybe, he was afraid that his own house would be searched. I declined. He was a Gandhiite. A devout Gandhiite, who had spent 16 years in jail. Experiences of that sort slowly made me look upon my past with irony when I started writing *Tamas*. I was a bit shocked that a Gandhiite should keep cartridges. I didn't want to keep them, but I didn't want to say no either. So I went to a friend of mine who was a civil supplies officer in Rawalpindi and asked him to keep them, and told him not to talk about them to anyone (laughs). And he too declined. So, I gave the bundle back to the Gandhiite.

AB : Was your disagreement with the Congress workers only over tactics?

BS : No. I also found myself asking ideological questions all the time.

AB : In *Tamas*, you also suggest that some of the Congress workers were corrupt. They were in the Congress, at least in part, because of personal gain.

BS : They were not corrupt. They made compromises. Their democratic spirit, however, was strong. Even ordinary members from the lower strata of society would speak out fearlessly. Let me take an example. There were provincial elections in 1945. The headquarters of the provincial Congress were in Lahore. The Congress leaders there decided to nominate a person to stand from our constituency—a man called Divan Chaman Lal. The local people resented that very much, since he was not a resident of Rawalpindi. 'Why should we support him?' they asked. I remember, with great admiration, a man who was very poor—he used to earn his living by selling soap and advertising goods, earning no more than two rupees a day—stood up at the meeting of the Congress and opposed Divan Chaman Lal's nomination. He said, 'We don't want a man from Lahore. We want to put up our own man.' He was, of course, made to shut up. So you see, a certain number of go-getters were there in the Congress party even at that time. But let me clarify. While there was a certain amount of corruption, it was nothing like what we have today. Indeed, there was no possibility of it at that time. Besides, Congressmen were devoted to the cause of India's freedom.

AB : In *Tamas,* there is a character called Dev Dutt. He is a Communist. What was your attitude at that time to the support extended by the Communist Party to the Muslim League and its demand for Pakistan?

BS : Now that I think about it, I must say that my attitude was very confused. I did not subscribe to what the Communists had resolved, but I also felt that I did not know enough. Dev Dutt, in *Tamas* is based on one of my friends. I was, as I told you, teaching as an honorary lecturer in a college in Rawalpindi. My friend, who was the prototype of Dev Dutt, was also teaching there. He was a very active member of the Communist Party. An organizer he did very good work. He used to give me books to read, books written by Rajani Palme Dutt and others. It was he who gave me a very good book about the rise of National Socialism and Hitler in Europe. I liked him because he was a very sincere and a very active man. But ideologically, I was not convinced by him. I should add that even after my brother, Balraj, came back from England in 1944-5 as a convinced Marxist, I did not agree with him either. Anyway, the stand of the Communist Party *vis-à-vis* Pakistan was not very convincing to me even at that time. That is why, I continued to work in the Congress party despite my friends. Later, the riots happened. The country was divided. I left Rawalpindi. . . . I have never been convinced of the desirability of the Partition of the country. . . . But, you know among the young Communists there was a strong feeling about it. They said two things that were self-contradictory. On the one hand, they did not believe in the Partition of the country. On the other hand, however, they said that the Muslim League was the sole representative of the Muslim masses. They were, I think mistaken. But they did not see the confusion in their thinking. In fact, I am still surprised that the Communist Party, which at that time had men like P.C. Joshi, who were otherwise so alert, should have subscribed to such a mode of thinking. But I am sure that they did not believe in Pakistan. Their entire emphasis was on finding a way of coming to terms with the Muslim League. That is why they boosted Jinnah also. Let me recite, for you, an IPTA song that we used to sing in those days.

Gandhi jayain dain, to Jinnah jaate hain bain,
Alag, alag hain, juda juda hain rahain,
Par Wavell ke ghar pey jatey dono bari bari . . .

[If Gandhi goes to the right, Jinnah goes to the left,
Their paths are different, their ways are distinct,
But both go to Wavell's house one after the other . . .]

The Communists equated the Congress with the Muslim League, and thereby gave credence to the 'two-nation theory'. I drew closer to the Left when I started working for the IPTA around 1945. My brother was by then an active member of IPTA. I watched IPTA plays—which were secularist in their convictions and fairly strong. I was very impressed.

AB : Wouldn't you say that at one level, Gandhi's strategy was not very much different from that of the Left? He was both an anti-imperialist and, despite his strong personal religious convictions, a genuinely secular man. But the IPTA people don't seem to have been attracted by him. Did they not mock at him?

BS : Not really. P.C. Joshi, in fact called him the Father of the Nation.

AB : There is a conversation in *Tamas* where someone says that he has loose motion because he has been drinking only milk. Were you also not mocking Gandhi in that section? The novel seems to suggest that by the time you came round to writing about the nationalist past, you had changed your mind about Gandhi and had become more critical.

BS : May be. But I was, perhaps, reflecting there a personal intellectual struggle over the years.

AB : Did you ever see Jinnah?

BS : Yes. Once. I never heard him speak, though I did read about what he said. I was once travelling by the Frontier Mail. When the train stopped at a station, I saw a number of people on the platform standing near the next compartment. I looked out of the window and saw Jinnah standing in the doorway of his compartment and addressing the crowd.

AB : What was your attitude towards Jinnah?

BS : I did not like him. But that sort of thing happens. At that time, I did not know about his contribution to the Congress party and the national movement. Later, I learnt that he was amenable to a settlement. But the attitudes on the eve of the Partition had become very rigid on all sides. Gandhi and Jinnah had very long meetings in Bombay, and every one hoped that something positive would emerge from them. It didn't.

AB : The attitudes towards Jinnah are very strong even now amongst the Indians, particularly amongst those who come from the present Pakistan region.

BS : You see, there is no political formulation behind the dislike. Jinnah is for them a symbol of the Partition. Remember, however, that Maulana Azad was very highly respected at that time, and continues to be respected.

AB : His presence was a sign of hope that there would be an amicable settlement.

BS : Yes. But he began to be very strongly condemned by the Muslim League. After his wife died, I remember that I heard a Muslim Leaguer talk about her death in bad taste.

AB : That happened regularly, didn't it? Muslims who opposed the Partition were maligned.

BS : Yes, Muslims working for the Congress were often called names. I remember that when I introduced a Muslim comrade working with me in the Congress to a Muslim neighbour of mine, he turned to me and said, 'I don't want to meet a Muslim Congressman, he is a dog of the Hindus.' I describe all this in *Tamas*.

AB : That kind of language was commonly used when it became apparent that Pakistan would be formed.

BS : Yes.

AB : When did you finally leave Rawalpindi?

BS : On 13 August 1947.

AB : What was Rawalpindi like in the last weeks before the Partition. I don't want gory details, because you really can't add to the stories of violence we already know. I am actually more concerned about why you stayed on for so long. This morning I was talking to Rajee Seth (she was a Fellow with us at the Indian Institute of Advanced Study in those days). She is, as you know, writing a novel about the Partition, based on her experiences of childhood in Lahore before 1947. She told me that her father refused to leave Lahore even after

15 August 1947. He finally left only in November, after he witnessed something truly horrible.

BS : My father, too, refused to leave.

AB : Why?

BS : Because he believed that even if the regimes change, populations don't. People don't leave. He said, 'I have a house here, my property is here. I will continue to live here.' So he stayed. I left Rawalpindi and came away in August. My father remained behind till November. He left by chance only after things had become difficult for him. By November, there were very few Hindus left in town. They were all moved into one street so that they could be protected, but my father refused to move from his house. He stayed where he was. We had good relations with our neighbours. They were all Muslims. One of my uncles had a transport company and used to ply trucks and cars between Rawalpindi and Kashmir. The younger brother of the Unionist Chief Minister of Punjab, Sikander Hayat Khan, was Barkat Hayat Khan, who happened to be going to Kashmir. My uncle sent a word to my father, 'Here is a chance. There is a seat in the car. I can help you get to Kashmir.' He also sent my father a Turkish cap. My father wore it when he left. . . . Remember the butchery that was going on everywhere at that time.

AB : Was there much killing in Rawalpindi?

BS : No, not much.

AB : Why did you leave?

BS : I wanted to see the Independence Day celebrations. I told my father, 'I will be back in a week's time.'

AB : In your story, 'Amritsar Aa Gaya Hai' (We Have Reached Amritsar), during the course of a conversation, someone says that Jinnah will never leave his home in Bombay, that he will commute between Bombay and Karachi. What is surprising about this conversation is that it takes place on 13 August 1947 while there are riots everywhere. As the train moves towards Amritsar, all the towns on the way are burning. You were, of course, a witness to all that, and yet were confident that you would he able to go to Delhi and return to Rawalpindi in a week?

BS : Yes let me tell you why. At first, the exodus was in the form of a trickle. A person or two would carry his luggage to the railway station. He would go past our house. Some people in the neighbourhood would get frightened, and say to themselves, 'If he is leaving, what will happen to us?' But, most people would simply laugh at the person who was leaving, 'Why is he running away?' they would say. 'There is no danger here.' After the first riots in Rawalpindi, things had settled down. There was a lull. In my town the riots had lasted for only five days. Even later, after the Muslim refugees from India had begun to arrive, ordinary life and work continued. Some people did leave, but many did not think it was necessary to do so. One day J.B. Kripalani came to Rawalpindi, a few days after a new outburst of riots. I was working in the Congress committee at that time. I met him along with the other members of the committee. At that time Kripalani did not see eye to eye with Nehru and others. One of the young men present asked Kripalani, 'Please tell us, should we stay on or go away?' Kripalani did not give a clear answer. And when the young man repeated the question, Kripalani snubbed him and said '*Tumaherey muhe par to abhi maan ka doodh naihi sookha hai, aur tum aisi batein karte ho!*' (Your lips are still wet with your mothers' milk and you dare to talk like that!) The reason was that no Congress leader was willing to say 'Leave your cities and go away.' At the same time, Kripalani knew that the conditions were bad and that we couldn't continue to live there.

AB : Did you ever hear any of the Muslim League leaders say to you, 'There is no reason for you to go'.

BS : No.

AB : In fact, I don't remember having read any account in which Muslim League sympathizers in Pakistan said to the Hindus who had been living there for generations, that there was no need for them to migrate. The same, of course, also holds true for the Hindu Mahasabha people.

BS : The exodus started from the villages, which were predominantly Muslim. The Sikhs and Hindus were small in numbers there. They were either traders or owners of small shops.

AB : Like Harnam Singh in *Tamas*.

BS : Yes. It is these people who left first because they were scared. They sought shelter in refugee camps. There was one near Rawalpindi. It was being looked after by a British officer. The Congress workers also helped in the relief work. People coming from remote areas preferred to go to refugee camps instead of taking help from their relatives. Soon after, people began to leave in larger numbers.

AB : What interests me in your description of the events, especially when I compare them to the experiences of members of my own family, is that most people initially seem to have asserted that they would not leave; that there was no need to leave. Most of them seem to have said, 'We'll not run away. We were born here. Nothing will happen to us.' Yet, of course, the worst carnage in Indian history happened during the Partition.

BS : The political situation was something utterly new; something which no one had expected. Of course, there had been massacres in the historical past, but for different reasons. For example, my great grandfather, who lived in Kabul a century ago, was forced to leave because of political conflicts. The carnage of the Partition was a different phenomenon, a new experience.

AB : What was your own response when you saw the carnage. Did you feel that there was something people like you could do to stop it, to intervene?

BS : Of course, but not in an organized way. I remember that we talked to people. Tried to persuade them not to leave. But, inevitably, we were told that life would never be congenial there ever again.

AB : You mentioned that your Muslim neighbours protected you; that your family felt safe. Similar experiences have been recorded in other fictional works about the Partition. Indeed, most of them assert that the threat always came from outside, from people who didn't live in their neighbourhood. Is that really true? Were there no attacks by people who knew each other?

BS : Yes. It is not that the people who protected us were non-communal. They could be very rabidly communal. But not with us. They protected us, because when it came to their neighbours, a different value system prevailed. But the same persons would go and kill in other areas.

AB : Did you know people like that?

BS : Yes.

AB : What puzzles me is how does one deal with somebody whom one has known, one has grown up with, who becomes a communal killer? You describe such people in *Tamas*, people who attack Harnam Singh. There are moving scenes in the novel in which Harnam Singh has to hide from people he has known all his life, because they have suddenly decided that he is a man who belongs to the wrong religion and, therefore, no longer deserves their neighbourly protection.

BS : In the novel, if you remember, there are elderly people who have lived with Harnam Singh for years and have established a certain degree of affectionate relationship with him. They are the ones who protect him, because they don't want their old relationship to be disturbed. But the younger people are sectarian and communal and have no sympathy for their father's friends. Harnam Singh is forced to leave not by his older friends but by the communalized young.

AB : Yes. After he is forced to leave his village, it is old Rajo who protects him.

BS : Although Rajo's husband does say, 'When I think of what the Hindus have done to the Muslims, my blood boils, but I still do not want to kill you.' He adds, however, that he would not be able to vouch for his son, who would probably not be so considerate. I think, in this regard, what Rajo's husband says is absolutely convincing. The old people may not have been warm towards each other and may have only tolerated one another, but they did value neighbourly relationships. It is the younger people, I think, who were more rabid in their outlook—not all of course. But the majority of them were not at all tolerant.

AB : Did your father stay back because of this sense of neighbourliness?

BS : Yes, he felt quite secure. Our neighbour was an old Muslim who had retired as a subedar from the army. I used to play hockey with his son. Both were always very warm towards us. Indeed, when my brother went to Pakistan, he met the son. They were overjoyed to meet each other. When my brother wrote a book about his journey to Pakistan, he published his photograph in it. Let me add that the Hindus living in the Rawalpindi area, where the population was predominantly Muslim, were not as rigid in the observances of Hindu rituals as the Hindus in other parts of the country. Punjabi Hindus are somewhat different from the UP Hindus. There was, in Punjab, a greater interaction between the two communities. My father had dealt with Muslim merchants all his life. He had also lived in Peshawar. So, while at the religious level, as an Arya Samaji, he observed his differences, at the practical level, he knew how to interact and get along with the Muslims. He did not permit his Arya Samaji views to interface with his business (laughs).

AB : So ideologies and civilities never came into great conflict in your father's generation. But there did come a time when old civilizational codes broke down and barbarism became the order of the day. Why and at what stage did the barbaric become a part of our history?

BS : As you were talking, I was trying to imagine my father becoming barbaric. I can't ever imagine him to have said to me 'Go and shoot that Muslim.' It is possible that middle class people nurse prejudices, but when it comes to killing, they hesitate, because of their past culture and education. The killings that took place in Rawalpindi was a result of the fanaticism of young people, but looting and molesting were confined, I think, to a small minority of people.

AB : Let's take the figure of Shahnawaz in *Tamas*. He is cultured and a rich man. He is a friend of Raghunath. Yet, at one stage, he gets so worked up that he kills Milkhi. He is surely an example of pathological behaviour that has nothing to do with either education or class. Isn't that so?

BS : Yes, I think human reaction keeps changing, keeps varying. The same Shahnawaz after the riots, becomes very active in the *aman* movement. He gives all the petrol for the bus, etc. At that time he is seemingly moved by a different kind of impulse. He wants to please the Deputy Commissioner and wants everyone to think of him as a man of peace. He does save Raghunath and his family, but he also kills that poor man, Milkhi. He is not a Muslim Leaguer. Was he deceiving himself, or was he deceiving others? I think, he is an example of the fact that human nature is not very consistent. Human beings in real life behave differently in different circumstances.

AB : You had earlier said that you couldn't imagine your father ordering you to kill. This was because you had learnt to expect a certain consistency of behaviour from him. So there are only certain kinds of people who behave in an unpredictable manner.

BS : There are certain kinds of people, as you know, who are willing to give money to get people killed, but would never kill themselves.

AB : Did you ever meet a man who was involved in the killings?

BS : I had met a man who had done a lot of killing.

AB : You had?

BS : Oh, yes.

AB : From what class was he?

BS : He was the son of a carpenter.

AB : In *Tamas*, Murad Ali is certainly not a poor man. He is one of the main organizers of the killings described in the novel. On the other hand, I can't imagine Nathu, the poor tanner, capable of killing a man. He can kill a pig as part of his profession, but not a man. In fact, even after he kills the pig, he feels that he has sinned and will have to pay for it.

BS : Quite right.

AB : During the Partition then, violence was not confined to a class.

BS : Not at all.

AB : If violence was neither class inspired nor the product of any particular religion, then what was responsible for it? I can understand your statement that violence could have been the result of personal pathologies. Thus, in *Tamas*, Shahnawaz may, in a moment of rage and disgust, kill a deformed servant. And a boy like Ranbir may kill because he sees aggression as a proof of his manhood. He may also kill because, inspired by religious fanaticism, he may want to establish a place for himself within a violent sect. What puzzles me, however, is that such violence was possible in a highly civilized society—from what you describe and others have described, up to 1947 no one could have imagined that such a holocaust could have occurred in India. Of course, there were always violent incidents in various areas before 1947—incidents that happen in every society. Yet, in India, 1947 represents a civilizational break. In 1947, every assumption we had about ourselves as a people and a culture—about the restraints and the mutualities that governed our daily behaviour—suddenly collapsed. Why did that happen? Incidentally, the same thing happened over the same period of time in a highly civilized society like Germany. What is puzzling about Germany, as it is about India, is that the collapse into barbarism took place during a time when the intellectual discourse was about how to make a rational society even less vulnerable to violent collapse. Consider that a book like the *Philosophy of Enlightenment* by Ernst Cassirer was published in 1940. Yet there is an undercurrent of barbarism in Germany of a kind that human societies had never experienced before. How do you explain it?

BS : I think barbarism is not a permanent feature of human conduct. It depends on a combination of circumstances, which somehow incite man's basic instincts. Under certain circumstances men lose all sense of decency and proportion, and indulge in butchery. After some time, the barbaric impulses slowly subside and give way to reason. Men begin to repent their actions. It is often said that the oriental people are excitable and bloodthirsty. Yet, Hitler's Europe undermines that assertion. I have seen the places where he had built gas chambers for the killing of civilians. How does one account for them. How did Hitler convince his followers that the Jews were the enemy and had to be exterminated? Yet, the German people are highly civilized. I, therefore, don't think that barbarism is a permanent feature of human behaviour. Human beings are incited to act like beasts. There are a number of circumstances which provoke people to kill. After all, as you know, marauders came from

Central Asia to India and butchered lakhs of people in a matter of days. That killing must also have been motivated. I am sure, however, that men are not naturally bestial.

AB : But conditions of war are different from what happened during the Partition. In *Tamas*, for instance, there is a brilliant scene in which you describe how Ranbir kills a man. The boy walks down a street beside an old Muslim who is a perfume-seller. The conversation between them is nerve-racking. The street is empty because of the fear of a riot. The conversation between them is a fine example of what one understands civilized behaviour to be all about. The Muslim peddler tells the boy that he should go home because the times are bad and that his parents would be worried—indeed all the things that make for human societies and relationships. Yet, the boy himself seems to be living in a world of murderous fantasies. The boy's action is clearly pathological. He is not fighting a war.

BS : Yes, you are right. The boy, however, has been incited. He doesn't know what he is doing and why he is doing it. He thinks he is performing a deed, which is heroic and patriotic. He is, however, very confused.

AB : Would you say that in 1947 the rhetoric of non-violence had lost its power?

BS : I did not try to analyse the cause of the Partition in *Tamas*. I was only interested in describing the incidents I had seen and heard about. I was also trying to record what people thought and felt at that time. If you, however, want to know my own opinion about what happened and why, I still may not be able to tell you. All I can say is that, as a humanist and a writer, I cherish certain values and modes of behaviour. I deplore the killings that took place. It was shameful that a large population should have indulged in so much violence.

AB : You had earlier said that people often repent their actions. You have probably seen the recent reports about some German leaders who have gone to Israel and made statements of regret. Why is that, that Indian and Pakistani leaders haven't made similar apologies for what happened in 1947? Why have we, as a people not asked each other for forgiveness for our past actions? Don't you think that such an act would help us find our way out of the present politics of anger and revenge.

BS : People in power have a vested interest in holding onto that power. But ordinary citizens of India and Pakistan have spoken up.

AB : Why has a similar kind of thing not happened at the political level?

BS : It will if there is sufficient pressure from below. Only then will the politicians begin to think. Already there is some talk of forming a confederation between India and Pakistan. There is a demand to stop the kind of confrontational politics we have been indulging in. Thirty years ago no one would have spoken about such a confederation. Now people are willing to ask for it. There are, of course, fewer such voices in Pakistan. But they are present.

AB : In Pakistan these voices are muted for a variety of internal reasons. . . . You haven't yet answered the question I asked at the beginning: 'Why did you write *Tamas* so many years after the Partition?'

BS : It was not a calculated decision. It never is. Many years later when I saw the riots in Bombay and Bhiwandi, I was reminded of my days in Pakistan. They compelled me to think about my old experiences. I also felt that the conditions that had caused the riots in 1947 were still present. The Partition of the country should have put an end to the riots, but it hadn't. I started writing. When I began, I had no well thought-out objective in mind. Perhaps, I merely wanted to recollect and relive my past.

AB : What I had in mind is something else. When I read accounts of similar experiences, I am struck by the fact that they are recalled in order to exorcise them—of course, they can also be evoked for nostalgic reasons. Writers try to overcome their troubling memories by objectifying them and giving them a shape.

BS : That is true at a personal level, perhaps. But I had no mental conflict or discord. I had lived in the midst of Muslims. Maybe, if I had lived in a place where I was isolated from them, I would have developed some hostility towards them. But I had lived with them both in India and Pakistan. Indeed, I had the opportunity of working with some very remarkable Muslim friends in the Progressive Writers' movement, Sajjad Zaheer and Faiz Ahmad Faiz, for example. Moreover, the Urdu writers were in the vanguard of the Progressive movement. I had a great regard for them. They were very impressive people, Faiz, in particular, both as a man and as a writer. I was not influenced by communal propaganda.

AB : Did you know that Faiz was one of the few people in Pakistan who flew into Delhi to attend Gandhi's funeral? That speaks of a very different kind of sensibility from what caused the Partition.

BS : Yes. Faiz once told me that during one of his visits to Delhi, he had received a message from Nehru at 1 a.m. requesting him (Faiz) to visit him. When he met Nehru, who was a great admirer of his work, Faiz told Nehru that he was a leader who had the authority to bring about change. Among the intellectuals there are very few Muslims or Hindus who are bigoted. This has to do both with our tradition, and our education and culture. We do have a liberal outlook. This is certainly so in our personal behaviour and attitudes. I am convinced that India is a multi-lingual, multi-religious and multi-racial society. It is important to maintain this liberal character. If it is upset we are in for trouble. This is true of the intellectuals also. Of course, there are some on both sides who are fanatics.

AB : Isn't this true at the non-intellectual level also?

BS : Yes. In our cultural life we do rub shoulders with people from different religions and different states. There is no communal attitude, for instance, in our films or plays. Ayodhya was an aberration. After all people did protest against it and reject it.

AB : That's a good point to make. In your novel the one character who speaks unambiguously in favour of a united people is the General. He is not the sanest of men. Did you know such a person in Rawalpindi?

BS : Yes. I knew the man. I loved him. Although he was regarded as a nitwit, he was a very dear person. As a matter of fact, when *Tamas* was made into a film, I received a letter from Patna informing me that the man was alive. The letter was resentful because in the film it was shown that the General had been killed. The writer informed me that the man had lived through the riots and had finally settled down in Ambala.

AB : The figure of the lunatic as a person of real goodness appears not only in your novel, but also in Manto's 'Toba Tek Singh' and in Krishna Baldev Vaid's *Guzara Hua Zamana*. But let me end the interview by asserting that lunacy is not our only hope (laughter). Thanks.

1947: The Great Migration

MRINAL PANDE

We saw a trainload of Hindus had been killed and in Dera Baba Nanak, a trainload of Musalmans who had come from the direction of Ludhiana had also been killed . . . they killed each other's people. We saw bodies of Musalmans, utensils lying in the mud, clothes . . . some people buried under others, and disease and illness all around. When we got to Dera Baba Nanak, they said to us, you have come home. But we thought, our home was over there. We have left it behind. How can this be home?[1]

Since self-preservation, aggression and a sense of one's own turf are basic human traits, all migrations, irrespective of their cause, nature and scale have caused bloody conflicts. The Partition of India in 1947 triggered off one of the biggest migrations in human history, it was also one of the bloodiest. It uprooted nearly 12 million people from the land of their birth and caused physical and mental scars that remain even after 50 years.

Looking at the life, literature and politics in the two countries, one feels that neither India nor Pakistan, has recovered entirely from the memories and aftermath of the great holocaust. In both the countries xenophobic Right wing groups have taken advantage of the communal hatred triggered off in 1947 and built up their cadres, whose anger and suspicion of the 'other' still feeds upon the real or imaginary tales of the communal tensions that brought about the Partition and the great migration of 1947. Neither country has chosen to raise a national monument to commemorate the tragic events, and its innocent victims, as for example, the Germans have after the Second World War or the Japanese have after Hiroshima. There is, to date, no formal ceremony or a national day of mourning, by which the two nations would remind the coming generations of the dangers of communal hatred and of the self-destructive venom that xenophobia generates. It almost seems as though both wish to bury those memories deep underground along with the lessons to be learnt from them.

* Based on Urvashi Butalia, *The Other Side of Silence* (New Delhi, 1998).

But is it possible to erase such a trauma totally? The fact is, that the common people, the men, women and children who lived through that terrible period have been whispering their stories into the ears of their progeny for half a century. Some of these stories have found their way into literary works of astounding quality, like Yashpal's *Jhootha Sach*, Bhisham Sahni's *Tamas*, Krishna Sobti's 'Daar Se Bichhudi', Manto's 'Toba Tek Singh', Amrita Pritam's 'Pinjar' and Dronvier Kohli's *Wah Camp.* The tales re-evoke the Partition before our eyes and at the same time remind us of the raw and naked emotions that may still smoulder beneath our new national identities. But literature is peripheral to our lives today. The midnight's children in both India and Pakistan, are now aging parents and grandparents and still harbour within them, most of the misgivings and biases of their parents and elders. The recent spurt in jingoism and firings in the air, when India detonated its nuclear device in Pokharan and Pakistan in Sind (evinced on TV screens in both countries), were eerie replays of the pre-Partition sentiments in more ways than one. They showed how in both countries not only the religious fundamentalists, but political leaders also, still look upon aggressive militarization as a symbol of their country's assertive and virile masculinity.

Looking at these images, it is not difficult to see why even after 50 years of independence, in both India and Pakistan, communalism instead of dying out, has mutated and taken on new forms. The media and ruling élite on the subcontinent may endlessly analyse the violent conflicts and attacks that erupt in various states periodically against minority groups. They may call them unfortunate and warn that the fair name of the country would be darkened in international circles, if such tribal and racial vendettas were to continue. But assaults on one religious or caste group by another, in both India and Pakistan, are more than just passing neighbourhood squabbles or frustrated bickerings among poor and illiterate groups. In India, the communal riots targeting Muslims, Sikhs or Christians or the caste wars that often erupt in villages between Dalits and Backwards, upper castes and lower castes are all assaults on liberty, equality and fraternity, the basic principles of democracy. In Pakistan, similarly, the assaults mounted periodically against Shias, Ahmediyas or Christians deny the basic concept of an egalitarian democratic brotherhood and solidarity, on which Pakistan was allegedly built. All these clashes in India and Pakistan reveal tribal tensions that half a century of democracy has been unable to wipe out, because the lessons about non-violence and brotherhood we had been taught by great leaders, during the anti-imperialist struggle and the spirit of public cooperation and mobilization of the 1940s, were all wiped out by the violence of the Partition. And until we honestly face the memories of the Partition and denounce communalism, we may never reclaim the earlier tolerance.

In a way what happened in Delhi in 1984 or in Mumbai in 1992, or what has been happening almost every day in Karachi and Lahore, since the *muhajirs* moved in there after Partition, bring home to sensitive minds on both sides of the border, that the socio-political forces responsible for driving out millions from the land of their ancestors, have not changed that much and that self-interest and xenophobia are still anthropological constants in both countries. The well-known Pakistani writer Intizar Hussain writes:

> In the wake of the birth of Pakistan . . . we were faced with the disturbing questions of our identity which prompted us to embark on a journey to the past. But which past—the past of our land, or our past as Muslims? Where do our roots lie? Is it the history of the land or our Muslim past which forms the basis of our culture?[2]

In a recent book, *The Other Side of Silence*, an Indian scholar, Urvashi Butalia has bravely tried to rake up the cinders of the history of the Partition, to highlight several burning questions. Today, when the dramatic and suffering centre of Punjab's past seems gradually to be fading into the mists of time or into a larger history of an academic kind, Butalia, whose own family had migrated from Punjab to Delhi in 1947, has sought out the common people to record the hitherto unrecorded memories of our joint past. They are simple working folk, men and women, who speak to her about how they saw history first hand, both as participants and witnesses. They have remained largely invisible in formal texts on both sides of the divide, because former scholarship mostly focuses on major leaders or major events. Butalia, in her search for truth, has sought to elbow aside the usual methodology and skirted largely clear of the Hindu, Muslim or Sikh movers and shakers in both countries, whose basic preoccupation anyway, was to fill the power vacuum left by the British masters and expedite the process of nation building. They all agreed to the Partition, quite unmindful of the trauma it would cause the peoples of the subcontinent. Butalia has, therefore, fleshed out the unsung human actors in that moving real life drama enacted half a century ago, recorded their memories, however disjointed or foggy they might have been and reproduced their version verbatim. The searing and moving indictment of leaders and the stories told by these simple people (mostly for the first time to a human ear) offer a valuable insight into the hopes, fears, joys and sorrows of a whole generation of migrants, whose lives were changed almost overnight when history catapulted them from the land of their origin to a new one that was destined to be their home and nation.

The book is a remarkable product of an individual's research spanning a decade and covering uncharted historic territory. It weaves together strands of oral accounts of the common out-groups (women, Dalits and children), parts of vital historical and official documents, parliamentary records, personal and official letters and diaries, into an interesting and moving tapestry of human suffering and dignity, bestiality and goodness, shame and pride.

Instead of going by purely scholarly concerns, Butalia has concentrated on recording stories that answer specific hitherto mostly unanswered questions, such as: Do the causes for present-day alienation between Hindus and Muslims go far back into the precarious self-consciousness of a past no one really knows much about? Why is it that after the Partition, both Hindus and Muslims have developed deep rifts and hostilities within their own groups? Why is it that all the world over, when countries have been divided and subdivided following political exigencies of the day, the choices for the unwanted millions have been limited between emigration, expulsion or staying on and risking being wiped out, and later, in retaliatory acts of mass genocide? What is honour? Whose honour is saved when women are first slaughtered like lambs and then declared martyrs?

Feminist history today, almost in the manner of literary writing, has developed a third subaltern eye, that glosses over accepted social mores and eminent personalities of the day, for the working-class women's version of what history and society look like from a worm's point of view. The stories Butalia's book reveal suddenly bring home to us how in times of stress identities based on clan, caste and religion, may override all the ideological baggage that constructs a national identity. Also, how the nation may proclaim itself secular and gender-neutral but the subterranean pull of the tribal mosaic underneath the 'national' identity may, time and again, lead the nation back into tribal ideologies and situations, because nations, as we see and identify them today, have been around for only about two centuries, whereas castes, clans and religions have existed for thousands of years.

Reading Butalia's book, it often strikes one, that the known Hindu and Muslim cultures may actually harbour within them so many other cultures, born of ancient castes and clans and languages that go back to thousands of years. We may think that on the national level all the people of one country may endorse a 'national' culture, but that is an illusion. Each cultural unit looked at closely through the lens of a climacteric event, such as the Partition, offers many perspectives, and the affected people are seen to have priorities that are clearly at odds with the view point of the larger society.

To enter the sealed minds of her protagonists, Butalia first returns to her own family and its past in Pakistan. Thus, she first recounts the haunting story of her own uncle, Rana *mama*, who chose to convert to Islam and stayed back with his mother, who also converted to Islam, when the rest of the family chose to protect their religious identity and migrated to India. Was Rana right in betraying the spiritual moorings of the family in preference for its material base? To what extent did he really belong to his new identity and national and familial ties? Can families really wipe their slates clean if they proclaim from rooftops that they have?

In recounting Rana *mama's* tale, Butalia has created a magnetic field through which thoughts and impressions of both communities can flow and in which traditional markers of caste, clan and religion take on a very different shape and colouring. In Rana *mama* we see at close quarters the rise of communal identity in an individual with all its human dilemmas; the contrapuntal pulls between kinship ties and ownership of assets.

The family Butalia faces when she eventually makes contact with her elusive uncle in Pakistan is, in part, a survival of the older collective and, in part, a microcosm of the new socio-political reality of Islam in an Islamic nation. To this family, Indian relatives are not sons of the soil anymore, but honoured guests at best and intruders at worst. The more artificial the genesis of the neo-converted, the more precarious and panic-stricken its reaction to family reunions of this kind. Possibly the heightened sensitivities and the anticipatory fear impair thought:

> I have not been able to decide whether Rana was telling the truth or not. Was his problem really one of conversion? . . . Or was he simply lying, choosing a method of survival he had resorted to many times earlier I don't really know.[3]

Of course, there have been great massacres and endemic poverty in every age in the Indian subcontinent. Yet it is only since the Partition that communal riots on both sides of the border have condemned whole groups of common citizens to uprootment. The seeds of this are traceable in the pre-Partition days:

> Partition the word itself is so inadequate. Partition is a simple division, a separation, but surely what happened in 1947 was much more than that . . . not only were people separated overnight, and friends became enemies, homes became strange places, strange places had to be claimed now as homes, a line was drawn to mark

a border and boundaries began to find reflection in people's lives and minds. Identities had suddenly to be redefined. And it is perhaps precisely for this reason that in some ways so many people who see themselves as victims, are complicit in the violence of Partition, that there is such reluctance to remember it.[4]

Since 1947 poverty, political corruption and religious discrimination, have led more and more groups in both India and Pakistan to insist on their 'identity' as specially underprivileged groups. Militant spokesmen raise separatist demands and when they do so, they often fall back on the legacy of 1947. There are confrontations not only with the majority but also between the minorities. Assamiyas want to expel Bengalis, but Bengalis and Assamiyas jointly crib about Bangladeshi infiltrators, Bangladeshis wish to eject Chakmas, Sindhis want to see the last of the *muhajirs*, Yadavs fight Kurmis and Dalits, Jats are against the Jatavs and Sunnis clash against the Shias regularly. Obviously the more fiercely a nation defends itself against threats from the 'others', and the higher it raises its walls against the 'intruders', the less, in the end, it has left to defend.

Perhaps, we need to make a national effort now to rewrite our histories more honestly. We can start by first facing our own creative works without flinching. We have to read again fiction and plays that we have tried to ban and censor, we have to see Maniratnam's films, Hussein's paintings and even listen to Rushdie's literary rantings, to purge the venom that is corroding our souls. Art, good art specially, always errs on the side of truth and liberalism. But, art seldom has had political allies. Neither India nor Pakistan has seen a major political leader speaking up for Rushdie, Manto, Ismat Chugtai or Rajinder Singh Bedi. Neither state has compensated artists for what vandals have destroyed: precious paintings, sculptures or manuscripts. It has not declared artistic works its national treasure, and artistic concerns a national priority. Most of our leaders would rather go with Plato and ban all artists from holding painfully vivid mirrors before the Republic. Mohan Congressi says:

> It was because our big leaders were in a hurry to sit on high chairs, that we have had to face the Partition. They are comfortable now but we, who have really paid for this freedom with our home and hearth, have been turned into unwanted refugees . . . all politicians failed us. (my translation)[5]

The rage of Kohli's hero on the eve of the Partition, is echoed across the border in Pakistani columnist Shahnaz Aijazuddin's lines, half a century later:

> To live in Pakistan today is to be at times as disconcerted and perplexed as Alice

was in the Looking Glass world. Nothing it quite what is seems. You have to recognize that each aspect, whether in law, or the bureaucracy or the political system, has an inner core that governs it. Mostly the dictates of this subterranean code of ethics are in sharp contradiction with the overt image of the institutions it controls. . . . In the confused collage of Pakistani politics today, . . . the state-controlled media prefers to remain silent on the most significant issues.[6]

The governments and state controlled media in both India and Pakistan wish similarly to banish the Partition from the subcontinent's collective psyche for the very existence of those thousands of real life stories, about the Partition, puts many of our declared values into question. The only way the two countries can face their future with any degree of confidence and honesty is if they let the floodgates of Partition memories open up on both sides, let the citizens soak up the painful facts and then face each other without inhibitions. Artists and writers who have already done so, could help people learn about human dignity and degradation, and genuine tolerance.

Do we wish to allow the wounds of Partition to fester within increasingly inadequate walls on both sides and plan to destroy each other continually; or do we wish to open up and remember our beginnings as modern nations, understand the great migration collectively and come to terms without grief and shame.

The choice is ours.

NOTES

1. Interview with Rajinder Singh, a three-wheeler scooter driver in Delhi, in Urvashi Butalia, *The Other Side of Silence* (New Delhi, 1998), p. 80.
2. Intizar Hussain in the preface to *Fires in an Autumn Garden, An Anthology of Short Stories from Pakistan*, compiled by Asif Farrukhi (Karachi, 1997).
3. Butalia, op.cit., p. 65.
4. Ibid., pp. 271-2.
5. Dronvir Kohli, *Wah Camp* (in Hindi) (New Delhi, 1998), pp. 203-4.
6. Shahnaz Aijazuddin, *Lost from View* (Lahore, 1994), p. 104.

Listening for a Change: Narratives of Partition

URVASHI BUTALIA

I would like to take as the starting point of this paper a small incident of violence that took place in Seelampur, in Delhi, soon after the demolition of the Babri Masjid in 1992. The beginnings of this incident lay in the alleged killing, by unknown persons (assumed to be Muslims) of a police constable (a Hindu), which then led to retaliation by the police and armed hoodlums on Muslim households, in the mixed lanes of Welcome and Janata colonies. Houses were burnt down and destroyed. Men were kept in illegal detention. It was estimated that there were 11 deaths and large-scale losses as a result of the burning down of the timber market, which bordered these residential areas. These were some of the apparent, visible losses.

Soon after, when activists from different groups in Delhi began to go to the area to help, other things emerged. Doctors working in the area found many women suffering from different kinds of medical problems related to stress and trauma. Two of them had actually aborted as a result of the trauma. Because their homes had been destroyed, most of the survivors, particularly women who feared sexual violence, had moved to the homes of friends and relatives some distance away. But home exercises a powerful pull, and they would come back, day after day, during the relaxation of curfew and just stare at the broken shells of their homes and weep. For many of them, however, there was no time for tears. There were, instead, all the processes that follow such sudden and violent loss and death to go through: filing reports, tracing lost family members, rebuilding homes, keeping families together, and all this in the restricted space of the two or so hours, when the curfew was relaxed. Many of the women were illiterate and completely at a loss about how to cope with filing reports with the police or getting their men out of detention, which sometimes meant that male representatives had to step in, while at other times, the women dealt with these problems on their own. While the loss of family and home was felt deeply by the women, I was struck, too, by the deep sense of insult many of them felt at being rudely pulled out of their houses during the violence. They protested that they were not even given the time to cover themselves with a veil, before being 'exposed' in the public space. They said '*hum ko be-pardah kar diya*' (we were forced to bare our faces).

A question that I asked myself at the time and one that continues to worry me today, is: When the history of this and other such events is written, say 50 years from now, will these experiences find a place in it? We may learn about the 11 deaths and the 500 men who were missing, but will we learn anything more? Indeed, are such things of any relevance to history? The number of deaths, the number of men who were missing, these will count among the 'facts' of history, but how the experience actually affected men, women and children, in some cases how it changed their lives, where will these things find a place? To put the question in another way: How, if at all, can history accommodate these experiences?

I have for long been concerned with, what I like to call the 'underside' of history. A question that preoccupies me is: Why is it that the history we know deals so much with the State, with government, with rulers and hardly ever with people? It is these and other similiar questions that have informed my research on Partition. As an historical event, Partition, for example, has ramifications that reach far beyond 1947, yet historical records make little mention of the dislocation of people's lives, the strategies they used to cope with loss, trauma, pain and violence. Why have historians been reluctant to address these? Are these questions of no use to history at all? Or can they inform and enrich history and historical practice? I realize too that if we pose these questions, we must inevitably pose others. If, for example, we are to attempt to recover the 'underside' of history, are there any satisfactory methods, any tools that we have, to undertake such an exercise? Moreover, is such an exercise of any use at all? Does it broaden or deepen our perception of issues? Can we put it to any use? How, indeed, is such research different from the supposedly more 'objective' research?

For me, these questions and this research carry particular meanings because of my own history as a child of Punjabi refugee parents. Like many children of my generation—first generation children after Partition—stories of Partition, stories in which love, friendship and sharing, seem to go hand-in-hand with brutality, violence and hatred, have formed the staple of my childhood. The fact that Hindus, Muslims and Sikhs shared a sort of common identity as Punjabis is something many Punjabis recall with a kind of nostalgia that is almost a yearning for a 'golden time' in the past, a notion which gains strength as current reality becomes more and more difficult to cope with.

However, precisely because these stories are so much a part of our lives, we barely listen to them. They are often dismissed as just stories and are seldom looked at as history. For me, the process of listening to family stories of Partition, my own and those of others, became especially important, in 1984, after the anti-Sikh riots in Delhi. At the time, hundreds of concerned citizens of Delhi worked in the outlying areas of the city, where the violence against Sikhs had been particularly harsh. They helped to file claims for compensation, report missing people and organize shelter, food and clothing for people, who had been ousted from their homes. I was also a part of these groups.

As we worked, we found people talking, again and again, about Partition, comparing what they had faced then to what they were facing now. It was then that I began to realize what a major trauma Partition had been for people who had lived through it. How could we have ignored the memories of that time? If the violence of 1984—so far away from those of us who merely worked with the survivors—could affect us so deeply, what must have Partition meant for the survivors? And how could we know this, if we were not willing to listen to what people had to say?

Oral narrative and oral history, I have come to realize since then, are important sources for the researcher, who wants to explore the 'hidden' dimensions of our history. Though not unproblematic or unexploitative, these sources are nonetheless important. A second possible source is journals, diaries, memoirs and personal accounts by people who were involved at the time. It is my belief that these sources lead us to a much more complete and complex view of history, than the 'standard' historical sources such as documents, reports, published papers, etc. While rich in themselves, these latter address only certain aspects of the historical experience. If we wish to explore other aspects, we need to look elsewhere. In what follows, I look at two different kinds of sources: written, personal accounts and oral narratives, to examine what it is they have to offer.

WRITTEN ACCOUNTS

Although I have spoken in general of memoirs and diaries, I want here to concentrate mainly on one. Anis Kidwai's memoir, *Azadi ki Chhaon Mein*,[1] is constructed from a detailed diary that she kept for about a year after Partition, and relates mainly to her work with Muslim refugees in Delhi. Kidwai came into relief work, in the way that many women of her generation did at the time—through their own or their family's political involvement, through contact with someone important (in this case Gandhi) or as a result of a personal loss or tragedy. All of these were true in some measure for Kidwai. Her husband was killed in communal rioting in Mussoorie. Despite being aware that it was dangerous for him to stay on there as a Muslim, Shafi Ahmad Kidwai refused to move and was killed on his way to the office while he was bringing salaries for his office employees. Kidwai was bereft and at the behest of her brother-in-law, Rafi Ahmad Kidwai, then with the Congress, went to see Gandhi, who advised her to take on some work.

Kidwai's memoir is rich in detail and provides fascinating insights. In the process of my research I met her daughter, Kishwar Kidwai, who had worked with her, and also several other members of her family. From them I learnt that although she herself was keen to publish her account, Kidwai had refrained from doing so, at the suggestion of her brother who felt, in the 1950s, that the time was 'not right'. Later, a small edition did come out (in Urdu), which Kidwai was not happy with and soon the book was out of print. It was only recently that it was republished.

Kidwai describes in detail the Purana Qila camp, where she worked. Displaced Muslims were housed there, while they waited to be sent to Pakistan. Many did not want to go, but they had very little choice. Conditions in the camp were abysmal—probably because they were Muslims waiting to be sent away, the State did not want to be bothered with them, even though until virtually the day before or the hour before, they may have been its citizens. Indeed, Kidwai points out that much of the food, etc., at the Purana Qila camp, was provided by the Pakistan Embassy.

Kidwai's memoir is doubly valuable because it provides information on what was happening with Muslims. It provides a valuable counterpoint to stories of Muslim 'atrocities', which are otherwise open to misrepresentation. She points out that while the Indian State was reluctant to offer any help to the refugees its workers were sometimes willing to help, for a price! She tells the story of a Muslim man in her camp who had 'lost' his wife. While visiting her parents she, along with them, had been forced to undergo *shuddhi* (purification, common at the time to 'convert' or 'reconvert' people to Hinduism) and become a Hindu. The husband, keen to recover her, bribed two of the camp guards and with their help, took a truck and brought his wife back. Kidwai was unaware of this until the next day when the police and district magistrate arrived at the camp, intent on recovering the woman who was now a Hindu and, therefore, belonged to India. Kidwai tried to argue with them, even suggested to them that they would be better off arresting the camp guards who had violated the law, but in the end was persuaded that they meant no harm and so, in turn, persuaded the man to send his wife back. At the time, she was convinced that the officials would send the woman back soon, having once made their report and fulfilled other formalities. But nothing of the sort happened and the bereft husband finally had no alternative but to leave for Pakistan, while Kidwai was left with a sense of deep failure and frustration.

Her memoir provides many other instances of people who were more or less forced to go to Pakistan because they had no alternative. A compounder in a local women's hospital had to move to the camp for safety. When things were a bit better he was keen to go back. Kidwai went to the hospital, where she discovered that everyone spoke of him with tremendous respect and agreed that he was one of the best and most popular workers they had had. But when she raised the subject of his coming back to the hospital, the warden made it clear that there was no way that could happen and the next day, his things were sent to the camp. The man had, perforce, to leave for Pakistan.

Elsewhere, I have looked at different dimensions of the experiences of women, during and as a result of Partition, and also at how the question of gender became a crucial one for the fragile Indian State in its quest for legitimacy.[2] Acting out its responsibility as the 'family' and, more specifically, as the patriarch, the Indian State mounted a massive and sustained 'recovery' operation, which lasted for nearly nine years after Partition and which was aimed at recovering and bringing back abducted women to their 'rightful' homes (which, in the eyes of the State, were linked with their religion). This basically meant bringing Hindu women to India and sending Muslim women to Pakistan. In the initial stages both countries were agreed on this and they reached an agreement (the Inter Dominion Treaty of 6 December 1947), to carry out search and recovery operations in each other's territories. Since the actual rescue operation could take several years (by the time the families filed reports, women were tracked down, etc.), and by the time the women were actually found they were often married, settled, with children, and perhaps living a new and different life. Some had been through so many hands that they no longer believed the fact that simply because their rescuers were from the same religion, they would be any safer with them. It is by now well known that several of them, therefore, did not want to return. Hindu and Sikh women, in particular, also feared that their families would not have taken them back. Gandhi and Nehru had to issue repeated appeals to people to do so, saying that abducted women should not be seen as polluted or sinful and that the families should take them in. Anis Kidwai describes the plight of these women in detail:

In all of this sometimes a girl would be killed or she would be wounded. The 'good stuff' would be shared among the police and army, the 'second rate stuff' would go to everyone else and then these girls would go from one hand to another and then another and after several would turn up in hotels to grace their decor, or they would be handed over to police officers, in some places to please them.

And every single one of these girls, because she had been the victim of a trick, she would begin to look upon her 'rescuer' perforce as an angel of mercy who had, in this time of loot and killing, rescued her, fought for her, and brought her away. And when this man would cover her naked body—whose clothes had become the loot of another thief—with his own loincloth or *banyan*, when he would put these on her, at that moment she would forget her mother's slit throat, her father's bloody body, her husband's trembling corpse. She would forget all this and instead, thank the man who had saved her. And why should she not do this? Rescuing her from the horror, this good man has brought her to his home. He is giving her respect, he offers to marry her. How can she not become his slave for life?

And it is only much later that the realization dawns that among the looters this man alone could not have been the innocent . . . all were tarred with the same brush. Each one had played with life and death to save the honour of some young women, and thousands of mothers and sisters must be cursing these supposedly 'brave men' who had abducted their daughters.

But by the time this realization came, it was too late. Now there was nowhere for her to go by this time she is about to become a mother, or she has passed through several hands. After seeing so many men's faces, this daughter of Hindustan, how will she ever look at the faces of her parents, her husband.[3]

To persuade those who were reluctant to return, the Government of India enacted a law, the Abducted Persons Recovery and Restoration Act, which effectively denied a woman the choice of where she could stay. Clauses 1 and 2 of the act, pointed out:

1. Every effort must be made to recover and restore abducted women and children within the shortest time possible.

2. Conversions by persons abducted after March 1947 will not be recognized and all such persons must be restored to their respective dominions. *The wishes of the persons concerned are irrelevant and consequently no statements of such persons shall be recorded before magistrates.*

Although the clause refers to 'persons' it became clear from the implementation of the act that the second clause referred mainly to women. For the two states of India and Pakistan, women also came to symbolize, in some way, both lost honour and lost property and, therefore, they had to be *recovered*. Thus, while it was crucial for the State to act as a patriarch for women, at the same time women were denied their rights as citizens of a State that was, at that very time in the process of drawing up an egalitarian and non-discriminatory Constitution. While women's rights were being violated with State sanction, the rights of minorities—in this case Muslims—were also being violated, if not in letter, certainly in spirit. This was something the State effectively sanctioned by its indifference as shown by the story cited above or by the fact that neither the Purana Qila nor the Humayun's Tomb camp merited the kind of attention that Hindu camps (as the Purana Qila camp was later to become) did. This, for a self-defined secular State, was a betrayal of its aims. It was as if, though still physically present on Indian soil, those Muslims who were in camps had, in the eyes of the Indian State, no longer any claim to it for they had already become the responsibility of the 'other' country. Since they were seen to have 'voluntarily' given up these claims, the State, therefore, had no responsibility to them.

Women like Kidwai were unique in that they felt for the abducted women. In her memoirs she records that 'the reader will not understand how I, as a woman, felt on hearing these things' (hearing about the problems of women, that is). Her feelings mirrored those of many other social workers, who had taken on the task of recovering abducted women. Acting as dutiful servants of the State, they nonetheless responded to the women as women and often helped to subvert the State's agenda, although most of the time they were also helpless and hampered by the fact that they had little choice but to carry out their assigned tasks. Kidwai describes her own feelings movingly:

> There were some women who had been born into poor homes and had not seen anything other than poverty. A half-full stomach and rags on their body. And now they had fallen into the hands of men who had bought them silken *salwars* and net *dupattas*, who taught them the pleasures of cold ice cream and hot coffee, who took them to the cinema. Why should they leave such men and go back to covering their bodies with rags and slaving in the hot sun in fields? If she leaves this smart, uniformed man, she will probably end up with a peasant in rags, in the filth, with a *danda* on his shoulder. And so they are happy to forget the frightening past, or the equally uncertain and fearful future and live only for the present.
>
> They also had another fear. The people who wanted to take them away, whether they were friend or foe, how did they know that they would not sell them to others? After all, she had been sold many times, how many more times would it happen? The same police informs, it was they that had, time and again, taken her from here to there. What was there to reassure her that she could believe in the authority of the turban, that the person who wore it came from her relative and not

someone who had come yet again to buy and sell her. The stigma did not go away until she was dragged away and made to live with her relatives for a few days.

There remained religion, and what did these girls know about that after all? Men can at least read the *namaz* the *alvida* they can go to the mosque to read the *namaz* at Id, and listen to the mullah. But the mullah has never allowed women to even stand there. The moment the men see young women the blood rises in their eyes. Be off with you, go away, what work do you have here? As if they were dogs to be pushed out of every place. The culprit is within them, but it is the women who are made to go away. If they come to the masjid everyone's *namaz* will be ruined. If they come to listen to the sermon, everyone's attention is distracted. If they go to the *dargah*, they will get pushed around by men, and if they participate in a *quwwali mehfil* the sufi's attention will be on worldly things rather than on God. And friend, the God of this religion has never kept her very comfortably. But the new man with whom she is, is like God. Let everyone talk, she will never leave this man who has filled her world with colour.[4]

There are many other stories in Kidwai's memoir, but I will mention only a few others here. One of the casualities of the mass migration, was that *karigars*, workers and crafts people of all sorts, went away to Pakistan, thus dealing a major blow to trade. In the camps, as people began to leave there was a serious shortage of midwives. Kishwar Kidwai, for example, remembered delivering a baby at the age of 16 with no training and no experience. She said:

I had never seen so much blood . . . and I was holding this little bloody child in my hands without knowing what to do. Then a man standing nearby, he tore a piece of cloth from his dhoti and gave it to me to cover the child and clean my hands.[5]

Clearly the business of birth (and death) had to go on. Kidwai's second story has to do with the dying. She tells of an old man who died, and who had no relatives, save a daughter and her young child, to perform the last rites. Kidwai and a friend, Jamila, tried to persuade various people to take on this task, but to no avail. They considered whether they should do the work themselves, but there was a problem: being women, they could not bathe a male body and, in any case, they were not familiar with the rituals that had to be performed. They were, however, willing to dig a grave. But, when all appeals for help failed, the two women decided to take on the task themselves. It was then that help came from an unexpected quarter, two old women walking past offered to take on the work: 'What difference did it make', they said, 'if the dead person was a male? All were equal before God, and after all, this was a day that came for everybody.'

As the violence continued in Delhi, in January 1948, Gandhi decided to go on an indefinite fast. Historical record is full of stories of how the

Mahatma was visited by major leaders every day. They were anxious about his health and worried about what might happen if he died. A story that is never told in history books is how, on the third day of the fast, truckloads of children, both Hindu and Muslim, from camps and schools set up by Jamia students, took a procession through the city, pleading for peace and the life of the Mahatma. On the next day, it was the turn of the women and Hindu, Sikh and Muslim women all wove their way through Chandni Chowk and its lanes, again making a plea for peace. For the public, which eventually responded to the Mahatma, these must have had much more significance than the visits to Gandhi, by major political leaders.

ORAL ACCOUNTS

In 1986, while working on a film, *A Division of Hearts*, I met Maya Rani, a sweeper, who worked in a school in Batala in Punjab. Maya was a young girl at the time of Partition—she remembered the time vividly. When she was being interviewed for the film, Maya recounted the confusion of the time. For a while it was unclear, she said, whether her village, Dinanagar, would go to Pakistan or Hindustan. Each time, when one sort of rumour took hold, the 'other' community would abandon their things and run away. Maya described how she and her friends watched this helter-skelter flight almost as if it were a game. She laughed as she told her story:

Weren't we frightened? No, we weren't frightened - everyone tried to scare us even our parents. But all the children of that area, none of us was scared. Often, we would leave our own roof and climb up onto a neighbour's, just to see. Then we all got together and started to go into people's houses. In some we found rice, in others almonds, *sevian* . . . we began to collect all these and pile them up in our house. Great big utensils, *patilas*, *parats* . . . we collected them all.

Yes we children did this. Then the city elders, Hindus, they felt this was not a good thing, this kind of looting, and it should be stopped, if possible without any ill feeling. About six or seven of the important ones got together and called us. We were all together, our people. They said, don't do this, you will also be searched later, all your things will be snatched away from you, you shouldn't do this. But we didn't stop, we just went on.

Our father also told us to stop, and each time he said that we'd say, yes, we'll stop. But as soon as the men went away to sit down and talk, we would start again . . . rice, food, all sorts of nice things. From one shop we stole pure ghee and almonds, at other places we found cloth. We collected so many utensils that we filled up a room as large at this one.

I kept lots of new utensils, *hamams*, etc., for my wedding, I brought a lot of utensils with me when I got married. I also looted many *razais*, quilts, some already made and some which I made later with the material we found. There were eleven of us girls, we all made our dowries with the stuff we collected . . . two of those girls were also married in Batala [where Maya also lived at the time of the interview].[6]

Maya's story seemed amazing to me. 'Didn't anyone try to harm you?' we asked. 'How did you escape the violence?' Maya did eventually admit to being somewhat frightened, while she and her friends looted their neighbours' houses. But, she said:

We kept doing this, going from street to street. Our parents were very worried, they kept trying to stop us, saying we would get killed, people would take us for Musalmaans. But we thought, who's going to take us away, who's going to kill us? We call ourselves Harijans, Hindus, Christians, no one can take us away. And like this we jumped from roof to roof, not really caring what happened.[7]

The first time I heard this, it came as a shock to me. Loot and theft are part of all situations of conflict, and for the economically disadvantaged, the chaos of the situation offered opportunities to amass goods and wealth. It was not that that worried me. But it was a different dimension to the experience of Partition in terms of caste, and particularly that the Dalits (whom, like most Hindus, I had been accustomed of thinking as part of 'us'), had felt themselves so separate from both communities, was something that I found surprising. I was reminded of a story that Anis Kidwai related, also about Dalits, that described a different aspect of their experience. She described how, in January 1948, she and Sushila Nayyar went to visit Tihar village on the outskirts of Delhi. They had heard that a rich Hindu from Pakistan had left behind huge properties when he had moved and had, therefore, like many people, effected an exchange of property, with a rich Muslim in Tihar to whom the land belonged. Each took the other's property, but neither was obliged to carry on with the other's business. The Hindu, therefore, threw out all previously employed workers from his newly-acquired piece of property. Most of these were Muslims, but about a third were Harijans. The Muslims made their way to one or the other of the two Muslim camps that had been set up in the city. But for the Harijans, displaced in a situation that was basically centered around Hindu and Muslim identities, there was nowhere to go. No camps to help them tide over the difficult times, no recourse to government—all official machinery was too preoccupied at the moment with looking after the interests of Muslims and Hindus. No help from political leaders either whose priorities were different at the time.

Maya Rani's interview and the stories in Anis Kidwai's account, made me realize how much, and how easily, we tend to think of Partition only in terms of the most visible identities: Hindus, Sikhs and Muslims. But Partition had touched the lives of many others: of Christians, of Dalits and of those who did not necessarily define themselves in terms of religion. It was thus this one interview that alerted me to the question of caste, during Partition. Maya had gone on to confirm (something, that is, borne out by documents from Dalit groups at the time) that the Dalits had been relatively safe from the violence. She said:

> There was no danger for us. Because we are Harijans. Whether it had become Pakistan or Hindustan it made no difference to us. We would stay where we were born. Our elders felt that whatever happened we wouldn't move from this place. This was our home. If anyone had tried to make us leave we would have shown our strength. After all, Harijans are not just anybody. We're also a very powerful group. If that had happened we would have asked for a separate state and they would have had to give it to us. We felt strong in this knowledge.[8]

In fact, Dalits did make a demand for a separate state, asserting that if the Hindus could be given Hindustan and the Muslims could get Pakistan, they too wanted a land of their own, and they gave this land a name, Achutistan, a fact that seldom figures in the histories of Partition. There were other paradoxes that emerged. Even though the history of Dalits has been marginalized from the mainstream histories of Partition, because the Dalits were an organized group, it is possible to trace this history through the documents and speeches (especially those of Ambedkar), which are available in various archives. What those documents do not tell us is whether the protective 'invisibility' that Maya speaks about, and that the documents confirm, also helped to protect Dalit women from rape and abduction. It does not, however, take much to guess the answer to this question. It was this exploration into the history of Dalits that also pointed to another important aspect of this history: because the Dalits were an organized group, in many ways they had the possibility of putting their demands before the State. Whether or not these were heard is another thing. Women, on the other hand, were not similarly organized and their histories remained individual, personal and unspeakable, something that would account for the much deeper silence in which they are shrouded.

Workers, harijans, women, children, soldiers and ordinary people, these were all bit players in the drama of Partition, yet we know so little about them. If today we have to deal with deep ethnic and communal division, and complex questions of fractured identities, surely the experiences of these people are something we can learn from. It is for this reason that I feel it is especially important that we 'listen' to what people have to say, to see how they remember those times. These memories are important because for the people who survived Partition, this is what the event meant, this is their recollection of that history and, therefore, for them, this is the history of Partition.

Stories of Partition are often full of nostalgia at the supposedly idyllic relations that existed between Hindus, Muslims and Sikhs. Some of the interviews I did, however, told a rather different story. Bir Bahadur Singh, a shopkeeper from Thoa Khalsa in Rawalpindi district, told us this about his village:

In our area the people used to live in towns, or in the *kasbahs*, or there were small villages where they would go to set up shop, and they used to live there with their families. And I remember that from the time I was admitted into school, in the first class, till class five, I studied there. . . . There was a Musalmaan woman, *dadi*, . . . *dadi* we used to call her. Her name was Ma Hussaini, and I would go and sit on one side in her lap, and her granddaughter would sit on the other side. I used to pull her plait and push her away and she would catch hold of my *jura*, my hair, and push me away. I would say she is my *dadi* and she would say she is her *dadi*. Look at this: that girl was small when we used to play together. I was in the fifth class, she was younger than me and now her son has become a young man, he was in Dubai and from there he wrote to me, calling me *mamuji*. The girl wasn't even married then, and her son is 40 now, he saw my letter in his grandparents' home and asked who is this. He was told . . . that this is also your *mama*, your uncle.

Such good relations we had that if there was any function that we had, then we used to call Musalmaans to our homes, they would eat in our houses, but we would not eat in theirs, and this is a bad thing, which I realize now. If they would come to our houses, we would have two utensils in one corner of our house, and we would tell them, pick these up and eat in them and they would then wash them and keep them aside and this was such a terrible thing. This was the reason Pakistan was created. If we went to their houses and took part in their weddings and ceremonies, they used to really respect and honour us. They would give us uncooked food, *ghee*, *atta*, *dal*, whatever *sabzis* they had, chicken and even mutton, all raw. And our dealings with them were so low that I am even ashamed to say it. A guest comes to our house and we say to him, bring those utensils and wash them, and if my mother or sister have to give him food, they will more or less throw the *roti* from such a distance, fearing that they may touch the dish and become polluted . . . the Musalmaans dealt with us so well and our dealings with them were so low.

If a Musalmaan was coming along the road, and we shook hands with him, and we had, say, a box of food or something in our hand, that would then become soiled and we would not eat it. If we are holding a dog in one hand and food in the other, there's nothing wrong with that food. But if a Musalmaan would come and shake hands, our *dadis* and mothers would say, 'Son, don't eat this food, it has become polluted'.

Such were the dealings: how can it be that there are two people living in the same village, and one treats the other with such respect and the other doesn't even give him the consideration due to a dog? How can this be? They would call our mothers and sisters *didi*, they would refer to us as brothers, sisters, fathers and when we needed them they were always there to help, yet when they came to our houses, we treated them so badly. This is really terrible. And this was the reason Pakistan was made. They thought, what is this, what has happened? How can this be?

Two people living in the same village and one loves the other so much while the other hates him so much that he will not eat food cooked by his hand and will not even touch him . . . if a Musalmaan shook hands with you and you had something in your hand, you could take it that the thing was finished, destroyed. . . .

We don't have such dealings with our lower castes as Hindus and Sikhs did with the Musalmaans. I'm really saying that today I feel ashamed of this.[9]

While this was a picture many people we interviewed gave us, there were also other dimensions. One day, quite by chance, I came across Dhan Raj Wadhwa, an auto rickshaw driver, who said his home was in Baluchistan and he had come away from there only recently, not because there was any problem in living there as a Hindu, but because he was fed up with his old and domineering father! According to Wadhwa, there was a whole community of Hindus in Baluchistan even today, living peacefully with the Muslims. The following is the account he gave us:

About Punjab I say this: I mean our western Pakistani Punjab or Sindh or the Frontier, riots took place here only then . . . when they began in UP and Bihar. In fact the riots began first in India, in Indian provinces, not in our Pakistan. First, they were in Bihar and UP and then they spread to Punjab, and there the crimes committed by the Sikhs, the rumours of that touched the Muslims and it was in response that they killed the Hindus. When they saw with their own eyes how children's chests had been pierced, their eyes torn out, when they saw this, they saw their hands and arms cut off, they saw them hanging between life and death, then the anger is natural, who can actually remain indifferent to this?[10]

Alongside stories of relations between the communities, there are stories of violence and horror. Kulwant Singh was a child at the time of Partition. He was in his *zila* Rawalpindi, *tehsil* Kahuta, when the 1947 riots took place. He remembers:

I was about ten years old and I used to study in the third class. When they attacked us, approximately seven days they kept attacking us. I was small, my mother . . .

when she saw my father being killed - they cut him up into a 100 pieces, the first blow they struck on his neck, and then they cut him into a 100 pieces—at that time I was trembling. At my feet there were many bodies, there was fire all around. I was dying of thirst, they heard my voice—my mother lifted my head and my *chhachhi* took my feet . . . the six-month old daughter, first of all they did *ardaas* and threw her into the fire, and then they said, '*bibis*, our *izzat* is in danger, will we save our honour or our children?' And then turn by turn they threw their children into the fire . . . my mother, she took me and put me down by my father's body, where there was fire all around and I felt so thirsty and because of the heat, my legs got burnt.[11]

Tales of brutality and violence by the other community are matched by similar tales within communities, effectively shattering the myth that the violence always comes from the 'other'. It was mostly women and children who suffered in these incidents. In Thoa Khalsa, a small village in Rawalpindi district, 90 women are said to have jumped into a well and drowned themselves to avoid rape and conversion. Bir Bahadur Singh and his mother, Basant Kaur, described two such incidents to us. The first was a story of women and men being killed.This is what they said:

There were some 1000-2000 people in the village. There was one Sardar Gulab Singh—we had all collected inside his *haveli*, it was a large house. All of us had collected there . . . in Gulab Singh's *haveli*. Twenty-six girls had been put aside. First of all, my father, Sant Raja Singh, when he brought his daughter, he brought her into the courtyard to kill her, first of all he prayed, he did *ardaas*, he said '*sachche padshah*, we have not allowed your *sikhni* to get stained, and in order to save your *sikhni* we are going to sacrifice our daughters, make them martyrs, please forgive us.' Then . . . there was one man who used to do coolie work in our village, he moved forward and . . . he stepped forward and caught my father's feet . . . Ram Singh caught his feet and he said, '*Bhapaji*, first you kill me because my knees are swollen and I can't run away . . . you will run away and I will not be able to and the Musalmaans will catch hold of me and make me into a Musalmaan.' So my father immediately hit him with his *kirpan* and cut his head off. After that, Justice Harnam Singh, who was Chief Justice of Punjab, his *behnoi*, meaning his father-in-law's *sala*, he, Sardar Nand Singh Dheer, he said to my father, 'Raja Singh, please martyr me first because my sons live in Lahore . . . do you think I will allow Musalmaans to cut this beard of mine and make me go to Lahore as a sheikh? For this reason, kill me.' My father then killed him. He killed two, and the third was my sister. Maan Kaur . . . my sister came, and sat in front of my father, and I stood there right next to him, clutching on to his *kurta* as children do. I was clinging to him . . . but when my father swung the *kirpan* [*vaar kita*] . . . perhaps some doubt or fear came in his mind, or perhaps the *kirpan* got stuck in her *dupatta* . . . no one can say . . . it was such a frightening, such a fearful scene. Then my sister, with her own hand she removed her plait and pulled it forward . . .

and my father with his own hands moved her *dupatta* aside and then he swung the *kirpan* and her head and neck rolled off and fell . . . there . . . far away. I crept downstairs, weeping, sobbing and all the while I could hear the regular swing and hit of the *kirpans* . . . 25 girls were killed, they were cut. One girl, my *taya's* daughter-in-law, who was pregnant . . . somehow she did't get killed and later my *taya's* son shot her with a pistol. Then he killed himself, he and his father both, they became *shaheeds*, martyrs. . . .[12]

And the second incident is an account of the mass drowning, related to us by Basant Kaur:

My name is Basant Kaur. My husband's name was Sant Raja Singh. We came away from our houses on 12 March and on the 13 we stayed out. At first we tried to show our strength, and then we realized that this would not work, so we joined the *morcha* to go away. . . . We went into the *morcha* inside the village, we all left our houses and collected together in the centre of the village, inside the *sardaran di haveli* where there was also a well. It was Lajjawanti's house . . . Then we talked and said we don't want to become Musalmaans, we would rather die . . . Mata Lajjawanti, she had a well near her house, in a sort of garden. Then all of us jumped into that, some 100 . . . 84 girls and boys. All of us, even boys, not only children, but grown up boys. . . .[13]

But there were other stories as well, stories in which people helped each other out, where religion did not matter. One of the most touching of these was told by Amrik Singh, a school teacher from Doberan. He said:

In Doberan . . . there was one girl. One Krishan Kaur, she was taken away by a Musalmaan by force. She kept crying and shouting. He took her some two *kos* away from our village. He had an old father. . . . He [the boy] kept the girl inside, he wanted to do all kinds of things with her. But the father was sitting outside. He said, 'Son, don't do these things, she is my daughter, if you do anything to her, you will be doing it to my daughter, you can take it as that. Take her back to where you brought her from and leave her there. I will not sleep while she is here. I will keep guard.' So the father protected the girl's honour. When the son fell asleep, the father said to her, 'Daughter, now you go away.' The girl then ran. She came back to our village . . . there she saw . . . she saw the village had been burnt down . . . she saw the bodies in the gurudwara, so what she did, she met . . . another girl, Prem, from the same village. They thought 'What should we do now?' and then they thought 'We should also burn ourselves, what else is there to do?' So they collected pieces of wood and other stuff . . . there was a *kolu* there . . . used to make *sarson ka tel* [mustard oil]. There was oil in the *kolu*, they collected lots of wood, put it next to the *kolu*, set fire to it, and sat down on the fire. But life is precious . . . when the flames licked them, they could not bear it.[14]

In 1981 I spoke to Damyanti Sahgal, a woman who had worked with her aunt, Premvati Thapar, in the relief and rescue operations for abducted women (the Central Recovery Operation). In the beginning, Damyanti kept insisting that she had nothing to say and interviewing her would be useless. When we finally met Damyanti, her sister Kamla, was also present at the interview. Halfway through Damyanti's recounting of her story, Kamla broke in with some questions. It was clear that Kamla knew little of the trials and tribulations Damyanti had been through. I reproduce below an excerpt from their conversation:

Kamla : What stories these are. You've never told us these stories. . . .

Damyanti : You don't know, Kamla, you don't know anything because you were in England.

Kamla : No, I mean we haven't had much time to talk . . . an hour here, and hour there... you used to come for short visits.

Damyanti : And after this, I had another life altogether, and things kept changing.

Kamla : I know, I've never asked you how you came away.

Damyanti : I came alone.

Kamla : We took it for granted because we came from England. We knew that everyone had come, no one asked how . . . we took it for granted. . . .

Damyanti : Kamla, no one was there to help. . . .

Kamla : No, I mean you came and went from *ashrams*. . . . We didn't know . . . the others came together.[15]

CONCLUSIONS

Perhaps the best way for me to begin pulling together the different strands of what I have been trying to say is to go back to the question I raised at the beginning of my paper. Throughout my work on Partition, I have been struck by the silences surrounding this important subject. Why is it that the kinds of experiences people wrote about or described in their oral accounts, hardly ever figure in what we call 'traditional history'? Why is it that these and other such accounts have found such little space in history? Is it that this is not the stuff history is made of? Pain, trauma, loss, grief, the minute of daily living and the violence of upheaval, is there any way in which these experiences can find a space in the way history is written?

In raising these questions, I do not mean to valorize one kind of history writing over the other. Over the years, I have come to understand that little purpose is served by doing this, as all kinds of historical sources are valuable and useful. When I began work, I was sceptical of the tools of conventional history. What, I asked myself, could documents, government reports and speeches, tell me about what I was trying to look at: feelings and emotions, those indefinable things, that make up the sense of an event? I learnt, however, in the course of my work that even what we see as 'conventional' tools can yield a great deal, for so much depends on the perspective you bring to bear on them. Thus, what I would like to argue for is not that the kinds of voices I am exploring in this paper be seen as voices that can replace, or even be put up against, conventional or factual histories of Partition. Rather I would like to suggest that they be placed alongside such histories, so that both can enrich and inform each other.

I say this because the kinds of sources I am arguing for, are those that rely heavily on people's memories of an event, a time or a place. I am deeply aware that the use of such a method of research and exploration is not unproblematic. There has been considerable research that shows that memory is never 'pure' or 'unmediated'. Much depends on who remembers, when, with whom, to whom and how. But to me, the way people choose to remember an event or a history, is at least as important as what one might call the 'facts' of that history. They are also interpretations, as remembered or recorded by one individual or another.

And both—or more—sorts of interpretations are important for these are the ways in which Partition is handed down to us, and these then are what make up the history of that event for us. I have come to believe, therefore, that there is no way we can begin to understand what Partition was about unless we look at how people remember it. I would like to end this paper then with a plea for more attention to the kinds of sources I have explored here. I make this plea with a full awareness of the problems that attach to such sources, but my belief is that as long as we are aware of those problems, we will be richer for turning to these sources, than if we were to ignore them altogether. It is true that memories are shifting, unreliable and changeable. However, as James Young says: 'Whatever "fictions" emerge from the survivors' accounts are not deviations from the "truth" but are part of the truth in any particular version. The fictiveness in testimony does not involve disputes about facts, but the inevitable variance in perceiving and representing these facts, witness by witness, language by language, culture by culture'.[16]

NOTES

1. Anis Kidwai, *Azadi ki Chhaon Mein* (in Hindi) (Delhi, 1990).
2. Urvashi Butalia, 'Community, State and Gender: On Women's Agency During the Partition', in *Economic and Political Weekly*, 24 April 1993, pp. WS12-WS24.
3. Kidwai, op. cit., p. 142.
4. Ibid., p. 143.

5. Personal Interview with Kishwar Kidwai.
6. Urvashi Butalia, *The Other Side of Silence: Voices from the Partition of India* (New Delhi, 1998).
7. Ibid., p. 300.
8. Ibid., p. 313.
9. Ibid., pp. 221-2.
10. Personal Interview with Dhan Raj Wadhwa in 1990, in Delhi.
11. Butalia, *The Other Side of Silence*, pp. 254-5.
12. Ibid., pp. 226-7.
13. Ibid., pp. 198-200.
14. Personal Interview with Amrik Singh in 1990 at Tihar Village, Delhi.
15. Butalia, *The Other Side of Silence*, p. 120.
16. James E.Young, *Writing and Rewriting the Holocaust: Narrative and the Consequences of Interpretation* (Bloomington, 1990).

Unknown Victims of a Major Holocaust

MONMAYEE BASU

A few years back, while visiting West Bengal, the Prime Minister Rajiv Gandhi, condemned Calcutta as a 'Dying City'. Unfortunately, however, beyond making callous and insensitive remarks, those in power never endeavour to find out where exactly the malady lies. Why is this untimely death of Calcutta (even if we are to believe Rajiv Gandhi) taking place at all? History provides us the answer to this. Apart from the continuous drain of wealth, which was a characteristic feature of the British period, the other catastrophe, which dealt a fatal blow to the economy as well as to morale, was the Partition of the country in 1947. Millions of Bengalis were grievously affected by this tragic event. Even after the pre-Partition migration, which amounted to about 4,50,000 coming to present day West Bengal and going to Assam and Tripura , about 13 million non-Muslims still remained in eastern Pakistan. By the end of 1947, about 4,25,000 Hindus had migrated from the area, which was then East Pakistan (now Bangladesh), to West Bengal.[1] The event was so traumatic that it still lives on as the most significant landmark for those who suffered the Partition. It exists in their lives as a deep wound from which blood still oozes. A big dividing line drastically changed the direction of life of a large number of people—life before Partition and life after it.

What really prompted me to take to writing on this subject was indeed the fact that nothing much has been written 50 years after independence on the woes of Bengal except a few articles here and there and a collection of essays, edited by Ranabir Samaddar,[2] though a sustained effort has been made by both historians and social scientists to focus on the tragedy of Punjab. The main reason behind this apathy must be the great impact on the minds of the people of the orgy of violence and carnage that rocked Punjab through the Partition days. Although, Bengal, too, fell a prey to the terrible communal mayhem on several occasions, the intensity, measured in terms of the number of people killed and the damage to property, was admittedly less than that in Punjab. But this cannot in any way reduce the horrors of the disaster that engulfed this unfortunate eastern province. The exodus of those millions of hapless people from their motherland, their trials and tribulations have perhaps, very few parallels in the history of civilization. Even Nehru who, for whatever reasons, failed to provide adequate relief to Bengal, acknowledged in a press conference at Nagpur, on 1 January 1950, the tragedy of Bengal in the following words:

> West Bengal has suffered more from Partition and its after effects than any province or any part of the country. The Punjab also suffered, but it suffered more in the sense of mass killing of the people while economically West Bengal has suffered more. The province has a heavy population and after Partition, it has become heavier. More than any province, West Bengal has a large number of lower middle class population, which suffers tremendously in the economic conditions of today. Consequently unemployment and scarcity and other factors have led to the present situation in the province. . . . The Punjab had a terrible blood bath. Nevertheless, the continuous pressure of problems on West Bengal is greater.[3]

The object of this paper is to reassess, against the backdrop of the Partition of Bengal in 1947, the extent of the suffering of the Hindu women of Bengal, directly affected by the impact of Partition, and to reconstruct a brief and fresh narrative based on oral evidence of their traumatic and painful experiences. It is relevant, to point out here, that my own family—paternal as well as maternal—were refugees, who migrated from the rich district of Barisal, in erstwhile East Bengal, now a part of Bangladesh, while my husband's family hailed from Dacca, presently the capital of Bangladesh. A lot of oral evidence through personal interviews, therefore, could be collected from my relatives who were direct victims of the holocaust. Narratives or accounts relating to the experiences of people belonging to any other community have been excluded, purposely, owing to lack of space.

Almost all my interviewees were unanimous in their grievance that the Government of India did not do as much as it should have done in order to redress the immeasurable sufferings of the displaced people from East Pakistan. On the basis of their oral evidence, some striking distinctions between the cases of West Pakistan and East Pakistan are brought to light. In the first place, as is well known, the migration from West Pakistan was large scale but was over by 1949. Horrendous carnage, mass exodus and exchange of population were the most important features of this migration. Exchange of population led to mass evacuation, which in turn made the process of rehabilitation comparatively less irksome. Evacuee property left by the migrating Muslims helped to settle them down. Apart from government jobs, a large number of Indians migrating from West Pakistan were absorbed in the armed forces. As Ranjit Roy points out, in *The Agony of West Bengal*, apart from compensation claims for immovable properties, the Government of India took into account, details of all other assets in order to compensate the refugees arriving from West Pakistan.[4]

The case of the Bengali refugee was completely different. Like their counterparts from West Pakistan, they also faced from time to time, though on a lesser scale, terrible violence and massacre, loot and arson, loss of kith, kin and ancestral property, like land and houses; but received no adequate compensation and rehabilitation. As against the mass migration in the West, in the East there was the continuous infiltration from East to West Bengal, till 1971. Most of my interviewees felt that the exchange of population would have solved the problem, and that their sufferings multiplied because of the overcrowding of West Bengal, which became a matter of grave concern. Nehru admitted this serious problem in several of his speeches and categorically stated at a press conference in New Delhi that 'West Bengal has suffered continuously'.[5] He further said that ever since Partition, there had been a constant migration of the minority communities from East Bengal and West Bengal, about 16,00,000 people having left East Bengal for India; subsequently this got reduced to a 'trickle' either way, until events in December 1949 and early 1950 had led to a new mass migration.[6]

On 23 February 1950, in the Parliament, Nehru provided some figures of migration from East to West Bengal, which ran as follows:[7]

	From East Bengal to West Bengal and Assam		From West Bengal, Assam and Tripura to East Bengal	
	Hindus	Muslims	Hindus	Muslims
From 7 February to 8 April 1950	8,57,579	6,847	65,537	3,78,778
From 9 April to 25 July 1950	12,84,623	2,97,408	5,41,251	4,49,968

These figures do not take into account those who migrated between East and West Bengal on foot or by country boats, as well as those who travelled by train between East Bengal and Jalpaiguri. These figures clearly show the sustained influx of refugees from East Pakistan and the mounting pressure of population on West Bengal in general and Calcutta in particular.

In the Bengal assembly, Dr B.C. Roy explained[8] on 9 August 1950 as to why the refugees preferred to live in and around Calcutta. Industry, business and trade had developed in Calcutta to the neglect of rural areas. Government offices were also concentrated in Calcutta, so were the large majority of educational institutions. The amenities of life were better. Calcutta, therefore, paid the penalty for this overgrowth.

Exchange of population, according to most of the women I interviewed, would, therefore, have been the only solution. This had also been stressed in a meeting of women held at Deshapriya Park in Calcutta on 8 February 1950 under the presidentship of Lila Roy.[9] Roy observed that mere resolution would not solve the refugee problem. She further said that they should do all that they could, but if all their efforts failed, there should be an exchange of population between the two countries. In another public meeting on the same day, Major General A.C. Chatterjee, formerly of the INA, who presided over the meeting, said that the only solution lay in the exchange of population and revision of the Radcliffe Award, so that the East Bengal Hindus might have at least a part of their province carved out where they could settle.[10] S.K.Ganguli, President of the New Bengal Society, also said that the only reasonable solution to the refugee problem was to increase the areas of West Bengal. According to him, the Bengali speaking areas of Bihar and parts of East Bengal should be added to West Bengal so that the refugees from East Bengal could be rehabilitated adequately.[11]

Nehru, however, deprecated an exchange of population as not only completely undesirable but also unfeasible, pointing out that even if carried out with complete cooperation of both governments and with all available facility, it would take about five and a half years to complete. What was needed, he felt, in order to 'relieve the tension, lessen the panic and give a little more security' was that 'the door should be open for anyone who wishes to travel from one part of Bengal to the other'.[12] With this end in view he opened his discussions with Liaquat Ali Khan, the Premier of Pakistan, in Delhi, on 2 April 1950 and the result was the agreement of 8 April 1950 (Nehru-Liaquat Pact), on the minority problem.

The pact was concluded against the backdrop of a fresh spurt of communal violence, which shook many parts of East and West Bengal in the last few days of December 1949 and the early part of 1950. The trouble started with an incident, which occurred in village Kalshira in the Bagerhat subdivision of Khulna district in East Bengal, on 20 December 1949. A police party went to arrest an alleged Communist suspect and, finding him absent, began to assault the inmates of the house, including the women. Attracted by the cries of the women, the neighbours ran to the scene and there was a free for all fight between the police party and the villagers.

One policeman was killed and another died of injuries. Two days later, assisted by the Ansars and other rowdy elements, the police, attacked not only that village, but 22 other neighbouring villages, which were mostly inhabited by the members of the Namasudra community. There was arson and looting on a large scale, men were murdered and women ravished. There were also forcible conversions and desecration of places of worship. The residents of those villages could not escape from the scene because of a rigid cordon thrown by the armed police and others. Even news of the incident could not filter through.

Only after about three weeks some of the victims managed to evade the cordon and cross into West Bengal. The arrival of these refugees and their stories of ill-treatment sent shock waves all over West Bengal. The President of the Council for Protection of Rights of Minorities, J.P. Mitter, sent a telegram on 2 February 1950 to President Truman on the reported atrocities committed by armed and police forces on the defenceless villagers of Khulna and neighbouring places. The telegram read:

> East Pakistan government enraged at complaint against them to UN for oppression on Hindus have now inaugurated unparalleled reign of terror and ruthless persecution of minorities. Pakistan armed and police forces recently burnt, destroyed and looted several Hindu villages in Khulna, Barisal and Rajshahi rendering 50,000 unarmed men, women and children destitute and homeless. Many were killed and *enceinte* women raped in the presence of husbands. Young girls ravished in presence of parents. There has been large scale abduction of women and forcible conversion. Month-old babies snatched away from panic stricken feeding mothers and thrown in the river. Army and civil officials openly threatening complete annihilation of Hindus. Immediate intervention of civilized governments imperative or else peace in this region will be jeopardized.[13]

This had repercussions in the state of West Bengal. Some isolated incidents took place in Murshidabad town and two or three villages nearby. The situation, however, was rapidly brought under control. The refugees from Khulna and the accounts of what they suffered created considerable concern in Calcutta and on 4 February a series of incidents began there. These were stray assaults on some Muslims and a number of Muslim *bastis* were burnt. On 8 February two Hindus were stabbed in front of a mosque in Ultadanga in north Calcutta. There was then a recrudescence of arson and looting in certain Muslim localities. There were also cases of stabbing of Muslims. Owing to all these disturbances a number of Muslims left their houses and went to other parts of Calcutta, notably the Park Circus area.

The incidents in Calcutta reechoed in East Bengal. On 10 February, there was a demonstration in Dhaka by East Bengal Secretariat employees. Rioting, looting, murder and arson started and spread all over Dhaka city. This widespread rioting also continued on the next day. On the 12 February, a crowd of Hindu passengers at the Karimtolla airport near Dhaka was attacked by an armed mob and a large number of passengers, including women and children, were killed. The tragedy took place within the stone's throw of Karimtolla military headquarters in the presence of Pakistani armed guards. A person who escaped from East Bengal, walked on foot from Belonia to Agartala and dispatched a telegram. This was forwarded by Nehru to Liaquat Ali Khan. The telegram containing the details of the incident at Karimtolla aerodrome in Dhaka, read as follows: 'Arson, looting, killing started at Feni at 3 p.m. of thirteenth and continued whole night. Prominent Hindu leaders done to death. Some burnt alive'.[14]

In view of the magnitude of violence in both the Bengals, Nehru wrote to Liaquat Ali Khan on 17 February 1950 urging the need for two joint commissions to visit East and West Bengal respectively in order to ascertain the facts of the situation. He felt that even the 'mere visit of such a joint commission would help in lessening the apprehension of many people and thus lessen the abnormalities of the situation'.[15] Liaquat Ali rejected Nehru's suggestion of these fact finding commissions which, he thought, would inevitably become nothing but a 'fault finding mission'. The only solution, he emphasized, was for both governments to 'win the confidence of minority communities on either side, and convince them that it was to their own Governments that they should look for redress of their wrongs, and not to Governments across the border'. The result was the conclusion of the Indo-Pakistan Agreement or the Nehru-Liaquat Pact, concluded on 8 April 1950, already referred to earlier. The main principle reiterated by this pact was that:

> The Governments of India and Pakistan solemnly agreed that each shall ensure to the minorities throughout its territory complete equality of citizenship, irrespective of religion, a full sense of security in respect of life, culture, property and personal honour, freedom of movement within each country, and freedom of occupation, speech and worship, subject to law and morality. Members of the minorities shall have equal opportunity with members of the majority community to participate in the public life of their country. . . .[16]

However, the agreement failed to solve the problems as far as the minorities in East Bengal were concerned. The Hindus there did not get their property back and those who ventured to go back found themselves unwelcome and unwanted. On the contrary, their position worsened and their lives were fraught with danger and insecurity. In fact, the Pakistan government issued an order on 7 July for large scale requisitioning of minority property, and in the three weeks that followed, 811 houses were requisitioned in East Bengal.[17] The result was that those who had gone back to East Bengal had to return further frustrated to West Bengal again. Even Nehru, who refused to accept the failure of the agreement, had to acknowledge that 'many of the Hindus, who returned from West Bengal to East Bengal subsequently came back to West Bengal . . .'.[18] However, he felt that the agreement did a lot of good by easing the tension, which existed between India and Pakistan and by giving immediate relief to millions of people in both countries. They were also now assured that the possibility of war between the two countries no longer existed. In his opinion, the very fact that people wanted to go back was a clear indication that the atmosphere that drove them out no longer existed, otherwise that would have overtaken all other considerations. Whatever mess existed, was due, according to him, to the inefficiency of the Pakistan government, which was left with second rate people to carry out the administration, since most of the competent officers had gone over to West Bengal after Partition.[19]

In this condescension of Nehru lay the crux of the problem. While the flow of refugees continued, relief and rehabilitation were hard to come by. Many of the respondents, especially those belonging to the educated middle class like Aparna Sengupta, Beethi Chatterjee, Geeta Saha, etc., hold the Nehru-Liaquat Pact to be squarely responsible for the lack of quick and proper rehabilitation schemes by the Government of India. It led to the continuance of the ill-treatment and persecution of the minorities in East Bengal, with the result that the exodus of Hindus continued throughout 1950 and also later. West Bengal began to crumble under this weight. Proper and effective rehabilitation schemes were not adopted because it was wrongly assumed that the Nehru-Liaquat Pact, had effectively solved the Bengal problem.

Syama Prasad Mookerjee, was entrusted with the task of travelling in various parts of East Bengal and Assam to assess the gravity of the situation. He pointed out in the Parliament on 7 August 1950 that so far as the pact aimed at enabling the Hindus to live in East Bengal fearlessly with a sense of security and encouraging those who had come away to go back to their homes, it had failed miserably. Between the date of the pact and 30 June 1950, he pointed out, that there had been 757 cases of dacoity, robbery and theft, 219 cases of extortion, 194 cases of trespassing, 180 cases of assault, harassment and threats, 129 cases of abduction, rape and outraging the modesty of females, 70 cases of murder, 70 cases of grievous injury, stabbing and looting, 67 cases of arson, 21 cases of wrongful confinement and restraint, 39 cases of defiling Hindu temples and places of worship and 72 cases of illegal possession of firearms.[20]

The position of women was pitiable in the extreme. S.P. Mookerjee referred to a number of cases, illustrating the inhuman torture suffered by Hindu women. He cited the examples of two girls in a village in the district of Barisal whose breasts were cut off and who died of injuries in the Barisal hospital.[21] He further referred to three families, which had gone back to East Bengal from Murshidabad district in West Bengal, only to suffer abduction, rape and butchery.[22] S.P. Mookerjee narrated the case of some school teachers who attempted to go back. They were forced to return immediately as their womenfolk were asked to go to a Muslim's house at night and return home the next morning. But there were others who were unable to counter the aggression consequent upon refusal.[23] Further, he stated that the house of the sister of a Hindu member of the Pakistan Assembly living in Khulna was attacked and an attempt was made to take her away at night. The attempt failed because she shut herself up in a room and the attackers could not enter it as the door was heavily bolted. No action was taken by the police against the offenders who were identified.

The events narrated by S.P. Mookerjee expose the failure of the Nehru-Liaquat Pact. Against this backdrop, I endeavoured to probe into the feelings, experiences and trauma of contemporary Hindu Bengali women and reconstruct an image of that time, based on the memory of those who had personally suffered. For this purpose, I interviewed about 50 displaced women. The interviewees included educated and uneducated women belonging to the upper, middle and lower strata of society, some economically well-off as well as some that were not. Questionnaires, containing queries regarding their personal experiences of the events before and after Partition, the impact of these events as well as the aftermath of the Partition on their lives, were distributed. Many came forward to answer while some chose to be reticent on the whole issue. Broadly speaking, the ways in which the Partition affected the displaced women could be identified as:

1. Physical violence, like abduction, outrage of modesty, rape and murder.
2. Forcible marriage with Muslims, after forced conversion to Islam.
3. Tremendous economic impact of such disruption, which was further aggravated by the post-Second World War scenario. The young Hindu

women who migrated not only lost their homes and livelihood, but often lost the opportunity of education as well as of timely marriage due to acute economic difficulties. Some of them had to spend their lives as spinsters with the concomitant social ramifications.

Most of the women I interviewed held that serious communal violence began with the Direct Action Day announced by the Muslim League on 16 August 1946. Ferocious fighting and killing continued in Calcutta for three days, bringing the life of the city to a complete standstill, and causing loss of thousands of lives. In the early morning of the same day, Muslim mobs scoured the city, beating up Hindu shopkeepers, looting and burning shops and offices, and assaulting innocuous pedestrians. The demonstrators set fire to the house of Dr B.C. Roy. Despite a broadcast appeal made by the governor, Sir Frederick Burrows, and also appeals made by the Muslim and Hindu leaders, and despite the presence of strong British reinforcements rushed to Calcutta, communal frenzy continued with unabated violence on the 17-18 August. The transport services was completely suspended and the fire brigade was unable to cope with thousands of conflagrations started by the rioters.

The Calcutta correspondent of the *Times*, made general comments without throwing aspersion on any particular community and described the situation on 20 August as follows:

> Direct Action Day surpasses in magnitude anything previously experienced in Indian history, including notorious communal butcheries that took place in the past in Cawnpore, Bombay, Ahmadabad, and Dacca. The actual number of dead will never be known owing to shambles to which the city had been reduced. . . . The incendiarism and the looting were of unparalleled intensity and extent. The immediate problems of Calcutta are food and sanitation. . . . Thousands have not had a square meal since August 16 owing to the closing or looting of the city. . . . The cessation of train services denied the citizens the daily supplies of milk, eggs, poultry, fish and vegetables for which they depend on the railways. . . . The city stinks. Though many have been removed, putrefying corpses lie about in profusion in many areas and are being eaten by vultures and dogs. Stench masks are being widely used. Garbage, not cleared since August 16, adds to the misery.[24]

Serious disturbances broke out in Dacca towards the end of August and in Calcutta in September. From then on, frequent communal strife and tension became an inextricable feature of the life of both Bengals. In fact, the atmosphere all over East Bengal became so tense that the Hindu minority started feeling extremely insecure and it was this that compelled them finally to leave their home and hearth and migrate to other places.

Sabitarani Dhar, a lady of about 70 years, says that her father, a resident and school headmaster of Chandpur subdivision of Tipperah district of East Pakistan, had been postponing the migration for a long time, although the situation was visibly deteriorating over the years. She says that changes were marked sharply from 1944 onwards; and after the Direct Action Day riots, people started migrating from their neighbourhood, especially those who had relations or some other provision for shelter elsewhere.

At this juncture, a gruesome and ghastly incident took place, which forced Sabitarani's father to take the final decision to migrate. He had a very close friend—Rajkumar Bhowmik—who was a doctor by profession and was also a resident of the same place. At a short distance from her house, there was a market called Rahimnagar. It was a Muslim-dominated area and 95 per cent of the customers of the market were Muslims. Her doctor-uncle (the doctor friend of her father), who was held in high esteem, had his dispensary within this market area. It was very popular and was visited by both Hindu and Muslim patients alike. Her father used to visit his friend's dispensary every evening and chat with him till late at night. Soon after the riots in Calcutta in 1946, one evening while her father was sitting with his friend in the dispensary, a chit written in red ink was thrown inside the chamber through the window asking the doctor to leave immediately. Sabitarani's father urged his friend to go home without delay. The doctor refused and said that he would go at his usual time and thus ignored the warning. At about 10 p.m. while the doctor was returning home, he was surrounded by several Muslims and brutally killed. His hands were chopped off, big nails were hammered into both sides of his head and his body after being thrust into a gunny bag was thrown into the river Meghna, which flows through the town. Several other Hindus were killed in the area that night and the whole market was ransacked by the Muslims, shouting 'Allah-ho-Akbar', etc.

Thereafter, the situation in the town rapidly worsened. The Hindu households began to be attacked indiscriminately. Sabitarani and her two sisters were sent off to a relative's house outside the district. Overwhelmed with grief, and highly alarmed at the deteriorating political and communal situation, her father immediately decided to leave for West Bengal. Meanwhile, attempts were also made to attack and loot their house, but their Muslim neighbours prevented it. They were advised by the Muslim farmers, who worked in their fields, to leave before it became too dangerous. Finally, the family left their homeland for good in October 1946.

As far as physical atrocities on women were concerned, they took the form of abduction, outrage of modesty and rape, followed by murder on many occasions. Many times, the kinsmen who tried to protect them were also killed. A large number of respondents preferred to remain silent on this point. This may be due to the social stigma generally associated with such incidents. I will narrate here the accounts of a few women who were prepared to talk about their experiences.

Promilla Das, aged about 75 years, narrated her nightmarish experience as follows:

> My husband was a doctor who lived in Shillong while his parental family was living jointly in a village named Kashipur in East Bengal. I used to live with my husband in Shillong and would regularly visit my in-laws' place in Kashipur once or twice a year along with my husband. Once when I was in Kashipur and my husband was away in Shillong, unprecedented communal violence engulfed the whole of our province. At midnight, a gang of Muslim marauders attacked our house, looted and seized all available assets in cash and kind. Over and above, they butchered every member of my family—male, female and child. I fled secretly through a backdoor, ran breathlessly and reached a neighbouring Muslim house. They were kind enough to hide and protect me as a family member. It was they who informed my husband who rescued and took me back to Shillong.

Physical atrocities, in fact, took different forms. In Purnima Sen's neighbourhood in Khulna district, a father and his daughter committed suicide as Muslim aggressors who stormed their house forced the father to rape the daughter in public. In Shobha Bhrahma's native place in Noakhali town, a Hindu girl was found by the peasants to be lying in the rice fields in an unconscious state after suffering repeated physical assaults. After she regained consciousness, it was found that she had lost her mental balance totally and kept on weeping incessantly. She committed suicide two days later. Her address or identity could not be ascertained.

Jayashree Saha's family lived in Barisal while she herself lived in Calcutta with her husband and in-laws. Her parent's house in Barisal was attacked and the intruders agreed to spare the lives of the inmates on the condition that their young and beautiful maiden girl (Jayashree's younger sister) should get converted to Islam and married off to one of the intruders. The girl immediately agreed and forced her parents to leave without delay, saw her family members off and committed suicide thereafter by consuming poison, which she secretly hid in her clothes. The family came away and settled more or less peacefully in Calcutta, but at the cost of their younger daughter, who saved their lives by sacrificing her own.

Several cases of abduction and forced marriages after conversion to Islam took place. In a note prepared by the Ministry of External Affairs and circulated on 4 August 1950 among members of Parliament, 80 women were reported by the East Bengal Search Bureau to have been either abducted or missing. Nehru mentioned in Parliament on 20 November 1950 that 190 abductions were reported to the East Bengal Bureau by their counterparts in West Bengal.[25]

Lila Mukherjee (a close friend of my mother aged about 67) narrated a tragic event from her own life. She belonged to a respected well-to-do family, in the district of Dhaka in East Bengal. Her father was a highly revered professor of English in a local college. As the orgy of violence started in East Bengal in the aftermath of Partition, her brother and sister fell prey to it. Her sister was attacked and her brother was killed when he went to her rescue. Her sister was then abducted and raped by the Muslim villagers. Later she was converted to Islam and was married to one of the abductors. Her parents died brokenhearted. Since then Mukherjee has lost all links with her sister, except hearing once in a while about her through those who happened to visit Bangladesh. She is a part of the Muslim family, a mother of four children and sternly refuses to keep any contact with or recognize anything related to her past. Several girls rendered destitute by the riots, embraced Islam and married Muslims.

The atmosphere of acute tension, apprehension, insecurity and danger compelled the Hindu population to move to other places. The mass evacuation began from 1946 onwards although the migration of individuals had started earlier. The migration itself was also a matter of great ordeal. Rivers had to be crossed by steamers to reach Khulna from where trains for Sealdah station in Calcutta had to be boarded. Juthika Biswas (a lady now about 75 years old), who migrated from Barisal district recollected vividly the pathetic sights at the steamer ghats. She recalled how thousands of homeless, hapless and unfortunate refugees waited there for days together. Each day fresh refugees accumulated in large numbers eager to cross the border. The number of steamers was very limited. As a result, people had to wait patiently for their turn—sometimes even 10 to 15 days. Old and infirm people, children crying with hunger and fatigue, weary parents with grown up children whose future hung in uncertainty, rich and affluent, poor and needy—all waited alike with anxiety writ large on their faces. Their anxiety did not end when they boarded a train because many a time the trains were attacked by irate Muslim mobs.

The economic fallout of such a massive holocaust can well be imagined. The Hindu society of East Bengal, like those in other parts of the country, could be classified broadly into three socio-economic groups—the rich or the landed class, the educated middle class or the professionals and the poorer sections. The middle class again could be divided into two sections—the affluent or the upper middle class comprising prosperous professionals like doctors, lawyers, well-to-do teachers, high government officials, engineers, etc., and lower middle class consisting of ordinary school teachers, petty government servants, etc. Then there were the poorer and the weaker sections like labourers, small farmers, share croppers, poor priests, artisans, fishermen, boatmen, etc. All these groups suffered in different ways. An analysis of the situation based on interviews would bear this out. The Muslims, though constituting the majority of the population, were economically far more handicapped than their Hindu counterparts. The lands in East Bengal mostly belonged to the Hindus. Muslim peasants worked on the lands and in return, they got money, crops, vegetables, fruits, etc. Farming was another means of livelihood and Muslim peasants sold their farm produce to the Hindu households. They were generally less educated.

Such being the socio-economic structure, the different sections of the Hindu population reacted to the Partition in different ways. The Ghosh's of Gabha, for example, were from the landed class in Barisal. Shefali Mitra hailed from this family and had stayed in Calcutta since her marriage in 1941. Her father, she said, had bought a double-storied, reasonably big house at Shyambazar, in Calcutta during the Second World War. When the communal situation began to worsen and Partition became imminent, he arranged, on his own, for a exchange of property with an affluent Muslim family in Calcutta. He managed to sell a considerable part of his property in East Bengal and, therefore, their migration became much smoother. Her brothers were well educated and got jobs in Calcutta. So their loss was basically at the psychological level of leaving one's homeland for good, which was indeed no small tragedy.

Many of the propertied and moneyed people attempted to stay on even after Partition, because they were extremely unwilling to detach themselves from their home and property. My mother's aunt, Sonapishi's case, is an example. She had acres of land and a beautiful palatial house in Dacca. While all her family members moved out, she (her husband was no more) stayed alone hoping against hope, to preserve her property. But in the end, it was her Muslim servants who advised her to migrate as it was rapidly getting unsafe for the Hindus to stay on. So she finally sold her property at a ludicrously low price and came away escorted by her Muslim servants, dressed in a *burkha* supplied by her Muslim neighbours.

Prabharani Bannerjee's story was of another kind. A retired official of the Indian Statistical Institute, Prabharani, now about 65 years of age, hailed from the Chittagong district of East Bengal. Her native town was called Sitakunda, almost the whole of which belonged to her family. Owners of a huge palatial house with several guest houses, acres of land, sprawling gardens, lakes, rows of shops, orchards, they were the wealthiest family in the district. Her father, Harakumar Mukherjee, an employee of the Forest Department , died quite young and her mother, Nirupama Devi, thereafter inherited the whole estate. Prabharani and her only brother had moved out to Comilla and Calcutta, respectively, for higher studies and their mother lived on in Sitakunda long after Partition, until 1971. She stayed with the help of her neighbours who respected and protected her. However, at the time of the Bangladesh War the situation became so unsafe that she had to leave; she was escorted across the hills and jungles, through a circuitous, uncommon route, by the son of the priest of the Bhairav temple of Sitakunda, which she had patronized. She reached her son's house in Calcutta after travelling for months, famished and exhausted. Before leaving she had donated her whole estate for the construction of a college in the name of her husband as there was no institution of higher education either in Sitakunda or in the neighbouring towns. Prabharani's grievance was that the Muslims took over her property, built a college, too, but named it Sitakunda College, not after the name of her father as was wished by her mother. They wiped out even the name of the owner who had given away such a huge property, expecting nothing in return except only a token of remembrance.

The middle class Bengalis who subsisted on service primarily had a little edge over others because those in government had the beneficial option of exchanging their jobs with those who were in the service of the Indian government and wanted to migrate to East Bengal. Apart from government servants many other educated people also managed to get some jobs in West Bengal, Assam, Tripura and other areas to which they migrated. My grandfather, for example, who was a professor of English in B.M. College in Barisal district, joined the City College in Calcutta. That , however, does not indicate the end of his problems, for he had left all his possessions in East Bengal and came with a few bare essentials. Moreover, many people got jobs far below their status, dignity and economic level, but were compelled to accept them owing to acute pecuniary pressures. The net result was that all the different socio-economic classes were dragged far below what they had enjoyed earlier. The rich became middle class, the middle class became needy and the poorer sections were overnight turned into beggars and vagabonds.

These crucial social and economic implications left an indelible impression on the lives of innumerable Bengali Hindu women. My own mother, and especially my aunt, were direct victims of the economic effects of Partition. My grandfather belonged to an educated and well-to-do family of East Bengal with sufficient ancestral property. He was a scholar in English literature and a Professor of English of a renowned college of Barisal. He had nine children and also younger brothers to look after. The eldest daughter was already married, my aunt was his second child and my mother was the third. Partition came when my mother was an undergraduate student. She and my aunt went to Calcutta to their relatives house for the continuation of their studies. Meanwhile, in 1948 my grandfather migrated to West Bengal with the rest of the family. He had been offered the post of the Principal of Basirhat College in West Bengal. He had to leave everything behind and come virtually as a pauper, with only Rs 500 in his pocket. An acute financial crisis ensued in the family, as his salary was not at all sufficient to make ends meet.

By this time both my mother and my aunt had reached marriageable age. But there was no hope of their marriage due to economic reasons. In fact, my aunt had to take up a job in order to supplement the family income. My grandfather had no money or savings to marry his daughters off. My mother got married later, but my aunt, who was five years older than my mother could never get married, because, by the time her father's position stabilized, she had crossed 30. And in those days it was nearly impossible for a 30 year old woman to get married, especially for someone whose father had very limited money, whose family was displaced and who herself was not very attractive to look at. As a result, she was forced to lead the life of a spinster working throughout her life, to add to her father's income and to help her younger brothers and sisters get educated and settled in life. There are innumerable instances of young lives affected in this way by this national calamity.

Another aspect of the problem was the intense psychological impact left on the minds of the victims. The Hindu women who migrated were totally shattered psychologically as a result of the uprooting. They were forced to leave their birthplace, their homeland, their home and hearth and most of their precious belongings for a new land, which offered no sympathy, no kindness but only a sullen resentment. A section of Hindus in West Bengal still hold that the people of East Bengal have adulterated the culture and tradition of West Bengal. As my mother and others narrate, they were often subjected to ridicule and caustic remarks by their neighbours in West Bengal. 'The city has become filthy due to the flooding of the refugees . . .' was their oft-repeated comment. The dialect of the refugees, their dress, their way of living—everything was sharply criticized. In fact, many of the refugees could hardly believe that they would never be able to return to their dear homeland. An interviewee, Renubala Ghosh, now an old lady of 80, says, 'I asked Rafiq [the Muslim farmer who worked on her land] to look after our house, land and cattle as long as we were away, because my husband kept on saying that we should return again shortly after the disturbances were over. But now almost 50 years have elapsed, my husband is no more. I have not seen my homeland ever since.'

Life for all the refugees, therefore, was in complete disarray. The worst hit, perhaps, were the economically handicapped people of East Bengal—small traders, artisans, masons, carpenters, labourers, fishermen, farmers, etc., who could find no means of livelihood for want of proper education in the places where they settled. They were forced to seek shelter on railway platforms and in transit refugee camps, which had been set up by the government in several places. In limited spaces inside these camps, thousands of people were squeezed in indefinitely for years together. Several families squatted on railway platforms of Sealdah station as well as in parks, pavements and in public buildings. Many women, while living in utter filth and squalor, took up jobs as maidservants in different households. Kusum, a maidservant in my grandmother's house and Kamala, in my aunt's house, were two such refugees. After spending months on the railway platform they finally set up unauthorized tenements on unauthorized land and took jobs that came by, which eventually became their permanent occupation. The Partition converted these housewives of yesterday—the wife of a farmer and a mason, respectively—into maidservants, leaving a deep impact on their whole psyche.

The condition of the refugees in the camps was miserable. Shivani Sen's cousin Nilima Sen was camping in Ranaghat Refugee Camp. Nilima Sen, who belonged to a small shopkeeper's family in East Bengal with a small house and a piece of land at Lamchar in Noakhali, migrated during the spate of communal violence that overtook Noakhali in the early 1950s. They had to flee one night in order to save their lives and could not therefore bring anything along and were forced to take shelter in camps. Many others found it below their dignity to stay in camps and took shelter in the houses of their relatives. As Shivani Sen recounts, the life in camps was awful. Several families were huddled together in one single room like cattle due to scarcity of accommodation. All of them had lost their homes and lands and overnight had turned into paupers and beggars. Owing to the paucity of proper schemes of rehabilitation, helpless people were forced to spend year after year—sometimes 20 years—in these camps, which witnessed many significant episodes of human life. Here babies were born, children grew up and the middle aged grew old, older people died, younger ones fell in love and marriages took place. As Mridula Sarabai pointed out, 'Life in the camp, its surroundings and the atmosphere, all reminded me of our prison life.'[26] According to Sushama Roy (the name has been changed not to disclose identity) a retired Deputy Director, Women's Resettlement, under the Refugee, Relief and Rehabilitation Department, Government of West Bengal, refugee camps existed even as late as 1987, 40 years after independence. In April 1987, the rate of dole was raised from Rs 58 to Rs 75 per person per month. The break-up of dole at this time was as follows:[27]

Cash in hand	Rs 45/=
Dry dole, that is, in the form of staple food like rice, dal, wheat, etc.	Rs 30/=
Total	Rs 75/=

Some of these refugee camps were later converted into homes, including children's and women's homes. Sushama Roy says that there was a special home for the mentally retarded women, called Kartikpur Women's Home, while Jyotimoyee Women's Home and All Bengal Women's Home were meant for recovered abducted women. A few of these abducted women had lost their mental balance. She referred to a case where a very beautiful girl, who had been abducted and had since then lost all track of her family, had been recovered and brought to Titagarh Women's Home. She developed an obsession that her husband and young son would come to take her back and, therefore, waited for them at the Titagarh Railway Station every morning. Except for this particular trait, however, she was very normal in her behaviour otherwise. The majority of the women refused to go back to their original homes for the fear of non-acceptance and preferred rather to stay on in the camps where they received vocational training in weaving, knitting, tailoring, nursing, etc. The marketing of their products was the government's responsibility and they were paid wages for their labour. Their young children also received education.

Many women succeeded in settling themselves in this hard way. Rupashree Mandal of Khulna district is one such example. She had lost all her family members—father-in-law, husband, brother-in-law—during the riots and fled with her two year old son. She had been escorted in a *burkha* across the border by a Muslim beggar woman of her neighbourhood and had secured shelter in Jyotirmoyee Women's Home. She learnt tailoring, brought up her son (the children could stay with their mothers till the age of 18), who passed the Intermediate examination, secured a small trading loan and with it started his own business. He later built a house in the refugee colony of Howrah.

As late as September 1993, the following refugee homes existed in West Bengal:[28]

Chamta Women's Home
Ranaghat Women's Home
Coopers P.L. Home (Mixed)
Chandmari Amalgamated Home (Mixed)
Titagarh Women's Home
Habra Amalgamated Home (Mixed)
Bhadrakali Women's Home
Bansbaria Women's Home
Kartikpur Women's Home
Dhubulia Home and Infirmary (Mixed)

Although my respondents hailed from different parts of East Pakistan, and from different socio-economic groups and went through different experiences, all of them, however, were unanimous on one point. They all felt that the Government of India was rather apathetic to their unbound miseries. The Ministry of Rehabilitation, on the other hand, in its publication entitled 'The Story of Rehabilitation' in 1967, proudly claimed to have formulated rehabilitation projects in Marichjhampi, Dandakaryana, Andaman, etc. 'Dandakaryana is the pride of the Rehabilitation Ministry, the most enduring monument to its dedicated labours—and the biggest. As an experiment in resettlement, it is, perhaps, the most ambitious of its kind in the world today.'[29] But the land in these places was rocky and unfertile and absolutely bereft of irrigation facilities. The refugees, therefore, came back and demanded land in better places. Consequently, the economic pressure on West Bengal mounted. This had been foreseen by Sarat Chandra Bose, as early as 1949, in his manifesto for the south Calcutta by-election to the West Bengal Assembly—'the very existence of West Bengal is at stake; her economy is in a perilous condition'.

The condition of Calcutta was particularly precarious. The capacity of the city in every way was stretched to the extreme in order to accommodate the excess population. Refugees were overflowing everywhere. The damage was so deep-rooted that large scale and thorough rehabilitation programmes alone could have salvaged the situation. But nothing of the kind came up with the result that economically as well as physically Calcutta was ruined. No serious attempt was even made to revitalize the metropolis. Ranjit Roy, in his book *The Agony of West Bengal* gives an elaborate account of the disparity in aid and resettlement policies pursued by the Government of India in the cases of Punjab and West Bengal. As Ranjit Roy thinks, and the majority of Bengalis join to support him, Nehru had all his sympathies for the migrants from the west. He dropped the Mongol-Dravidians from the east like hot bricks and allowed them to perish.[30] Now all this is conveniently overlooked and forgotten and Calcutta is condemned for her handicaps.

A rather strange generalization emerged from the case studies. Although it was Muslim aggression, which was the root cause of their agony, many of the women I interviewed did not nurture any deep-seated grievance against the Muslims. They all unanimously agreed that the relation between the two communities was extremely cordial earlier. The Hindus were economically much better off, but economic factors could not in any way impinge upon their amicable, brotherly relationship. During Holi and Durga Puja, the Muslims cheerfully participated and were always invited for almost all festivals and other functions in the Hindu houses. Moreover, respondents said, the Muslims were very docile and submissive by nature. According to Anupama Deb, the Muslims were, in general, very honest in their dealings. For example, the milk, ghee, etc., which the Muslim milkmen brought were generally very good and pure. The Hindus could never imagine that the Muslims, with whom they had lived side by side so peacefully for generations, could all of a sudden become so ferocious and bloodthirsty. Anupama Deb, Sabitarani Dhar, Sushama Roy, all think that the economic and cultural backwardness of the Muslim community might have been responsible for the latent, subconscious ember of resentment, which existed and burst into flames flaring up into a ravaging conflagration transcending boundaries and splitting up the whole nation. In Sabitarani's view, the initial intention of the rioters was economic. Enriching themselves by looting and grabbing Hindu property was the main objective. Religious fanaticism evolved later. However, according to a large number of respondents, including my aunt, once the religious factor seeped in and riots started in full scale, it was the Muslims who displayed far greater intolerance.

At the same time, however, it was repeated again and again by respondents that it were the Muslims who saved and protected innumerable Hindu lives. When my grandfather migrated in 1948, it was his Muslim student Bahauddin, who escorted him and his family upto Khulna so that no mishap befell them on the way. Anupama Deb says that the atmosphere became very tense in Dacca in 1950 following the mayhem in Calcutta, with the result that the Hindu families were escorted from their mohallas by the army and were given shelter in a place called Baldar Bagan. While leaving her house, she could take only a few clothes with her and she handed over her favourite sewing machine to her Muslim neighbour for safe custody till her return. When she came back to her home for a short while before finally migrating to Dehradun, she found her house ransacked and looted of all valuables. However, before her departure, her Muslim neighbour gave back her sewing machine and wept profusely to see her go. Prabha Bannerjee's mother stayed on in her ancestral home in Chittagong till 1971 with the help, respect, love and protection of her Muslim neighbours. Pramilla Das was protected by her neighbours, a Muslim family, when all her family members were hacked to death by rioters. Samira Datta and her family, stayed on in the riot-ridden Khulna district till 1971 only under the protection of her brother's influential Muslim friend, Sabhur Mian, who was a prominent Muslim leader and a member of the Muslim League. When they finally migrated, they were escorted across the border safely, the women travelling in *burkhas* given to them by Sabhur Mian's female relations. Monica Basak and her family were given shelter, when riots broke out, by their Muslim neighbours—the Khans—with whom they had been very close for generations. Before leaving, Monica's mother gave away the key of her house to Mrs Khan with tears in her eyes and said '*Didi, ami to chailya jaitachhi, amar gharbari tomare diya gelam*' (Elder sister, I'm going away. My ancestral house is yours from now). Mrs. Khan threw the key into the well in her courtyard and said, '*Bahan, dakhla to, chabi phalayia dilam. Okhaneyi roilo. Tumi abar aishya bair kairya loiyo*' (Sister, can you see, I've thrown away the key into the well. Let it be there. You'll take it out yourself when you come back again). Mrs Basak says tearfully stated, ' I've lost all contact with her. I consider her my own sister, I yearn so much to see her face once before my death.'

The passions of the Muslims were aroused by political leaders in the name of religion to satisfy their political interests resulting in extreme misery and untold sufferings. It was the political game in which the masses were used merely as pawns. But, at any rate, the Partition, as a historical event, though a national loss beyond redemption, holds little significance for the section of Hindu women, who were affected by it. They were petrified with shock and trauma with remembering what they underwent. No other tragic story they felt, could sting their hearts any longer, because, according to them 'they had seen the worst'. And the irony is that the genesis of Partition—the two-nation theory, propounded by the Muslim

League and acquiesced to by the Congress leaders like Gandhi and Nehru, eventually proved to be a myth ; because a large number of Muslims still reside in India. According to the 1991 census, the Muslim population in India was 95.2 million.[31]

NOTES

1. *Recurrent Exodus of Minorities from East Pakistan and Disturbances in India: A Report to the Indian Commission of the Jurists by its Committee of Enquiry* (New Delhi, 1965), pp. 2-3.
2. Ranabir Samaddar, *Reflections on the Partition in the East* (New Delhi, 1997).
3. S. Gopal, ed., *Selected Works of Jawaharlal Nehru*, Vol. XIV, Part I (New Delhi, 1992), pp. 6 and 23.
4. Ranjit Roy, *The Agony of West Bengal: A Study in Union-State Relations* (Calcutta, 1971), pp. 165-76.
5. *Amrita Bazar Patrika*, 7 January 1950.
6. *Keesing's Contemporary Archives*, Vol. VII, *1948-50* (London), p. 10738.
7. *Appendices to Parliamentary Debates*, July-August 1950, Appendix I, Annexure No. 19.
8. *Amrita Bazar Patrika*, 10 February 1950.
9. Ibid., 9 February 1950.
10. Ibid.
11. Ibid.
12. *Keesing's Contemporary Archives*, op. cit.
13. *Amrita Bazar Patrika*, 4 February 1950.
14. S. Gopal, ed., op.cit., p. 43.
15. Ibid., p.40.
16. *Keesing's Contemporary Archives*, op.cit.
17. Nehru's letter to Liaquat Ali Khan, S. Gopal, ed., Vol. XV, Part I, (New Delhi, 1993), pp. 256-7.
18. Nehru's Statement in Parliament, 1 August 1950, *Parliament Debates*, *Official Report*, 1950, Vol. IV, Part I, Cols 7-14.
19. Nehru's Statement in Parliament, 7 August 1950 in ibid., Vol. V, Part II, Cols 407-8.
20. Ibid., Col. 430.
21. Ibid., Col. 434.
22. Ibid., Col. 435.
23. Ibid., Col. 435-6.
24. *Keesing's Contemporary Archives*, Vol. VI, *1946-48*, p. 8082.
25. S. Gopal, ed., Vol. XV, Part II (New Delhi, 1993), p. 327.
26. *Hindustan Times*, 27 July 1948.
27. Old files lying with Sushama Roy, Refugee, Relief and Rehabilitation Department, Government of West Bengal.
28. Ibid.
29. U. Bhaskar Rao, *The Story of Rehabilitation* (Department of Rehabilitation, Ministry of Labour, Employment and Rehabilitation, Government of India, 1967), p. 198.
30. Ranjit Roy, op.cit., p. 198.
31. *Manorama Yearbook*, 1997 (Malayala Manorama), pp. 456 and 459.

The Half-Shut Door in Punjabi Writing

K. S. DUGGAL

Not long after the Partition of Punjab, I brought out a collection of poems, called *Band Darwaze* (The Shut Doors),[1] then a collection of short stories in 1976, which was entitled *Dhoya Hoya Booha* (The Half-Shut Door).[2] To my mind, the two titles reflect the unending agony of the people of the Punjab on either side of the border. Fifty years ago, we left our hearths and homes in the hope that we would return after the communal frenzy, which had overtaken the land of the five rivers, would abate. Five decades have gone by, but we find that the doors continue to be sometimes shut and at other times still half-shut.

I remember my old grandmother forbidding my mother to purchase an oversize basket, three years after the Partition, saying, 'How will you carry it when we return to our village back in Rawalpindi?' The poor simple lady did not know that there was no going back. Far from going back to live where one was born or brought up, it is not possible even today for an ordinary citizen to go across the border without fulfilling untold preconditions that make it well-nigh impossible to undertake even a short-duration visit to one's erstwhile neighbours and friends. It is easier to go to Poland or Peru than to go to Pakistan, our next door neighbour. The blame cannot be apportioned. The responsibility lies equally with the people on either side.

It is cruel indeed. And it is more painful for people with sensitivities: writers, poets and artists. There has been a spate of literary and artistic activity on the Partition of the Punjab. Satish Gujral painted a cow stabbed during the communal riots. It haunted the Punjabis for several years. There are novels narrating the tragic saga, including those by leading fiction writers like Nanak Singh. There are a large number of short stories, subtle and perceptive, telling of the harrowing experiences of uprooted humanity on either side of the border. There are plays, both short and full length, on the trauma of the refugees and their rehabilitation. But, perhaps, the most significant writing relating to the Partition of 1947 is found in Punjabi verse.

It was the heart of a mother, in Amrita Pritam, that shed tears of blood immediately after the Partition at the insensate massacre of innocent men and women on both sides of the border. I have it on the testimony of the poetess herself who at the time was a refugee from Lahore, heading for Dehradun, in search of an asylum. 'Those days, as it was, you had to wade through blood and walk over dead bodies to reach the railway station', said the poetess, 'and you needed all the luck for the train to take you to your destination without bloodshed or rape at the intermediate stations. The night was dark.' She continued to relate that she was alone in an overcrowded compartment, full of homeless people, who had walked through the shadow of death. The Muslims were massacring the Hindus and the Hindus were hungry for Muslim heads. It was as if all decency and all good-neighbourliness was sinking around her. Suddenly the poetess found her lips moving and, with tears gushing down her face, she invoked Waris Shah, the great bard of Punjab:

Today I ask Waris Shah
Speak from your grave;
Open a new chapter
In the Book of Love.

A daughter of the Punjab once wept;
You wrote her long story for her.
Today millions of daughters weep,
Waris Shah, they're calling you.

Oh friend of sorrow
Look at the Punjab,
The village square heaped with corpses,
The Chenab flooded with blood!

Someone mixed poison
In the five rivers,
Their flow
Watered the Punjab.

Poison has sprouted
From the fertile land.
Look how far the red has spread,
Curse how far the red has spread!

Poisoned air
Floated into the jungles
Turning all bamboo flutes
Into snakes.

Biting everyone's lips
Their tongue tips rose up
And quickly all parts
Of the Punjab turned blue.

Song is crushed in every throat;
Every spinning-wheel's thread is snapped;
Friends parted from one another;
The hum of spinning-wheels fell silent.

Oars have left all boats
And float in the current.
Peepal branches with swings
Lie broken.

Where is the grave where love songs
Used to echo, where is the flute?
All Ranjha's brothers
Have forgotten how to play the flute.

Blood keeps falling upon the earth,
Oozing out drop by drop from graves.
The queens of love
Weep in tombs.

It seems all people have become *kaidos*,
Thieves of beauty and love.
Where should I search out
Another Waris Shah?

Waris Shah!
Open your grave;
Write a new page
In the Book of Love.[3]

It is easy to write about a traumatic experience, like the Partition of the Punjab, and the consequent dislocation, torture and misery it inflicted upon the affected people. And yet it is not so easy as it appears. Many of the writers and artists, who attempted to write on this theme seem to have been carried away so much by what they had witnessed that they lost all sense of balance. The tendency is to hold one side, or the other, totally responsible for the holocaust. If the writer was a Hindu, he laid the entire blame at the door of his Muslim neighbours and if he happened to be a Muslim, he held the Hindus or the Sikhs totally responsible for all those shameful happenings. Mercifully, I have been spared this charge, both in India and in Pakistan. I have a major novel, called *Ab Na Bason Eh Gaon*

(I'll Live in This Village No More),[4] relating to the Partition and the subsequent three wars, fought with Pakistan, until the liberation of Bangladesh. It attempts to give a lie to Jinnah's two-nation theory. I have a number of short stories about the uprooting of the refugees, their eventual rehabilitation and the entire gamut of the emotional ups and downs they underwent, in between. I, too, have some tender poems, bemoaning the cruel gulf created on the basis of religion, which should unite, and not alienate, people. I quote:

A vessel here overflows with tears,
A pair of eyes there are riveted on the threshold,
Again the moon has come down
Leaving the stars behind.
And in the apron of the moonlight
Are found tied messages of the love-lorn.

Held by the hauteur of her people,
Bound by the borders of her country,
Restrained by the taboos of her religion,
Helpless Heer sheds tears of blood.

The eyes on that side are wet.
The eyes on this side are drenched
The eyelids flutter and remind
Someone remembers someone.[5]

Rather than getting closer, whether it was Liaquat Ali Khan coming to Delhi, Jawaharlal Nehru going to Lahore or Z.A. Bhutto making a trip to Shimla, every such attempt found us drifting further apart. In a period of 50 years, we have fought with each other three bloody wars, if not four. And yet when the Pakistan forces surrendered to the Indian Army, in Dacca, in 1971, it brought tears to the eyes of a Punjabi neighbour, this side of the border, on finding his neighbouring country defeated and humiliated. Sohan Singh Misha, winner of the Sahitya Akademi Award, 1977, has depicted this sensitive moment with a remarkable feeling of tenderness:

Strange is the story of this enmity
If I were to tell a stranger, he wouldn't believe it.
When your armies
Surrendered arms to our armies.
It was a sad day indeed
And something to feel sorry about.
You must have shed tears
It was so natural
But why did tears gush out in my eyes?[6]

However, it was left to the late Mohan Singh to write, perhaps, the most poignant and the most beautiful poem portraying the spiritual agony of the Punjabis. It is one of his last few poems, written before his passing away, saying how God in all his benevolence comes to the poet when he is young. But the poet has nothing to ask for. God visits the poet again in his middle age. The poet still has no use for God's grace. He asks, 'Why opt for an unknown tyrant in place of the known tyrants here?' And then comes a time when the poet is old, his end is near, he himself goes to God and asks:

I come to you, my Lord
With a beggar's bowl in my hand
At the day's end I ask your blessings
For the severed limbs of the Punjab!
Let its towns flourish manifold
Peopled with hearts without rancour![7]

The Punjabis uprooted from West Punjab have indeed done well. It is seldom that one comes across a refugee who is not better off than what he was in the undivided Punjab. And yet their hearts bleed when they remember their homes and their playing fields. They long to go back, if for nothing else, to have one wistful look at what they had left behind. It continues to be reflected in their poetry, fiction and other works of art.

NOTES

1. K.S. Duggal, *Band Darwaze* (The Shut Doors) (New Delhi, 1959).
2. Idem., *Dhoya Hoya Booha* (The Half Shut Door) (New Delhi, 1976).
3. Amrita Pritam, 'Waris Shah Nun', translated by Kiron Bajaj and Carlo Copploa, *Lamian Watan* (Long Marches) (1949).
4. K.S. Duggal, *Ab Na Bason Eh Gaon* (I'll Live in this Village No More). This novel was published under the title *Ma Pio Laye* (Born of the Same Parents) (New Delhi, 1974).
5. Idem., *Band Darwaze*, op. cit.
6. S.S. Misha, 'Dushmani Di Dastan' (The Story of Enmity), in *Kach de Vistar* (Garments of Glass) (1972).
7. Mohan Singh, 'Khair' (Alms), in idem., ed., *Panj Darya* (a magazine brought out from Ludhiana, 1972).

Memories of a Fragmented Nation: Rewriting the Histories of India's Partition

MUSHIRUL HASAN

Today I am asking Waris Shah to speak from the grave,
To turn the page of the book of love. Once the daughter of the Punjab wept, and you wrote endlessly.
Today lakhs of daughters are weeping and they are imploring you Waris Shah
Get up, you who sympathise with our grief, get up and see your Punjab.
Today there are corpses everywhere, and the Chenab is filled with blood.
Somebody has mixed poison in all the five rivers,
The rivers we use to water our fields. . . .[1]

When I think of Lahore, I go back to the days of my youth just before the Partition. Life then was so romantic, slow, deep and beautiful. Really, they were good times, they were great times.[2]

I hope that one day . . . displaced families on both sides of the fence will at least be able to freely cross the borders and show their grandchildren where their grandparents had once lived and belonged. The day such a change comes about, I shall be the first to cross the Wagah or Hussainiwallah border posts to take my granddaughter to Lahore, and show her the home of my youthful dreams.[3]

The countdown to 15 August 1997, India's fiftieth year of independence, generated an extraordinary interest in plotting the history of Partition.[4] One wonders why painful memories and traumatic experiences were revived on such an occasion, why the nostalgia and the celebration of the dead.[5] Was it because there was not much to celebrate? Or did the occasion itself finally sensitize sections of the intelligentsia to the painful legacy of a brutal past? Amrita Pritam, the noted Punjabi writer, who lived in

*This paper does not cover the historical writings on the Bengal province, especially Bangladesh where the histories of Partition are being written differently since 1971. For a recent insight and references to other works, see Willem van Schendel and Eric Jan Znrcher, eds, *Opting Out of the Nation: Identity Politics in Central, South and West Asia* (London, 1998).

Lahore before moving to Delhi in 1947 and whose celebrated poem, quoted in the epigraph, became one of the most influential and representative works of Partition, recalled:

> What I am against is religion—the Partition saw to that. Everything I had been taught—about morals, values and the importance of religion—was shattered. I saw, heard and read about so many atrocities committed in the name of religion that it turned me against any kind of religion and revolution.[6]

Sure enough, a common refrain in popular and scholarly writings was that the country's division was a colossal tragedy, a man-made catastrophe brought about by hot-headed and cynical politicians, who failed to grasp the implications of division along religious lines.[7] For a change, the focus was on the popular experiences of violence and displacement,[8] on the impact of Partition on the lives of hundreds of millions, including the trauma of women,[9] and on the great variety of meanings they attached to the upheaval in and around their homes, fields and factories.[10] Although one should not make much of this shift in emphasis, the inclination to sideline the tall poppies in the Partition debates was, in a large part, an expression of the growing disillusionment with high politics and its post-colonial practitioners.

The mood reflected in popular literature was decisively against the leaders of the subcontinent and their inability to resolve their perennial disputes over power-sharing. Doubtless, the colonial government's role in heightening Hindu-Muslim rivalries and the 'communal' implications of Bengal's partition in 1905 were recounted. So also were the political blunders committed by Wavell, during his inglorious years in the Viceregal Lodge, the impetuousness of Mountbatten, who revelled in his role as arbiter, playing with the destiny of millions, the collapse of the law and order machinery, which was kept in a state of readiness to protect the Europeans but not the hapless victims of a civil war and, finally, the arbitrary demarcation of the border by a British jurist who was neither familiar with India nor had shown interest in Indian affairs.[11] 'Nothing could illustrate', commented the senior journalist Ajit Bhattacharjea, 'the callous haste with which Partition was pushed through more strikingly than the last-minute arrangements to demarcate the border'.[12]

According to the same writer, the onus nonetheless rested on the Indian leaders, many of whom were primarily interested in ensuring that the transfer of power was not delayed and were, therefore, 'unaware and uncaring of the human cost of cutting a border through the heart of populous provinces'.[13] Illustrating Jawaharlal Nehru's 'lack of touch with grassroots reality' and his 'self-delusion' that Pakistan would be compelled by its limitations to return to the greater Indian fold,[14] Bhattacharjea recalled what Nehru told the author, Leonard Mosley, in 1960:

> We were tired men, we were getting on in years too. Few of us could stand the prospect of going to prison again—and if we had stood out for a united India as we wished it, prison obviously awaited us. We saw the fires burning in the Punjab and heard of the killings. The plan of Partition offered a way out and we took it. . . . We expected that Partition would be temporary, that Pakistan was bound to come back to us.[15]

With the focus on high politics, the same old story does the rounds with unfailing regularity. The engagement continues to be with the 'major' political actors of the 1930s and 1940s, who conducted their deliberations lazily in cosy surroundings and presided over the destiny of millions without their mandate. One is still encumbered with the details of what went wrong and who said what, from the time the First Round Table Conference was held in London in 1930. Thanks to the publication of the voluminous transfer of power documents and the works of Gandhi, Nehru, Mohammad Ali Jinnah, Vallabhbhai Patel and Rajendra Prasad, the spotlight remains on the 'mystery' behind the protracted and tortuous negotiations triggered by the Cripps offer and the Cabinet Mission.[16] The bitter and acrimonious exchanges thereafter, which have all along dominated the historiography on 'nationalism', 'communalism' and 'Muslim separatism', continue to haunt present day writers. The search for the 'guilty men', based on personal reflections/memories or the blunt testimony of the Socialist leader, Ram Manohar Lohia, and the guarded 'revelations' of Maulana Abul Kalam Azad, goes on relentlessly.[17] As a result, the historians' history of Partition 'is not a history of the lives and experiences of the people who lived through that time, of the way in which events of the 1940s were constructed in their minds, of the identities and uncertainties that Partition created or reinforced'.[18]

The concerns are not so widely reflected in Pakistan, where it is conveniently assumed that the 'Partition issue', so to speak, was resolved well before 1947 by the weight of the two-nation theory.[19] The result is for everybody to see. Although Jinnah of Pakistan has been elevated to a high pedestal by the Cambridge-based scholar Akbar Ahmad, he would remain, unless rescued from his uncritical admirers, a lonely figure in the pages of history and in the gallery of nation builders. If the desire is to come to terms with his political engagement and explain his extraordinary success, it is not at all helpful to press him into service to establish

Pakistan's identity as an Islamic state. Likewise, the use of religious symbols, long forsaken by that country's bureaucracy and military establishment, can hardly serve as the starting point for a meaningful dialogue on Partition.

The engagement of several writers in India, though sometimes marred by a majoritarian perspective, centres around 'secular nationalism', the main inspiration behind much of liberal Left activism from the 1920s onwards. Their chief concern, though nowadays pooh-poohed in the 'post-modernist' discourse, is to examine why the secular élites and their ideologues, whose presence is grudgingly recognized across the ideological divide, failed to mediate between those warring factions/groups, who used religion as a cover to pursue their worldly goals and ambitions. While detailing the cynical games played out on the Indian turf by the British, the League and the self-proclaimed 'nationalists' of every variety, they do not spare the Congress stalwarts, Gandhi, Nehru and Patel included, for their failure to guide the movements they initiated away from the forces of reactionary communalism.[20] They marshal a wide array of sources to comment on Hindu communalists disguising themselves as Congressmen and preventing the national movement from becoming truly inclusive. They also point to Gandhi's role in introducing religion into politics, the anti-Muslim proclivities of the Hindu right, led by Patel in the 1940s, the Hindutva agenda of the Hindu Mahasabha, the Arya Samaj and the RSS (Rashtriya Swayamsewak Sangh), and Nehru's arrogance and haughtiness in dealing with Jinnah and the Muslim League. At a time when the Muslim League was flexing its muscles, India's first Prime Minister is said to have jettisoned the plan for a Congress-League coalition in 1937 and dimmed the prospect of an enduring Hindu-Muslim coalition in Indian politics. Thus the mainstay of the argument is that the country's vivisection could have been avoided had Nehru acted judiciously on this and at other critical junctures in the 1940s.[21]

Though such impressions rest on questionable assumptions, they cannot be brushed aside.[22] The real difficulty lies with the grand narrative itself and the tendency to generalize on the basis of the actions of a few. While the grand narrative illuminates several facets of the Pakistan story, it fails to incorporate the complexities and subtleties of institutional and structural changes, introduced by the colonial government, as also the impact of the socio-economic processes on caste, class and religion-based alignments. One does not, moreover, get a sense of why the two-nation theory was floated in March 1940 and not earlier, why and how different forms of identities and consciousness got translated into a powerful campaign for a separate Muslim homeland, why Partition created ten million refugees, led to the death of over a million people and resulted in sexual savagery, including the rape and abduction of 75,000 women. Finally, the grand narrative does not reveal how the momentous happenings in August-September 1947 affected millions, uprooted from home and field and driven by sheer fear of death to seek safety across a line they had neither drawn nor desired. Clearly, the issue is not whether a million or more died or whether only 3 per cent of the country's population was affected by the communal eruption. The essential facts, as pointed out by the Chief of the Governor-General's staff, were that 'there is human misery on a colossal scale all around and millions are bereaved, destitute, homeless, hungry, thirsty—and worst of all desperately anxious and almost hopeless about their future'.

In order to explore some of these aspects and probe those areas, which directly or indirectly impinged on the sudden and total breakdown of long-standing inter-community networks and alliances, it is necessary to locate the Partition debates outside the conference chambers. Without being swayed by the paradigms set by the two-nation theory or the rhetoric of Indian nationalism, it is important to examine why most people, who had so much in common and had lived together for generations, could turn against their neighbours, friends and members of the same caste and class within hours and days. Such tragedies have taken place in the former state of Yugoslavia, but it is unclear why they have gone unnoticed at research centres in the subcontinent, especially in areas worst affected by gruesome violence and migration. Is it because the ghosts of Partition should be put to rest and not exhumed for request post-mortems? Or, is scholarship on the subject itself so woefully inadequate and contentious that it fails to excite the imagination of young graduates?

The perspective and attitudes on such vexed matters are bound to differ, though scholars in Pakistan tenaciouly adhere to the belief that the creation of a Muslim nation was a legitimate act, the culmination of a historical process. Perhaps, it is hazardous to contest such inherited wisdom in a society where nationality is still defined, often clumsily, in purely Islamic terms and religious minorities, Hindus and Ahmadiyas (Qadianis) included, are left to stew in their own juice. Perhaps, Partition does not convey the same meaning in Lahore and Islamabad as it does to some people living in Delhi, Lucknow, Calcutta and Dacca. It is not bemoaned, for understandable reasons, as an epic tragedy but celebrated as a spectacular triumph of Islamic nationalism. After all, why should people inhabiting the fertile districts of western Punjab or the rugged Frontier region mourn the break-up of India's fragile unity or lament the collapse of a common cultural and intellectual inheritance? Some beleaguered *muhajirs* may still want to recall their friendships and associations in Hindustan (*guzashata bada-paraston ki yaadgaar koi*), trace their intellectual and cultural links with Lucknow or Delhi and, occasionally, revive memories of a bygone era by dipping into the writing of Saadat Hasan Manto, Ahmed Ali, Josh Malihabadi, Qurratulain Hyder and Intizar Hussain.[23] Yet the nostalgia for what has already become an imaginary homeland or the identification with Lucknow's grand *imambaras*, with the sufi shrines of Khwaja Muinuddin Chishti at Ajmer and Nizamuddin Auliya in Delhi, is gradually fading away with the passage of time and the passing of a generation. The Badshahi Mosque, standing majestically as a symbol of India's secular dream, is as distant and remote as the *Masjid-i-Qartaba*, the theme of Mohammad Iqbal's melodious poem. Aminabad in Lucknow or Ballimaran in Old Delhi, are far removed from the imagination of a generation that has grown up in a different social and cultural milieu.

The differences in approaches and perspectives should not, however, stand in the way of developing a common reference point for rewriting the *histories* of an event that cast its shadow over many aspects of state and society in the subcontinent. Despite decades of mutual suspicions and antipathies that has led to a mindless arms build up and contributed to the backwardness and appalling poverty of the region, it is still possible for the peoples, rather than the governments, to make sense of the poignant writings of creative writers and poets and to reflect on how and why a generation was caught up in the crossfire of religious bigotry, intolerance and sectarianism. Such an exercise can be undertaken without calling into question the legitimacy of one or the other varieties of nationalisms.

For the initiative to get off the ground, it may be useful to revisit the old fashioned theories on the syncretic and composite trajectory of Indian society and define, as the writer Krishna Sobti does in her recent interview, the shared values and traditions that had enabled diverse communities to live harmoniously for centuries.[24] It is not necessary to be swayed, as is often the case, by the 'nationalist' historians, who portrayed an idyllic picture of Hindu-Muslim relations during the pre-colonial days in order to strengthen inter-community ties during the liberation struggle. It is nonetheless important to underline, despite valiant attempts to uncover the 'pre-history of communalism', the fusion and integration of the Hindu communities at different levels and the value they attached to religious tolerance and pluralism in their day-to-day living.[25] In doing so, one can put to rest those speculative theories that are designed to lend respectability to British colonialism and offer corrective to the distorted Islamist or the Hindutva world views which have, in equal measure, created widespread confusion in the minds of the common people and, in the process, caused incalculable damage to state and civil society.

The conclusions flowing from such formulations are bound to differ, yet the urgency to underline the commonality of interests amongst large segments of the population must be felt in India, where Hindutva could well be the new *mantra* of civil society, in the foreseeable future, and in neighbouring Pakistan, where ethnic and sectarian strife, combined with deep-seated regional and linguistic cleavage, reveals the limits of an agenda, that is, tied to wild and imaginary notions of Muslim/Islamic brotherhood or solidarity.

II

The following three impressions are drawn from a period when Hindu-Muslim relations had reached their lowest watermark. The first is that of Malcolm Darling, a civil servant in Punjab for many years. During his travels in 1945-6, he found much similarity between the Hindu and Muslim communities in the tract between the Beas and Sutlej and the Chenab and Ravi rivers. He noticed, on numerous occasions, during his long career as a British civil servant, how often Hindus, Muslims and Sikhs had a common ancestor in a village, how a Hindu from Karnal proudly announced that the Muslim inhabitants of the 50 neighbouring villages, belonged to his clan and were prepared to return to the Hindu fold on the one condition that the Hindus would give them their daughters in marriage. Although the condition was refused, Hindus and Muslims of the area continued to interchange civilities at marriages, inviting the mullah or the Brahmin, to share in the feasting. Malcolm Darling wondered how Pakistan was to be fitted into these conditions. 'What a hash politics threatens to make of this tract', he observed, 'where Hindu, Muslim and Sikh are as mixed up as the ingredients of a well-made *pilau* (rice cooked with fowl or meat).'[26]

Mohammad Mujeeb, the Vice-Chancellor of Delhi's Jamia Millia Islamia, had a similar experience in Bihar soon after the orgy of violence had taken a heavy toll of human lives. While visiting the grave of a Sufi saint on the banks of the river Ganga, he found that the Muslims, living in the shrine, had already abandoned the place. But soon a group of Hindu women appeared. They performed the same rituals that they and their ancestors had observed for generations. It appeared 'as if nothing had happened that affected their sentiments of veneration for the tomb of a Muslim saint'.[27]

Finally, consider the reports of Phillips Talbot, written for the Institute of Current World Affairs, New York, on the eve of independence, and published recently in the daily newspaper, *Hindu*. For one thing, Talbot was struck by the countrywide expression of Hindu-Muslim cordiality during the independence celebrations. He wrote:

> For twenty long and bloody weeks after 16 August 1946, Hindus avoided entering Muslim neighbourhoods and *vice versa*. Communal clashes and deaths were daily occurrences. Yet at the climax of Independence celebrations this week, Hindus and Muslims mixed together freely. Many Hindus visited mosques on the eighteenth and distributed sweets to Muslims who were observing their Id festival. . . . It was a spectacular truce, if not a peace treaty, between the two communities. Similarly, in Delhi and Bombay I saw Hindus and Muslims playing hand in hand. Reports of the same nature came from most places except the still-troubled Punjab.[28]

Talbot's own explanation was that the political parties desired peace and friendship between the communities, though he laid greater stress on 'the popular revulsion against the constant dislocation and actual fear of life during the last year'. He added:

> Terror is an enervating emotion. I've seen neighbourhoods so distraught by the medieval lack of personal security that they could think of nothing else. I think that people everywhere used the excitement of the celebrations to try to break the vicious cycle of communal attacks and retaliations. How permanent the change may be is yet to be seen.[29]

Such impressions need to be drawn into the discussions on Partition so that the past is not judged through our recent encounters with Hindu-Muslim violence in India. It is just as important to delineate the multiple strands in the Muslim League movement, underline its complexity, assess its ideological orientation afresh and explore the mobilization strategies adopted by Jinnah, after he returned from his home in Hampstead to plunge into the humdrum of Indian politics. In addition to having greater access to source materials, this is an opportune moment, 50 years after independence, to revise and reconsider established theories on Partition, introduce a more nuanced discourse and stay clear of the conventional wisdom that we, the generation born after independence, have inherited on the theme of 'communal' politics, generally, and on the Pakistan movement, in particular. As 'old orthodoxies recede before the flood of fresh historical evidence and earlier certitudes are overturned by newly detected contradiction', this is the time to heal 'the multiple fractures which turned the promised dawn of freedom into a painful moment of separation'.[30]

For example, one of the points adequately documented, though not sufficiently considered in secondary literature, is that not everyone who raised or rallied around the green flag was uniformly wedded to, or inspired by, a shared ideal of creating an Islamic society. The reality is that many were pushed into taking religious/Islamic positions, while many others, especially the landed classes in Punjab and the United Provinces (UP), used the Muslim League as a vehicle to articulate, defend and promote their material interests. In fact, the intensity of emotions expressed in the 1940s, which is so often invoked in the subcontinent to create popular myths and stereotypical images, had more to do with the political and economic anxieties of various social classes, than with a profound urge to create a *sharia*-based society. Today, the issue is not the legitimacy of a movement but to place in perspective the dynamics of power politics in a colonial context. In fact, a rounded picture of the Pakistan movement is possible only if we are able to contest the exaggerated claims made in the name of Islam, then and now, by the Islamists and the proponents of the two-nation theory.

In sum, the clamour for a separate nation, though pressed vigorously in the post-war years with much popular backing and enthusiasm, was raised not so much by the Muslim divines, many of whom were waiting on the fringes of Indian politics to intervene on behalf of Islam, but by the vociferous professional groups in UP, Bihar, the princely state of Hyderabad and the small, but upcoming, trading and banking communities in Gujarat, Bombay and Calcutta. Interestingly enough, the Muslim landlords of UP were the first to raise the banner of revolt against the League; in fact, the Nawab of Chattari and Nawab Mohammad Yusuf of Jaunpur broke away from the Muslim League Parliamentary Board, in April 1936, in order to revive 'a mixed party in preference to a Muslim communal organisation'.[31] They changed course once the Congress Ministry adopted the UP Tenancy Bill and Nehru and his comrades became more and more strident in their Socialistic pronouncements. These men were not concerned to defend the Koranic injunctions, which they probably flouted every day of their life. Nor were they interested in the welfare of the poor Muslims, who were victims of their oppression and exploitation. Their chief goal was to defend their landholdings, orchards, *havelis*, palaces and, above all, the *nawabi* paraphernalia built through the courtesy of their British benefactors. Notice the following conversation, between Saleem and his father Hamid in Attia Hosain's (died in January 1998) celebrated novel, *Sunlight on a Broken Column:*

Saleem was saying, 'In the final analysis, what you are facing is the struggle for power by the bourgeoisie. It is not really a peasant's movement, but when it comes to a division of spoils even class interests are forgotten. For example the four hundred or so *Taluqdars* insisted the British should give them higher representation than the thousands of other landlords.'

'It is not a question of numbers alone', protested Uncle Hamid, sitting up and waving his pipe in negation. 'We *Taluqdars* have ancient rights and privileges, given by a special charter, which we have to safeguard. . . .'

'Yes, yes, of course. One respects tradition. One fights for one's self, one's interests. But you cannot expect the tenants to love you for it.'

'That is because so-called reforms are destroying the personal ties between landlord and peasant. Surely a government and its changing officers cannot have personal relations or traditional ties with the tenants? With whom are the people in constant touch? Their landlords or local political leaders? . . .'

'How can landlords but be uneasy at the thought of such reserves of power being vested in officials at a time when it is uncertain what class of persons will obtain political power? . . .' (Uncle Hamid)

Saleem could not let an argument die an unnatural death. He began, 'What you said, father, about the landlords' fear of abolition is the crux of the matter. This fear for their existence is the basis for the formation of a new party which is interested in keeping the *status quo* intact, that is favoured by the British and is fundamentally opposed to progressive, national movements.'

'Words! Theories! Irresponsible talk!' Uncle Hamid burst out. 'I am a part of feudalism, and proud to be. I shall fight for it. It is my heritage—and yours. Let me remind you of that. And that you enjoy its "reactionary" advantages. You talk very glibly of its destruction, but you live by its existence. It is, in fact, your only livelihood.'[32]

No wonder, the landed elements in UP, as also the Jamaat-i Islami and sections of the ulama connected with the Barelwi 'school', Nadwat al-ulama, Firangi Mahal and Deoband, hitched their fortunes to the Muslim League at different points of time and for different reasons. Their overall strategy, one that suited the Raj during and after the Second World War, was to masquerade their hidden agenda and project the Congress, as their main rival in the political world, and also as a 'Hindu' party inimical to Islam. Once the League bandwagon rolled on, other aggrieved groups, especially those who failed to secure employment, contracts or seats on regional and local bodies, jumped into the fray as the defenders of the faith.

Still, Pakistan was not everybody's dream. Nor was Jinnah everyone's *Qaid* (leader).[33] In this respect, one should not, as is generally the case with both the Hindu and Muslim majoritarian discourses, lose sight of the perspectives of those who were intellectually committed to secular nationalism or were actively engaged in repudiating the two-nation theory.

Their voices, which have been stifled by 'secular' as well as 'communal' histories, should not be relegated to a historian's footnote. Indeed, the part played by those Muslims, who are patronizingly described as 'Nationalist Muslims', the Khudai Khidmatgars, in the North West Frontier region, who were eventually let down by the dispirited Congress leadership, on the eve of independence, the ulama of Deoband and the Momins in Bihar, should not be submerged beneath the rationalization of the 'victors'. Their main contribution, exemplified by Maulana Abul Kalam Azad's exemplary conduct and performance,[34] was to keep alive the vision of a secular India. These 'marginal' voices should be recovered to rewrite the histories of Partition.[35]

For these and other reasons, it is appropriate to ask if the Muslim League movement was as cohesive and unified as it is made out to be, by some writers in India and Pakistan. If the Congress was faction-ridden and ideologically fragmented, so was the League.[36] This is illustrated by the depth and intensity of jealousies and internal discord in the organization, the regional groupings, the *Ajlaf-Ashraf* divide, the Shia-Sunni strife in many places and the unending doctrinal disputes between the theologians and the followers of the Barelwi and the Deobandi 'schools'. Such differences, which are conveniently overlooked in the histories of the freedom movement in Pakistan, were real and not imaginary. If so, it will not do to portray the Muslim Leaguers as earnest and self-sacrificing crusaders or equate them with the *muhajirs* or *Ansars* of the Prophet Muhammad. What is perhaps challenging, as indeed intellectually rewarding, is to probe those critical areas where the 'faithful', despite having projected themselves as a community acting in unison, were themselves so hopelessly split. Such an exercise, far from reducing or tarnishing the reputation of historic figures, would enrich our knowledge and understanding of a complex phenomena. Arguably, if we know our leaders better and question their reading of the authentic and vibrant histories of shared memories and experiences, we may not repeat their mistakes and errors of judgement, which cost the nation dearly at the stroke of the midnight hour of 14-15 August 1947.

III

The decision about the creation of Pakistan had just been announced and people were indulging in all kinds of surmises about the pattern of life that would emerge. But no one's imagination could go very far. . . . The Sardarji sitting in front of me repeatedly asked me whether I thought Mr Jinnah would continue to live in Bombay after the creation of Pakistan or whether he would resettle in Pakistan. Each time my answer would be the same, 'Why should he leave Bombay? I think he'll continue to live in Bombay and continue visiting Pakistan.' Similar guesses were being made about the towns of Lahore and Gurdaspur too, and no one knew which town would fall to the share of India and which to Pakistan.[37]

In the specific context of the Pakistan movement, the professed ideology of the nation state itself, though celebrated on both sides of the border, had no significant impact on, or relevance to, the millions living in India or Pakistan. Contrary to the exaggerated claims made in both the countries, most people were either indifferent to, or unconcerned with, the national borders or the newly created geographical entities that were being laboriously created. National borders were political constructs, imagined projections of territorial power. Although they appeared in deceptively precise forms, they reflected, at least initially, merely the mental images of politicians, lawyers and intellectuals. Their practical consequences for most people were quite different.[38] Rajinder Sachar, jurist and human rights activist, who has spent a lifetime struggling with his memories of Lahore, recalled:

> One day I ran into a Muslim villager who had come to Lahore all the way from Sargodha looking for my grandfather, a well-known criminal lawyer. Poor chap he didn't realise that Partition had taken place and that the Hindus had left. It just shows how long it took for the implications of Partition to sink in.[39]

Indeed, though such people were repeatedly fed with ill-informed and biased views and interpretations about the 'other', they were neither committed to the land of Aryavarta nor the *dar al-Islam.* They had no destination to reach, no mirage to follow. Even though the trains had started carrying people to their death traps, they were unclear whether Lahore, with its splendid Mughal monuments, beautiful gardens and boulevards, would be part of India or Pakistan. They did not know whether Delhi, the city of Mir Taqi Mir and Mirza Ghalib, would remain in Gandhi's India or Jinnah's Pakistan. Manto captures this mood in his brilliant story 'Toba Tek Singh', based on a character from a lunatic asylum. This is what he writes:

> As to where Pakistan was located the inmates knew nothing. That was why both the mad and the partially mad were unable to decide whether they were now in India or in Pakistan. If they were in India where on earth was Pakistan? And if they were in Pakistan, then how come that until only the other day it was India . . .?
>
> Those who had tried to solve this mystery had become utterly confused when told that Sialkot, which used to be in India, was now in Pakistan. It was anybody's guess what was going to happen to Lahore, which was currently in Pakistan, but

could slide into India any moment. It was still possible that the entire subcontinent of India might become Pakistan. And who could say if both India and Pakistan might not entirely vanish from the map of the world one day . . .?

Just before sunrise, Bisham Singh, the man who had stood on his legs for fifteen years, screamed and as officials from the two sides rushed towards him, he collapsed on the ground.

There, behind barbed wire, on one side, lay India and behind more barbed wire, on the other side, lay Pakistan. In between, on a bit of earth which had no name, lay Toba Tek Singh.

The paradox of how borders simultaneously separate and unite is discussed elsewhere.[40] The significance of Manto's description lies in describing an existentialist reality—the separation of people living on both sides, who had a long history of cultural and social contact—and the paradoxical character of borders being a metaphor of the ambiguities of nation building.[41] He was, in essence, offering a way of correcting the distortions inherent in state-centred national histories. 'India' or 'Pakistan' were mere territorial abstractions to most people, who were ignorant of how Mountbatten's Plan or the Radcliffe Award, would change their destinies and tear them apart from their social and cultural moorings. In their world view, there was no nationalism, religious or composite. They were blissfully unaware that their fate, which had rested in the hands of the exploiting classes for centuries, would be settled after Mountbatten's three days of 'diplomacy' leading to the 3 June Plan, and that the frontiers would be decided by Cyril Radcliffe in just seven weeks and 'a continent for better or worse divided'.[42] They had no clue, whatsoever, that these vain, insensitive and conceited representatives of the Crown, having received the mandate from Clement Atlee's Labour government to preside over the liquidation of the most important imperial possession of all time, would abandon them in mid ocean 'with a fire in the deck and ammunition in the hold'. Nobody had warned them how Mountbatten's mentor Winston Churchill had, likewise, sat with T.E. Lawrence and Emir Faisal, in Cairo, as Colonial Secretary, in 1922, drawing nation states on the map of what had previously been the Ottoman Empire. But, then, how were they to know that the colonial powers divide people and territories when in ascendancy, as also in retreat.

IV

For a long time I refused to accept the consequences of the revolution, which was set off by the Partition of the country. I still feel the same way; but I suppose, in the end, I came to accept this nightmarish reality without self-pity or despair. In the process I tried to retrieve from this man-made sea of blood, pearls of a rare hue, by writing about the single-minded dedication with which men had killed men, about the remorse felt by some of them, about the tears shed by murderers who could not understand why they still had some human feelings left. All this and more, I put in my book *Siyah Hashye*.[43]

Everytime I visited Amritsar, I felt captivated. But the city this time presented the look of a cremation *ghat*, eerie and stinking. . . .The silence was so perfect that even the faint hiss of steam from the stationary engine sounded a shriek. . . . The brief stoppage seemed to have lingered into eternity till the engine whistled and gave a gentle pull. . . . We left Chheharta behind and then Atari and when we entered Wagah and then Harbanspura everyone in the train felt uplifted. A journey through a virtual valley of destruction has ended when finally the train came to a halt at platform No. 2—Lahore, the moment was as gratifying as the consummation of a dream.[44]

Scores of writers reveal the other face of freedom, the woes of divided families, the agony and trauma of abducted women, the plight of migrants and the harrowing experiences of countless people who board the train that they thought would take them to the realization of their dream, but of whom not a man, woman or child survive the journey. A Zahid in Attia Hosain's *Sunlight on a Broken Column* or a Saddan in Rahi Masoom Reza's *Aadha Gaon* (Half-a-Village), offers a vivid and powerful portrayal of a fragmented and wounded society.[45] What political debate will never fully do—and the reason we so badly need literature—is to defeat the urge to lay the blame, which keeps the animosity alive. Only literature can truly evoke the sufferings of the innocent, whose pain is more universal and ultimately a vehicle of more honest reconciliation than political discourse.[46]

Board the 'Peshawar Express' or the *Train to Pakistan* to discover the implications of what happened before and after the fateful, midnight hour. Consider the exchanges between Chaudhri Mohammad Ali, a well-known landlord of Rudauli, in Barabanki district (UP), and his daughter, who left her father to settle in Karachi or the correspondence of Brahm Nath Dutt, father of the historian V.N. Datta, to capture the poignancy of the moment. Turn to Rahi's Gangauli village—a world where people are seen to be wrestling to come to terms with competing ideologies—in order to uncover how the intricate and almost imperceptible way in which the politics of Partition worked its way into the interstices of people's consciousness.[47] Read Attia Hosain's *Sunlight on a Broken Column* or *Phoenix Fled* to discover how the Pakistan movement split families on ideological lines and created fears and uncertainties in the minds of people.

To read her novel and collection of short stories is 'as if one had parted a curtain, or opened a door, and strayed into the past'.[48]

Indeed, if the histories of Partition are to be rewritten, there are several reasons why we must judiciously draw upon the intellectual resources made available to us by such creative writers. They expose the inadequacy of numerous narratives on independence and Partition, compel us to explore fresh themes and adopt new approaches that have eluded the grasp of social scientists and provide a foundation for developing an alternative discourse to current expositions of a general theory on inter-community relations. Their strength lies in representing a grim and sordid contemporary reality without drawing religion or a particular community as the principal reference point. In their stories, the experiences of each community distinctly mirror one another, indeed reach out to and clutch at one another. No crime, no despair and no grief in exile belongs uniquely to anyone.[49] In the words of Krishna Sobti, whose best-known Hindi writings on Partition are 'Sikka Badal Gaya' and *Zindaginama*, the fiction written about that cataclysmic event preserved 'essential human values'.[50] That is probably why:

> We emerge from the literature with a mistrust towards group solidarity of an oppositional bent. If so, we must emerge at the same time, paradoxically, with a conviction to oppose such mistrust with trust in the goodness of the human life-urge wherever we find it. Indeed, we emerge from the literature as searchers of such trust. If we find it in the solitary dissidence of even a single person, we feel obliged to offer him or her our companionship. And if we find it stitched into whole communities, we come away not necessarily more pious, but inspired. The literature as a whole seeds pathos for the suffering and inhumanity of the Partition, and related instances of cultural chauvinism, but not merely so. It also sprouts a countervailing protest, a voice of justice that must be the surging of our humanity itself—something greater than our bestiality—within us. In this sense the literature does what religious leaders in each community failed to do: to make communities forces for the affirmation of humanity broadly. . . . If religious politics worked nefariously in favour of Partition, it was because ecumenical religious politics never developed. We are in a different position than the men and women of August, 1947. Our choices are not limited to exile, death or resignation.[51]

In other words, if creative writings can still stir the individual and collective imagination of sensitive readers in the subcontinent, there is no reason why people on both sides of the Wagah border cannot share the anguish of Faiz Ahmad Faiz[52] and, at the same time, echo the optimism and plea of Ali Sardar Jafri in the following lines:

Tum aoo Gulshan-i Lahore se chaman bardosh
Hum ayen subha Banaras ki raushni lekar
Himalaya ki hawaon ki taazgi lekar
Phir uske baad ye puchain ke kaun dushman hai?

(You come covered with flowers from the Garden of Lahore
We bring to you the light and radiance of the morning of Banaras
The freshness of the winds of Himalayas
And then we ask who the enemy is?)

NOTES

1. Amrita Pritam, *Aj Akhan Waris Shah Nun* (in Punjabi) (I Say Unto Waris Shah).
2. Krishna Sobti, in Conversation with Alok Bhalla, in Geeti Sen, ed., *Crossing Boundaries* (Delhi, 1997), p. 78.
3. N.N. Vohra, '91, Garden Town', in ibid., p. 54.
4. Some years ago, historian Gyanendra Pandey complained that the history of violence accompanying Partition had not been written. Recently, Ashis Nandy bemoaned that the finest creative minds of India had maintained a profound, almost cultivated silence about Partition and the bloodbath, *Times of India*, 20 July 1997. See, also Urvashi Butalia on the 'Official Silence', in *Hindu*, 21 September 1997. My principal interest in this essay centres around articles published in newspapers, magazines and journals during the fiftieth year of independence. I have, however, used scholarly writings, mostly published in 1996-7, to comment on the theme of Partition.

   The Delhi based weekly news magazine, *Outlook*, brought out a special issue on 28 May 1997. The *Asian Age*, edited by M.J. Akbar, published extracts from books on Partition, personal memories and recollections and interviews. See, for example, the reports of the Reuters correspondent, Don Campbell, who arrived in India in March 1947 and spent the next 15 months in Delhi. The coverage in the newspaper *Hindu* was also quite extensive. The impressions of Phillips Talbot, an American, were particularly interesting.
5. For example, Urvashi Butalia, 'Blood', in *Granta* (London, March 1997); Sunil Mehra, 'Sufferers and Survivors', in *Outlook*, 28 May 1997, pp. 32-3; 'Bridging a Great Divide', in *India Today*, 18 August 1997; Anita Mukhopadhya, 'The Last Journey', in *Hindu*, 31 August 1997; Ajeet Cour, 'I've Seen Rootless Trees Wobbling and Walking', in *Hindustan Times*, 4 January 1998 (courtesy, Nonica Datta); C.M. Naim, 'Pakistan or Hindustan', in *Communalism Combat*, September 1997; 'India's Unforgettable Divide', in *Guardian* (London), 30 July 1997; Iqbal Masud, *Dream Merchants, Politicians and Partition: Memoirs of an Indian Muslim* (Delhi, 1997).
6. *Femina* (Bombay), 1 August 1997. I am grateful to Nonica Datta for this reference.
7. For example, Patrick French, *Liberty or Death: India's Journey to Independence and Division* (London, 1997).
8. See, for example, the scholarly contributions of Gyanendra Pandey, 'Community and Violence', *Economic and Political Weekly* (hereafter *EPW*), 9 August 1997, and idem, 'Partition and Independence in Delhi: 1947-48', in ibid., 6 September 1997; also, Azhar Abbas, 'The Twice Displaced', in *Outlook*, 28 May 1997, p. 66. For insights into ethnic violence in Sri Lanka in 1983 that had many features in common with the Hindu-Muslim

riots before and after independence, see S.J. Tambiah, *Ethnic Fratricide and the Dismantling of Democracy* (Chicago, 1986).

9. Butalia, 'Blood', op.cit.; Ritu Menon and Kamla Bhasin, *Borders and Boundaries: Women in India's Partition* (Delhi, 1998).
10. Mushirul Hasan, *Legacy of a Divided Nation: India's Muslims Since Independence* (London, 1997); and idem, ed., *India Partitioned: The Other Face of Freedom*, 2 Vols (Delhi, 1997, 2nd rev. edn).
11. For a critique of Mountbatten, see N.N. Vohra, op.cit.; and F.S. Aijazuddin 'Same to Same' from a different perspective, in Geeti Sen, ed., op.cit.
12. *Outlook*, 28 May 1997. Notice the following letter of Cyril Radcliffe to his son: 'I thought you would like to get a letter from India with a crown on the envelope. After tomorrow evening nobody will ever again be allowed to use such stationery and after 150 years British rule will be over in India. . . . I am going to see Mountbatten sworn as the first governor-general of the Indian Union. . . and then I station myself firmly on the Delhi airport until an aeroplane from England comes along. Nobody in India will love me for the award about the Punjab and Bengal and there will be roughly 80 million people with a grievance who will begin looking for me. I do not want them to find me. I have worked and travelled and sweated. . . oh I have sweated the whole time', quoted in Sunil Khilnani, *The Idea of India* (London, 1997), p. 201.
13. Ajit Bhattacharjea, 'Cyril's Scalpel', in *Outlook*, 23 July 1997, p. 8.
14. Thus the following view: 'Looking back 50 years, the haste and self-delusion of Congress and Muslim leaders that contributed to the bloodiest religious cleansing in history emerges with disturbing clarity', in ibid., 28 May 1997.
15. Leonard Mosley, *The Last Days of the Raj* (London, 1961), p. 77.
16. For example, the Presidential Address delivered by Professor V.N. Datta, at the Indian History Congress, held in Madras in December 1996.
17. Kuldip Nayyar, 'Was Pakistan Necessary?', in *Indian Express*, 15 August 1997, and idem, 'Partition: An Inevitability', in *Hindu*, Special Issue on 'India!', August 1997. For earlier accounts of who is to blame, see Chimanlal Setalvad, *India Divided* (Bombay, n.d.), pp. 4-7.
18. Gyanendra Pandey, 'The Prose of Otherness', in David Arnold and David Hardiman, eds, *Subaltern Studies VIII: Essays in Honour of Ranajit Guha* (Delhi, 1994), p. 194.
19. This is the common refrain in the writings of Ayesha Jalal and Farzana Shaikh. For Pandey's critique of Jalal's work, see ibid. And for her response, see 'Secularists, Subalterns and the Stigma of "Communalism": Partition Historiography Revisited', in *The Indian Economic and Social History Review*, Vol. XXXIII, No. 1 (1996), pp. 93-103. The tendency to exaggerate the difference in perspectives and to castigate each other for that reason is the hallmark of recent historiography on South Asia. Young and upcoming social scientists, many of whom have not even written their doctoral dissertations, are engaged in polemical writings. They regard this as a short cut to establishing their scholarly reputation in the West. Ayesha Jalal's critique of my introduction to *India's Partition: Process Strategy and Mobilisation* (Delhi, 1998, 4th impression) is based on a misunderstanding of my overall argument. Yet, I respect her views and her understanding of a highly complex phenomena which should not, incidentally, be reduced to polemical exchanges among fellow historians.
20. In a perceptive article, Aijaz Ahmad has offered a powerful critique of 'the Congress-inspired mythology'. His analysis suggests: (a) that the politics of caste and communalism was inherent in the structure of the colonial society itself; (b) that the reform

movements usually contributed to solidifying such identities rather than weakening them in favour of ecumenical culture and non-denominational politics; and (c) that the national movement itself, including the majority of the Congress under Gandhi, was deeply 'complicit in a transactional mode of politics which involved bargaining among the elites and a conception of secularism which was little more than an accommodation of the self-enclosed orthodoxies. *Given the immensity of this historical weight, the wonder is not that there was a Partition but that there was one*' (emphasis added), in *Hindu*, 'India', op.cit., p. 28.

21. The judgement is harsh, although many contemporary observers believed that Jinnah may not have had the space to press his campaign in the UP if the coalition issue was amicably resolved. The Governor of UP felt that way, Harry Haig to Linlithgow, 3 June 1939, File No. 115/16, India Office Library and Records (hereafter IOLR). See also, my introduction to *India's Partition*, op.cit., pp. 12-15.
22. On the coalition issue, there is unmistakable evidence to suggest that talks of a Congress-Muslim League alliance were initiated sometime in March-April 1937. Although Nehru had opposed 'all pacts and coalitions with small groups at the top' (Nehru to Abul Wali, 30 March 1937, All India Congress Committee [hereafter AICC] Papers, G-5, K.W.i, 1937, Nehru Memorial Museum & Library), Abdul Wali of Barabanki (UP), referred to a scheme 'being hatched with the help of Pantji [G.B. Pant] and Mohanlal [Saxena] to bring about coalition between the Congress and League parties in the Assembly', Abdul Wali to Nehru, 28 March 1937, AICC Papers. The Governor of UP reported on 7 April that the League was looking forward to an alliance with the Congress and felt that 'at present it looks as if the new government will gradually attract to itself a fair number of the Muslim Leaguers'.
23. See Masud Hasan Shahab Dehlavi, in Mushirul Hasan, ed., *India Partitioned*, Vol. II, op.cit., pp. 184-95.
24. Krishna Sobti in Conversation with Alok Bhalla, op.cit., p. 66. And the comment of J.S. Butalia, a retired journalist: 'I was born and brought up in a predominantly Muslim village, Butala. There were 300 Muslim families and only 10 or 15 Hindu homes but we lived in such close harmony that it was difficult to make out who was who. A Hindu-Muslim conflict was something we had not imagined even in our worst dreams. It is with a sense of horror and shame that I look back . . . but, finally, I am overwhelmed by nostalgia', in *Hindu*, 'India', op.cit., 15 August 1997, p. 32. For Bengal, see Mukhopadhya, 'The Last Journey', in *Hindu*, 31 August 1997.
25. See the contributions of Rakshat Puri, Muchkund Dubey and Sumanta Banerjee, in Geeti Sen, ed., op.cit.
26. This is quoted in full in Mushirul Hasan, *Legacy of a Divided Nation*, op.cit., p. 168.
27. See idem, *India's Partition:* op.cit., p. 405. For Punjab, see Krishna Sobti, in Conversation with Alok Bhalla, op.cit., pp. 67-70. For Bengal, see Ranabir Samaddar, ed., *Reflections on Partition in the East* (Delhi, 1997); the review of the book by Sumanta Banerjee in *Biblio* (Delhi), July-August 1997, pp. 40-1; and Peter van der Veer, 'Playing or Praying: A Sufi Saint's Day in Surat', in *The Journal of Asian Studies*, Vol. LI, No. 3 (August 1992), pp. 545-64.
28. Phillips Talbot, 'Thus Independence Came to India', in *Hindu*, 4 and 24 August 1997.
29. Talbot filed this report on 10 August 1947.
30. I have borrowed these lines from Ayesha Jalal, 'Secularists, Subalterns and the Stigma of "Communalism" ', op.cit., p. 1.

31. Nawab of Chattari to Hailey, 28 October 1936, Malcolm Hailey Papers, File No. 28c, IOLR.
32. Attia Hosain, *Sunlight on a Broken Column* (Delhi, 1992), pp. 231-3 and 234.
33. In this respect, my reading of the Pakistan movement is different from that of Ayesha Jalal.
34. The following impression of Azad by Kanji Dwarkadas is interesting, 'Abul Kalam Azad', he wrote, 'is dignified and level-headed, but his health is giving way. Jinnah dislikes him heartily and a few years ago he called him the "show boy" of the Congress and in private conversations Jinnah says much worse things about Abul Kalam Azad,' 'India—April 1944 to November 1945: What Next?', 28 November 1945 (Typescript), George Lumley Papers, IOLR.
35. See Pandey, 'The Prose of Otherness', op.cit., p. 214.
36. In fact, Jinnah exhorted various regional groups and other factions to overcome their differences and rival claims so that the Muslim League could concentrate all its energies towards the achievement of Pakistan. 'We shall have time to quarrel ourselves', he said, 'and we shall have time when these differences will have to be remedied. We shall have time for domestic programmes and politics, but first get the government. This is a nation without any territory or any government', quoted in Khalid B. Sayeed, *Pakistan: The Formative Phase, 1857-1948* (London, 1968), p. 297.
37. Bhisham Sahni, 'We Have Arrived in Amritsar', in Stephen Alter and Vimal Dissanayake, eds, *The Penguin Book of Modern Short Stories* (Delhi, 1989), pp. 180-7.
38. These lines are based on Michiel Baud and Willem van Schendel, 'Towards a Comparative History of Borderlands', in *Journal of World History*, Vol. VIII, No. 2 (1997), pp. 211-42.
39. Quoted in *Hindu*, 'India', op.cit., p. 28.
40. Baud and Schendel, op.cit., p. 242.
41. Benedict Anderson, *Imagined Communities: Reflections on the Origin and Spread of Nationalism* (1983, repr., New York, 1991); E.J. Hobsbawm and Terence Ramger, eds, *The Invention of Tradition* (Cambridge, 1983).
42. This is a line from W.H. Auden, see Khilnani, op.cit., p. 200.
43. For my translation of Saadat Hasan Manto, *Siyah Hashye* (Black Margins), see Mushirul Hasan, ed., *India Partitioned*, Vol. I, op.cit., pp. 88-101.
44. Mohammad Saeed, *Lahore: A Memoir* (Lahore, 1989), p. 94.
45. On *Aadha Gaon*, see Sudhir Chandra, 'The Harvest of Fear: A Retrospective Critique of Hindu-Muslim Relations in Two Hindi Novels', in T.V. Sathyamurthy, *Region, Religion, Caste, Gender and Culture in Contemporary India*, Vol. III (Delhi 1996).
46. Jason Francisco, 'In the Heat of Fratricide: The Literature of India's Partition Burning Freshly' (A Review Article), in *The Annual of Urdu Studies*, No. 2 (Madison, 1996), p. 250.
47. Sudhir Chandra, op.cit., p. 195.
48. Anita Desai, 'Indroduction', *Phoenix Fled* (Delhi, 1988), p. viii.
49. Francisco, op.cit., p. 250.
50. Geeti Sen, ed., op.cit., p. 77; and Alok Bhalla, ed., *Stories About the Partition of India*, Vols. I, II and III (Delhi, 1994).
51. Francisco, op.cit., p. 250.

52. This leprous daybreak, dawn night's fangs have mangled—
This is not that long-looked-for break of that day
Not that clear dawn in quest of which those comrades
Set out, believing that in heaven's wide void
Somewhere must be the stars' last halting place,
Somewhere the verge of night's slow-washing tide,
Somewhere an anchorage for the ship of heartache.

How Long Does Lahore Burn? History, Memory and Literary Representations of the Partition

NANDI BHATIA

How long does Lahore burn? Weeks? Months?

Despite all the ruptured dreams, broken lives, buried gold, bricked-in rupees, secreted jewelry, lingering hopes . . . the fire could not have burned for months and months . . .

But in my memory it is branded over an inordinate length of time: memory demands poetic license.[1]

Alluding to a burning Lahore on the eve of the subcontinental Partition in 1947, the above passage from Bapsi Sidhwa's *Cracking India* speaks of the consciousness of a subject positioned within this particular historical moment, whose location in that history involves a configuration of memory in order for the event to be reconstructed. However, instead of letting her fractured memory undermine her experience, the Pakistani writer of this passage reminds her readers of the critical importance of memory as a site that enables an alternative interpretation of this history, however partial and subjective it may be. 'Branded over an inordinate length of time', as Sidhwa says, these memories are fragments of the experiences of millions of people traumatized by the Partition. Revived and manifested in literature, such memories, in the words of Foucault, lead to the resurgence of hidden or suppressed histories that destabilize and challenge official ones.[2]

Sidhwa's recollection of Lahore through the literary devices of interrogation, introspection and commentary in her novels is emblematic

* Many people have contributed to the development of this paper through their thoughts and ideas. In particular, I would like to thank Preet Aulakh, Kathleen Kane and Indira Baptista Gupta for critical input on earlier versions and Prabhjot Parmar, Raja Seera, Ruby Singh, Vishal Bhatia and Shyama Bhatia for discussions and encouragement. I would especially like to thank my father, Harbans Singh Bhatia, for telling those numerous stories that have kept the memories of the Partition alive.

of the larger role literature can play in challenging official histories of the Partition as is evident in the vast archive of literary writing, journalism, films and plays, some of them recounting events as remembered by those who were first hand witnesses to the Partition. Khushwant Singh's *Train to Pakistan*,[3] Attia Hosain's *Sunlight on a Broken Column*,[4] Manohar Malgonkar's *A Bend in the Ganges*,[5] Bhisham Sahni's *Tamas*,[6] telecast by Doordarshan several years later under controversial circumstances, Chaman Nahal's *Azadi*,[7] R.K. Narayan's *Waiting for the Mahatma*,[8] Anita Desai's *Clear Light of Day*[9] and Harwant Singh Bains' *Blood*[10] are only a few examples that constitute the corpus of Partition literature available in English. This list extends into Urdu, Hindi and Punjabi, including the works of Saadat Hasan Manto, Yashpal, Amrita Pritam, and numerous other writers, some of which have been recovered and compiled into collections and anthologies. Drawing on published diaries, excerpts from autobiographies, personal accounts, poems, stories and interviews, Mushirul Hasan,[11] for instance, provides a wide array of individual and collective experiences of migration, nostalgia, refugee trauma, during and after the Partition, as do the collection of Partition stories, edited by Alok Bhalla.[12] In recounting the role of these stories, Bhalla emphasizes the multiple uses of memory. While in some instances, memory offers a vision to 'counter violence' in other cases, memory of the past 'becomes a source of dignity in the present'. Says Bhalla: 'the history of atrocities is not forgotten, but neither is a life of connectedness. The archives of memory are used, not only to explore the life of greed and violence, but also as a source for a life of communal togetherness again'.[13]

In the context of the Partition and the historical writing on the event, the role of memory and literary representations become especially relevant. As Gyanendra Pandey has argued, the Partition was, 'for a majority of people living in what is the now divided territories of Northern India, Pakistan, and Bangladesh, the event of the twentieth century—equivalent in terms of trauma and consequence to the first world war [the "great" War] for Britain or the second world war for Japan'.[14] As a moment that witnessed unprecedented violence, the Partition, which involved dislocation and relocation of about 12 million people who moved across borders to their newly identified homes in India and the east and west wings of Pakistan, cost approximately one million lives in riots and resulted in the abduction of nearly 75,000 women.[15] Descriptions of violence by survivors include those of trains filled with corpses as they arrived on both sides of the border, mutilated bodies, women and men paraded naked on streets, women's bodies 'tattooed with marks and symbols of the other religion',[16] forced religious conversions, separation of families and the abandonment of homes.

In my own conversations with friends and family members who witnessed the Partition, I have been struck by the profound significance they attached to the event, during their recollections even after four decades.[17] Also striking for me is the vividness with which these individuals recounted the event with the utmost detail—from the horror of violence to being witness to mob killings and frenzy, and the emotions that they felt during those days. Some of them recalled travelling for days by whatever means of transportation they could secure before reaching their destination. The more fortunate ones were rescued in cars, buses or lorries; others walked on foot for days with or without their belongings, and many lost family members and personal belongings along the way. During these migrations on foot, women and men went behind crops in the fields to hide from the enemy, and others, to escape frenzied mobs that entered their homes, hid in attics or trunks. At times their recollections were accompanied by analyses of the situation—ranging from blaming the British to police complicity in the violence to suspicion of opposing religious groups. As I recorded the conversations on tape, at certain moments a few asked me to switch off the tape recorder, as they simply did not want certain instances of trauma, humiliation and embarrassment recorded for posterity. Also, the women were sometimes hesitant to participate in discussions and, on occasion, gave instances when people helped each other at times of extreme uncertainty. Needless to say, the recollection of these events was wrought in emotion, anger, sadness and trauma.[18]

This then is the personal side of Partition, which, for the most part, resides primarily in the memory of those who lived through, witnessed and were thoroughly traumatized by the moment. On the other hand, historical scholarship on the Partition—official records, documents, private papers and political historical resources—is marked by a crisis in which the personal and social histories of the 'people' receive 'short shrift'.[19] While the high politics of India's Partition has been reevaluated in the works of Mushirul Hasan,[20] Ayesha Jalal,[21] Stanley Wolpert[22] and Anita Inder Singh,[23] among others, the task of recovering the histories of the 'people' continues to pose a challenge for scholars. In their attempts to rewrite this history from the margins, scholars have repeatedly emphasized the centrality of personal narratives, testimonies, eyewitness accounts, literary narratives and the role of memory.[24] Turning his attention to literary narratives, Pandey argues that 'the historian needs to struggle to recover "marginal" voices and memories, forgotten dreams and signs of resistance, if history is to be anything more than a celebratory account of the march of certain victorious concepts and powers like the nation-state, bureaucratic rationalism, capitalism, science and progress'.[25] However, even scholars recording personal experiences through testimonies or literary writings are confounded by the question of the 'authenticity' of texts and the reliability of personal narratives. It is to this problem that I seek to refer, to uncover the relevance of literary representations.

From a historian's viewpoint, personal stories, steeped as they are in emotion and sentimentality, are difficult to lay down simply as 'facts'. Filtered as these instances are, through memory and the space of distance, and mediated by the ongoing communal crises in post colonial India, traditional historical methodologies perceive recollections as bearing the imprint of bias, distortion and even exaggeration. As Pandey asserts, perusal of the personal creates difficulty regarding the 'nature of evidence and the modes of analysis and representation employed in historical discourse'.[26] Part of the difficulty, as Pandey and Huma Ibrahim assert, lies in the emotions and sentiments attached to the personal. Yet as Ibrahim herself points out, sentimentality 'did have a lot to do with the Partition'.[27] Moreover, the trauma of being severed from families, friends, land and nation only compounded the grief that has crystallized into an intense emotion over the decades. Methodologically, how are these testimonies to be accounted for and analysed? For a generation that went through the Partition and for whom these events are of enormous significance, are they to be dismissed or obliterated simply on account of their emotional, sentimental or anecdotal nature? For in addition to being personal emotional recollections, the statements do provide insights into sectarian strife, violence and trauma—issues that are of central concern to the historian. If these records are an inadequate means of representing the trauma and the violence, what place do we find for these statements and why else do we retrieve them?

Urvashi Butalia, Ritu Menon and Kamla Bhasin who have engaged in the much needed task of reconstructing a 'people's history' of the Partition, through personal interviews with survivors, witnesses and social workers, argue that in the absence of official records about a 'people's history' and the difficulty of framing and establishing historical 'truths', personal testimonies become crucial to the revisionist historiographer's task of reconstructing an alternative history of the Partition. As Menon and Bhasin assert:

> When one is trying to unravel the complexity of an event that took place 45 years ago but that still reverberates in the general consciousness . . . without such an attempt [to retrieve testimonies] the myriad individual and collective histories that simultaneously run parallel to official accounts of historic moments and their sequel, almost inevitably get submerged; with them may also be submerged the countering of accepted—and acceptable versions to be buried eventually in the rubble of what Gyan Pandey has called the 'aberrations' of history.[28]

Accordingly, they foreground personal testimonies of destitute women to communicate an experience of the Partition through voices that have remained silent.[29] Such recovery of what Butalia calls 'hidden histories' of the people, especially women and children about whose stories of atrocities there continues to be a resounding silence, makes an important intervention in the dominant historiographical discourses about the Partition.[30]

Yet the fear of some survivors to confront the past and their inability to write and circulate these stories limits our access to such histories. Further, experiences as recounted in testimonies are ideologically constituted, depending on the personal location of the subject in that history and mediated by a wide array of factors: gender, religion, class-position, ethnicity or the political configuration of the moment within which they may be recalled.[31] The recollections of those with whom I spoke seemed mediated by these factors. One person, for example, while talking about the Partition, commented on the discriminatory policies of the present government against Sikh minorities. Another, whose family had once again experienced the trauma of the Indo-Pakistan War, held Muslims responsible for the problems. The women I spoke with, focused more on their own methods of orchestrating escape from the violence that apparently endangered their lives. Given these complexities, the reinscription of such testimonies into historical frames demands attention to their specific locations. However, our own lack of access to the personal, public, political or gendered circumstances within which they are located may handicap our reading of these testimonies.

Within this context, literary representations, that narrate the historical circumstances and insert the experiences of the people within specific sociological frames, become critical tools for reconstructing fragmented histories. Through the literary techniques of storytelling, dialogue, flashback and description they weave meaningful stories in which they debate and discuss questions of violence, agency and communalism. To make sense of personal testimonies, therefore, we need to return to the vast literary archives that both affirm the experiences of those who suffered during the Partition and function as a discursive space that allows the silenced subjects to speak, interpret and raise critical questions. By giving meaning to the stories of those whose struggles or acts of solidarity may otherwise remain obscure, literary and cultural artifacts, thus, signal the elaboration of an important archive and make a valuable contribution to the revisionist historiographer's project of recovering alternative histories. This is not because these texts make a claim to 'authenticity' or 'accuracy'. Rather, I believe that the poetic license assumed by literature affords the fictional means to corroborate the dark and compelling experiences of the time that remain etched in the collective consciousness of the millions affected by the Partition and allows writers to assume responsibility for what is forgotten and what they can reconstruct.

Bhisham Sahni in *Tamas* and Bapsi Sidhwa in *Cracking India*, both of whom saw Partition as the articulation of a painful historical moment, piece together memories of a history that speaks of those whose stories remain outside the orbit of the official historical discourse and rigorously question the precepts of official narratives. Written several decades after the Partition by those whose personal experiences are themselves located in the historical process of the Partition, the narratives engage a strategy of remembering the past to undertake the much needed task of historical reconstruction and analysis of events on the two sides of the Punjab. As such, they can be categorized as what David K. Herzeberger has termed, in the context of Spanish literature, the 'novel[s] of memory', albeit 'those fictions that evoke past time through subjective remembering, most often through first person narration'.[32] Further, since the project of recovery in this case is inscribed in the form of literary representation, the politics of the form are also critical. Set in a small town in the North West Frontier Province, Sahni's *Tamas*, is presented through a narrative fragmented into episodes which acquaint its readers with stories of territorial, religious, national and familial fragmentation. Seen through the eyes and mind of a child, Sidhwa's *Cracking India* presents a world that begins to disintegrate as the political, personal, communal and territorial parameters begin to develop cracks and fissures on the eve of the Partition in Lahore and its surrounding villages. Through a discussion of *Tamas* and *Cracking India*, the rest of the article discusses the role of literary representations in retrieving alternative narratives of the Partition and their intervention in dominant historiography.

II

> We want statistics, nothing but statistics. Just try to understand. I don't want stories. I want the bare figures—how many died, how many were injured and the extent of their financial loss! [33]

All the data collected in the course of the day was tabulated and classified in the late hours of the evening when the representatives of various newspapers turned up to collect the latest figures. One copy of the figures was sent to the Congress office. One copy was retained on file.[34]

These two excerpts from Sahni's novel *Tamas*, the first, a statement by the Record Clerk of the Relief Committee at the refugee camp after the riots, and the second, which is the author's comment about the purpose of this knowledge, encapsulate the problems underlying the dominant historiography of the Partition. Preoccupied with statistical analysis, data and the 'bare truth', this historiography imposes a methodology to produce a narrative that bears little resemblance to people's experiences and memories. Yet, it is precisely this commentary that allows Sahni's fiction to critically question the authority of dominant historiography in repressing and representing the Partition and to render official historical accounts contentious. An analysis of the Sidhwa and Sahni novels warrant, a return to the representation of the Partition in some of its dominant modes.

Dominant historiography of the Partition remains, for the most part, aligned with nationalist interests and focuses primarily on the origins of the Partition debates among the leaders and decision-makers; the role played by the Gandhis, Nehrus and Jinnahs in bringing the freedom struggle to completion through their numerous sacrifices and political acumen; their arguments and disagreements; divisions between political parties, such as the Congress and the Muslim League; the intervention of Mountbatten in effecting the division of the subcontinent; and the subsequent transfer of power to the governments of India and Pakistan. Such history writing continues to suppress the terrible human suffering and through such suppression seeks to engender a 'collective amnesia' about the past and create a myth about the illustrious achievements and glories of the nation and its leaders.[35] Furthermore, most histories, as Pandey points out, write the story of the Partition as a story of communalism. The reasons for this problem with historiography, he writes lie in the complicity between colonialist history writing and nationalist historiography. Marked by the dominance of the nationalist paradigm and based primarily on a reliance on the colonialist system of information retrieval, such historiography constructs a 'prose of Otherness' in which violence is only treated as 'mass sectarian violence' and 'reduce[s] history to a more or less generalized triumphant account of the triumphant march of modernity and progress'.[36] In the interest of producing seamless 'biographies of the nation state', such writings, as Pandey argues, plays a major role in shaping and organizing memory about significant events—in this case a kind of forgetting of the horrors of the Partition.

Such forgetting is further induced by a lack of official memorialization of the Partition. As Urvashi Butalia points out, the reason for this absence lies in the State's complicity in the horrors that ensued during the Partition, the complicity of brothers and fathers in killing women in the name of their 'honour' and the participation of men in raping women, not only from the other community and religion, but even those belonging to their own. Says Butalia, 'No matter how much Indian politicians, members of the Congress Party, tried to see themselves as reluctant players in the game, they could not escape the knowledge that they accepted Partition as the cost of freedom. Such histories are not easily memorialized.'[37] It is hardly surprising, then, as Butalia points out, to find the absence of an institutional memory of the Partition. She writes:

> The State has not seen fit to construct any memorials, to mark particular places—as has been done, say in the case of the holocaust memorials or memorials for the Vietnam war. There is nothing at the border [of India and Pakistan] that marks it as a place where millions of people crossed, no plaque or memorials at any of the sites of the camps, nothing that marks a particular spot as a place where Partition memories are collected.[38]

That nationalist interests continue to dominate the process of history writing also became visible during the year-long national commemoration of India's golden jubilee celebrations in 1997, which contributed largely to this myth-making about the nation and accorded little space to the tragic consequences of the Partition. A glance at two newspapers, one national and one regional, in English and Hindi—the *Times of India* and *Amar Ujala*—for the month of August 1997, provides at least a partial reflection of how the event was relegated to the margins during the euphoric commemorations of India's 50 years of independence from colonial rule.[39] The jubilant and celebratory accounts of India's independence in these newspapers, emphasized national heritage and 'unity in diversity' to instill in their readers pride in the nation's ideals of secularism and democracy. In all their euphoria they conveniently forgot to fully engage with the accompanying historical event of the Partition. With the global reach of the media and its ability to maintain links with the large Indian diaspora, such celebratory narratives were also disseminated internationally.

Special issues of an academic nature commemorating India's 50 years of independence also focused largely on the role of the statesmen and the politics of the Raj in discussions of the Partition. An example from a special issue of *History Today*, on the subcontinent during the 50 years after the Raj, illustrates this point. With the exception of Mushirul Hasan's

'Partition: The Human Cost',[40] the articles in this issue engage in the discourses and debates among the leadership, eschewing largely any discussion of the people.[41] Though *Granta* attempts to be more inclusive of the histories of the people, in Sanjeev Saith's photomemoirs of a largely heterogeneous group of people it, nonetheless, opens with an epigraph of Nehru's famous 'Tryst with Destiny' speech delivered on the eve of independence in 1947.[42] The epigraph apparently, is intended to dramatize the contrast between Nehru's reference to India's fulfillment of its 'tryst with destiny' at the much awaited hour of independence, with the simultaneous outburst of violence, massacre and dislocation in the partitioned states of Bengal and Punjab. However, in the absence of any commentary from the author, the epigraph suggests a reaffirmation of the mythical status accorded by dominant historiography and the State to India's first Prime Minister. As such, it functions as a reminder of the firm hold that the 'glorious' achievements of Nehru continue to have on the literate imagination.

Setting their novels on the eve of the Partition, Sahni and Sidhwa engage in the historical project of writing unrecorded histories and exposing the orthodoxies of the dominant historiography. Like the accounts that have survived in biographies, autobiographies, memoirs, diaries and personal testimonies of survivors, their novels recall similar stories with tremendous vividness and clarity and function as sites of cultural memory about a shared experience. The stories presented in both *Tamas* and *Cracking India* contribute to the recovery of the silenced voices, recalling significant moments as they were experienced and witnessed: riots, murder, brutality, suicide, dislocation, relocation, abduction, rape and exile. In recounting the incidents, the writers do not describe the events in a vacuum, but also provide a historical sense of the circumstances in which identities—religious, familial, communal, gendered and national—were continually formed, deformed and reconstructed in the process. For example, Hindus persecuted or were forcibly converted to Islam, Muslims persecuted or were persecuted and women's identities changed from being wives, mothers and sisters, to that of 'harlots', 'martyrs' or 'dishonored' women as thousands were raped and abducted.

As summarized in the blurb on the back cover of the English translation of *Tamas*, it is:

> Based on actual events, following the tragedies that unfold in the town when a pig, considered unclean by the Muslims, is found slaughtered on the steps of the local mosque. The enraged Muslims massacre scores of the town's Hindus and Sikhs who, in turn, kill every Muslim they can find. Finally, the area's British

administrators call out the army to prevent further violence. The killing stops but nothing can ever erase the awful memories from the mind of the survivors, nor will the various communities trust one another again.[43]

To provide possibilities for understanding the subjectivities of those who became victims and aggressors at the same time, depending upon the context and the location, Sahni recollects these memories. Yet inspite of the allegations made by certain special interest groups about *Tamas* being Communist propaganda, a distortion of history or an inflammatory tool against Hindus, when the novel was first televised as a mini-series in 1988, Sahni's text comes through as neither a piece of political propaganda nor a distortion of history.[44] Nor is the novel complicit with nationalist and official narratives in generating a 'collective amnesia', that Pandey has accused it of. In a comment on *Tamas*, Pandey claims:

> The story marks a return to a less subtle nationalist statement in which *agent provocateurs* and mysterious evil folk pulling the strings from behind the scenes mislead an innocent and bewildered, but brave people. Partition is represented here, moreover in the likeness of natural disaster in which human actions play little part; far removed from the run of daily life . . . this is also the line that respectable, academic nationalist historiography has followed.[45]

Contrary to Pandey's claim, I would like to argue that *Tamas* is a critique directed at the writing of a history that consciously engages in censoring the human side of this reality. Through the stories of Ranvir, eager to use his newly-acquired skill of taking a life after he kills a hen; the trepidation of Nathu, manipulated into killing a pig that sparks off the riots; apathy of the colonial administrator whose interest in India is restricted to the Taxila Museum so he can write his book after retiring to England; the political debates among self-serving representatives of the Congress, Hindu Mahasabha, Communist Party and the Muslim League; lackadaisical police vigilance; the persecution of men, women and children in large numbers; and the courage of those who helped others in times of great uncertainty, the novel opens a window to the highly complex, strained and historically contained realities of the politically explosive times.

Nowhere is the containment of this 'dark' side of history more visible than towards the end of the narrative in a refugee camp where, after exhaustion from several days of walking, rioting and witnessing the loss of properties, homes and loved ones, the refugees await the resolution of their futures. Here the Record Clerk in charge of collecting and compiling information to aid the government's relief operations is only interested in what he calls 'facts'. His statistical surveys have no room for the human drama. Sahni here seeks to reveal both the limitations of the Record Clerk's survey and to inscribe the stories of the men and women within the official records. Hence, the Record Clerk of the Relief Committee, whose quest for minimal information wipes the stories of the refugees out from his statistical compilations is constantly interrupted by Harnam Singh with his story about his and his wife's escape, about the fate of their son and daughter, of the many Sikh women and children who jumped into a well and about the women who were abducted or raped. As the frustrated clerk accumulates 'facts', for newspapers and the 'Congress Office', he systematically attempts to silence Harnam Singh:

> The Babu questioned the next man without taking his eyes off his register.
>
> 'Name?'
>
> 'Harnam Singh.'
>
> 'Father's name?'
>
> 'Sardar Gurdial Singh.'
>
> 'Village?'
>
> 'Dhok Ilahi Buksh.'
>
> 'Tehsil?'
>
> 'Noorpur.'
>
> 'How many Hindu and Sikh homes?'
>
> 'Only one Sikh house. My house.'
>
> The scribe raised his head from the register and looked at the man. He was old and tired. 'Rather surprising. How did you escape?'
>
> 'I was on good terms with Karim Khan. In the evening when. . . .'
>
> The scribe raised his finger gesturing him to stop. 'Any loss of life?'
>
> 'No. My wife and I escaped, complete in our limbs. My son, Iqbal Singh, was in Noorpur. But I've no news of him. My daughter, Jasbir Kaur was in Sayyedpur. She jumped into a well and died.'
>
> The scribe again raised an admonitory finger. 'I'm asking you, was there any loss of life?'
>
> 'I've told you my daughter jumped into . . .'
>
> 'But she didn't die in your village?'
>
> 'No, not in my village.'
>
> 'Then keep to the facts.'[46]

Through the alternating stylistic registers of language, Sahni seeks to unsettle the reader and draw attention to the problems encountered in official discourse. Bearing the characteristics of simultaneous reporting and emotionally laden testimony, such language provides a discursive interpretation to the official archive. It counters the officially proclaimed truths as recorded by the clerk, with the personal stories of the silenced subjects whose realities and their meanings are differently located within that history. Even though the Babu writes Harnam Singh's stories out of his records, the language Sahni uses in the exchange cited above, exposes the disjunctures between official record and personal narration. Through the relentless attempts of Harnam Singh to write in the story of his family, the conversation prevents the disclosure that he wants to make and displays what the official documentation seeks to achieve.

In *Cracking India*, the narrative shapes up in the form of the autobiographical voice of an eight year old girl, Lenny, whose observations of the details of the intense human and psychological relationships as they develop before, during and after the Partition, function as a self-consciously deployed tool that mediates the process of remembering and provides an interpretive meaning to historical events. The darling of her *ayah*, and of everyone else around her, Lenny, through the numerous relationships among the community of men, women and children that surrounds her, achieves an awareness of the connection between the politics of territorial boundaries, British imperialism and the complex formation of identities—religious, communal, gender and national. As the inevitability of the cracking up of India draws closer, a strong sense of religious identity seizes the characters. The eight year old Lenny, who does not comprehend fully the complexities of the political process, none the less senses a link between the politics of the Partition and identity politics. In recounting the situation, Lenny says:

> There is much disturbing talk. India is going to be broken. Can one break a country? . . .
>
> Gandhi, Jinnah, Nehru, Iqbal, Tara Singh, Mountbatten are names I hear.
>
> And I become aware of religious differences.
>
> It is sudden. One day everybody is themselves—and the next day they are Hindu, Muslim, Sikh, Christian. People shrink, dwindling into symbols. Ayah is no longer my all-encompassing Ayah—she is also a token. A Hindu.
>
> Imam Din and Yousaf, turning into religious zealots, warn Mother they will take Friday afternoons off for the Jumha prayers.[47]

These memories are later drawn upon and sorted out by the adult narrator who connects her personal life with imperial history:

> Playing British gods under the ceiling fans of the Faletti's Hotel—behind Queen Victoria's gardened skirt—the Radcliffe Commission deal out Indian cities like a pack of cards. Lahore is dealt to Pakistan. Amritsar to India. Sialkot to Pakistan. Pathankot to India.[48]

As these decisions made by colonial and national leaders finally split the nation, Lenny's world—surrounded by servants, her parents, *ayah*, Rodgers and her neighbours—collapses as well, severing personal ties and forcing new identities. 'In a snap', as Sidhwa says, the *dhoti*-clad Hari with a *bodhi* on his head, a mark of his caste for generations, becomes Himmat Ali. Also 'in a snap' the barber removes Hari's foreskin. He is forced to take up the *kalma* and replace his *dhoti* with the *shalwar*. And shortly thereafter, her beloved Hindu *ayah*, Shanta, becomes a 'fallen woman'. Like the thousands of women who were condemned as they were raped, tortured and 'dishonored' by the other community, the *ayah*, after being kidnapped and gangraped by the men she had known all her life, is forced into a life of prostitution in Hira Mandi, the red light district of Lahore, and renamed Mumtaz by the ice-candy man.[49] 'In a snap', Lenny's identity also changes: 'I am a Pakistani', she says. 'In a snap. Just like that. A new nation is born. India has been divided after all.'[50] Etched in her memory and recalled through the technique of storytelling, these and numerous other stories—about the gardener, her family, slave-sister, godmother, Rodgers, Bharucha, cousin, the ice-candy man and *ayah*—allow the narrator (and the author) to emplot the past, both as a way of recovering their untold stories and to highlight the complexities of identity, nationhood and history against the singular claims of historiographical authority about 'facts' and 'truths'.

In doing so, the author generates a sense of the historical circumstances, provides the contours and details of the several members of Lenny's family and community and establishes the differentiated contexts of economics, class, caste and ethnicity, transforming these details into useful webs of information for the readers' potential historical knowledge. For instance, by virtue of their class position, neither godmother, slave-sister nor Lenny's mother is subjected to the same fate as her *ayah*. Nor is her family faced with the same degree of violence as the servants. Further, the numerous discussions, interactions and changing relationships among the circle of family, friends and servants provide Lenny and the reader with a sense of the tensions and anxieties building up before the Partition. And through the patchwork of allusions to the British, the Quit India movement and leaders including Nehru, Jinnah and Gandhi, she situates the ongoing tensions before, during and after the country's Partition in a context that is inseparable from the imperial centre. References to the political figures and the cartographic violence inflicted on the subcontinent also usefully situate the human scale of violence in its socio-political context, disrupting, in the process, the claims of the dominant historiography that presents the Partition violence as a natural consequence of communal strife and sectarianism.

But none of the stories in the narrative build towards any coherent explanation. On the contrary, Lenny's questions and queries and her attempt to search for answers constantly interrupt the narrative. This refusal to impose coherence on the narrative through its fragmentary emplotment is part of a storytelling technique that can only rely on memories to evoke the past. Memories themselves being fragmentary and changing, the narrative too, as a consequence, veers between bits and pieces of the lives of various characters and presents the past not in fixed or static terms but one that makes itself open to reinterpretation, everytime an untold story is inscribed onto it.

Nowhere is the desire to disrupt a coherent narration challenged more forcefully than in 'Ranna's Story', a section that stands out as a separate piece in Sidhwa's novel. As a tale based on the personal experience of someone who Sidhwa thanks in her acknowledgements, Sidhwa carefully separates her own (and Lenny's) narrative from that of Ranna's chilling memories. On an emotional level, Ranna's life is inextricably bound up with Lenny's own childhood memories: early in the novel she recalls her visits to Ranna's village with Imam Din. Having had the protection of her upper middle class privilege and her Parsi ethnicity, Lenny, as a consequence, is not subjected to the same fate as Ranna. Even though the Parsis of Bombay had played an instrumental role in the nationalist struggle, the 300 or so Parsis in Lahore at the time of the Partition were 'distanced from the Hindus, Muslims, and Sikhs [and] sought a neutral position in the nationalist agitation surrounding them'.[51] Hence, the adult narrator who understands these socially constituted differences seeks not to trivialize Ranna's story. Instead, Sidhwa inscribes the narrator's narrative into her own literary representation to emplot, through this intertextuality, Ranna and numerous others subjected to a similar fate, as historical subjects whose identities and experiences are profoundly connected to their class, religion, ethnicity and the position of their community within the complex power relations in their villages. In giving a separate space to Ranna's story, Sidhwa teaches us invaluable lessons about her own careful intervention and representation of the stories of others. Her message is that this story is to be listened to and understood on its own terms.

III

Tamas and *Cracking India* are only two examples from the vast corpus of literary writing that offer a critique of the distortions of official histories. Simultaneously, scholars, oral historians and activists have embarked upon the much needed task of reconstructing a 'people's history' by gathering the stories and personal recollections of survivors and social workers. However, the difficulty of obtaining testimonies and making them available in the form of written accounts constantly limits our access to them. Until the latter undertaking shapes up into a distinctive genre of its own through the practice of writing out these testimonies, we need to continue to examine literary texts where we can find a fuller elaboration of personal stories as they are revived through the process of writing. The conventions of autobiography, storytelling, popular memory, description and the languages of reportage, insert personal stories into sociological frames and historical contexts to broaden the readers' understanding of the event and highlight the crucial place of these stories in the historiography of the Partition. Therefore, literary representations function as an important step in the process of making contact with the silenced voices on two counts. First, as evidenced in 'Ranna's Story', they engage in a dialogue with personal testimonies. And, secondly, through this intertextual dialogue between personal stories and fictional representation, they provide meaningful frames that function as sources of knowledge about the unknown stories of the Partition, marking in this way a critical intervention in the orthodoxies of official histories.

In the present post colonial milieu that has witnessed a resurgence of communalism and political strife in India, texts such as *Tamas* and *Cracking India* acquire a special relevance. As both Pandey and Butalia assert, with the new and emerging political contexts and configurations of power—the 1984 mass killings of Sikhs, following Indira Gandhi's assassination, the harassment of Muslims in India in the wake of a resurgent Hindu fundamentalism and the persecution of the *muhajirs* who moved back to Pakistan to reclaim their lost 'homeland'—the same theoretical questions about violence, agency and history resonate again.[52] It is to this urgency that literary works of the Partition continue to speak and raise questions regarding colonialism, democracy, secularism and violence, both state-orchestrated and otherwise. As real as the stories that I heard from my own family and friends, as well as those recorded by Butalia, Menon and Bhasin,[53] the stories recounted by Sahni and Sidhwa, thus, carry both historic and symbolic importance in the present. Recollected through memory, and elaborated through a multitude of social, cultural and linguistic registers, they remind their readers of the need to remember that which has been forgotten and aid the work of those engaged in attempting to reconstruct a 'people's history' of the Partition.

NOTES

1. Bapsi Sidhwa's novel first appeared in 1988 as *Ice-Candy Man* and was republished in 1991 under the new title *Cracking India* (USA, 1991), p. 149.
2. Michel Foucault, *Language, Counter-Memory, Practice, Selected Essays and Interviews*, trans. by Donald Bouchard and Sherry Simon (New York, 1980).
3. Khushwant Singh, *Train to Pakistan* (New York, 1956, also New Delhi, 1956)
4. Attia Hosain, *Sunlight on a Broken Column* (London, 1988).
5. Manohar Malgonkar, *A Bend in the Ganges* (Delhi, 1964).
6. Bhisham Sahni, *Tamas*, trans. by Jai Ratan (New Delhi, 1988).
7. Chaman Nahal, *Azadi* (New Delhi, 1979).
8. R.K. Narayan, *Waiting for the Mahatma* (East Lansing, 1955).
9. Anita Desai, *Clear Light of Day* (London, 1980).
10. Harwant Singh Bains, *Blood* (London, 1989).
11. Mushirul Hasan, *India Partitioned: The Other Face of Freedom*, Vols I and II (Delhi, 1995, 2nd edn 1997).
12. However, not all fictional texts contend with the problems that beset dominant historiography. As Alok Bhalla in his introduction to *Stories about the Partition of India*, 3 vols (New Delhi, 1994), points out, some writings underscore the assumptions of dominant historiography, presenting the Partition violence in terms of sectarian strife and communalism.
13. Ibid, pp. xxx-xxxi.
14. Gyanendra Pandey, 'In Defence of a Fragment. Writing about Hindu-Muslim Riots in India Today', *Economic and Political Weekly*, Vol. XXVI, 1991, p. 560.
15. Urvashi Butalia, 'Community, State and Gender: On Women's Agency During the Partition', ibid., Vol. XXVIII, No. 17, 24 April 1993, pp. WS12-WS24; and Ritu Menon and Kamla Bhasin, *Borders and Boundaries, Women in India's Partition* (Delhi, 1998).
16. Urvashi Butalia, 'Breach of Faiths', *Far Eastern Economic Review*, 28 August 1997, p. 45.
17. Being part of the generation that grew up on stories that pervaded dinner time conversations and circulated in social gatherings among family and friends who were personally affected by the Partition, I felt the need to write about their stories. A class on 'Poetry and Partition' at the University of Texas in 1992 led me to record the stories of some friends and family members. I would like to acknowledge the Barbara Harlow's 'Poetry and Partition' seminar that led me to think about the subject further and in critical terms.
18. I would like to thank Amrik Singh Seera, Harbans Singh Bhatia, Leelavanti Bhatia, Amro Dhillon and Dalbir Singh Aulakh for sharing their experience.
19. Pandey, op.cit.; Butalia, 'Community, State and Gender', op.cit.; and Ritu Menon and Kamla Bhasin, 'Recover, Rupture, Resistance: Indian State and Abduction of Women During Partition', *Economic and Political Weekly*, Vol. XXVIII, No. 17, 24 April 1993, WS2-WS12.
20. Mushirul Hasan, *India's Partition: Process, Strategy and Mobilization* (Delhi, 1993).
21. Ayesha Jalal, *The Sole Spokesman: Jinnah, the Muslim League and the Demand for Pakistan* (Cambridge, 1985).
22. Stanley Wolpert, *Jinnah of Pakistan* (New York, 1994).
23. Anita Inder Singh, *The Origins of the Partition of India, 1936-1947* (Delhi, 1991).
24. See the works of Butalia, Menon and Bhasin and Pandey cited elsewhere.

25. Gyanendra Pandey, 'The Prose of Otherness', in David Arnold and David Hardiman, eds, *Subaltern Studies VIII* (Delhi, 1994), p. 214.
26. Idem., 'In Defence of a Fragment', op.cit., p. 559.
27. Huma Ibrahim, 'The Troubled Past, Literature of Severing and the Viewer/Viewed Dialectic', in Deepika Bahri and Mary Vasudeva, eds, *Between the Lines, South Asians and Postcoloniality* (USA, 1996), p. 308.
28. Menon and Bhasin, 'Recover, Rupture, Resistance', op.cit., WS 2.
29. Also see idem, *Borders and Boundaries*, op.cit. The authors argue that while there is no dearth of material on the Partition, there remains an absence of a feminist historiography. To compensate for this absence, they compile interviews with women survivors of the Partition.
30. Urvashi Butalia, 'Hidden Histories', *Index on Censorship*, Vol. IV (1995), pp. 81-8.
31. I do not mean to suggest that scholars have not thought through the issue of cultural memory. In fact, Menon and Bhasin, Butalia and Pandey carefully ground the complexity of the process of memory retrieval.
32. David K. Herzeberger, 'Narrating the Past: History and the Novel of Memory in Postwar Spain', *PMLA*, Vol. LVI, No. 1, 1991, pp. 34-45.
33. Bhisham Sahni, op.cit., p. 214.
34. Ibid., p. 220.
35. Pandey, 'The Prose of Otherness', op.cit.
36. Ibid., p. 193.
37. Urvashi Butalia, *The Other Side of Silence: Voices From the Partition of India* (Delhi, 1998), p. 272.
38. Ibid.
39. Both newspapers, the *Times of India*, a national daily published in English, and *Amar Ujala* a regional newspaper in Hindi published in Bareilly, Uttar Pradesh, enjoy a wide readership. However, I should mention *Outlook* for its special issue on the Partition and *India Today* for special features in its issue on 50 years of independence. My thanks to Tarun Tejpal for bringing to my attention the Partition issue of *Outlook*.
40. Mushirul Hasan, 'Partition: the Human Cost', in *History Today*, Vol. XCVII, No. 9 (1997).
41. See Jean Alphonse Bernard, 'Bengal and Panjab: Before and Beyond', in ibid., pp. 28-33; Alan Campbell-Johnson, 'Mountbatten and the Transfer of Power', in ibid., pp. 34-40; and Francis Robinson, 'The Muslims and Partition', in ibid.
42. Sanjeev Saith, 'Freedom', *Granta*, Vol. CVII, 1997, pp. 23-36.
43. Bhisham Sahni, op.cit.
44. Govind Nihalani, 'Introduction', in Bhisham Sahni, op.cit., p. 8.
45. Pandey, in 'Defence of a Fragment', op.cit., p. 561. For a discussion of the 'the literary' as a resource for historical research see Jill Didur, 'Fragments of Imagination: Re-thinking the Literary in Historiography through Narratives of India's Partition', http://152.1.96.5/jouvert/issue2/Didur.htm.
46. Bhisham Sahni, op.cit., p. 215.
47. Sidhwa, op.cit., p. 101.
48. Ibid., p. 180.
49. For a detailed study of abducted women, see Menon and Bhasin, *Borders and Boundaries*, op.cit.
50. Sidhwa, op.cit., p. 180.

51. For an in-depth study on the Parsis in India, See T.M. Luhrmann *The Good Parsi*, *The Fate of a Colonial Elite in a Postcolonial Society* (Massachusetts, 1996).
52. Pandey, in 'Defence of a Fragment', op.cit., and Butalia, 'Community, State and Gender', op.cit.
53. See Menon and Bhasin, 'Recovery, Rupture, Resistance: Indian State and Abduction of Women during Partition', op.cit., idem, *Borders and Boundaries*, op.cit., Butalia, 'Community, State and Gender: On Women's Agency During the Partition', op.cit., and idem, *The Other Side of Silence*, op.cit.

Partition Relived in Literature

ANINDITA MUKHOPADHYAY

The other face of India's independence in 1947 was Partition. The terrible human tragedy created around a total of 12 million refugees on both sides and left around a million dead. They had left their homes for a safer haven, but with uncertainty at their journey's end: many women had been exposed *en route* to the savagery of communal violence, were raped or were killed. Yet, references to the Partition in literature are not as plentiful as they should be. For Ashis Nandy it is a national trauma that had to be forgotten, because memory could not relive the traumatic experience and still remain focused on the national issues of governance and security both external and internal. Tormented voices mourning for the dead, for the lost, had to be swept out of hearing, denied their histories, just so that the task of nation building could be carried on uninterrupted. Urvashi Butalia, even with her personal background of a refugee family history, has attested to the lack of meaning of Partition to her own generation.[1] Her exposure to the stories of Partition that circulated in her family in her formative years had not prepared her for the reality of the communal riots that murdered more than 3,000 Sikhs in 1984, in the wake of Indira Gandhi's assassination.[2] The year 1984 had opened the floodgates of memory, with all the bitterness of coming full circle for many. Yet, without this trigger, these memories might have remained buried. Literature had allowed itself to forget them.

This silence has also remained unexamined. Was it because even an acknowledgement of the deeper roots of the Hindu-Muslim communal conflict, beyond the machinations of a foreign ruler, at the very moment of the assertion of the people's right to rule themselves, would nullify all that was fought for over the last 70 years? The cause, therefore, had to be seen as political, had to be the manoeuvering of a third party with imperialistic designs, it could not be the lack of understanding within the two communities. Authors maintained a near total silence on the subject because at this point, when the national agenda of nation building was so clear, their doubts and fears had to suffer the fate of the national memory—they had to be buried into oblivion. Partition, therefore, remained the proverbial Pandora's Box even for authors like Tarashankar Bandyopadhyaya, a classic example of a forceful pen remaining almost mute on Partition. This was especially ironic as this silence followed hard on the heels of many passionate representations of India's struggle for freedom in his novels. The final gory rupture after three decades of hope for an ultimate harmony between the two communities proved too painful to be addressed. An author like Sadaat Hasan Manto could express the phobias of the two communities, starkly and brutally, but not many had the courage to do so, even if they had so desired.

An author who shilly-shallied between the political language of *divide et impera*, the accepted template for dealing with the Partition as a political event, that passed into the history textbooks of free India, and the deeper *malaise* hidden underneath, was a Bengali—Sharadindu Bandopadhyaya. Strangely, he himself was not aware of the ambiguity of his position as a recorder of deep subconscious schisms and the superficial, much toted political reason given by all the leaders of the Indian freedom struggle. He hardly dared to gaze at the violence that had ripped through the underbelly of the country but managed to take a few sidelong glances. Symbolically, he never took up the issue of Partition directly in any one of his stories or plays. In five stories, however, the brooding, malignant presence of communal passions in the background, waiting to be fanned to a blaze, underscore his thematic handling of violence and the tremendous feeling of insecurity this generated amongst the middle classes in Bengal. Only two of his detective stories, *Adim Ripu* (Primeval Enemy) and *Rakter Daag* (The Bloodstain), a novel, *Rimjhim* (Pitter Patter) and two short stories, 'Bisher Dhnoya' (The Poisonous Smoke) and 'Dui Dik' (Both Sides),[3] have the theme of Partition violence as a grim and cheerless background music.

It is apparent that Bandopadhyaya was completely caught between the spectacle of the violence that was played out in the two new countries and the immense task the Partition presented to the new India. The effect is weird. It is almost as if the author is trying his best to keep his pen and vision focused on the unfolding of the story, but the explosion of the raw passions of his times would keep bursting in onto his story-line, forcing the pace, goading the central characters to act, ruminate and judge. Citizens of the country, before the new nation had even counted one day of freedom, had to think of damage control. And this came in the shape, for many, especially the literati, in the dream of a secular India—the Nehruvian vision of all religions coexisting peacefully in the public sphere, while people quietly explored different religious paths in private, an idyllic middle class solution to all the problems that communal passions could throw up. The beauty of this vision lay in the fact that communal hatred could be relegated mainly to the lower classes who, it was believed, could be goaded by unscrupulous politicians and criminal elements of either religious hue into a mad fury against each other because of an unenlightened approach to religion. The élite could profess tolerance and armour themselves with a flawless brand of secularism, devoid of the vulgarity of religious passions, a mental state described well by Satish Deshpande:

> Giving all religions a secular status would obviate the need for communalism. Thus the Nehruvian era created the privileged, pan Indian elite that could, by and large, afford to cut loose its regional moorings. Not only did this elite seem to be placeless, it also appeared to be casteless, classless, a truly secular modern elite. It spoke in the idiom of secular nationalism, scientific technology, and economic development. By adopting this idiom the elite was able to render invisible its own ascriptive markers. The fact [was] that it was almost exclusively upper caste and middle class, and that it came from a very select cultural background.[4]

Bandopadhyaya fits into this mould well. A successful author, he had stripped himself of any obvious label of overt religiousity. He was the quintessential patriarchal and a liberal Hindu, whose writings reveal the layers of middle class life through the genre of detective fiction, short stories and novels. The national and familial events merge smoothly into seamless pieces of writing, and these five stories are no exception. Of these perhaps the most significant is *Adim Ripu*, because it personifies the struggle of the author to face the chaotic movement of history that had brought the two communities, Hindus and Muslims, face to face with each other without the intervening imperial power, Britain. In this story he has captured the intense feelings of euphoria and doom mingling in the same moment. It was a time of contradictory emotions pulling in different directions, when at least 30 years of hope for a free India were realized, though a sense of deep loss and for some, even a sense of deep betrayal, made the moment bitter. There was an upsurge of hate as communal frenzy gripped the Bengali community and there was a rush of hope in a new future without that constant thorn in the flesh—the other community. This story possibly could only have been written in 1955, for by then the author had acquired a certain distance from the events of the 1940s and could look at the two sides with detachment. He could even distance himself from the violence that had ripped through Bengal:

Ever since the Second World War, in Bengal, especially in the city of Calcutta, the premium put on human lives has been very low indeed. We had enslaved Life and Death to our whimsical fancies during the Bengal Famine of 1943. But when Direct Action Day was declared by Jinnah Saheb, we fell completely in love with the God of Death.[5]

The author's favourite detective protagonist, Bomkesh Bakshi, the possessor of a razor-sharp intelligence that penetrated all mysteries, and his dear friend Ajit, were rendered helpless before the communal violence that turned men into demons. Murder and mayhem needed here no keen-eyed detective to unravel its motives and twists of events—they were celebrated as bold deeds. Dead bodies littered the roads one moment, they were taken away by police vans the next—and life continued for the citizens of Calcutta under the pall of heavy menace and lurking danger. Where was the mystery and awe of death?

The underworld came alive under the cover of communal violence. To the fear of the knife held in the hands of the other community was added the fear of the *goonda* who exacted his own charge for the continued safety of the Calcuttans who lived in his locality. Caught between the devil and the deep blue sea, Ajit and Bomkesh also paid the price of safety and kept the line of communication open with the underworld with a steady supply of cigarettes and tea when the local *goonda* came to collect his forced levy. 'While in Rome do as the Romans do' became the idiom of the day for survival. Also, as far as practicable, 'take care of your own' was yet another key to survival and Bomkesh took no chances with his wife and son—they remained safely in Patna, away from the communal violence and criminal lawlessness alike.

Bandopadhyaya gives us voices, from both the Hindu and the Muslim sides, speaking in various tones, expressing their own views about the march of events and telling their stories in their own way. Bandopadhyaya's own anxieties about the nature of the violence resonate through the convictions and doubts of his characters that he captures in cameos. One class he has no doubt about, is the *goonda*, and here the Hindus and the Muslims are so similar, that not even the difference of a pin is to be found between them. In *Adim Ripu*, it is a Hindu, Bantul *sardar*, who wields the stick in a Hindu majority area and whose word is law in both the alleys and in respectable homes. In 'Dui Dik', it is Noor Mian who is the uncrowned king of crime in a Muslim majority area. They are conscienceless and motiveless and are violence personified. They just take *danga* as a convenient shield and indulge themselves behind it. The subtext to this *goonda* raj is that they are the ones who keep the *danga* alive by putting together their private armies of cutthroats and launching attacks and counter attacks.

Bantul *sardar* is the tamer of the two. Short, with a red smear of vermilion on his oily forehead, he is content with terrorizing respectable people and inducing them to part with their hard-earned money. The more ominous armed expeditions into enemy territory is merely hinted at—for, after all, he is the self-styled protector of the locality and is supposed to conduct these activities on the war zones of Calcutta just to maintain his self-respect as a self-sustaining *goonda*. He has a secret hoard of revolvers and rifles bought from the American soldiers during the war. These he tries to sell to his more favoured clients, like Ajit and Bomkesh, unctuously saying that revolvers are useful things to have in times of turmoil, for he could not be on guard all the time. A benign well-wisher, he seems to hold the motto of the Delhi police of the 1990s, 'With you, for you, always' close to his heart.

When Noor Mian comes onto the scene, the concept of violence changes. Noor Mian is captured through the eyes of a young Hindu doctor who had set up his dispensary in a Muslim majority area at the junction between Mechobazaar and Badurbagan. It turned into an epicentre of communal violence, principally because of Noor Mian. Years later, one lazy evening, when his friends had gathered for an evening chat, the doctor, with professional success behind him, recalled those days of horror. Without any rhyme or reason, he said, one fine morning suddenly the Muslims and the local *marwaris* started cutting each other's throats. The initial violence escalated into a blood bath and the doctor witnessed three to four murders on his very doorstep. His consciousness of his helpless position, as a lone Hindu in a Muslim majority area, prevented him from helping the unfortunate victims.

The man who masterminded all these murders was Noor Mian. He had become a byword for lawlessness in the area, the undisputed king of the jungle. He had three or four mistresses, all forcibly kidnapped from respectable houses. He openly ran an illegal business of cocaine, yet the police dared not put him behind bars. During the riots Noor Mian would lie in wait for an unwary Hindu in a convenient alley quite close to the dispensary. Any unsuspecting Hindu passing through the locality, would inevitably end up with Noor Mian's one and a half foot knife stuck either in his stomach or his back. After a number of these murders had been committed, the Hindus became wiser and came as hunters instead, armed to the teeth, much to the relief of the doctor. Noor Mian and his cronies, under these circumstances, would disappear perforce into their lairs, and reappear only when the rival group had left. When Noor Mian became unemployed; conversely, the locality became relatively peaceful.

The doctor, in this reconstruction of the past, dwells on his own reactions to Noor Mian. As the lone Hindu in a Muslim dominanted area, he had to reluctantly submerge his Hindu identity and live as inconspicuously as possible. He only kept alive his identity as a doctor who saved lives regardless of the Hindu or Muslim identities of the wounded thronging to his dispensary at all hours. But this deliberate scissoring of an essential part of his identity had filled his mind with resentment, a resentment that was only tempered by his refusing to buckle down as a professional. If his fear had got the better of him at that juncture, he felt that he could never have faced himself again, whatever the world outside might have thought of him. But this intense sense of helplessness and shame could not be hidden years later before his friends, to whom the memories of those days were also just as real. The deeply felt fear was a shared memory, before which all the finer feelings of human beings had fled and in its stead was a desire to survive at all costs, whatever the price. It was almost as if the doctor and the friends shared a bond of remembrance that excluded all those who did not know, who could not know and, therefore, must be for ever locked out of the charmed circle. No amount of storytelling could compensate for the void in the memory: it was a pointless exercise to retell and relive what the others had seen; while the obverse of it was the pointlessness of retelling and reliving the memories when there was no latent memory to jog one into the present. So when the doctor said, 'I do not see the least necessity of describing the macabre sights in detail: you had all been in Calcutta in those days, you have all witnessed a little or much of that I have seen', not a single voice asked for more details of 'those days'. The circuit of remembrance, through a shared silence, was complete.

To see human beings killed would have been a disturbing experience for anyone, but to have witnessed wholesale murder of Hindus in riots, being a Hindu himself, had devastated the doctor. His mind was filled with hate and contempt for Noor Mian and he felt a keen sense of empathy for the hapless victims. Nobody was more relieved than the doctor when the Hindus outside the locality got the danger signals loud and clear and stopped coming alone. But to his horror and dismay, after two days of inactivity, Noor Mian suddenly had another opportunity of killing a Hindu. This time it was a up-country Hindustani (a *pashchimi khotta*), wrapped in a shawl, with a tuft of hair on his head like a flag, proudly flaunting his Hindu identity to all and sundry. With heavy *nagra* shoes on his feet, he came walking down Noor Mian's hunting ground. The doctor, a typical product of Bengali respectability, in normal times would never have had a feature in common with a '*chotidhari* [tufted] Hindustani', but now all the doctor's suppressed Hindutva flared in alarm and admiration at this deliberate provocation. This instant identification with someone who was brave enough to be blatantly Hindu was apparent when he reminisced: 'As soon as I set eyes on him, my heart jumped into my mouth! Oh, my God! Surely, Noor Mian is going to come now with his one and a half foot long knife.' And come he did. He sprang on his victim from behind but then suddenly the scales turned. The victim whirled round, whipped out two knives from underneath the shawl, plunged both into Noor Mian, and left with both his hands tucked innocently under his shawl.

Then began the doctor's own personal battle—his instincts to let Noor Mian die fought hard with his desire to save a critically wounded man. His own mental applause and a sense of vindication when he witnessed a Hindu killing a Muslim in front of his eyes was the reaction of a triumphant Hindu, not that of an ethical doctor. From the moment the man crawled to the door of his dispensary, covered in blood and mud, the doctor wrestled with himself—'I felt like letting the wretch lie there and die—as you sow, so shall you reap! Let him atone for his sins with his face ground down into the mud! But as a doctor I just could not do that.' A brief conversation with the man did nothing to improve his state of mind—for Noor Mian was trying to buy his life and safety: '*Dagdarsaheb*, save my life, I will give you one lakh rupees.' The doctor was irritated: 'That's what I am trying to do, I am sending you to Medical College.' But the man pleaded, 'Don't send me to *Mitiya* College *babu*, they are all Hindu doctors there—they will poison me.' This aspersion on his profession further irritated the doctor—he taunted him with all the hate of the past few days, packed in a few syllables: 'Sure they can, all the doctors of *Mitiya* College are like you. But I can also poison you, I am also a Hindu.' With his last breath, before he fainted, Noor Mian said 'No, *dagdarsaheb*, you will not do that.'[6]

An injured sick Muslim man who trusted him—here was a situation where the doctor was torn between his hate and his professional duty to save a life. He himself professed amazement at the way his conscious mind at every step was divided into two—when he wanted to give Noor Mian poison, he gave him fruit juice, when the delirious man yelled out, '*Maaro* Hindu, *maaro* Hindu' he pressed ice bags to his head. The doctor in him won even this time, the Hindu in him lost. In no other story dealing with Partition has Sharadindu Bandopadhyaya explored the limitless potential of the human mind. The doctor knew that there was a dialogic space within his mind, where a vengeful Hindu identity was being appealed to with every step of the diffusion of violence against his imbibed professional ethics.

Adim Ripu, written much earlier, has also looked at the Partition but, because it bore the imprint of a political crisis that suspended judgement, there is a lack of clarity in many of its ideological convictions. Partition and independence at this point had collapsed into historical time and space, back to back, and the retrieval of the former could only be partial. The restrictive corset of colonial historiography was also responsible for this. History meant political events and political figures. The capturing of people's voices, not just the recorded voices of the leaders, had not been perceived to be necessary. Thus, the accepted norm of a political reason behind the Hindu-Muslim tension was not even questioned. Instead of looking into the depths of the problem, the author all too readily, like the other intellectuals of his time, tried to see the Partition as a political move forced on the Indians by an alien ruler, albeit one with tragic consequences. He avoids the questions—'Why the violence? Where does it come from?' Yet a deep disquiet refused to be allayed with his own vapid political rhetoric and would rear up its head at unexpected moments—telling the reader that the author was aware that 'Something is rotten in the state of Denmark.'[7]

In *Adim Ripu*, the degree of preparedness of the protagonist, Bomkesh and his friend Ajit, to meet any eventuality as a consequence of Direct Action Day, was such that even on the night of the worship of Goddess Kali, they would not venture out of doors. The *Deepavali* festivities, the milling people in the streets, the constant noise, fire and flash of fire crackers, the loud gaiety, was resonant for them with a very different kind of noise—the beating of the war-drums heralding communal violence. Ajit, with the excitement of the festivities throbbing in the air, dismissed the celebrations as idiocy:

> Countless people were roaming about in the streets. . . . The poised sword of communal riots were hanging over our heads, but the people were heedless of danger. . . . We certainly would not object to anyone calling us cowards, but we have a strong objection to dancing about in ignorant bliss like a garlanded kid [of the four legged variety] consecrated to the sacrificial stocks.[8]

Uncertain times, indeed, when the exuberant noise of festivities could be loaded with menace and the hubbub of many voices could portend something other than mere enjoyment. A frenzied banging on the door that very night breaking into their sleep, immediately brought the possibility of Direct Action finally at their very doorstep. It made them leap out of their beds with heavy sticks, prepared to fight to the last. Yet, it merely turned out to be a part of their lives in normal times—a man murdered, a corpse to be accounted for. At times like this, Bandopadhyaya's indictment of the selfishness of the British rulers dividing up the country, rings hollow:

Independence, in a bloody form, was approaching with hesitant steps on wounded feet, crossing near-impassable barriers. To keep it alive, every Indian would have to wring out their heart's blood . . . may be it would remain alive even though rent asunder by the sword wielded by the foreign rulers made cruel by self-interest.[9]

In a strange way, Bandhopadhyaya does try to come to grips with the question that just could not be wished away. Whose responsibility was this bloodbath? In a little cameo he captures the state of his own troubled mind. Ajit's dear childhood friend, Fajloor Rehman, bursts into the scene, complete with *sherwani* and *pyjamas*, an advocate in the Patna High Court and a committed Pakistani. Immediately after bearhugs have been exchanged, both the friends engage in a verbal bout, totally playful and sadly also totally serious. In one moment they take the debate of the inevitability of the Partition, between India and Pakistan, to the playground where they have grown up and scrapped together and where, naively (and to the reader, forlornly), they felt that the terribly costly debate could be resolved. In the next moment, they come straight to the heart of the matter—when there is trust, friends are capable of doing just that, and touch the rawest of wounds with lightheartedness and laughter:

Ajit [sticking his neck out]: 'Fajlu, here is my neck, take out your knife!'

Fajlu [handing his own heavy stick to Ajit and bending his head down]: 'Ajit, here is my stick, feel free to hit me on my head. You people can do anything!'[10]

A joke between friends, but with a lingering aftertaste of the bitter. As the two friends went hammer and tongs at the two-nation debate, it was again ironical that the two friends arrived at an impasse. Ajit was a liberal Hindu and an ardent nationalist, while Fajlu wanted Pakistan but both wanted to apportion responsibility. Fajlu dismissed his friend with familiarity: 'Bomkeshbabu, it is useless to argue with Ajit, he never did have any brains, but you are an intellectual, tell me now, whose fault is all this—Hindus or the Muslims?' It is surely the author's own voice, through the dispassionate remark of Bomkesh, that the reader can hear:

Ashes and cinders all,
Faults or virtues of either cannot be told.[11]

Bandopadhyaya, while unable to commit himself to any side, either Hindu or Muslim, does not even mention the British—they had slipped out of his mind! The magic cloak that hid an uncomfortable truth had been forgotten. He came to the conclusion that friendship, understanding and gentle humour would make the necessary space for the different point of view. But sadly, only in the case of individual spaces, for community spaces it seemed a distant dream, as the 'mad jealousies and burning rage' culminated again and again in the 'demonic dance of death and destruction'. This was the domain of incomprehension, which rational minds could not understand, when 'one fine morning the Muslims and the *marwaris*, without any warning, could just start cutting each other's throats'. Implicit in the statement was a contempt for the 'mob', which in Bengali middle class parlance meant the unreasonable illiterate and easily incited fanatic low-class elements, both Hindu and Muslim. It also shows the panic which mindless violence could evoke in a rational professional like the doctor. When such rabid suspicion and hate took over, people like Fajloor Rehman could be murdered in cold blood just because he was convinced about the rightness of his cause and had the courage to profess his views openly. Where was the space for dialogue here? Or when the old, harmless bookbinder, Ishaq Khan, could be murdered and his shop gutted because he happened to be a Muslim. Educated people on either side could not indulge in such atrocities in cold blood, there was a chance of communication, but some others, who refused to see the other point of view, were eaten up with hate and distrust.

Sharadindu Bandopadhyaya, in yet another story, *Rakter Daag*, tells us of the form this hate could take in an educated, college going young man, cerebral enough to read Gorky's *Lower Depths* in the silent hours of the night. Conducting investigations of the murder of his client, Bomkesh had to interview the murdered man's cousin, Sitangshu. Both Ajit and Bomkesh were struck by the young man's eyes, which held 'all the sharp, meditative intentness of an owl'. This unflinching gaze led Bomkesh to ask for more information about the young man from the police officer investigating the case. The police officer informed him of the boy's police record. He said, 'He was a very nice boy, but in the last riots in Calcutta [1946], his father was murdered by the Muslims, and since then, his nature has changed completely. To my sure knowledge, he has killed at least three Muslims, but I have no proof.' Later Bomkesh asked Sitangshu outright about the veracity of the rumour. Sitangshu did not deny it—'his neck swelled with passion as he answered—"Yes, they were murdered . . ." "I know", said Bomkesh—"How did you murder them?"

Sitangshu replied without any hesitation,"With a knife".'[12] Unknown people falling prey to a knife wielded by a person who had sworn vengeance for a public/private tragedy. There was a tragic element to such a complete severing in communication. Bandhopadhyaya explores the tragic dimensions of the cost of such a lack of communication both at the domestic site and at the national level in a love story, 'Bisher Dhnoya'.[13]

The protagonist Kishor falls in love with Suhashini, a neighbourhood girl and everything is set in train for their wedding, when mistrust breaks up the perfect understanding between the young couple. Neither of them can communicate their desire for a reconciliation. The girl believed she had been betrayed by a faithless fiance. Kishor, likewise, withdrew into a hurt silence, considering it beneath his dignity to proclaim his fidelity. When matters are poised on the brink of an irreversible rupture between the two, the riots intervene, shattering like glass an artificially created situation, showing in the hour of need everybody in their true colours. The story assumes almost allegorical proportions, when the mad jealousies and hate raging through the national scene find echoes in the familial jealousies and misunderstandings that threaten to disrupt domestic happiness. The author seems to suggest that lack of communication lay at the root of all mistrust, vitiating personal and community relationships alike. The closure of communication lines by communities could unleash limitless violence, by engendering a spiralling and growing intensity of mistrust and hate within communities. Flash points of crisis only deepen the rift and the hate.

The flaring violence in the wider social context also had the power of imploding into domestic space, inflicting intense mental and physical hardships on the members of a family. The author seems to mourn, that there are no remedies for the breakdown of communication between communities and this only results in tragic consequences for the nation. The volcanic eruption of hate on Direct Action Day on 16 August 1946, sent violent convulsions rippling through the city. Even though the militia from Fort William was guarding all the main crossroads, the killings went on unabated in the alleys and bylanes of Calcutta. Murder on the streets became painful reminders, poisoning the well of good feeling and trust shared by communities. Kishor, gazing at the deserted streets, reflected sorrowfully, 'A little distance away, there was a long rusty blood-stain on the footpath. Some wretch had fallen under the knife and had breathed his last on the spot. On the empty street, that stain looked like a raw wound festering within the very bosom of the earth.'[14]

At the individual level, there were chances of reconciliation. A sudden crisis could drive individuals closer together. Thus, when the threat of annihilation in the face of erupting violence, prevented even trusted servants from going out to bring the necessary medication for her ailing father, all the jealousies and suspicions of Suhashini are scattered and, of course, Kishor gets the medicine. But he is seriously hurt in the process, a prey to a nameless hand wielding a heavy stick. As a victim of the larger violence outside, Kishor's injury at the hands of a fanatic turns into a domestic crisis, the public wrong turns dramatically into private pain and paradoxically, helps to lay the domestic jealousies and bitterness at rest.

Tragically at the national level, what was perpetrated on the streets had no private remedy, the public could not or was unable to purge itself of the traumatic memories. Nelson Mandela and South Africa were still waiting in the future to unlock the secret of forgiveness. What Bandopadhyaya hoped for was a parting of ways, a nation-state without such strife, a happily-ever-after expectation in the future. The past had to be forgotten in the march towards the future. Marching instructions 'Ey-y-y-e-e-s front, left, left, left-right-left' neatly symbolized this desire not to look backwards. The hope lay in the citizen of new India, with equal parts of good and bad mixed in him. Bomkesh exhorted one such new citizen of new India, Prabhat, to believe in himself as a human being and forget his own past, which should then hide for ever the fact that he had killed his own father, who had been a scoundrel and a criminal:

> Be brave, Prabhat *babu*. Who does not have tainted blood in his veins? Don't forget, the human race has evolved from animals. After a long evolution stretching over millions of years, man has partly rid himself of his apishness . . . if one really tries, it is not difficult to overcome the ties of blood. Forget the past. . . . You are the new citizen of new India, you are independent from both within and without.[15]

But this did not mean that Sharadindu Bandopadhyaya had no place for memories in his brave new world. 'Bisher Dhnoya' ends with the young child of Suhashini and Kishor being told for the umpteenth time the bloody story of his parents reconciliation during the riots, by his aunt, a much-repeated and favourite reward for being a good boy and for getting into bed without any fuss. The storyteller and the listener knew each and every word of story and the storytelling itself was a ritual, for the listener prompted the aunt with the past events if she showed signs of being overwhelmed by her own rush of memories. The parents, wondering at the sound of voices, would go up to investigate and would be drawn, in their turn, into the past, a past wrapped in the warm and fragrant present. The tight family circle was complete and memory was passing onto the future. The implications of this individual family memory is for the reader to guess. It might be presumed that traces of memory, with these aids to remembrance passing on through family history, would shape an individual's mental topography when it came to relations with and opinions about the 'other'. While exclusion of people from the shared memory of a common experience shut out vicarious participation in the event by the like-minded, individual histories of pain and violence passed on through the conduit of family histories, shaped individual opinions and prejudices.[16] The author, too, in his reconstruction of the happy-ever-after situation and in his portrayal of the idyllic family unit, has slipped into a subconscious world of envisaging the 'other' as the enemy, the potential destroyer of domestic happiness. Insidiously and surreptitiously his prejudices have stained the lives of his protagonists; the author has unconsciously betrayed himself.

However, all this was in the context of violence and the loss of human lives. The author had to confront other problems in his capacity as an intellectual who straddled a period that arched over the immediate years before the Partition and independence, a period that collapsed both the events together and defied all attempts at separation and the post-independence period. The refugees pouring into West Bengal around this time could not be ignored but there is a half-hearted attempt to put them into the picture. The majority of the victims were suffering from some kind of deprivation or the other—loss of homes, employment, land, property, honour, for many women, and loss of family members. About all these there is near total silence. The silence is broken only at rare moments, and at these points some of the prejudices of the author come through, in a vignette or two. First, these families are poor, had known better days in East Bengal, but because they are uprooted, they have fallen upon evil days in independent India. And second, they are completely unscrupulous as to where they get their money from.

In *Adim Ripu*, there is one such man from Dhaka in East Bengal, called Dayalhari Majumdar, who had all the faults of duplicity and cupidity. Reduced to selling his daughter's musical talents in public, he was quick to take advantage of the men who lusted after Shiuli and planned her marriage with at least two such candidates, needless to say, for a hefty monetary consideration. Finally, he turned a blind eye at the elopement of his daughter with a third person, who he presumably knew about. Before he could be nabbed by one of the irate suitors, he fled with the cash which had been paid to him. Not a very pleasant portrayal, but the prejudices of the resident Bengalis reverberate through such pen sketches. As sufferers of violence, when the violence spilled over into West Bengal, there was a core of common experience that stirred both East and West Bengalis. But that was a far cry from socially accepting the refugees who were seen as interlopers in the social networks of the resident Bengalis.

In two stories, *Adim Ripu* and *Rimjhim*,[17] where the problems of young women, who had come away from East Bengal, have been marked with a certain degree of sympathy, both of them have been shown as earning their own living. Shiuli, as Dayalhari Majumdar's daughter, was responsible for the family's upkeep. Her father saw no objection to his daughter appearing in public, and being a target of every tout in town, for many were on the look-out for pretty young faces for the silver screen, something which a resident Bengali father would never have dreamt of doing. In *Rimjhim*, the young woman, Priyamvada Bhowmik had spent her first 16 years in East Bengal and was a matriculate. Her father, a doctor trained in Indian medicine (*kaviraj*), who had a flourishing practice in Dhaka, getting a whiff of the impending political trouble, decided to come away to Calcutta. That was the end of his flourishing practice. He did not attempt to educate his young daughter further, but tried to marry her to 'a decent and deserving boy'. But by then the riots had already broken out in East Bengal and hoards of refugees were swarming into Bengal. Empathy with victims of violence was there, but to receive a possible female victim of marauding Muslim male violence into the family fold strained the liberalism of any self-respecting resident Bengali family. Priyamvada cynically observed:

> But a decent house and husband was not for me. I was fair-skinned, face, eyes, build, all were as they should be, but I had one terrible fault. I was a refugee from East Bengal. All the prospective in-laws had only this [rape] at the back of their minds when they rejected me—they had doubts about my physical chastity.[18]

When Priyamvada's father saw that his daughter would remain unmarried, at least during his lifetime, he urged her to take a diploma course in nursing. This was a bitter pill to swallow for any middle class Bengali father: to acknowledge to himself and to his offspring that it was beyond his power to provide for his daughter, and, therefore, deliberately equipping her for self-employment. This also marked off the girls from East Bengal from the girls of West Bengal. The latter, when they stepped out of their homes, were driven by economic need, by ambition or a desire to be free of domestic shackles. The former were driven to self-employment because of dire necessity—they would be homeless if they were not self-employed. And this precisely would have been Priyamvada's fate if she was not trained to strike out on her own. Beyond this the author refuses to go. Whether Priyamvada Bhowmik spoke with a East Bengali accent or whether Shiuli's songs were tinged with her Dhakai pronunciation he does not tell the reader. His silence on this subject is far more eloquent than any words. Like Priyamvada Bhowmik's prospective in-laws, he also did not quite welcome the East Bengalis into the fold, for they were different. The cultural dividing line was clearly drawn between the girls of the two Bengals. For Bandhopadhyaya, so far and no further.

To end on this note, however, would be to belittle the author. This was not all that Bandopadhyaya as a writer and an intellectual was all about. In *Adim Ripu*, the idealization of nationhood, of the perfect moral citizen, the importance of every citizen doing his bit for the new nation and, thereby, steering it through troubled times to a bright and truly independent India would have delighted Nehru. But by 1964, his story 'Dui Dik' had moved away from the conviction in the inevitability and desirability of progress, that the writer seemed to share with Jawaharlal Nehru in the 1950s.

His protagonist in 'Dui Dik', the doctor, had reached a more mature phase of his life. He could actually appreciate the *goonda*, Noor Mian, from the comfortable distance of 16 years and admit something that he might have never have done in his younger days—his own sneaky feeling of admiration for Noor Mian. He knew he had survived as a Hindu and as a doctor with a deep commitment to life when he tended the Muslim whom he had witnessed killing several Hindus. When Noor Mian had recovered somewhat he was shocked afresh by his wickedness. In order to scare Noor Mian into a more law-abiding frame of mind, the doctor brought up the subject of the police but there was no panic-stricken reaction. Noor Mian merely made a dismissive grimace and warned the doctor that if he ever did anything so foolhardy, he would get into trouble, for on the day the murder was committed, he had been in the police lockup and even his thumb impression was there in the register to bear out his statement. To have actually arranged for his own alibi with the police overwhelmed the doctor—such depravity was beyond his understanding. Yet, when the *goonda* insisted that the doctor receive payment for having saved his life, the doctor again could not resist the temptation to show him the right path, with a mildly malicious touch of self-righteousness. He said, with the hint of a challenge, 'You can't repay me with money but you can repay me with something far more difficult than that.' Noor Mian professed readiness to do anything in his power only, he warned, he would not give up his religion. The doctor then demanded he should give up his career as a *goonda* and also give up his habit of imbibing cocaine. Noor Mian was stunned, but after a while he said, '*Malik*, you have just robbed me of the only life I have ever known, but your demand I will do my best to obey.'

Noor Mian gave up his lucrative career and took a whole year to conquer his hunger for cocaine, then he came and thanked the doctor for doing him such a favour. Noor Mian opened a *paan* shop and every morning he would *salaam* the doctor before beginning his day. The *goonda* had an honourable soul, and he kept his *iman kasam*! Yet, one cannot help making a further probe into the motives of the protagonist. Surely there was a tinge of moral superiority in the final triumph of the doctor over the Muslim *goonda*: there was also something seemingly ridiculous in a powerful man who had inspired fear in the police being reduced to a local *paanwala*. This revelling in gratitude and obeisance from a fearsome figure who represented the elemental brutality of the 'other' surely revealed the desire to dominate in the breast of the Hindu doctor/author. Therefore, the sequel of the story can be read both ways: an admiration for 'honour' so rigidly maintained or a subtle restoration of the natural order, the Hindu at the top, the Muslim at the bottom. This natural order was what the liberal Hindu felt to be right in independent India.

Sharadindu Bandopadhyaya, in his more soul-searching moments, had he spoken his mind freely about this last story, would have acknowledged two things. First, that the doctor had found the right answer to the vexing question of the nature of the 'secular' in his instinctive reaction to human suffering. Whatever came welling up deep out of his heart was beyond the dogmatic certainty of an identity—whether of any religion or of a lack of it (the later desire to reform the Muslim was an after thought, initially it had not been present in the doctor's mind). Terms like 'secularism' attach virtues immediately to persons professing it. Instant labels of being 'progressive', 'tolerant' and 'good' are acquired without effort. There is a blinkered certitude in the assumption that secularism cannot mean anything else. No 'lower depths' need to be sounded for doubts and fears, of constant battles fought and won with one's self for the control and suppression of a baser instinct crying out for blood, only the eternal and lofty serenity of the heights of an unshaken mental equanimity.[19] Such a perfect assumption kills the possibility of improvement. Gwendoline, in *The Importance of Being Earnest*, reproved an ardent admirer who had called her perfect, 'Oh! I hope I am not that. It would leave no room for development. . . .'[20] And sure enough, the limited possibilities of a perfect ideological position gradually starts resembling fish swimming in tighter and tighter circles in a rapidly freezing lake. Second, that the doctor having sunk to the 'lower depths', for feeling the punitive desire to hurt, poison, to obliterate the hated 'other', had gradually swum to the surface, understood with every fibre of his finer feelings that a human life could not be snuffed out at will, and at the same time understood that as a Hindu he could desire vengeance. Even to become closely acquainted with one's self involves a risk, which holistic terms like 'secularism' blank out as too unsafe.

To the modern reader, this is slippery ground. Used to the politics of avoidance, where comforting euphemisms are employed—sex-workers for prostitutes, misconduct for corruption, alleged crime for guilty as hell, taking responsibility for one's good and bad feelings, to admit that 'communal' and 'secular' are terms that have to be expanded in meaning, to take away the derogatory tone attached to the first and the laudatory nature of the second, sounds a difficult and dangerous thing to do. But from the example set by Sharadindu Bandopadhyaya's doctor, one feels instinctively that to duck from one's own prejudices is the worst form of self-induced amnesia. The secular and Hindu identities of the doctor fold back into each other. Only the combined presence of both allow for a full play of a dialogic encounter within the self. Anodyne, correct ideological positions, by erasing this possibility, are cabalistic, for they also impose rigid conformity and homogeneity on the people professing 'secularism' in the laudatory sense of the term. Bandopadhyaya, in that sense, reminds the reader of the necessity of treading on the razor's edge in one's mind: that prevents the mind from sinking into comfortable certitude, into the conviction that one is always right, merely by the virtue of possessing a perspective on the world.

NOTES

1. Urvashi Butalia, *The Other Side of Silence, Voices From the Partition of India* (Delhi, 1998).
2. This remembrance of the horrors of the past, flooding back after the carnage of 1984, linking the trauma of the immediate present with the past, especially for the families who had survived the Partition, has also been reflected in the studies conducted by the research team led by Ashis Nandy.
3. Sharadindu Bandopadhyaya, *Sharadindu Omnibus*, Vols I-XII (Calcutta, 1977). All references to Sharadindu Bandopadhyaya in this article have been taken from this set. *Adim Ripu* was written in 1955, *Rakter Daag* was written in 1961, *Rimjhim* and 'Bisher Dhnoya' were written in 1961 and 'Dui Dik' was written in 1964. All translations from the original in Bengali are mine.

4. Satish Deshpande, 'Hegemonic Spatial Strategies, in *Society for Transnational Cultural Studies*, Vol. XXV (1998), p. 261.
5. Bandopadhyaya, *Adim Ripu*, in *Sharadindu Omnibus*, Vol. II, p. 1.
6. Idem, *Dui Dik*, ibid., Vol. VI, p. 295.
7. William Shakespeare, 'Hamlet, Prince of Denmark', in *The Complete Works of William Shakespeare* (Avenel), Act 1, Scene IV, Marcellus' comment, p. 1078.
8. Bandopadhyaya, *Adim Ripu*, op.cit., p. 62.
9. Ibid.
10. Ibid.
11. Ibid.
12. Idem, *Rakter Daag*, in *Sharadindu Omnibus*, Vol. II, pp. 152, 155 and 159-60.
13. Idem, 'Bisher Dhnoya', in ibid., Vol. VIII, op.cit.
14. Ibid., p. 108.
15. Idem, *Adim Ripu*, op.cit., p. 85.
16. James E. Young, *Textures of Memory* (New York, 1993).
17. Bandopadhyay, *Rimjhim*, in *Sharadindu Omnibus*, Vol. X.
18. Ibid., p. 4
19. Shiv Visvanathan has used this concept in a different context. See his paper on 'Democracy, Plurality and the Indian University', presented at the Tri-National Seminar on Campus Diversity, South Africa, 13-21 March 1998. I quote, 'Tolerance as absolute neutrality is both necessary and inadequate. It is the lazy man's solution to the problem of plurality and can be construed as indifference' (p. 7), and 'If the nation-state constructs the other as an object of hate, extermination or violence, education must be the dialogue with the other' (p. 28).
20. Oscar Wilde, 'The Importance of Being Earnest', in *Complete Works of Oscar Wilde*, (London), p. 327.

On Narrativizing Partition

SUKRITA PAUL KUMAR

The experience of human suffering and the gruesome reality of the division of the country got recorded in a variety of ways, through diaries and memoirs as well as historical and official documentation. As for the tropes of forgetting, exclusion and silence, as also marginalization, these have been constantly attended to by sensitive narratives produced by those writers deeply affected by Partition. These narratives offer insights into the new sense of subjectivity, the profound sense of rupture and the deep personal meanings emerging from the grotesque human massacre and the mass exodus of panic-stricken people from one side of the country to the other to be close to their own religious group. The long awaited 'freedom' brought to a whole people not merely the exhilaration of political freedom but also a tragic snapping of their roots grown over centuries within specific geographical, cultural and social boundaries.

The province of Punjab went totally berserk with one of the greatest migrations in human history. There was a display of irrational savagery at the same time when India had set to prove to the world how 'colonialism' could be defeated and freedom won by non-violent Gandhian means. Indeed, such historical contradictions offer tremendous creative potentialities and possibilities. Whether it be in Hindi, Urdu, Punjabi, Bengali or English, the aesthetic distillation of the horrendous experiences of Partition is found to be represented. An account of the same in history can, perhaps, be summed up in objective terms in just one or two volumes, but the scope of exploring the range of experiences in the creative arts seems to be almost unending.

There was hatred, mutual suspicion, arson, loot, abduction of women, a scenario of mass hysteria, homelessness and insecurity all around. In just a few years, the sheer primitive bestiality demonstrated by the Indian people ripped open the very social fabric firmly woven by traditional values, religious faith and a steady sense of protection yielded by

* This article is based on a chapter from my book, *The New Story* (Indian Institute of Advanced Study, Shimla, 1991).

commitment to one's *mohalla*. It is, perhaps, the incomprehensibility of the situation that has been a constant source of energy to the creativity of a large number of writers. A mere official history cannot offer any understanding of the complex and strange workings of the human mind when relationships suddenly collapse. The writer's intrigued sensitivity was repeatedly led into exploring the phenomenon of Partition in experiential terms, a partition, which was much more than a mere political divide.

In fact, creative literature focusing on the theme of Partition presents the underside of history. It brings out the continuities of human consciousness. And Partition cannot just be historicized as an event of the past. In actuality, that 'past' has been perpetually digging into the present. The creative writer in the subcontinent has been working and reworking Partition in fiction, if only to come to grips with the dynamic thrust of human consciousness struck by both the collective as well as individual tragedy. For the relation between the actual social conditions and the reality of the individual's experience to be understood, the writer has had constantly to evolve a new strategy to confront the actuality of the historical and cultural 'accident' of Partition. Human relationships were re-evaluated, values were re-examined and a new sensibility emerged.

Apart from giving rise to macabre scenes of death, the Radcliffe axe, as it was called, caused a complete dislocation, be it places of pilgrimage, historical associations or economic activities. Radcliffe realized, of course, the extent to which the people of the Punjab were aggrieved: 'People sometimes ask me whether I would like to go back and see India as it really is, God forbid. Not even if they asked me. I'd suspect they'd shoot me out of hand both sides.'[1]

Partition, did not merely mean two new geographical dominions, as the examination of creative literature proves, it gave birth to a new psychic dominion as well. For the expression of this new sensibility, the short story was adopted as the most suitable form of expression of the varied dimensions of the anguish of the people. Concepts and ideas evolved in Europe's 'mono-lingual, non-colonized, non-balkanized cultures are bound to undergo important ideological mutations when employed in an essentially tolerant polytheistic and eclectic Indian culture'.[2] Various aspects of modernism, as it shaped itself in Western literature, located an appropriately dishevelled ground in the post-Partition Indian situation. Ideas were imbibed and had to be localized for an authentic and aesthetically satisfying expression.

Ashfaque Ahmed's story 'Gadariya' (The Goatherd) is a classic example of a narrative capturing a very poignant moment. A sturdy and robust communal integration within an individual psyche is assaulted by an insane and ignorant mob. The essentially, according to G.N. Devy, 'tolerant, eclectic and polytheistic' society is encapsuled, as it were, in the psyche of Dauji whose knowledge of Islamic religion, history and culture makes him conversant with Muslim culture, even though he is a conscientious Hindu. Dauji, who is a perfect example of communal synthesis, becomes the victim of frenzied Muslim gangsterism! His *choti*, which stands for his Hindu identity, is clipped and he is made to read the *kalma*. He, of course, knows the *kalma* better than those Muslims. But all his Islamic scholarship is nullified in the face of his own image as a Hindu. His lifelong commitment and learning may have diffused his own insulated Hindu self-consciousness, but this capacity to participate in the other's religion becomes quite meaningless *vis-à-vis* the fanatical and crude proclamations of the rowdy rioters, who were classifying the people into Hindus and Muslims. The story ends with the powerful image of Dauji condemned to become a goatherd walking, like the long-haired Farida, behind the goats.

Although Dauji never forfeits his formal identity as a Hindu, he is entrenched in Islamic studies and imbued with the Muslim faith. He often recalls amidst ecstasies of reverential joy and gratitude that all his knowledge is a gift from Hazrat Maulana, his benevolent ailing teacher, whom he daily carried on his back to show around in their small town. It was a miracle wrought by Hazrat Maulana, that had made him Munshi Chintram from mere Chinto, the ignorant and savage goatherd of the family of Abu Jehel. Interestingly, the image of Dauji as a goatherd emerges off and on in the story. Has Dauji then really been able to shed the past to which he had been attached? The *gadariya* has been assigned his original vocation perhaps unwittingly by the rioters. The symbolic connotation of the role of having to tend goats cannot be missed by him now. But the humiliation undergone by him with the clipping of his *choti* is a painful reality. His humble stark simplicity is a formidable front against all those assaults on his physical and psychological being. He has to confront the present somewhere in his consciousness. The fact of partition, the separating line between the Hindus and the Muslims, within his own psyche has to be recognized. Or, does he transcend this need by going the way of Farida, the Sufi saint at the end of the story, an image that haunts the reader long after the story is over! It is this ambivalence, which when narrativized by the writer in a literary form, accommodates such a perception. Historical documentation would normally fail to contain such an account of a similar 'real' experience.

In as far as the immediate effect of the declaration of the Partition on the human psyche is concerned, Saadat Hasan Manto's well-known story 'Toba Tek Singh' seems to take off from where 'Gadariya' ends. The situation outside the lunatic asylum projects much more insanity than that of the inside. When one of the lunatics climbing high up a tree is asked to come down, he says: 'I don't want to live in Hindustan or Pakistan. They mean nothing to me. I am going to make my abode right here on this tree.'[3] When he does come down he cannot bear the thought of his Hindu and Sikh friends deserting him and going away to Hindustan. The emphasis on shared inter-community life makes the 'rigmarole of Pakistan and Hindustan' appear absurd even to the lunatics. 'Were they in Hindustan or Pakistan? If they were in Pakistan how could it be possible that only a short while ago they were in Hindustan? How could they be in two places at the same time? In Hindustan a short while ago and now suddenly in Pakistan.'[4]

As though with an X-ray vision, Manto's perception of madness delicately brings out the painful psychic reception of the idea of Partition. The demarcation of the boundaries evokes utter panic and insecurity amongst the people. When Bishan Singh, now called Toba Tek Singh, asks an inmate of the asylum, who considers himself God, where Toba Tek Singh is, in Hindustan or Pakistan, the 'God' claims not to have taken any decision about the location. Immediately, Bishan Singh places him in the enemy camp as being merely a God of the Muslims for otherwise he would surely have given him the information. This shows, that in a sense, the reality of the new boundaries is obviously getting injected into their perception.

Therefore, when the exchange of lunatics takes place and the police ascertain that Toba Tek Singh is in Pakistan and that Bishan has to be handed over to India, 'the man who had always stood erect on his legs for the last fifteen years was now lying on his face. . . . On one side behind him stood together the lunatics of Hindustan and on the other side across the road the lunatics of Pakistan. Between them on no-man's land, Toba Tek Singh lay stretched.'[5] The last scene of the story rejects Partition outright by making 'sanity' lie flat on no-man's land, while those who seem to accept the new boundaries by migrating, even though under pressure, remain lunatics. It is a well-known fact that many people particularly in rural areas, in their simplicity and unawareness of the reality of political division, had never anticipated the havoc of Partition. The inbuilt resistance to leave one's home and the desire to believe in the transient nature of the disturbances had made them stay in their homes and lands only to be massacred or uprooted in thousands, in the wake of the Partition.

So then, where is sanity? Is it in resisting the uprooting and dying, or, in escaping the slaughter and fleeing as a refugee? 'Toba Tek Singh' offers a fine perception of the thin line dividing sanity from lunacy. The predicament of becoming a refugee can indeed permanently damage the psyche. For the person who refuses to accept the imposition of a political decision and protests, the result could be death.

Partition has been articulated in sensitive and artistic narratives over and over again in the last 50 years as an evolving tragedy operating on various levels of consciousness in diverse contexts. To narrativize an event from the distant past demands a very strong use of imagination, which can transform the historical truth into a fictionalized one with all its rights of autonomous existence. But it may not directly help in perceiving the reality of a phenomenon in relatively objective terms. Since Partition is recent history and many from amongst the affected people are still alive, to narrativize Partition is not really a reconstruction of the past, it is in fact a recording of a continuous present. In that sense Partition is an enduring fact, living in the present as much as in the past. Nostalgia and a feverish desire to build up a new life generated a host of emotional as well as socio-cultural orientations. Partition has also created a new political consciousness in Hindu-Muslim relations. The history of communal strife demonstrated in the last 50 years in India and Pakistan is also a fall-out. This is consistently captured in literature. The narratives thus created tell the history of the emotional make-up of these regions and bring out vital dimensions of new life emerging from total devastation. The continuous present carries within its folds the devastated past.

Joginder Paul's Urdu story 'Dariyaon Pyas' (The Thirst of the Rivers) unfolds the acute pathos embodied in the personality of Bebe, a grandmother. The pain injected in her by the Partition is described as follows: 'The bundle of pain lies open in the womb of mother earth; from which are born twin children soaked in blood, causing the death of the mother. There is no one to wash and clothe the newborn and, there is no one to give them shelter or food.'[6] Now, with the death of this mother earth, the story's most powerful character, Bebe, forfeits her present as much as her future. Urged by her dead husband, who is for Bebe more than alive in his *haveli*, through hundreds of associative memories, she leaves the ancestral house populated, as it were, by the ghosts of a long string of relations—

husband's father, his father's father, and so on. Even though she physically leaves the *haveli,* mentally she is rooted in the warmth of the *haveli*, filled with the memories and the spirits of the ancestors, even though she lives in her son's house.

This story was written more than three decades after the Partition but even from this distance the author sensitively records the extent to which Bebe's consciousness is stirred by the holocaust. The author's perception and style are contemporary, while the ethos and the orientation of the main character remain traditional. Bebe's bunch of keys stands as a symbol of authority and the confidence manifested in her by the family. This is central to the story. For decades together, Bebe has always carried the bunch of keys on her person, tied to one end of her sari, the key of the kitchen door urges her to cook on time, the one to the office of the husband, seems to extend a welcome to her. Desperate and unsympathetic, her son cannot see why she is unable to reconcile to the changed circumstance and open the locks of her psyche. But then, new keys have to be located to match the new locks of the present. The old ones are now redundant. Bebe is found trying out all her old keys to open the lock of her son's new bungalow, which remains closed to her. She never manages to come face to face with the new reality represented by the new bungalow.

The story begins with Bebe brooding alone outside her son's new house, the wrinkles of her face hanging heavily as if with her memories. Her psychological make-up is rooted in the traditional cultural pattern. She defines herself always in the context of familial relationships in the world of the *haveli*, which had its own ethics and laws of existence. To have her come out of that world meant a total disintegration of her self. In refusing to accept her separation from that existence, she keeps her past intact through her attachment to the bunch of keys. The suddenness of Partition gives her no time to comprehend the changing reality, make new psychic adjustments and, in effect, reconstruct her identity. However, her son has moved on in life and the dynamism of modernization has pulled him into its folds away from the tradition-bound *haveli* and into a new modern bungalow. In locking Bebe outside the bungalow, perhaps lies the suggestion that if tradition cannot be totally destroyed, it can at least be resisted, dismissed or even ignored. Since 'Dariyaon Pyas' is a story written in the late 1970s, the writer has clearly come a long way from wanting to merely record the sensational hysteria of the times.

Krishna Sobti's story 'Sikka Badal Gaya' was written in 1948 in Hindi with a similar theme of having to leave behind the ancestral house. The chief character Shahni wants to maintain the dignity of her Shahji's house by stepping out of the door respectfully and not in tears. The familial status and dignity of her ancestors, she thinks, is in her custody. Having to migrate and leave that *haveli* meant a kind of betrayal of the family trust bestowed upon her, but she must move from the house into the refugee camp. While she is shedding tears in distress, there is bloodshed in the surrounding villages. Shahni has to save herself from the very people she has helped just a few weeks ago by contributing generously towards the building of their *masjid*. The story focuses on the pangs of separation at the individual level through the utter bafflement of somebody like Dauji Khan, who does not know how to respond to Shahni's departure. Such narratives, reveal the confusion both at the individual and social plane caused by the announcement of Partition. The history of the human psyche recorded through such stories help one understand many of the resultant problems and the new orientations of modern Indian society.

Novels written on Partition in English, such as Khushwant Singh's *Train to Pakistan,* Kartar Singh Duggal's *Twice Born, Twice Dead,* B. Rajan's *The Dark Dancer* and Chaman Nahal's *Azadi* point towards a rather romanticized picture of communal harmony of pre-Partition days. But Kamla of *The Dark Dancer* offers an interesting clue to the understanding of the basis of that horrifying violence. She attributes the sudden eruption of violence to prolonged repression:

> You couldn't have brought it out if it wasn't in us. It's all in us, in many many years of occupation, submission to the state, obedience to the family, every inch of our lives completely calculated, every step down to the relief of the grave. And if we wanted to protest, there was only the pitiless discipline of non-violence. Then all of a sudden, the garden belongs to us, and we reach up into the blossoming tree to pluck the ashes.[7]

The poetic truth of such an interpretation is unwound in Mohan Rakesh's 'Malbe ka Malik' (The Owner of the Debris) in his sensitive presentation of Gani Mian's visit to Amritsar seven and a half years after Partition and the replaying of the story of the fate of his family during the Partition riots. Gani Mian's visit to bazaar Mansa, which had been a locality of the poor Muslims in pre-Partition times, seems to ignite again the most ravaging fire, which had swallowed the majority of the Muslims in the area in 1947. He goes there in search of his house. Manori shows him the past in its present shape, in the form of the debris with broken and burnt bricks sticking out here and there. Ironically, a half-burnt frame of the door sticks out as though inviting him to enter it and pick out memories from his own wreckage. With the touch of his head against it, he only manages to create another refugee, he disturbs an earthworm who runs in fright to save himself. It fails to get into another hole or a home. The tell-tale debris of his house is now under the proprietorship of Rakkha who has actually murdered Gani's son, Chirag, with the intention of taking over the house. In the background to the current ruins we see earlier the Hindu-Muslim brotherhood and shared community life within that *mohalla*.

The self-interest and greed on the part of the many 'Rakkhas' had made them seize opportunities to become barbaric under the cover of religion. Strangely, Rakkha had even collected the concomitants necessary to hold a *havan* (oblation by fire) to consecrate the house after acquiring it from the Muslim family. And now, for the past seven and a half years, he has regarded himself as the proprietor of that debris. He sits on top of it almost as though time has frozen at the moment he had taken the decision that it belonged to him. When Gani Mian comes back there with his total ignorance about the present truth, the good old days of 'brotherhood' are revived, arousing in Rakkha the pangs of guilt more so with Gani's persistent declaration of faith in him. It is essential for Gani to confront both, the reality of the conversion of his house into a debris as also the reality of the death of his son and his family. Similarly, Rakkha's meeting with Gani diverts the stream of Rakkha's consciousness back to his 'feeling self'. He suffers now for the brutality of the action he had earlier committed.

The moral dimension of the situation begins to reveal itself to Rakkha. In the night, instead of teaching people gambling tricks, he indulges in narrating the story of his pilgrimage to Vaishno Devi, as if in repentance. As he approaches his 'debris' and sits at its 'doorstep' in the silence of the night, a variety of live sounds emerge from the heap of the wreckage. It is as though the debris was coming alive. Rakkha is now aroused and feels that the barking of a dog is directed at him, perhaps reprimanding him. He feels compelled to dislodge himself from the debris and seems to surrender his right over it. Like the frustrated earthworm, he has to change his direction and search for a new home.

In his critical survey, Alok Rai discusses how enlightened explanations break down, in the face of a monstrous upsurge of mass violence.[8] And, one of the crudest consequences of this process, he says, is a kind of literary indulgence in horror, which he also calls a pornography of violence. In the cataclysmic events of Partition, epitomized by scenes of carnage, devastation and utter chaos, reality itself became a melodrama. And a mere slavish imitation of it in fiction or art would mean indulgence in horror. The artistic representation of emotionally charged experiences requires a composure and a balance. It is in this that the difference between a historical narrative and a literary narrative becomes obvious. In the literary narrative, though the historical aspect remains intact, the experience is likely to transcend historicity and becomes a universal experience. The appeal is far reaching and the event narrated has an enduring impact rather than getting merely recorded in memory.

Though Kamleshwar's story 'Kitne Pakistan'? (How many Pakistans?) may here and there demonstrate, as some critics opine, a hypnotic fascination with horror, it is a story that yields an insight into the causes of this horror and the particular kind of human psyche it creates. Most stories on this theme remain trapped in mere descriptions of horror that can only feed further horror. A zone of silence between two lovers caused by a rupture of communication is represented by Kamleshwar as the 'birth of Pakistan'. The author successfully ascribes various shades to the meaning of Pakistan. The artistic representation of the symbol of Pakistan and its ravaging effect on the smooth natural flow of emotion is described as follows: 'Perhaps the lack caused in the power of feeling is Pakistan'.[9]

Many 'Pakistans' erupt in individual psyches with the creation of one Pakistan, complicating and disturbing the harmony of thousands of relationships. Pakistan then is not a mere territory for the masses, who associate nightmarish scenes of violence with its birth. 'Supposing the suppressed flames of my Pakistan flare up and burst from within me?'[10] Burdened with such a question, the protagonist of the story addresses Banno, his lost love, and says, 'In you, another Pakistan sobs. Each of us is restless for one's own Pakistan, seeking it broken, incomplete, in bits and pieces.'[11] The desperate quest for a place where there would be no Pakistan ends with the conclusion that everywhere there is a Pakistan that constantly beats, humiliates and desensitizes an individual. The story effectively projects the process of internalization of the creation of Pakistan depicted in the narrator's monologue.

There is a similar suggestion in Mohan Rakesh's story 'Malbe ka Malik' in which while Rakkha is murdering Chirag, he abuses him and says, 'Why do you scream? I am only giving you your Pakistan, here take it.'[12] And, as Mohan Rakesh the author, specifies, the womenfolk are given their Pakistan in another style: they are abducted and then killed. It is interesting to observe the identity 'Pakistan' acquires in various minds and the dehumanizing factors associated with it. The creation of a new political territory is seen as causing massive upheaval. Thus in these stories, Pakistan acquires the symbolic connotations of violence and barbarism.

'Why a refuge for Muslims suddenly?' and 'Why should Hindus and Muslims become enemies after Hindustan gets free?'—asks someone in Gangauli, UP, in Rahi Masoom Reza's novel, *Aadha Gaon*. Questions like these of the common man could only be heard through a literary narrative, not through tomes of historical texts.

Krishan Chander's book of short stories called *Hum Vahshi Hain* (We are Barbarians), published in 1948, exploits the novel technique of using unconventional narrators, such as a 'train' or a 'hired killer'. It is as though these stories attempt to relieve the shame and guilt of the times through an imaginative delineation of atrocities perpetrated by each of the communities. This sense of guilt is also overtly seen at the end of Chaman Nahal's novel *Azadi*, through Lala Kanshi Ram's statement made with reference to two scenes in which naked women are paraded—Hindu and Sikh women at Narowal and Muslim women at Amritsar—and the massacre on both sides: 'We are all equally guilty. Each one of those girls in that procession at Amritsar was someone's Madhu. . . .'[13] This brings to our mind, what Quentin says in Arthur Miller's play *After the Fall*: 'Who can be innocent again on this mountain of skulls?'[14] This proves that the people living through the horrors of the Second World War, those who killed as well as those who did not, in some way or the other, carried a sense of guilt for the rest of their lives. Khushwant Singh in his essay on 'Compulsion to Write' makes the same point in his personal confession: 'The Partition theme was born out of a sense of guilt that I had done nothing to save the lives of innocent people and behaved like a coward.'[15] There are a multitude of stories written precisely due to such an awareness, perhaps to exorcise one's self of the hatred that one felt for the other community or for indulging in the horrors during the Partition.

Agyeya published a collection of stories and poems in 1948, entitled *Sharnarthi* (Refugee), revealing the deeply felt pain at the hysterical and the irrational display of violence. Manto in 'Tithwal ka Kutta' takes the representation of such violence to its absurd extreme. A dog moving around on no-man's land is shot down by both Hindu and Muslim soldiers, as each is suspicious about which country the dog belongs to. The pertinent question to be asked is: Has all this to be attributed to a failing in nature or in man?

Shaken to the roots of their being, some of the writers of the Partition narratives indulged in a fundamental reflection on human existence. The experience of uprooting, for example, leads Munir Ahmed Sheikh's main character in the story 'Apni Shakl' (One's Own Face), to ask: 'Who am I? Where have I come from? Where did I start from? Where do I have to go?'[16] Such philosophic stirrings were indeed a consequence of sudden physical displacement causing a paralyzed dread, an acute apprehension of what was to come and a total incomprehension of the situation. In a story called 'Sapoliye', published in *Hans* in May 1948, the situation reveals an even more complex historical context. In the backdrop of the Second World War, two soldiers, one Hindu and one Muslim, after having won the war for the Allies are killed by communal rioters, on coming back home. International politics combine with national politics and condemn the common man into a state of helplessness.

Cynicism, helplessness, decaying human values and spiritual sterility together produced a sense of absurdity amongst the people. An existentialism of sorts too, in the later short stories, was bound to emerge from such a psychological climate. Macabre scenes of massacres led to frustration, negating any faith that might have been upheld so far. Manik Bandhopadhyaya in his 'Swadhinatar Swad' (The Taste of Freedom), 1951, refers to this era as a period of sudden deaths taken so casually. There is a great deal of literature available in Bengali which deals with the theme of the loss of kinship ties. Banaphool's 'Dangar Shamay' (When the Riots Come) depicts the genesis of a sudden distrust and communal belligerence. Socio-political crisis and anxiety creep into every household, weighing everyone down with moments of dread and unstability. Initially, the Partition of the country caused a tremendous political confusion; eventually it hit hard at the basic values, beliefs and attitudes of the people affected by it. Also, this triggered off a process of change in the patterns of human relationships with the availability of newer perspectives and new life styles. The aesthetic expression and articulation of these changes showed up quite clearly about eight or nine years later in the literary movement, termed as the 'new story'.

Nai Kahani in Hindi and *Naya Afsana* in Urdu, appear in the 1960s as a crystallization of the writer's need to re-examine and re-evaluate human existence and relationships in the context of the new evolving reality. The fragmentation and dispersal of domestic and social as well as cultural identity caused by the division of the country made Jainendra Kumar's philosophical approach, Agyeya's experimentalism and Yashpal's progressivism look inadequate for the expression of the new mental landscape of the people in their changed contexts. The consciousness to explore new ways of expressing and defining the new sensibility was reflected in these two publications.

From the wreckage of Partition, gradually rises a new order. The beautiful merger of the past with the present and a fine treatment of human history with private sentiment are revealed through the fresh and new sensibility displayed by Qurratulain Hyder in her Urdu stories, 'Patjhar ki Awaz' (The Sound of the Falling Leaves) and 'Saint Flora of Georgia ke Etrafaat' (Confessions of Saint Flora of Georgia). The educated young woman of 'Patjhar ki Awaz' becomes a monument of indifference. There are subtle hints of the effect of Partition on her relationships, her approach to her men, her aspirations and the slow dampening of her spirits. To her, everything now seems absolutely colourless, insignificant, purposeless and unnecessary. The writer subtly poses queries about contemporary life and relationships.

The new realities had not only to be confronted, they were also to be accepted. In Joginder Paul's story, 'Those Who Stayed Behind', no matter what Mohan might have felt after Partition, he has to face the current reality some time or the other.[17] The movement in time is possible only if there is a psychic acceptance of it. For a Hindu migrant from Pakistan, Mohan's Sialkot is lodged safely in his very being. He visits the city of his birth 36 years after having left it and he brings along his well-preserved dreams and old memories. An actual trip around his earlier haunts steadily demolishes his warm associations with them. He does not feel like himself when he knocks at the door of his old house. Ironically, no one opens the door since 'the inmates are out'. He has just had a vision of his own old self, opening the door, the present self being an outsider. The inmate-turned-exile comes face-to-face with this actuality. If the uprooted plant fails to take roots in the new soil, the writer tells us, that would be the end of the story. Sialkot gradually exposes its alien and new ethos to Mohan's psyche.

After Partition, Mohan's friend Jamal has occupied a house that was originally the temple of Lord Krishna. While Mohan is mentally involved in that past, with images of the celebration of the Krishna festivals floating in his mind, the awareness of the new present expresses itself in his Muslim mode of greeting, *aslama ulaikum* extended to a cockroach, crawling in the wash-basin. Towards the end of the story, he grieves for Lord Krishna, who seems to stand in front of him stripped of his flute, his crown and his glory, looking lonely and strange.

The pre-Partition Sialkot, which has survived in Mohan, and from which he had earlier drawn sustenance for inter-community amity, now makes him conscious of his own religious identity, different from post-Partition Sialkot. So then Partition, it is suggested, does not merely draw new geographical boundaries, it disregards the common cultural heritage and instead emphasizes communal separatism. There is a need for the cognition of the new emergent identities, through a detachment from the comfortable past, or else, the individual will no longer be able to relate with the present.

This examination of the Partition stories reveals that the Partition of the country is a past that has continued to feed into our present in a variety of ways. The present has, of course, evolved from the past. And for an understanding of the history of the people, it would undoubtedly be rewarding to scan the rich repository of diverse experiences recorded sensitively by the creative writer in the long and short narratives. These experiences tell the story of Partition, both in the past tense, as also in the present continuous.

NOTES

1. Leonard Mosley, *Last Days of the British Raj* (London, 1962), p. 200.
2. G.N. Devy, 'Comparative Literature in India - I', in *New Quest* (May-June 1987), pp. 133-47.
3. Saadat Hasan Manto, 'Toba Tek Singh', in Jai Ratan, ed., *Modern Urdu Short Stories,* (New Delhi, 1987), p. 21.
4. Ibid.
5. Ibid., p. 27.
6. Joginder Paul, 'Dariyaon Pyas', in *Samkaleen Bharatiya Sahitya* (January-March 1983), p. 18.
7. Balchandran Rajan, *The Dark Dancer* (New Delhi, 1976), pp. 74-5.
8. Alok Rai, 'The Trauma of Independence: Some Aspects of Hindi Literature, 1945-47', in Amit Kumar Gupta, ed., *Myth and Reality: The Struggle for Freedom in India 1945-47* (New Delhi, 1987), pp. 309-27.
9. Kamleshwar, 'Kitne Pakistan', in Narendra Mohan, ed., *Bharat Vibhajan: Hindi Ki Shresht Kahaniyan* (Delhi, 1984), p. 34.
10. Ibid., p. 41.
11. Ibid., p. 50.
12. Mohan Rakesh, 'Malbe ka Malik', in ibid., p. 103.
13. Chaman Nahal, *Azadi* (Boston, 1975), p. 339.
14. Arthur Miller, *After the Fall* (1968), p. 119.
15. Khushwant Singh, 'Compulsion to Write', in R.K. Dhawan, ed., *Explorations in Modern Indo-English Fiction* (New Delhi, 1982), p. 195.
16. Narendra Mohan, ed., *Bharat Vibhajan: Urdu Ki Shresht Kahaniyan* (Delhi, 1984), p. 133.
17. Joginder Paul, 'Those Who Stayed Behind', in *Indian Literature,* Vol. XXVI, No. 6 (November-December 1983), pp. 26-37.

The Politics of Translation: Manto's Partition Stories and Khalid Hasan's English Version

ALOK BHALLA

At one level translating Saadat Hasan Manto into English is not very difficult. As a storyteller he never retreats from the complexity of lived experience to find easy refuge in political posturing or moral and religious sermonizing. That is why the style of his best stories, devoid of all metaphoric excess and sentimental inflections, is always precise, bare-boned and conversational. Most of his narrators are either hard drinking and whoring men who live in cities, which have neither space for graciousness nor time for romance, or are men who have seen so much horror that they can only offer a disenchanted and cynical vision of the world. Their descriptions, ironic and cold-eyed, seem to be authentic versions of life at a particular historical moment, because they have the feel of the real and the pitilessness of stone. It should not, therefore, be impossible for a translator to find verbal and cultural equivalents for his stories in English.

Structurally, Manto's tales are idiosyncratic but should not make a translator anxious. He often disrupts the linear and chronological flow of his stories by using the same kind of parenthetical interruptions, digressions or elisions that are common to all ordinary conversations. Since he is not conducting political or ethical arguments, he does not worry about constructing well-argued paragraphs whose internal coherence is essential to convince us of some abstract proposition. Instead, with the fine cunning of a master storyteller, he disrupts the narrative at times to increase suspense, or breaks the story's spell to remind us that life always frustrates our longing for completion; at other times, he offers different narrative possibilities within the same story and invites us to puzzle them out, or merely writes a fragment, which emerges from silence like a scream. That is why his stories seem to have the structural sharpness of barbed wires and shards—and like them they can wound those who are not alert to their existence. Instead of being problematic, the narrative quirkiness of his stories should be exciting for any contemporary translator who is conscious of its jaggedness and fissures, its shifts and silences, its blanks and absences.

There is, however, one aspect of Manto's literary intelligence that can prove fatal for any translator. Manto's language may be economical, but it has the sting and precision of a whiplash. An English translation of his stories may be accurate, but may still fail to capture the grating roughness of his diction, the sardonic irony of his images and the rough rhythms of his prose. In order to be effective, it would have to cause the same nightmarish pain, the same sharp lacerations on the reader's soul as Manto's Urdu original. Otherwise, he could appear to be only sentimental, or obscene and cynical, not a writer who has a deeply troubled but profoundly moral concern with human experiences and actions in a world which has lost its political sense and social reason.

Khalid Hasan is the best known and the most well received of all the translators of Manto in English. Unfortunately, his collection, *Mottled Dawn: Fifty Sketches and Stories of Partition*,[1] is deeply flawed. There are two serious problems with the book. One, its translations are highly inaccurate and disfigure the original. Two, it has no recognizable editorial policy. The result is a slow moving and an unimaginative book, which fails to deal with the range of Manto's responses to the Partition. If Manto's initial response to the Partition was that of disgust at the brutality, he later tried to make a more historically conscious attempt to understand its causes, and then find a way to assert that citizenship is the right of anyone who has lived for long within certain boundaries and feels at home within its geographical and cultural spaces.

Mottled Dawn is, with one minor change, an unrevised reprint of *Partition: Stories and Sketches*, published by Penguin in 1991.[2] It contains only one new text, 'Mere Sahib' (Jinnah Sahib). Hasan makes no attempt to explain his selection of stories, nor does he offer any explanation for his radical structural transformation into their new avatars. Thus, for example, we are not told why the story 'Naya Kanoon' (New Constitution) has been included even though it has nothing to do with Partition. The story was written in 1937, a few years before the demand for Pakistan was raised, and refers to the promulgation of the Government of India Act, 1935. What makes the choice strange is that well-known pieces about the Partition, like 'Gurumukh Singh ki Vasiyat', 'Ramkhilavan' and 'Shahay', find no place in the volume. Since the selection is obviously whimsical, it is not surprising that Hasan does not accommodate Manto's later and more complex stories. He does not, for example, include '1919 Ki Ek Baat', a difficult and bleak tale in which Manto seems to conclude that, despite the presence of Gandhi, the foolish and the brutal characterized every instance of our nationalist past.[3] Nor does he include tales like 'Fauda Haramda' and 'Shahdauley Da Chuha', where Manto suggests that a disparate group of exiles, who have neither shared myths nor a common language, can never stand together to form a nation; carrying nothing more than their different memories, such people can only live in the half-lit spaces of nostalgia.

What is editorially most puzzling, however, is the manner in which 28 of the brief sketches are presented in this volume. Hasan does not mention that they form a part of a strange and unique text, called *Siyah Hashiye* (Black Margins), which is actually made up of 32 pieces designed to be read together. There is, of course, no reason given for the exclusion of the remaining fragments. Hasan's procedure is misleading and damaging, because Manto deliberately composes a splintered text in order to convey his terrified sense that the Partition was a time of phantasmagoria. The 32 pieces in *Siyah Hashiye* together create a nightmare landscape of random violence; a scandalous world where victims and predators interchange places endlessly and unpredictably. To present them as unrelated and individual sketches is to rob them of their cumulative irony and abrasive force.

If Hasan as an editor offers us a Manto whose writings on the Partition are considerably diluted, as a translator he recreates for us a Manto who is substantially compromised and damaged as a writer. Not only does he give to Manto's stories English titles, which have no recognizable relationship with the original ones in Urdu, he also dismembers and scrambles their structures, deletes paragraphs, summarizes significant dialogues, omits details about characters, transforms long monologues into comfortable paragraphs, converts broken sentences and hesitant speeches into smoothly flowing prose and adds information about Islamic history and the formation of Pakistan for *kafirs*, so as to make Manto both into a communal partisan and a weak storyteller.[4] Hasan does not trust Manto. He forgets that Manto, at his best, knows the measure of a story and is always cautious not to reduce the difficult craft of storytelling into one of the duller forms of politics and theology. Manto's mode of narration is not separable from his vision of our moral condition during the Partition; it is rather a part of his exploration of the social and psychological conditions, which can lead all of us into evil. Hasan's violations of Manto's narrative strategies so distort the originals as to nearly succeed in making his sardonic and complex responses to the Partition seem ordinary and predictable. Manto survives the translation because his stories are powerful and perturbing.

Hasan's translation of some of the brief pieces in *Siyah Hashiye* provides examples of the problems with his method. Manto's text is made up of a series of instances of atrocity; each new atrocity merely replaces the previous one and is equally unprecedented. Given the fact that Manto wants to record the randomness of terror, it is obvious that these brief tales cannot be arranged in any recognizable order. Yet they must be read together, for only then can they create a phantasmagoric landscape where there is neither reason nor hope. Many of the fragmentary pieces are deliberately constructed out of broken sentences or simple words so as to suggest that they have been carefully incised on the page—like epitaphs on tombstones. Their brevity of form and their restrained tone are continuously threatened by the frenzy of the events described. One is forced to read them with slow and painful deliberation. Only then does one notice how single words or sentences fragment in one line, crumble into the words in the next, before finally collapsing into sneering laughter, horrified silence or screams. Hasan's prose translation, without Manto's careful lineation, in which words simply slide into one another as in any conventional sentence, erases the spasmodic quality of the tales and, thereby, denies them their vituperative quality.

Take, for instance, the text entitled 'Sorry'. The original is arranged as follows:

Sorry

Churi
paet chak karti hui
naaf ke neeche tak chali gai
izarband kat gaya.
Churi maarnevale ke
munh se
dafatan
kalma-e-taassuf nikla
'Chi, Chi, Chi . . . mishtake ho gaya.'

(*Dastavez*, II, p. 304)[5]

Hasan translates it as follows:

Mishtake

Ripping the belly cleanly, the knife moved in a straight line down the midriff, in the process slashing the cord which held the man's pyjamas in place.

The man with the knife took one look and exclaimed regretfully, 'Oh no! . . . Mishtake!' (p. 207)

It is amusing to note that Hasan 'translates' the original title 'Sorry'. What is involved here is more than an error of judgement. By retitling the story, 'Mishtake', Hasan suggests that Manto is doing nothing more than casually recording a grotesque incident as an example of the quirkiness of those days. The change, unfortunately, turns a grim story into a weak anecdote. Surely it is obvious from the careful manner in which the lineation of the text has been crafted, that Manto is not merely taking a note of a singularly absurd event, but is trying to draw attention to an infinite series of mindless and anonymous killings, which had made life into a nightmare. The changed title suggests that Hasan's attitude towards the text is flippant. Indeed, one suspects that Hasan changes the title partly because he wants to snigger, rather arrogantly, at the lumpenization of language, and partly because he thinks that Manto wants to point to the murderous propensities of the Punjabis in order to affirm ethnic stereotypes (the inability of many Punjabis to pronounce 's' has been the subject of endless jokes).

Manto's title, however, is quite deliberately chosen. It is rather unbecoming of a translator to reduce the text, which is a serious attempt at analysing human behaviour during times of mob frenzy and misrule to the level of a racial slur. One of the characteristic features of Manto's stories about the Partition is that they refuse to pass communally or ethnically charged judgements. That is why Manto either erases all religious or regional markers, or makes one uncomfortable with them wherever they occur. His attitude towards the Partition, and of the capacity of human beings to deal with crises, is utterly cynical. He is convinced that there are times when appeals to reason or morality can do nothing to prevent human beings—Hindus, Muslims and Sikhs, equally—from becoming murderers and living like fools. The title, 'Sorry', therefore, seems to have been deliberately chosen. On the one hand, its formality is mocked by the coarseness of the last exclamation of the killer. On the other hand, it warns us not to mock at the assassin's inability to pronounce a simple word, lest we should forget his victim and become accomplices in the slaughter. If we have to retain our humanity, we have to feel shocked and ashamed at the casual murder and the equally casual expression of apology for having killed the wrong man; we cannot turn away without remorse to laugh.

In the structural arrangement of the original text the object which is given priority is the knife. It hovers like a threatening presence over the text and controls it thematically. Manto deliberately places it in an isolated line surrounded by empty spaces so as to make it a metaphor for Partition as an annihilating event. What makes the knife terrifying to contemplate is that it has a remorseless and mechanical force of its own; it requires no human agency; it kills automatically, pitilessly and repeatedly. The man who wields it is merely a part of the mechanism of slaughter, he has no will of his own and no religion or nationality, which defines him. And the victim, whose body it cuts open, is only a cadaver. By giving the knife such a powerful presence, Manto wants to suggest that Partition has nothing to do with freedom or religiosity. He is sure that those who want Partition are only concerned with might—with all its intoxication, pride and humiliation.[6] It is because of his strong condemnation of the Partition as a political act, which trifled with the life, religion and culture of the people, that the protagonists of Pakistan still continue to find him difficult to deal with.

Hasan, however, shifts the attention away from the knife. He removes it from its predominant position in the original and slips it into one of the secondary clauses in a tedious sentence made up of melodramatic assertions. Instead of gazing at the knife with fear, we are made to watch, rather voyeuristically, the quivering flesh of the victim who is being slit open. The suspense of the original is created out of a series of brief, harsh and brutally factual sentence fragments. The translation slides along casually from one phrase to the next, describing how the man's pyjamas are held up by a cord and the knife rips through his belly 'cleanly'. Manto is a better storyteller and a more subtle thinker than the translator. He understands the economy of words and does not pause to give explanation or information. A story of violence requires a certain degree of asceticism of language; it is precisely Manto's restraint, which makes the original so disturbing. Manto also understands that in times of extreme violence, instruments of torture and murder acquire a life of their own and people who use them become servile to them. By discarding the lineation of the original text, Hasan destroys its meaning and ruins its dramatic impact. Perhaps, the first sentence of the story could have been translated more effectively as follows:

The knife
plunged into the stomach
ripped through the abdomen
cut the string of the pyjama.

The second sentence is equally poorly translated. Manto intentionally breaks it up into five distinct and fragmentary units. The first three lines are sharp, harsh and spasmodic. Their quickness of movement dramatizes both the wild plunging of the knife and the shocked surprise of the killer—it is typical of Manto's irony that the victim is left unacknowledged; he merely strays into a lethal historical time. The convulsive quality of the writing makes it apparent that for the knife wielding man, killing is merely a reflex action and the Partition an excuse. In the original, there is no hint that he is capable of expressing 'regret' or remorse—terms which give him a capacity for moral judgement and atonement. Manto is sure that Partition is neither a result of some recognizable ethical impulse nor of some profound religious need. Indeed, what is always scandalous about Manto is that, against all the weighty arguments in favour of the Partition, he is willing to take the risk of asserting, with mordant laughter, that a whole civilization was ripped apart for something extremely trivial and obscene—that the only way of distinguishing a true Muslim from a true Hindu was a man's foreskin. Therefore, the translation should suggest that when the killer realizes that the victim belongs to his own community, he is either 'aghast' or 'disgusted'—words which are closer to the original intention and indicate that during the Partition murder was no more than an instinct, a mindless passion, which hardly ever left a trace of remorse in the killer.

The sense that the man kills because he is moved by some innate bestial urge, is affirmed by the last exclamation, when he splutters incoherently, '*Chi, chi, chi* . . .' The vulgar and aggressive theatricality of the expletives cannot be replaced by the decorous and effete, 'Oh, no . . .' Unlike Hasan, Manto understood that the Partition not only deformed men, it also debased language. Indeed, one must hear the slow spitting sound of '*Chi, chi, chi* . . .' before one reaches the slurred consonant in 'mishtake'. The catch here is : Should one laugh at the lumpenization of language, or feel ashamed at the pornography of casual murder? Hasan, obviously, chooses easily and opts for the former.

Further, in keeping with his normal practice, Hasan, underplays all religious references which Pakistani nationalists or Muslim fundamentalists may find problematic. That is why, one suspects, he ignores the complexity of one of the following lines and erases Manto's bitter mockery of communal politics. By refusing to find an imaginative way of translating the compound phrase, *kalma-i-taassuf*, he directs attention away from the strong religious undertow in the phrase. It would surely have been pointless for Manto to write about the massacres during the Partition without clearly indicating, with all the contempt at his disposal, that the killers belonged to religious communities—that killing gave them a sense of identity and destiny. The Partition may have, to some measure, been the result of economic concerns or political fears, but it was primarily caused by religious intolerance and contempt—a fact which is yet to be fully investigated by the historians of the period.[7] Manto would have read with grim laughter the recent assertions by some Pakistani critics, like Muhammad Umar Memon and Salim-ur-Rehman, that for the Muslims, 1947 was a moment 'filled with grace', and that they rejoiced in the Partition because it was 'the telos of burgeoning historical expectations'.[8] Manto would have found this language, as all of us must, morally disgraceful. He would have rejected with equal vehemence, the claims of the Hindu fundamentalists that they alone were the embodiments of culture and holiness. Indeed, if ethicality can only be tested in the visible civil and political spaces of a society, such apocalyptic statements about the Partition should be made in the middle of streets, littered with corpses—then at least we should know that doom is a part of all such teleological dreams.

There is, hence, a deliberateness of purpose in Manto's use of the phrase *kalma-i-taassuf.* The liturgical ring of the phrase calls attention to itself because it is placed between the dramatic briskness of the previous lines and the staccato sounds that follow. It is a sonorous phrase, which acquires a strange preternatural force because of its ironic placement between a brutal murder and its casual dismissal; all the shards of reasons for the Partition seem to gather around it and make it into a shameful, causeless and demented historical event. A historian, like Ayesha Jalal, thinks of the Partition merely as 'the theatre of the absurd'—a metaphor which accepts the Partition as politically senseless, but fails to acknowledge the enormity of the human suffering involved.[9] Fiction writers like Manto, however, insist that any action should be judged by its moral consequences. We must ask, for instance, if we can approve of a political demand which leads to genocide. What makes the usage of the phrase *kalma-i-taassuf* even more interesting is that it persuades us to think about the ritual repetition of holy words uttered to save us from following the path of sin (the Hindi editors of Manto's *Dastavez* notice this, but they seem to be alone in doing so). The words which the killer utters, however, indicate how completely incapable he is of reciting the *kalma*, how far removed he is from grace.

The greatest damage Hasan does to Manto is to communalize him. He does so systematically, with design and in bad faith. In nearly every story he translates, there is an apparent communal purpose behind his omissions, shifts and quiet additions. Take, for instance, the translation of 'Thanda Gosht', a story that got Manto into trouble with the new Pakistani government for obscenity. Hasan translates the title as 'Colder than Ice', instead of the more obvious 'Cold Meat' so as to avoid Manto's blunt association between sexual sadism, necrophilia and the politics of defiling women. Unlike Hasan, Manto is neither an amoral prig nor is he afraid of giving offence (there are other instances of Hasan's concern with the censors: he translates the title 'Mootri', as 'Three Simple Statements', instead of 'Urinal'; the title 'Khol Do', which in the story refers to the automatic response a rape victim makes, by lowering her pyjamas and spreading her legs, when she hears those words, as 'The Return', instead of 'Open It', etc.). What is, however, more disturbing about Hasan's translation is that he slips in phrases, which are not there in the original, so as to give the story a nasty religious edge. Manto is painful to many because for him murder is murder, and no amount of religious mantras can swindle him into believing otherwise. Yet, Hasan would have us believe that 'Thanda Gosht' is Manto's particular condemnation of Sikh atrocities against the Muslims. Consider the following confession Ishar Singh makes to his wife in the Urdu version:

> *Kulwant meri jan! Main tumhein nahin bata sakta, mere saath kya hua. . . ? Insan kudiya bhi ek ajeeb cheez hai . . . Shahar mein loot machi to sabhi kee tarah mainey bhi usmein hissa liya . . . Gahne-patte aur rupaiye-paise jo bhi hath lagay, veh maine tumhein dey diye . . . Lekin ek baat tumhein na bataee. . .'* (*Dastavez*, II, p. 272)

Hasan edits out Ishar Singh's general assessment of human nature and omits stating that everyone was looting. Instead, he assumes that Ishar Singh is talking about targeting the Muslims and becoming a member of one of the gangs engaged in causing all the torment. His translation reads as follows:

> Kulwant, jani, you can have no idea what happened to me. When they began to loot Muslim shops and houses in the city, I joined one of the gangs. All the cash and ornaments that fell to my share, I brought back to you. There was only one thing I hid from you. (p. 28)

Even from the fragmentary example taken from the Urdu text, it should be clear that Manto's concern is not with laying blame on a particular community, but with trying to record a world in which anyone can drift into cruelty and slaughter. He crafts nightmares, not communal texts; he is difficult precisely because he does not suggest a religious solution to the politics of pain that was enacted during the Partition.

The trivializing impulse in Hasan is at its demonstrative best in his translation of 'Yazid'. This is a pity because 'Yazid', which is an enduring story, has rarely been translated. Included in one of the last collection of stories Manto published in his lifetime, in a volume entitled *Yazid* (1951), it marks a major departure from the mournful and damning stories he had written about the Partition earlier. 'Yazid' signals both an end to a long period of mourning over the Partition and a search for a new secular faith in life-giving energies and associations. What makes the story deeply interesting is that, while Manto refuses to take his eyes off the actualities of suffering, he offers a fine reformulation of 'faith' as that which human beings do out of affectionate regard for each other. This shift in the definition of faith enables him to suggest two things: that we give up our rage for ritual and religious identities, in order to escape, both from the fated programmes of life that we think are inscribed in religious texts and the melodramas of power; and that we begin to regard our little rituals of marriage, childbirth, friendship or burial as acts of moral care, which are sufficient for our common survival. 'Yazid' is a compelling and a brave story because it is Manto's most convincing refutation of the two-nation theory.

Hasan changes the title of the story and calls it 'The Great Divide'. By doing so he radically alters the essential thrust of Manto's text. The phrase, 'the great divide', is a cliché commonly used to argue that, since there was a long history of irreconcilable differences between the Hindus and the Muslims, the demand for Pakistan was historically inevitable and politically necessary. Hasan's title suggests that the story is important, not because it makes a moral and an existential investigation of the ways in which we can stop living theologically and mythically, and hence less fatally, but because it offers yet another legitimization of Muslim League politics. Hasan tries to divert attention away from Manto's harsh assertion that religious bigotry destroyed comities, which sustained Hindus and Muslims together, in order to persuade us that Manto only wants to describe the plight of a few Punjabi villagers in Pakistan living in fear of renewed Hindu aggression a few years after 1947. As usual, therefore, he simplifies Manto and transforms the story into an anecdote. He fails to notice that the real significance of the story lies in the fact that Manto, who sees himself as an exile, is moving toward a new ethical position, which is radically distinct from everything he had held before: that those who have suffered great political wrong have a responsibility to ensure that *caritas* is never erased from our visible civil spaces; that migrants from a past of nightmares must cease to be fascinated with their own weakness and refuse to surrender, ever again, the autonomy of the self either to nostalgia or hate; and that it is possible for exiles of a partition to remake their communities provided they give up their dependence on that which is merely religious or political, and instead ask themselves what it is that is immediately necessary and what will suffice to sustain life in a community.

By calling the story 'Yazid', Manto draws upon one of the foundational events of Islam. It is said that Yazid denies Hasan, Hussain and their followers water in Karbala and so ensures their defeat and death.[10] Like Satan and Ravana, he is the figure of primal evil, the demon of unreason who threatens with destruction all that is virtuous. Manto invokes Yazid and the origins of Islam for two complex and interwoven reasons. One, he uses Yazid analogically in order to re-examine the historical assertion that hatred between the Muslims and the Hindus is a fact, which has always defined the relations between them from the very beginning of their contract with each other on the Indian subcontinent. Two, he uses the figure of Yazid ethically so as to reject the claim of the protagonists of the two-nation theory that their migration was a *hijrat* in search of an Islamic homeland free from the threat of contamination by the Hindu *kafirs* (Yazids), just as the wanderings of the earliest disciples of Muhammad were an aspect of the necessary rites of passage towards a sanctified place. Manto, in contradiction, wants to suggest that Yazid is not out there only in a community whose faith is different from the Muslims, but a part of each of us, Hindus and Muslims alike—that we are Yazids when we refuse to take responsibility for our actions or when we dream of killing as a way of proving our holiness; and, that the history of relations between the Hindus and the Muslims was as complicated a mixture of harmony and antagonism as is the case with any group of people who have lived together for ages. Thus, he uses Yazid, not to strengthen the historical or religious claims of a few survivors of the riots in Pakistan, but to replace the language of religion by the practice of a mode of analysis which is concrete, moral and psychological, and in the service of community making.

It is difficult to enumerate the variety of ways in which Hasan's translation damages the text of the story. His changes, additions, deletions, misreadings and summaries are so extensive and arbitrary that the English version of the story resembles the original only in its essential outline. It is, however, worth describing a few of Hasan's intrusions and elisions, which twist the story in ways antithetical to Manto's intentions.

In the opening sentence, the narrator (who is not necessarily Manto—he is after all not writing an autobiographical anecdote but a work of fiction) suggests that the troubles of the Partition were disruptions in the daily lives of the villagers, they came and went like a few days of unseasonable weather in any normal cycle of seasons. The context of the story makes it clear that the narrator's reasons for making an equation between the riots that disturbed the peace in 1947 and unexpected hours of inclement weather are two-fold: he is offering his own version of Fernand Braudel's notion of the *longue duree* of history in which 1947 seems to be less atrocious than it does to those who are caught in the immediate catastrophe; and he is hinting at the singular ability of the central character of the story, Karim Dad, to deal with suffering as an integral part of the process of living and to assert that in any life there are seasons of sorrow and seasons for celebration. The opening sentence, thus, provides the historical and ethical presupposition of the story and is crucial for our understanding of Karim Dad's actions.

In the original the opening sentence reads as follows:

San saintalees ke hungamey aaye aur guzar gaye, bilkul usee tarah jis tarah mausam mein khilafe-mamool chand din kharab aayein aur chale jayein . . .

(*Dastavez*, II, p. 183)

Hasan translates the sentence as follows:

The 1947 upheavals came and went, much like the few bad days you get in an otherwise sunny Punjabi winter. (p. 132)

Hasan's translation of the sentence is deaf to its nuances and its fictional purpose. Without any sanction from the original, he converts it into a localized observation: 'a few bad days you get in an otherwise sunny Punjabi winter'. He, thus, transforms an important statement about character and history into a personal report on provincial weather. There is no mention about the sunny winters of Punjab in the Urdu text, nor does the narrator address any listener or reader directly in order to seek his approval of, or complicity in, his trite observation. In any case, Manto knows better than to provoke us to ask whom the pronoun 'you' refers to and where is he located in the fictional structure. The narrator's statement is addressed to anyone who has meditated upon human affairs and, perhaps, sought consolation by locating them within the larger stability of either nature or culture. Such thinking, he knows, does not lessen the suffering or erase the memory of loss, but it does make sorrow a little more endurable.

Manto knows, with the usual intelligence of a good short story writer, that cadences of speech and qualities of diction and action are inextricable aspects of making a character. Hasan, on the other hand, with his continuous disregard for the requirements of fictional narratives, thinks that a few random verbal strokes, made without paying attention to tone and diction, are sufficient to indicate a character's role in carrying the action forward. The fact that the purpose of the story may not lie only in the incidents described but in the character's complex presence within them is of no consequence to him. Thus, in the original, after Karim Dad buries his father, who dies fighting during the riots, he stands by his father's grave near a village well and says: '*Yaar, tumney theek nahin kia . . . Mainey tumse kaha tha ki eik-aadha hathiyaar apne pass zaroor rakha karo* . . . !' (*Dastavez*, II, p. 183). If one has to convey the coarse poetry and informality of Karim Dad's speech in English, one should perhaps translate it as: 'Yaar, what you did wasn't right . . . Didn't I tell you to keep a weapon or two with you . . . !' Hasan, however, translates it prosaically as an address to no one in particular: 'He should have listened to me. Didn't I tell him one must keep at least one weapon on one's person these days?' (p.133). The original is a direct admonition to his father as someone familiar and a friend. There is sorrow in it, but there is also a jauntiness of spirit and an ability to accept life's difficulties—indeed, all the qualities which later enable Karim Dad to find the resources within himself and his immediate surroundings to leave behind his memories of pain. Hasan's translation, on the other hand, is cliché-soaked. It flattens out the rhythmic particularity of Karim Dad's speech that distinguishes him from his neighbours who are equally distraught. Hasan drags him down to the level of the commonplace and so produces a disjunction between what Karim Dad appeared to be then and what he would do later.

Like all finer works of fiction, 'Yazid' is shaped by paradoxes, which undermine the expected and the ideologically determined. In nearly every story about sexual desire that Manto wrote before the Partition, he presented sexuality as an extension of the loathsomeness of the social realm. In 'Yazid', surprisingly, he writes a rare story in which the erotic is joyous and exuberant. Carnal delight, he seems to suggest with a deliberate wink at the clergy and the judge, may be the earthly equivalent of grace.

In the story, Karim Dad insists on celebrating his marriage with lights and music even before the villagers had completed the rites for the dead and ceased to weep. Others are still absorbed by their fears, which makes them once again susceptible to jingoism, indoctrination and hysterical action. They think that his marriage procession is a march of ghosts through their village. Karim Dad knows that in their refusal to make a rational analysis of the actual relations between the Hindus and the Muslims, they had once confused the ghosts of history and religion with reality and so had caused the Partition and its agony. He, therefore, laughs at them and refuses to make religion and hate the basis of his new existence. Instead, he attempts to remake his life through sexual and familial love. His wonderfully gross vocabulary, which mixes crude sensuality with tenderness, sets into motion the celebrative process of generativity. Hasan's translation retains some of the gentleness of Karim Dad's love for Jeena, but makes it sentimental by deleting long sections in which Manto insists on revealing how desperately hard-won their love for each other really is, how long a period of mourning they had to work through in order to win for themselves some 'moral time'[11] for pleasure, irreverence, laughter and children. Manto intercuts the description of their maturing love, with constant reminders of the massacres of their relatives and friends, in order to show how they had come to realise that the claims of human desire are far more worthy than the claims of religious texts and tribal identities. Hasan not only edits the text in order to tell a simple love story, he also adds a long paragraph explaining who Hasan and Hussain were and how Yazid had caused their defeat, in order to give an Islamic frame of reference to the narrative. If in Manto's version Karim Dad and Jeena, slowly and painfully, learn through experience to make a commitment to a moral life, in Hasan's version they become a part of a Muslim narrative and a political statement.

Just as he longs for a life of fulfilled desire, Karim Dad also longs for a life of social coherence. Given the history of recent times, he understands the fragility of civil reason, yet he seeks to recreate life around the traditional institutions of marriage and village community. Driven both by what Robert Jay Lifton calls the self's instinctual urge for immortality,[12] as well as his own worldliness and realism, he argues with his friends and neighbours who have survived, that their present suffering is as much a result of their own logic and decisions as it is of the action of the people they now regard as their enemies. He urges them to understand that the Partition is a social and political event, instead of thinking about it as a religious melodrama in which Hindu villains are fated to play out their role as killers. Political history, he tells them, is radically different from a mythic narrative. In the first, antagonism of the moment has historical causes and one can find a solution to it; in the second, deliverance from evil is impossible and all one can do is either to pray or curse.

The argument between Karim Dad and the villagers, about the untrustworthiness of the Hindus and the necessity of revenge, is an elaborate one. It is conducted in the village square, through a series of brief exchanges that are colloquial, robust and earthy. While the village headman, Choudhry Nathoo, is jingoistic and abusive, Karim Dad speaks with irony and humour, cold logic and frankness. Manto crafts the dialogue between them and others very carefully in order to show how important it is to restore civil spaces where people can begin to learn once again that any moral and political dialogue can always be conducted without the use of force or the language of self-righteous anger. What is important here is to notice how Karim Dad's voice of calm reasonableness begins to be heard over the noisy rhetoric of the Choudhry, and finally gains a hearing.

Unfortunately, Hasan radically rewrites this section of the story. He cuts and pastes the original text so drastically that it is impossible to compare his version with the Urdu one in any meaningful way. He deletes the gestures Karim Dad repeatedly makes, which not only establish him as a man of self-assured grace and friendliness, but also affirm that he has worked his way towards a sense of psychic and communal confidence. Further, he transforms Karim Dad's insistent voice of reasonableness, which tries to persuade others dialogically, into a sermonizing voice which imposes itself through assertion.

The section is too long to quote here in its entirety, but what is distressing about the translation of the last conversational cluster and the manner in which it ends is that Hasan almost completely edits the presence of Karim Dad's childhood friend, Meeranbaksh, out of the debate, a move that both distorts the way the dialogue progresses and ends, and alters the basic intention of the story. In Hasan's text, Nathoo withdraws from the discussion pleading helplessness to offer any further argument, while Karim Dad merely gets up and leaves. The last part of the conversation reads as follows in Hasan's version:

'You are talking nonsense', was all that the headman could counter Karim Dad with.

But Karim Dad had not finished. 'It just so happens that the Indians are now in a position to take our water away from us. So, let's do something about it, instead of sitting here and abusing them. Don't expect the enemy to dig canals for you and fill them with milk and honey; expect him to poison your water so that you drink it and die. You will call it barbarism. I don't. If it is war, then war is, not a wedding contract with pre-conditions and the rest of it. You can't say, all right we will go to war, provided you don't starve us or take away our food.

If you must fire at us, use only a certain brand of cartridge. Be reasonable.'

'And how do I do that?' Choudhry Nathoo asked. Karim Dad did not answer, but rose and left. (p. 141)

Manto's original text, however, is radically different and reads as follows:

Choudhry Nathoo bhun gaya: 'Yeh tu kya bakwas kar raha hai?'

Meeranbaksh ne bhi haule-se Karim Dad se poochcha: 'Han yaar, yeh kya bakwas hai?'

'Bakwas nahin hai Meeranbaksha . . .' Karim Dad ne samjhane ke undaz mein Meeranbaksh se kaha: 'Tu zara soch to sahi ladai mein dono phareek ek-dusarey ko pachchadney ke leya kya kuchch nahin kartey . . . . Pahalwan jab lungar-lungot kaskey akhade mein uttar aatey hain to unhain har daainv istaymaal karney ka haq hot hai.'

Meeranbaksh ne upna ghuta sir hilaya: 'Yeh to theek hai.'

Karim Dad muskaraya: 'To fir dariya band karna bhi theek hai. . . . Hamarey leya yeh zulm hai, magar unkey leya rava hai.'

'Rava kya hai . . . Jab teree jeeb pyas key marey latakkar zameen tak aa jayegi to phir main puchchoonga key zulm rava hai ja narava . . . Jab tere baal-bachche annaj kay ek-ek dane ko tarasaingey to phir bhi yahi kahena ki dariya band karna bilkul theek tha.'

Karim Dad nein upney khushk honthon par zabaan pheri aur kaha: 'Main jab bhi kahoonga Choudhry . . . Tum yeh kyon bhool jaatey ho ki sirph veh hamaarey dushman nahin, hum bhee to unkey dushman hain . . . Agar hamarey ikhtyaar main hota to humnein bhi unka dana-pani band kar diya hota . . . Aab jaab ki veh aiysa kar sakta hain, aur karneywala hain to hum zaroor uska koi tord sochainegey . . . Bekar galiyan daney se kya hota hai . . . Dushman tumahre leeya doodh ki nahrein jari nahin kareya Choudhry Nathoo . . . Us sey agar ho saka to vey tumhari paani ki haar boond mein zahar mila dega . . . Tum us sey zulm kahogey, vehshiyanapan kahogey, isleye ki marney ka yeh tareeka tumhey pasand nahin . . . Ajeeb-si baat hai ki ladayi shuroo karney sey pahaley dushman sey nikha kisi shartein manvayi jayen . . . Us sey kaha jaye ki dekho, mujhey bhookha na marna . . . Bandook si aur veh bhi itney bore ki bandook se, albaata tum mujhey shock se halay kar saktey ho . . . Aasal bakwas to yeh hai . . . Zara thandey dil se socho!'

Choudhry Nathoo jhunjhulahaat ki aakhari haad tak pahunch gaya: 'Baraf la ke rakh mere dil par.'

'Yeh bhi main hi laun?' Yeh kehkar Karim Dad hansa. Veh Meeranbaksh key kandhey par thapki deykar utha aur chaupaal sey chala gaya. (*Dastavez*, II, p. 189-90)

This section can, perhaps, be translated as follows:

Irritated, Choudhry Nathoo said, 'You are talking rubbish.'

Meeranbaksh also said quietly, 'That's right, yaar, you are talking rubbish.'

'I am not talking rubbish . . .' Karim Dad said, trying to make Meeranbaksh see reason. 'Why don't you understand that in a war enemies try to do everything possible to defeat each other . . . When a wrestler tightens his loin-cloth and steps into the wrestling pit, doesn't he have the right to use any subterfuge, any hold . . . ?'

Still tense, Meeranbaksh nodded his head in agreement, 'Yes, he has the right.'

Karim Dad smiled, 'Then it follows that an enemy also has the right to dam a river . . . We may think it's unjust, but he thinks it's just . . .'

'How is it just . . .? When your mouth is dry and your tongue hangs down to the ground, then I'll ask you if it's just or unjust . . . I hope that when your children are dying for a grain of wheat, you'll still say that it's just to dam a river.'

Karim Dad ran his tongue across his parched lips, 'Even then I'll say it, Choudhry! You forget that if they are our enemy, we are their enemy too . . . If we had the power, we'd also dam their river and destroy their crops . . . Since they can dam the river, and are about to do so, we should do something about it . . . There's no point in cursing . . . Your enemy will not dig a canal for you and fill it with milk, Choudhry Nathoo . . . If he can, he'll mix poison in every drop of water you drink . . . You may think it's barbaric, because you don't want to be killed like that . . . But isn't it strange that even before you go to war, you want to lay down conditions, as if you are negotiating a marriage contract . . .? You want to plead, don't let me starve to death. Shoot me but only with a gun of a certain size . . . That, surely, is rubbish . . . Think about it with a cool head.'

By then Choudhry Nathoo was at his wits end, 'Why don't you get a slab of ice and place it on my head!'

'Am I supposed to do even that?' Karim Dad laughed. Then he patted Meeranbaksh on his shoulder, stood up and left the village square.

In Hasan's version, Karim Dad's attempt to find a language of community making is suddenly aborted. There is no sanction for such an abrupt end to a dialogue whose texture and intention, clearly suggest that Manto is exploring the possibilities of human renewal. Nor is there any sanction for naming Indians as enemies. In Manto's version, Karim Dad does not walk away in triumphant silence. Instead, his witty repartee and final gesture ensure that the village square remains open for companionship and conversation. It is clear, as he teases Nathoo, that he knows how difficult it is to convert men like Nathoo to the side of reason—if the task had been easy then the horror of the Partition may never have happened, nor would the continued history of communal violence have demanded our attention. Without the last smile and embrace, 'Yazid', as a story, remains an interesting addition to Manto's fictional history of a time when religion clawed its way across all that a civilization had created, instead of being what it significantly is—a fine meditation on the fate of reason and sympathetic imagination in times of political and moral disaster.

The importance of Manto's stories about the Partition lies in the fact that he is neither a moralist nor an ideologue, neither a sermonizer nor a nationalist. Like a good fiction writer, he refuses to turn his gaze away from what he sees, even though he is bewildered and shocked by the pain human beings, in their frenzy of small claims and neurotic resentments, are willing to inflict on each other. The best of his Partition stories surprise us by bringing together, in darkly illuminating moments of existential understanding, terrible violence and the beauty of the human yearning for sex, children, home and community, which refuse to yield its instinctual energy to the death-traps religious fanaticism and extremist politics lay for us. It is, therefore, important to translate his stories with care in order to reveal how they are constructed out of a complex variety of strong voices—voices of protest and anguish, mockery and nostalgia, mourning and longing—voices that clash against each other and jostle for a hearing. Khalid Hasan's translation, unfortunately, is much too weak and sentimental, partisan and censorious to show us why Manto is the kind of witness whose work may help us understand our shattered past.

NOTES

1. Sadaat Hasan Manto, *Mottled Dawn: Fifty Sketches and Stories of Partition* (New Delhi, 1997) (hereafter, all references to this volume are included in the text). While Hasan's translations have been praised, the reasons for approval are curious. There are two clichés that are generally used about thése translations. The first says that the translations are in 'idiomatic English', and the second, that they capture the 'flavour' of the original. No reviewer, however, bothers to explain what is so worthy about 'idiomatic English', or what precisely it is. Nor does any reviewer ever pause to wonder whether the task of 'capturing' flavour should not be left to cooks and writers on culinary matters—that translators have a different kind of work to do.
2. Twelve of the stories included in these editions are taken from an earlier volume edited by Hasan. See *Kingdom's End and Other Stories* (London, 1987).
3. For a detailed analysis of the story see Alok Bhalla, 'A Dance of Grotesque Masks: A Critical Reading of Manto's "1919 Ki Ek Baat" ', in Alok Bhalla, ed., *Life and Works of Saadat Hasan Manto* (Shimla, 1997), pp. 28-54. See also my translation of the story in *Kunapipi*, Vol. XIII, No. 3 (1997), pp. 16-22.
4. Many of these aspects of Hasan's translation have also been listed by M. Asaduddin in an article published in Alok Bhalla, ed., op.cit., pp. 159-71.
5. All references to Manto's writings are from Balraj Manra and Sharad Dutt, ed., *Dastavez*, Vols I-V(New Delhi, 1993) (hereafter, references are included in the text).
6. For a discussion of the relation between might and humiliation, see Simone Weil's wonderful essay, 'The *Iliad*, Poem of Might', in *Imitations of Christianity Among the Ancient Greeks* (London, 1987), pp. 24-55.
7. Recently, Gyanendra Pandey has drawn attention to the curious fact that the history of religious politics in India has found little place in the accounts of the Partition being written. See, 'Memory, History and the Question of Violence: Reflections on the

Reconstruction of Partition' (1998). This essay, in two parts, was consulted when it was in manuscript.

8. These remarks by Memon are taken from his unpublished article 'The World of Intizar Hussain'. Memon's Pakistani nationalism and aggressive Islamic identity politics are, however, apparent in all his published writings. Thus, in an article entitled 'Partition Literature: A Study of Intizar Hussain', *Modern Asian Studies*, Vol. XIV, No. 3 (1980), pp. 377- 410, he says that, whereas the Muslim writers of the Progressive Movement remained attached to 'Nehru's sentimental attachment to a united India' (p. 348), the Muslim leadership 'had the common sense' to realise that the idea of 'communal harmony' was 'unattainable' (pp. 383-4). The 'course of history', he says, has shown 'the Progressives to be wrong' (p. 396).

   Memon feels himself under no obligation to say that a significant number of Muslim leaders did not feel that the demand for Pakistan was either commonsensical or justified by history—and continued to feel that way even after the Partition. Indeed, if the new biographies of Jinnah are to be believed, there is sufficient evidence to show that even the Quaid-i-Azam was ambivalent towards the demands for Pakistan. Memon, however, does not have to be worried about the complexities and paradoxes of history. For him the history of Partition is nothing more than a *feeling* for the aspiration of some Muslims who supported Muslim League politics. As a counter to people like Memon, see Mushirul Hasan's *The Legacy of a Nation Divided* (New Delhi, 1997).

   In his recent 'Introduction' to *An Epic Unwritten: Urdu Stories About Partition* (New Delhi, 1998), Memon advises his Indian colleagues to be aware of deconstructive strategies while writing about the Partition. Perhaps. But it would have been better if Memon, instead of spending a good number of pages in name-calling and mud-slinging had taken his own advice to heart and done precisely that.

9. Ayesha Jalal, *The Sole Spokesman: Jinnah, the Muslim League and the Demand for Pakistan* (Lahore, 1992), pp. 96-7.

10. It would not be surprising if one were to discover that Manto used the foundational story of Islam deliberately to counter the use of the same story for propaganda purposes by a major Urdu writer, Ahmed Nadeem Qasmi, who was once a Progressive thinker, but after migration to Lahore in 1947 had decided to write diatribes against India. Qasmi's poem, which is of concern here, is a battle cry of the Kashmiri freedom fighter. Later, the great Pakistani writer, Intizar Hussain, was to use the idea of *hijrat* for his complex exploration of the idea of homeland and civilization.

11. Robert Coles defines 'moral time' as a time of the awakening of conscience. See, *The Political Life of Children* (Boston, 1986), p. 71.

12. Robert J. Lifton, *The Life of the Self: Toward a New Psychology* (New York, 1961), pp. 91-142.

The Paradox of a Fleeting Presence: Partition and Bengali Literature

TAPATI CHAKRAVARTY

Between 1961 and 1971, Satyajit Ray toyed with the idea of making a film on what had perhaps been the most cataclysmic event in the history of modern Bengal, the Partition. Yet, the project never materialized, apparently due to the lack of adequate time and opportunity.[1] His notebook reveals that Ray had even prepared a draft outline of the script, including detailed shot divisions and dialogues for a few scenes. Finally, he abandoned the project and began writing the screenplay for his now famous film on the Bengal famine of 1943, *Ashani Sanket*. Interestingly, he used the same notebook for the two scripts.

The silent bulwarks of Satyajit Ray's genius were the short stories and novels on which his films were based. The *Apu* trilogy and *Ashani Sanket*, written by Bibhutibhushan Bandyopadhyaya, *Charulata*, *Teen Kanya* and *Ghare Baire* based on Tagore's short stories and novels, *Jalshaghar* by Tarashankar Bandyopadhyaya, are some examples, to name a few. Here perhaps one finds the secret of Ray's reluctance to make a film on the Partition. There are virtually no short stories or novels of note[2] in the Bengali language that deal with the Partition as its main theme. On the other hand, even a most cursory glance at poetry of the contemporary period, reveals the overwhelming presence of the Partition as a central leitmotif. The historian of literature is then faced with this enormous paradox, the almost total absence of the Partition in fiction and its recurrent presence in poetry. This essay, I hope, would be a contribution to the unravelling of this paradox.

*I would like to thank my son, Aunindyo, for critical comments on an earlier draft of this paper and also for translating the extracts from poems of Dinesh Das, Mangalacharan Chattopadhyaya and Bishnu Dey.

I

I shall begin by posing a question: how did realistic literature of the first half of the twentieth century, deal with the issues raised within contemporary history? The central themes in Bengali fiction of the first four decades of this century, could be classified into four basic themes: (i) questions of nationalism, the ideal nation, the right path to freedom and the possibility of an ideal society; (ii) the encounter of tradition with modernity, its impact on social institutions (most importantly, the family), behavioural codes and the ethics of *bhadralok* existence, in short the question of samaj; (iii) the gender issue, women's individuality, position within the family, etc.; and (iv) the transition from a feudal/primitive economy to a capitalist/industrial society. To this last theme were related the disintegration of rural communities, the concomitant migration to cities and the attendant effects of a peculiar late colonial urbanization.

It is here that one would also find fiction operating on a different but converging axis. Its themes were, once again, those of the trauma and impact of modernization and economic transition, with the important difference that it was not restricted to *bhadralok* existence in terms of its subject matter. This type of literature, which made its first appearance in the literary journal, *Kallol* (1923), became the dominant literary tradition towards the end of the 1930s. The immediate background to the emergence of this type of literature, which, for want of a better term, I shall call radical fiction, was the changing nature of political mobilization and practice in Bengal.

Mainstream or élite politics in Bengal has diverged to a significant extent from the course taken by the Gandhian Congress. Its punctuation (the so-called 'movements') did not generally coincide with those of the Congress-led national movement and this fact has shown up in nationalist historiography as the recurrent 'failures' of the national movement in Bengal. Here, nationalist politics was dominated by the Swaraj Party, which sought to carve out an independent path from that of the Congress. By the 1920s the question of mass political mobilization had begun to occupy an important position in political debates.[3] The specific character of predatory commercialization in Bengal had resulted in the sharpening of the agrarian question, especially after the slump in jute prices in the early 1930s.[4] It is within this process that the two interrelated but different political processes took shape—agrarian struggles revolving around the Krishak Praja Party and the Bangiya Pradeshik Kishan Sabha and the crystallization of communalism as a political ideology.[5] Simultaneously, with the emergence of the Communist Party and the leftward tilt of trade unions, Socialist and Communist ideas found greater acceptance among the radical elements of the *bhadralok*. Preliminary attempts were being made to utilize Marxist concepts to understand society and social processes. Situations and relationships between fictional characters were increasingly treated in a self-consciously materialistic manner. The aesthetic-romantic vision of Rabindranath Tagore was giving way to an equally romantic, anti-aestheticism. This romantic veneration of the cruel, the sensual and the grotesque, is best exemplified in the classic fiction of one of the famous 'three Bandyopadhyayas' of Bengali literature, Manik Bandyopadhyaya.

Fiction increasingly began to deal with the issues of rural and urban poverty, rising unemployment, retrenchment, hardships associated with the great depression, shrinking returns from rents, etc. Rising prices, adulteration of goods, hoarding, the flesh trade, etc., had become important literary themes even before the 1940s when the war and famine, brought them directly into *bhadralok* homesteads. Along with the large-scale economic disruption caused by the war and famine, there came the increasing frequency of riots and communal disturbances.[6] The issue of communal harmony too became a regular theme, especially in short stories revolving around incidents of communal violence.

By all accounts then, Bengali fiction was extremely reflective of all the major events and processes that have come to be identified as the constitutive elements of Bengal's history in the first half of the twentieth century. Indeed, the historian would find contemporary history almost mirrored in the pages of Bengali fiction, of this period. Yet, when it comes to the Partition, one is faced by an almost all-pervasive, uneasy silence. It would be easy to explain this, as some critics have done, in terms of the territorial origins of major novelists and litterateurs. It is true that some of the best known names in the world of Bengali literature were from the western part of Bengal, and hence the Partition did not affect them. Such an argument, however, reveals a rather naive notion about the relationship between an author's immediate experience and the subject matter of his writing and can be only a partial explanation. After all one would then have to explain why migrant *bhadralok* from East Bengal did not take to writing novels or short stories about their own experiences of the Partition. The answer, as I see it, lies in the very structure of the ideological fields within which the litterateurs 'experienced' their lived world and the discursive fields within which they formulated themes of fiction.

II

The list of major themes that I presented in the previous section appears to mirror the actual processes of contemporary history rather comprehensively.[7] What one takes to be the reflection of the history of Bengal in Bengali literature is indeed the reflection of the way in which that history has been written and understood. It is no coincidence that one would find the same motif in nationalist and Left-nationalist historiography, that one finds in literature. What this indicates is the much larger connection between nationalist discourse and the knowledge of history, a connection that neither emanates from nor is restricted to history textbooks. Instead the notion of history enters into everyday speech, saturates it and forms its organizing principle.[8]

The ideological collective of the nation is a peculiar one since it is not a community. Indeed, the essential difference between a community and a nation lies in the specific way in which the concrete individual and the collective are related. While in the ideological collective of the nation, the relationship between the individual-as-subject and the collective appears to be an external and a constituted relation, within the collective of the community, the collective and the individual appear to be contiguous. Within the nation, based as it is on the modern civil society, the absence of a community, which subsumes the individual, necessitates the formation of identities, not in the present collective, but in an imagined past. Nationalist discourse thus must continuously search for the historical roots of the present, and construct a history, in which the self acquires a distinct continuity with the past, as well as a distinct difference in being the realization of a process of development. In the nationalist discourse, thus, a nation is always already a potential nation, a potential it contains in its very origin. What is perceived as the true course of history then, is the realization of this process inherent in the origin. The truth of a nationalist history of a nation, thus is the formation of the nation-state.

The novel is considered to be a modern literary form due to its secular-rational content. At the same time, what distinguishes a novel from other literary forms is that its subject matter, the interrelationship of characters, its canvas are all structured by a notion of history, which simultaneously form its backdrop. The novel is thus always deeply imbued with history in its choice of subject matter and in the way in which the subject matter is posed as a problem. This same notion of history becomes the silent condition for both the structuration, as well as the comprehension, of short stories. The literary form of the short story is subordinated to the existence of the novel.

The novels and short stories written in the Bengali language, in the first half of the present century, have been very closely tied to contemporary notions of history. And here one can draw out three basic discursive or politico-ideological formations[9] within which the Bengali literati identified their themes, posed contemporary problems and deployed the narrative artefacts within the structure of the literary text. Two of these are identifiably modern: that of nationalism and Left rationalism. Not only were these two discursive formations interrelated, but also they were often found combined in the same text. The third discursive formation, which haunted literary texts with its fleeting subterranean presence, was that of pre-rationalist, hierarchical-communitarian, discourses. It was a presence, which could not be exorcized and was especially recurrent in the novels, dealing with the rural *bhadralok*. Within these discursive formations there were infinite thematic variations, which allowed for differences between the ways in which authors constructed their texts. To understand the specific ways in which fiction could have been constructed in the period of the Partition, one would, thus, have to take a closer look at Bengali literature of the 1940s.[10]

III

Many authors wrote about the famine of 1943 with great sensitivity, though *Ashani Sanket* by Bibhutibhushan Bandyopadhyaya[11] was the most famous. The writings of this period were self-consciously realistic and remarkably sensitive to their contemporary world. Sympathies with the rural poor and Left rationalism[12] were very much a part of the changing political climate of Bengal though the class orientation of the authors bound them to the familiar nationalist bourgeois/liberal ideological framework. Yet what forced the pace of attitudinal changes was the violence inherent within the repressive imperialist state—a violence which found full expression in the 1930s and the 1940s, not just in India but as a world wide phenomena. This spilled over and permeated the militant Indian youth, transforming a whole generation.[13]

To give an example, Satinath's 'Jagori' (While Awake), 1945, was caught between the radical Left and the bourgeois nationalist politics of which the Congress was the symbol.[14] Diverging politico-ideological principles that pulled two brothers into totally different political worlds also made them act in total contradiction to each other. It attempts to portray the conflict between dedication to an ideology (and loyalty to the Party) and 'natural' human values is sincere, no doubt. Yet, it would not be an exaggeration to say that his characterization of politics and the interrelationship between social relations/processes and the novel's 'events' are products of a very naive and uncritical acceptance of liberal-nationalist (in other words, the Indian National Congress) notions of society and history. The relationship between the brothers and their respective political choices appear as independent choices made by autonomous individuals, a notion which is a product of straightforward imputation of the ideal of a civil-society.

What a survey of the fiction of this period reveals is the growing tendency towards a mode of organization of the subject matter, which is self-consciously sociological. Stories about the famine tended to revolve around issues of price rise, unemployment, hoarding, prostitution, breakdown of social institutions and, significantly, personal liberation through an identification with the masses. The influence of an economic understanding of society is evident from both a bourgeois as well as a Left Socialist perspective. Equally noteworthy is the radical questioning of institutions, which have emerged along with bourgeois society, especially in regard to the position of women within the family and the larger world.[15]

Yet, on the issue of what constituted a nation and a nation-state, there was a remarkable degree of agreement, between nationalist and Left radical thought. For the nationalist discourse of the mid-twentieth century, the legitimate and stable basis for a nation-state was a loose cultural homogeneity within a territorially specific area. Thus, India that is Bharat was the natural territorial basis for the Indian nation-state. For the Communists (and those allied to them) the socio-historical basis for a nation was a linguistic community, bound by a single market; hence India was a 'multinational' state. In both these discursive systems, the question of a nation was, more or less, settled. It was a problem, which had been resolved in the past in the history of development of modern Indian thought. Despite subtle differences in approach, all secular thinkers agreed that religious identity could not be the basis for a nation-state. The belief that people sharing a religious identity form a community and this community is the true basis for the establishment of a just and sovereign nation-state, was what came to be termed as communalism.

Manoranjan Hazra's *Managare Dabanol* (The Prairie Fire in the City), 1946, is one of the only two novels with a communal riot as its theme. The Muslim League's call for Direct Action is seen as the immediate cause of the riot. The Calcuttan's experience of the preceding years—of quickly organizing demonstrations, barricades or guerrilla battles—was now being used, in the novel, for raising overnight an armed nucleus of communal organizations in different localities. The newspapers did not report the redeeming unity of the factory workers and their bold defence of the girls' hostel. Probir, a Communist, joins hands with his friend Osman, a former Muslim Leaguer, to resist the rioters and to organize relief for the riot-stricken. In the second novel dealing with the riots, while describing the events of 16 August 1946, Saroj Kumar Raychaudhuri in *Mahakal* (The Ominous Times), 1946, says:

> The situation rapidly went out of control. Looting and plunder, burning, murder, rape, mob violence—nothing was left to the imagination. One felt, that the traditional values and culture that have developed over hundreds of years had been shorn-off in a matter of moments, and the people of Bengal had returned to those pre-historic barbaric days of the past.[16]

Communalism, equated with communal riots, appears as a 'moment of madness', a moment at which civilization gives way to barbarism, humanity to animalistic behaviour. This treatment of communalism as an abnormal, accidental moment of an otherwise 'natural' course of history, is characteristic of nationalist historiography.[17] The 'cause' of the riots remains imperialist machinations, divide and rule and 'outside instigation' by vested interests.

The riots, which fed on a growing lumpenization of the unemployed poor, become the theme in 'Ijjat' (Prestige), 1950, a short story by Baren Basu. A young unemployed boy, a member of the lower middle class, represents this lumpenization. His father says:

> Wretched riot, it made my son a beast. He has committed murders, looted. . . . His mother has become mad. . . . Tell me, what do you want? Do you want your son to go around killing people, putting their houses on fire, dumping looted property in your house . . . does not that affect your prestige? . . . I don't need any prestige—only let my son become a man.[18]

The active part in the riot is that of a 'lumpen', who has become one because of his unemployed status and his poverty. His father retains a sense of position and prestige within his immediate society. Yet he is ready to trade off all his *ijjat* for his son's return to the folds of humanity, to become a man from a beast. Once again, riots are seen as the product of an inhuman existence, which arouses the primeval beast in man, a momentary slide into anarchic 'barbarism'.

The genesis of a sudden distrust and communal belligerence is the theme of 'Dangar Shamay' (When Riots Come), a short story by Balai Chand Mukhopadhyaya, who wrote under the pseudonym Banaphool.

Apprehending an attack from the neighbouring Muslims (and rumours are easily believed in such an atmosphere), the Hindus persuade the hero to use his gun. Two figures attempt to enter the compound of his house in the dark through a breach in the wall, and gunshots hit the targets accurately. One dies instantly and the other is seriously injured. The injured one is an old Muslim friend who had chosen this house as the only safe shelter and the one that died is the hero's old foster mother, who had given the milk of her breast to the hero in his early childhood (since his own mother could not).[19] The extremely powerful and convincing manner in which the author has managed to portray his own ideas of the genesis of a communal situation, makes it difficult to unravel the text's conditions of production. It is a difficulty redoubled by the nature of the narrative structure itself—which attempts to efface any manifest presence of the author. In the very sequencing of the narrative and its 'shocking' closure one finds the underlying notions of 'natural human bonds', 'love' and their 'accidental violation'. Yet, the structuring of the narrative is such that the very notions of love and human bonds are brought into question by the fact that they can so easily and accidentally be destroyed. Indeed, amongst the numerous stories on the riots, Banaphool's short stories come closest to operating as somewhat tentative ideological critiques.

But the majority of the fiction relating to the riots and to communalism remained within an identifiably nationalist and a bourgeois-rationalist perspective. Even the Communist litterateurs worked within a bourgeois-economistic notion of communalism as a false consciousness whose real basis was rising prices, unemployment, etc. The capitalists and the agents of imperialism saw communalism as a divisive ideology foisted upon the people to divert them from the real struggle. Indeed, these notions formed the basis for a conscious 'literary policy' directed towards the representation of communalism in literature. For example, Dipen Bandyopadhyaya, at that time a young Communist writer, deemed it fit to 'change the plot' of a Banaphool short story, before publishing it, on the grounds that the original plot was one of 'outright communal incitement'.[20] But, it was not a subjective incomprehension on Bandyopadhyaya's part, rather, it was an incomprehension determined by the discursive space within which he understood communalism. For communalism, and its manifestation in communal riots, are events that violate the self-contained logic of the ideology of nationalism, so that as events they can be thought of only as so many aberrations. The lack of comprehension that is inherent here marks the literature dealing with communalism. In fact, it becomes a victim of the unavailability of adequate conceptual tools for understanding communalism in terms outside of the nationalist discourse. And it is this same dumbfounding, stultifying incomprehension, which is evident in the Bengali literature on the Partition.

IV

An immediate look at Bengali literature of the post-Partition era seems to belie our argument that the Bengali litterateur has largely neglected the Partition, as a theme. In fact there are, at least, 15 novels and novelettes which deal with the Partition. Yet, most of these either just mention the Partition as an event or use it as a backdrop for a different narrative, with different concerns. In fact, strictly speaking, there are only three novels and one novelette, which are constructed around the event of the Partition. It is only in these novels that the Partition is posed as a 'problem', as an object to be constructed by the structured whole of the narrative.[21] In the rest, the Partition appears as just another event, indistinguishable from other important events in the history of Bengal, such as the famine, riots, the war, etc. It is known only through its effects: refugee problems, real estate frauds, inflation, hoarding, unemployment, etc. More importantly, fiction has treated these as effects of a continuous process in history, wherein the 'disjunctive' character of the Partition finds no place.

Of the three Partition novels, the first was written by the outstanding Bengali poet, Jibanananda Das. Written in 1948, but published posthumously, the novel titled *Jalpaihati* begins in a small town of the same name, in the times just preceding the Partition. The fate of Jalpaihati, has not yet been decided; whether it is to be a part of the Indian Union or of Pakistan. The novel deals with the lives of the Hindus of Jalpaihati, the potential refugees. The main characters are Nishith, a professor of English in the local college and his son Harit, a radical who intends to be self-employed. Nishith's resolve to find a job in Calcutta is strengthened by the anticipation of the impending Partition. In Calcutta he meets Joynath, the sole owner of a huge college (*birat ek colleger ek matro pita*), who is out to make money out of the plight of the Hindu students from East Bengal. As thousands of students come seeking admission in Calcutta colleges, Joynath becomes richer. The imagery used in describing this process is—'night and day Joynath smokes his cheroots, while he drinks his habitual wine' (*dinraat chooroot khachchhe Joynath, niyomito mod khachche Joynath*).[22]

Meanwhile, Harit too is in Calcutta, but with a different objective. A Left radical, Harit believes that 'although the nation is free, its true freedom and independence would require a major revolution indeed, if necessary, by reforming that revolution itself'. Yet he knows that 'today no one would be ready to sacrifice anew, for true freedom and peace for man. Most believe that formal independence is enough . . . what more does one need? Now each would trample the other underfoot, and with faces flushed with effort, run forward to savour and enjoy life.'[23] Yet, Harit is unable to return to Jalpaihati where 'uncertainty and dazed bafflement' stares people in the face. Unthinking, people are leaving their homes like 'moths diving from a fire into an inferno. There are no houses, jobs or food in Calcutta. Death certainly lies waiting—yet like deformed children, they come, only to fall flat on their faces in the alleys, corners and footpaths of Calcutta.'[24]

Back in Jalpaihati, there is the Congress leader, Abani Khastagir, who appeals to people not to leave their homesteads. He advises all to walk on the path of truth, ahimsa, and with fearless hearts, help each other in this time of distress. But ironically, Khastagir himself lives in Calcutta.[25] 'It is easier to believe in Wajed Ali . . . from Harit's Party. A Calcuttan, who has come here [Jalpaihati], and is roaming from door to door, asking people not to leave Pakistan.'[26] Yet, in Hindu homes, Muslim men who had hitherto been underlings, were entering bedrooms, asking for *bidis* and even wanting to be married to Hindu women. It is this attack on the class distinctions in cultural practices and the reversal of rituals of deference, which becomes the 'moment' of realization of the inevitability of migration, for the *bhadralok* families. Jibanananda's struggle with this cultural problem is best seen in his inherent identification with the plight of the *bhadra mahila*, and his simultaneous attempt to 'resolve' the issue through the marriage of Wajed Ali to a Hindu girl, Sulekha.

The second novel is *Swaralipi* (Musical Notations), 1952, by Sabitri Roy. The novel is set in the period between 1946 and 1951. While the Partition forms one of the main themes, among others, its presence is important enough for it to be considered a Partition novel. The Partition becomes the main theme in the narrative, from 1950 onwards, when Prithvi, the hero of the novel, is expelled from the Communist Party for criticizing its militant stand. He comes to hear about the renewed violence in East Pakistan. He asks 'Riots again? Has not the blood of '46 quenched their blood-thirst?'[27] When Prithvi comes to the Sealdah railway station for news of his beloved Sita who has been caught up in the midst of the troubles in Pakistan: 'Passengers spill out of the packed Barisal Express, infants clinging to their limbs, ravaged and torn luggage on their heads.... [Their] pale, colourless faces sunken with terror. Like a looming shadow of a grief embodied. A bloodless ghoulish shadow.'[28] And again:

Terror spreads, humming across the whole of Calcutta . . . the heart-rending stories of the unfortunate passengers from the Barisal Express, spreads across the city from one person to another . . . The Dhaka Mail arrived jam-packed. Even the carriage roofs are crowded with passengers. . . . people are also coming from Netrokona and Kishoreganj. 'No there is no trouble there. But how long would it take to flare up? You can't trust those louts [*shaalas*]'.[29]

Fearing trouble the government prohibited the reporting of rioting in Pakistan,[30] but it was not heeded:

The newspapers refuse to obey. It is impossible to suppress news. Blood drips forth from every letter. Riots in Barisal. What a hair-raising story. Hundreds of Hindu women remain missing. It hurts to look into the abnormal faces of half-crazed relatives who have returned, faces blackened with shame. Someone's sister, another's wife, somebody's sister-in-law, snatched away by Muslim hooligans. . . . Nationalist journals print endless poisonous lines . . . read by every office-going bhadralok. Uncontrollable rage in their eyes, their faces. Even if the government quietly suffers these atrocities, the people shall not sit quiet. Vengeance must be wreaked upon the Muslims on this side—they say amongst themselves.[31]

In the midst of all this the demoralized Communists[32] play the role of agents of peace. They organize peace committees in every neighbourhood. The *agent provocateur*, Madhu Mukherjee [an ex-detenu], and his 'Swastika Club' fail to spark off a communal riot. Defeated, he summons the *goonda* Kalu, and tells him: 'I hear that they [the Communists] have established a peace committee. They are agents [*dalals*] of the Muslims. Why else would they speak of peace even after the humiliation of our mothers and sisters in Pakistan. . . . It is essential to destroy their hauteur.'[33] The next day, Hanshia, a girl from a poor Muslim family, becomes the victim of a gang rape.[34]

Back in Pakistan, Sita, the heroine, and the other Hindus of the area take refuge in the former's ancestral zamindari estate. They are protected, day in and day out, by a group of young men organized by an old retainer, Kashimuddin. Despite anxious moments, things were 'gradually returning to normalcy. A truce has been signed between Hindustan and Pakistan.'[35] The novel then moves on to describe how the Partition had changed the economy, social institutions and traditional ties in 'both of the Bengals [*Dui Bangla*]'. It describes the plight of the refugees in India and the problems faced by the erstwhile retainers of Hindu zamindars in Pakistan.

Sabitri Roy's novel would clearly fit into the discursive categories I have mentioned above. The notion of the Communists as 'organizing' the 'natural' peaceful bonds between the poor of both communities is a standard Left radical conception. Just as is the idea of the Swastika Club and its *goondas* being elemental in spreading communal violence. There is an interesting part where the discourse of Left radicalism combines with that of Bengali national chauvinism, when the author describes the meeting at Calcutta's Deshapriya Park, where 'the majority are non-Bengalis'. The Marwari plays an important role in constructing the narrative link between the 'rich', 'vested interests' and 'communal hatred'. It is however in its rich description of the Partition and its aftermath, that Roy's novel destabilizes the narrative's internal structure. An interesting example is the way in which the uprooting of a whole people [36] is seen through the eyes of the old ailing Bisheshwar:

> The people of east Bengal are floating about like a kite which has broken off from its anchoring thread—their culture and their immense specificity of character [*birat boishishto*] is fast disappearing in this manner. These nomads shall never again find secure roots on this earth. This immeasurable pain cannot be described in words. . . . It is not just a pain of a nostalgic memory. It is the mourning for an ancient heritage.[37]

The event, which had led to a sharp disjunction in the lives of millions, finds its place in this literature only in such peripheries of the narrative.

The third novel in this genre is that by Pratibha Basu, called *Samudra Hriday* (The Oceanic Heart), 1959. It would be more proper to club it under 'romantic fiction', since the actual subject matter is the romance between a Hindu girl, Sulekha, and the Muslim *nawabzada*, Sultan Ahmed. But since the romance is itself constructed through the events of the Partition, I have included it within the category of Partition novels. Sulekha, out to avenge the death of the Hindus in the Dhaka riots, plans to assassinate Sultan Ahmed, who she believes is the chief instigator of the riots. She finds herself held captive by the *nawabzada*, and his charm gradually turns her hatred into love. When her family flees to Calcutta, the *nawabzada* takes it upon himself to return Sulekha to the safety of Calcutta. On reaching the city he is killed by Hindu assassins. The story ends with Sulekha, identifying the dead Sultan Ahmed as her husband. The melodramatic overtones of the story, which stretch the limits of the reader's credulousness, certainly weaken the novel. Its literary merits notwithstanding the novel deals with the Partition within the typical motifs of instigated riots, loss of humanity and human love and recovery of humanity. The simplistic oppositions that inform the novel's narrative structure, make it the ideal ground for the operation of all the motifs of a 'humanist' understanding of the Partition.

Dipen Bandyopadhyaya's 'Maajhi' (The Boatman), the first part of his novel *Aagami* (The Future), 1951, deals directly with the Partition as an historical event. It tries to explain the causes behind the Partition, in terms of 'instigation by the Colonial masters and their local agents'. These riots 'do not take much time to spread. The poisonous current swept everyone along with it.' The *maajhis* however did not lose their humanity (*manushyatva*) and they refuse to be sucked into the vortex of communal violence. The conscious usage of the Communist Party's understanding of communalism and the Partition, that is, the idea of the natural ties of the poor of both communities, the effect of instigation from the outside by vested interests, etc., seems the result of youthful enthusiasm. Yet, the novelette reads more like a pamphlet than any critique of ideology that good literature would require it to be.

Other novels such as *Pranganga*, 1949, by Abinash Saha, *Durobhashini*, 1951, by Narendranath Mitra, *Pancha Parba*, 1954, by Banaphool, *Pub Theke Pashchime*, 1956, by Ramesh Chandra Sen, *God Shrikhanda*, 1957, by Amiya Bhushan Majumdar, *Bolmik*, 1958, by Narayan Sanyal, *Tabu Bihanga*, 1960, by Shaktipada Rajguru, *Neel Aagun*, 1963, by Sarojkumar Roy Choudhury and *Panka Palbal*, 1964, by Bibhutibhushan Mukhopadhyaya, deal with the Partition, directly or indirectly. Yet, as I have argued above, the Partition appears not so much as a decisive moment in the history of Bengal, but rather as just another event. Indeed, what one would identify, as effects directly linked to the Partition, appear as autonomous processes, to be dealt with in isolation from the event that shaped them. Thus the refugee problem is treated repeatedly as a problem of the 'present', without trying to unravel the process of its genesis. Indeed, refugee colonies and refugee existence become the backdrop for narrating other stories—stories of women's struggles, of the poor, of family life, of interpersonal relations, etc. This is what I have tried to capture, the 'fleeting presence' of the Partition in Bengali literature. In fact, the three major novelists of this period, the three Bandyopadhyayas, almost wholly ignore the Partition, except in two short stories by Bibhutibhushan Bandyopadhyaya,[38] and one by Manik Bandhopadhyaya,[39] all of which, once again, picture the Partition within the standard radical-nationalist discourse, seeing it as a result of the people's momentary lapse into madness and betrayal at the level of high politics.

I believe that the inability to break away from the 'normal' on the part of even the most sensitive litterateurs was a result of the unavailability of an adequate 'language' for literary representation, a language which could adequately comprehend and represent the disjunctive role of the Partition in the lived history of Bengal. While the 1930s and 1940s saw a more self-conscious attempt to present the contemporary world and to write fiction in, what I have called, a sociological mode, the post-Partition post-independence period marks a change in literary responses to the lived world. The 1950s witnessed an important, and somewhat bitter, debate between litterateur groups over questions of what would count as relevant and desirable themes for literature. The division took the form of a tripartite division among litterateurs: writers aligned with the Congress, the Marxists and those who wanted to revive the liberal-aesthetic tradition in Bengali literature.[40] It may be unfair to conclude that there were more debates among litterateurs than there was the writing of good fiction in this period.

Yet, more importantly, these debates not only remained unsettled between the three groups, but they also did not effect a rethinking within these groups as to the problems of literary production. Thus, the Partition novels that we have discussed suffered from this same inadequacy, that is, of a language for an alternative narrativization of new experiences. This can be seen in the two novels of Jibanananda Das and Pratibha Basu. In both of these, one would find a marked degree of disjointedness in the sequencing of the narratives; description of events, of images and emotions, which are somehow peripheral to the structure of the novel as a whole. The Partition enters more as description than as a unified aesthetic comprehension. The authorial structuration of the narratives reveals the same images of the nationalist/radical-rationalist discursive formations. It is through this peripheral description of the Partition and its effects, that another unstructured voice speaks, a voice which does not have a language to 'understand' but borrows the existing conceptual/ideational forms to describe a disjunction in a lived experience. It is the absence of this language, which lies at the heart of the litterateurs' inability to deal with the Partition, even if that litterateur be as accomplished as Tarashankar or Manik Bandhopadhyaya. Indeed both Tarashankar and Bibhutibhushan Bandyopadhyaya, who had been at the forefront of raising contemporary issues in literature, took up nineteenth century subjects to write about. It is tempting to think that this return to the past was an attempt to redefine its history and to search for a different, but modern, language to write about the new experiences in their contemporary world, a language which had gradually been banished by the advance and spread of the nationalist discourse in the twentieth century.

V

I have argued that of the 15 novels that deal with the Partition, only three can qualify as Partition novels. Even here the Partition has appeared more as description than as a unified aesthetic-literary object. At a time when Bengali litterateurs were taking pride in the 'realism' and the contemporaneity of their subject matter, this 'fleeting presence' of the Partition seems paradoxical. In fact, it is my contention that it is precisely this 'realist-contemporaneity' of Bengali literature, which explains the relative absence of the Partition in Bengali fiction.

This realism in literature is essentially a product of the litterateurs' self-conscious use of the prevalent notions of history, in organizing the structure of his narrative. In its very conditions of production, realistic fiction, as a modern literary form is closely tied to the modern rationalist notions of history, which inform the imaginary collective of the nation and the identities of nationalism. The emergence of parallel and antagonistic modern discursive formations, such as those of Left radicalism and Marxism, have provided possible conditions for criticizing and fighting the discourses of the liberal-bourgeois rationalist and nationalist thought.

In Bengal, Left radicalism provided the discursive conditions for criticizing and 'laying bare' the discourses of the right, especially on economic and women issues. Realist literature, when addressing such issues had tended to organize them within a Left radical sociological perspective. Attempts to write about the people, itself marks a move parallel to the writing of Left radical and Marxist-influenced histories, which broke with the nationalist tradition of focusing on national leaders and movements.

Yet, when it came to writing the history of 'nationalism', there was very little difference between nationalist and Left radical historians. I shall argue that, while Left radical discourses provided the ground for thinking about the 'economy' and the family in ways which were different and antagonistic to the discourses of the right, it had not yet developed the language for the specificity of the 'political' in a colonial situation like India. Political practice was conceived in terms of the modern nation-state and the bourgeois representative democracy. Even within radical thought, the nation-state was accepted as a 'fact'.

One would also have to accept that there was a somewhat uncritical acceptance of the institutions, ideologies and practices of 'modernity', especially on the part of the Left, and the survival of pre-modern ideologies was treated with suspicion. There was a fear that the pre-modern was 'feudal' and hence to be opposed at all costs. This transformation of the 'rational' into 'rationalism' played an important role in the failure to have an understanding of communalism. The Partition, seen as an inevitable consequence of communalism, could then be understood only in terms of imperialist conspiracies and, therefore, was as an aberration.

Thus, in both nationalist as well as radical-rationalist discursive formations, the Partition appeared as an anomaly, as a 'price' to be paid for independence. It was an event that subtracted a part from freedom, but was not a constitutive moment of that independence. Yet, as an event, it led to the uprooting of millions of people and a complete change in their lived world. Realist literature, which had developed a strong tradition in twentieth-century Bengal, became a victim of the ways in which history had been understood, both on the right and the Left. The absence of the conceptual wherewithal to understand this uprooting, this cataclysmic and violent transformation of millions of lives has meant that this important historical process found almost no place in fiction.

VI

Let me end with the point I had begun with: the fact that the Partition did find place in Bengali poetry of that period, even when it was absent in fiction. Almost all of the major poets, Jibanananda Das, Bishnu Dey, Mangalacharan Chattopadhyaya, Jyotindranath Sengupta, wrote about the Partition. I shall quote a few representative lines from Bishnu Dey, Dinesh Das and Mangalacharan Chattopadhyaya:

My eyes overflow this day,
With the endless waters of the Padma.
The call of the Meghna,
Stunned into silence like a torrent of clouds . . .
Here we are balancing on the edge of a precipice
As the days pass by upon the razor's edge.
Blood congealed mark out the borders
Like Kalnemi dividing the kingdom of Lanka.

'Panoroi August 1947' (Fifteenth August 1947), by Dinesh Das[41]

. . . Yet can one's own brother be a foe?—The wounded heart
That has crossed this blood-sea, has faith still, still sheds tears,
And at last alert with the real-enemy's gleeful smile
It wonders, when would that day be—when
Even our tear-emeralds shall spew forth, lightning and thunder?

'Kannar Pannao Thhikrabe' (Even the Emeralds of Tears Shall Glitter), August 1947, by Mangalacharan Chattopadhyaya[42]

Everyday I see on the streets, on footpaths, in disorderly homes
Parched faces, dishevelled hair,
On the platforms of Sealdah, tripped-over refugee households,
Forlorn dejected figures
Mother you have no home!

'Aashwine Aakash' (The Autumn Sky),
by Mangalacharan Chattopadhyaya[43]

. . . I came away, left you and came away.
Those lost days of my fearful timid loving, my love,
Yet I left you and came away.

'Megh Brishti Jhar' (Cloud-Rain-Storm),
by Mangalacharan Chattopadhyaya[44]

And here are a few lines, which bring together the questions of the Partition and the plight of the refugees:

The summer heat has scorched the Gulmohar of its ancient lustre;
The Krishnachuda's vibrance stings the eye. . . .
And everywhere, exhausted refugees sit panting,
In the shades on the pavements by park-sides,
Under alcoves and ledges, on roads and the streets
They sit thinking; who knows what they think!
Evicted, they seek out new lands.
Some here, some in Barisal and yet others in Dhaka.

'Jal Dao' (Give me Water), by Bishnu Dey[45]

There are numerous others which are difficult to translate, dealing with motifs which are identifiably linked with the Partition. This recurrent presence of the Partition in Bengali poetry, requires a tentative explanation. I believe that the answer lies in the difference between the specific historical development of fiction and poetry as literary forms. Historically, fiction in twentieth century Bengal, developed by evolving a specific 'realist' literary language, moving towards increasing simplicity of narrativization of increasingly complex social processes. This culminated in the literature of the 1940s, when fiction became more and more self-consciously contemporary in the choice of its subject matter. Poetry, on the other hand, while being historically rooted, did not require using experientially concrete history, to construct its diction. The development of 'counter-experiential' imagery and abstract linguistic formulations, best found in the poetry of Jibanananda Das and Bishnu Dey, respectively, effected the emergence of a distance between the discursive conditions of the production of a poem as a text, and the text's formal structure. It is this inherent (and necessary) pliability of poetry as a literary form, which allowed for a distance between the historical conditions of the emergence of the poet's concerns and themes, and their presentation within the form of the poem. This rootedness and the simultaneous distance from history, enabled poets to depict the Partition. The very nature of the contemporary poetic forms, which relied on the usage of compound images and fragments, freed the poet from 'narrating'. Poetry could thus reveal an instinct, where fiction would have required a comprehension. The fragmented consciousness of the world in the poetic mode of its appropriation in thought was better suited to destabilize the discourse of the nation-state, humanism, reason, etc. It is perhaps understandable then that one of the few Partition novels to be written in this period was by Bengal's foremost poet, Jibanananda Das. And it is equally understandable, one should add, that even here the specificity of the Partition appeared only as a fragmented consciousness, at the peripheries of the narrative, as a text.

NOTES

1. Sandip Ray, 'Keno Lekha Hoyechhilo Chitranatya, Keno Chhobi Hoyeni', in *Sananda*, 24 April 1998, p. 14.
2. In what is recognized as one of the most comprehensive works of literary criticism in Bengali, Sreekumar Bandyopadhyaya has written that there have been no significant (*sharthak*) novels in Bengali, dealing with the Partition as a theme, S. Bandyopadhyaya, *Bango Shahitye Upanasyer Dhara* (Calcutta, 1984), p. 710. Out of the 129 novels published between 1947 and 1950, only three deal with the Partition. A list of the 50 best novels and 50 best short stories published in the last 50 years, brought out recently by the Bengali literary magazine, *Desh*, has not a single novel or short story with the Partition as a theme. Also see, T. Chakravarty, 'Within Spectrum: Partition in Bengali Literature', in S.R. Chakravarty and Mazhar Hussain, ed., *Partition of India: Literary Responses* (Delhi, 1998), where I have discussed the relationship between literature, dealing with refugee issues, and what can be called 'Partition literature' in the strict sense of the term. I have argued that for a historian 'Refugee' literature is a useful source material for gauging the impact of the Partition. Here, however, I am more concerned with analysing the historical conditions for the writing of this literature, and it is my task to pose the question of the absence of Partition literature, in the strict sense, rather than write a history of the Partition from literary 'sources'.
3. The question of mass mobilization had of course been an important issue in Tagore's intervention in the post-swadeshi phase.
4. See P. Chatterjee, 'Agrarian Structure in Pre-Partition Bengal', in A. Sen, et al., *Perspectives in Social Sciences, Vol. II: Three Studies on the Agrarian Structure in Bengal, 1850-1947* (Calcutta, 1982); and O. Goswami 'Agriculture in Slump: The Peasant Economy of East and North Bengal in the 1930s', in *Indian Economic and Social History Review*, Vol. XX, No. 3; and 'Collaboration and Conflict: European and Indian Capitalists in the Jute Industry of Bengal 1919-39', ibid., Vol. XIX, No. 2.

5. See P. Chatterjee, 'Agrarian Relations and Communalism in Bengal, 1926-1935', in R. Guha, ed., *Subaltern Studies, Vol. I: Writings on South Asian History and Society* (Delhi, 1982).
6. On riots, see Suranjan Das, *Communal Riots in Bengal 1905-1947* (Delhi, 1993).
7. 'History' is used both for the knowledge of society and for real social processes.
8. For two separate analyses of the relationship between notions of history and modernity, see P. Chatterjee, *The Nation and its Fragments: Colonial and Post-Colonial Histories* (Delhi, 1993), Chapters IV and V; and S. Sarkar, *Writing Social History* (Delhi, 1997), Chapter I.
9. By 'discursive formation' I shall mean, a set of interrelated discourses, with a definite hierarchical structure of this interrelationship.
10. For a more detailed analyses of Bengali literature of the 1930s and 1940s, see T. Chakravarty, 'Freedom Struggle and the Bengali Literature of the 1940s', in A. Gupta, ed., *Myth and Reality: The Struggle for Freedom in India, 1945-47* (Delhi, 1987).
11. Ibid.
12. *Tarashankar Rachanabali*, Vol. V (Calcutta, 1984, 1st edn, 1973), p. 418.
13. Ibid., Vol. VIII (Calcutta, 1985, 1st edn, 1974), p. 50.
14. *Satinath Bhadurir Nirbachita Rachana* (Calcutta, 1985), p. 41.
15. For details, see T. Chakravarty, 'Freedom Struggle and the Bengali Literature of the 1940s', op.cit.
16. Saroj K. Raychaudhuri, *Mahakal* (Calcutta, 1946), p. 202. In Jyotirmoyee Devi's *Epar Ganga Opar Ganga* (The Ganga on Both Sides) (1968), a novel based on the Noakhali riots of October 1946, similar themes of rape, looting, murder, etc., have been depicted in much greater detail.
17. See Gyanendra Pandey, *Construction of Communalism in Colonial North India* (Delhi, 1990).
18. Baren Basu, 'Ijjat', in *Parichaya* (October-November1950).
19. *Banaphooler Galpasangraha Dwitia Shatak* (Calcutta, 1965), p. 236. It is noteworthy that Banaphool himself was brought up on the breast milk of the wife of their Muslim servant, Chamru, Sukumar Sen, *Banaphooler Phoolbana* (Calcutta, 1983), p. 26.
20. See 'Dipendranath Bandyopadhya Sankhya', in *Dibaratrir Kabya* (July-September/ October-December 1997), p. 370.
21. I am excluding the two novels written in the contemporary period—one by Debdas Ghosh, called *Udbastu* (The Refugee), 1948, and the other *Bhangchhe Shudhu Bhangchhe* (Crumbling Just Crumbling) by Amarendu Ghosh—which I have been unable to locate.
22. 'Jalpaihati', in *Jibanananda Samagra* (Calcutta, 1985), p. 295.
23. Ibid., p. 300.
24. Ibid., p. 301. Prafulla Chakrabarti, *The Marginal Men* (Kalyani, 1990), which may be regarded as the first adequately comprehensive history of the refugees from East Pakistan, observed that: 'It was a time of trouble for West Bengal. The entire state was groaning under the load of refugees; the Central Government was indifferent and did not even recognize the existence of refugees. Dr. Roy [the then chief minister of West Bengal] was sore at the attitude of the Central Government as his correspondence with Nehru demonstrates clearly enough', p. 37. The refugees, who had taken shelter on the 'The Gateway of Hell', as the platforms of Sealdah Station, were called, were regarded as intruders. Indeed, they were considered to be no better than a swarm of locusts, eating away the already scarce foodstuff in West Bengal. The local Press

ascribed the scarcity of food to the presence of those unwanted mouths, *Amrita Bazar Patrika*, 30 June 1948, cited in ibid., p. 23.

25. Dr P.C. Ghosh, the first post-Partition Chief Minister of West Bengal, toured the different districts of East Pakistan and addressed meetings of Hindus. The substance of his speeches were that 'Hindus should not migrate to the Indian Union as everything would settle down with time', in ibid., p. 38. In a memorandum to the Prime Minister Jawaharlal Nehru, he expressed the view that the 'fugitives' would see reason and soon go back to their deserted homes. That suited Nehru. In his 'reply to a question in Parliament, he said that his Government was aware that a considerable number of Hindus had migrated from East to West Bengal. But migrations were not desirable and should not be encouraged, as they would bring a great deal of suffering in their train', in *Amrita Bazar Patrika*, 22 March 1948, cited in Prafulla Chakrabarti, op.cit., p. 16.
26. 'Jalpaihati', op cit., p. 321.
27. Sabitri Roy, *Swaralipi* (Calcutta, 1952), p. 293.
28. Ibid., p. 294.
29. Ibid., p. 297.
30. In August 1948, Nehru wrote in reply to Dr Roy's letter, 'I have been quite certain right from the beginning that everything should be done to prevent Hindus in East Bengal from migrating to West Bengal. . . . Running away is never a solution to a problem. I think the Hindu leaders of East Bengal who have come away have done no service to their people.' See P. Chakrabarti, op. cit., p. 20.
31. Sabitri Roy, op.cit. p. 294.
32. See Joya Chatterjee, *Bengal Divided: Hindu Communalism and Parties 1932-47* (Delhi, 1995). Even after the Partition, the Communist Party of India, decided that there would be one party for both Dominions. The Communists believed that a revolution would be possible only after removing communalism, which had spread among the masses, especially among the Muslims.
33. Sabitri Roy, op.cit., p. 303.
34. Ibid.
35. Nehru and his counterpart, the Prime Minister of Pakistan, Liaquat Ali, signed the 'Delhi Pact', in April 1950. The Pact provided for the return of the migrants on both sides of the border to their homelands and somewhat checked the influx temporarily. See Saileshkumar Bandyopadhyaya, *Swadhinatar Panchas Bachhar* (Calcutta, 1997), p. 55.
36. It is estimated that, after the Noakhali riots of 1946, 58,602 persons came to West Bengal from East Bengal. After independence, unlike what happened in Punjab the 'uprooting' of East Bengal's Hindus was not effected in 'one swift swipe through massive pogroms on both sides of the border, nor was it a two-way traffic'. Migrants came to West Bengal in waves. In the first phase, by June 1948, the number of migrants reached 1.1 million. More than a lakh of the 11 lakhs migrants were peasants. At least nine lakhs belonged to the 'urban and rural middle class' and less than one lakh were artisans. See P. Chakrabarti, op.cit., p. 1. However, this exodus was not caused by communal violence alone. Hiranmaya Bandyopadhyaya, the then Rehabilitation Commissioner of West Bengal, noted that the migration from East Bengal was largely due to harassment, dishonour and insecurity of Hindu women, as well as the violation of the 'dignity' and 'self-respect' of Hindu men by Muslims who traditionally had an inferior social position. See, H. Bandyopadhyaya, *Udvastu* (Calcutta), pp. 92-3. After

the Inter-Dominion Conference held in April 1948 produced an Indo-Pakistan Agreement for the settlement of the minorities' problem, a West Bengal Government Press Note declared that persons arriving in West Bengal from East Pakistan, after 25 June 1948 would not be entitled to registration as 'refugees'. The second phase of migration started early in January 1949. Widespread violence, organized killing of Hindus and looting of their property in many parts of East Pakistan, were the immediate causes for this mass flight. For the first time even the Namasudras, who were culturally close to the Muslim peasantry, were not spared. 'This time the refugees came in like an avalanche', *Bharatbarsha* (Calcutta, 15 August 1950), p. 254. The Census of 1951 shows that there were at least 3.5 million refugees in West Bengal, according to P. Chakrabarti, op.cit., p. 3.

37. Sabitri Roy, op.cit, p. 209.
38. 'Acharya Kriplani Colony' (1948) and 'Jawaharlal O God'(1949).
39. 'Sthane O Stane' (1948).
40. See D. Das, ed., *Marxbadi Sahitya Bitarka*, Vol. I-III (Calcutta, 1975-8); and idem, ed., *Banglar Sanskritite Marxbadi Chetanar Dhara* (Calcutta, 1992). Also see Buddhadeb Basu, ed, *Kabita*, Vols I-III (compiled by Meenakshi Dutta) (Calcutta, 1987-9).
41. Dinesh Das, *Dinesh Daser Kabyasangraha* (Calcutta, 1984), p. 102.
42. *Mangalacharan Chattopadhyayer Shresthha Kabita* (Calcutta, 1983), pp. 4-5.
43. Ibid., p. 46.
44. Ibid., p. 7.
45. *Anwishta Bachhar Pachish* (Calcutta, 1973), p. 350.

The Muslim Polyphony in Attia Hosain's Sunlight on a Broken Column

NARESH JAIN

How can we live together as a nation if all the time only the differences between the different communities are being preached?[1]

Attia Hosain's *Sunlight on a Broken Column* is one of those few Partition novels that are both aesthetically satisfying and at the same time present the tragedy of Partition with great objectivity and sympathetic understanding. It is also perhaps the only novel in English that gives us a close-up of the attitudes of Muslims towards the cataclysmic event and of the forces leading up to it. These different attitudes come to us filtered through the consciousness of a young Muslim girl belonging to a *taluqdari* family, who lives through the tumultuous decades of the 1930s and 1940s of pre-Partition India. In expressing these attitudes the writer exploits the well-known capacity of a novel to incorporate multiple voices. As a result, though the novel reflects the writer's commitment to the ideals of secularism and shared identity, it does not stifle other dissenting voices. This enables the writer to achieve a delicate balance. In the process the novel demolishes certain stereotypes about Muslims in India and raises questions that are, even to this day, relevant.

Attia Hosain locates her first person narrative in the consciousness of Laila. She is young and idealistic and, as an orphan, lives on the periphery of a large family. And though she leads a sheltered existence behind the high walls of the family seat at Ashiana in Lucknow, she has a questioning mind and is alive to the social and political changes taking place around her. Besides she is engaged in her own long lonely battle to achieve selfhood and independence. Rebelling against the claustrophobic traditions of the family, she marries a commoner. There is a suggestive parallel between the tragedy of Partition following independence and her own

* Based on Attia Hosain, *Sunlight on a Broken Column* (1st edn, 1961, repr., New Delhi, 1992).

story; for her dearly beloved husband dies. This brings together the personal and the political in her consciousness, which makes her narrative at once more intimate and more authentic.

Partition figures prominently only in Part IV, which is also the last part of the novel. But the first three parts are important for they give us an idea of Attia Hosain's understanding of the communal relations as they develop during the period covered by the novel. Perhaps, because of the national commitment to secularism or for some other reason, Partition novelists generally tend to romanticize these relations in pre-Partition India or play down differences or divisions between Hindus and Muslims. An extreme example of what could be called 'sentimental evasion' is furnished by Khushwant Singh's *Train to Pakistan* (1956), which presents an impossibly idyllic picture of Sikh/Hindu-Muslim amity in the Indian border village of Mano Majra before all hell breaks loose. Whatever the compulsions of the writer in presenting Mano Majra as an 'oasis of peace', the fact remains that the idealized picture is more facile than true and leads to cliched thinking. Whether it is an artistic deficiency on the part of the writer or whether it underscores 'a national inability to introspect, analyse and face up to a most intractable problem of our political, social and cultural life',[2] is a matter of deeper analysis than is possible here.

In this respect, however, Attia Hosain's presentation is largely refreshing. Saleem rhetorically asks: 'What can you expect from a religion which forbids people to eat and drink together? When even a man's shadow can defile another? How is real friendship or understanding possible?' (p. 197). Though this does not need corroboration, it would be interesting to hear what one of the persons interviewed by Urvashi Butalia has to say on the subject:

> Such good relations we had that if there was any function that we had, then we used to call Musalmaans to our homes, they would eat in our houses, but we did not eat in theirs, and this is a bad thing, which I realize now. If they would come to our house, we would have two utensils in one corner of our house, and we would tell them pick these up and eat in them and they would then wash them and keep them aside and this was such a terrible thing. This was the reason Pakistan was created. . . . [Interview with Bir Bahadur Singh of village Thoa Khalsa in Rawalpindi district].[3]

At the community level Hindu festivals of Diwali and Holi were celebrated in some Muslim homes, but Attia Hosain, realistically hints at the subterranean tensions between the two communities that surfaced on occasions, such as Muharram.

The writer's treatment of the Sita-Kemal love affair is also closer to the ground realities. The romantic impulse is wayward all right—*ishk par zor nahin, hai yeh woh aatish Ghalib*—but most inter-religious love affairs simply had no chance of flowering, Partition or no Partition, and interweaving these into Partition novels gives them a false melodramatic touch. In this respect also this writer is more realistic for though the novel contains the mandatory formula of a Hindu-Muslim love affair, the Sita-Kemal relationship is shown as doomed from the start. Instead, the writer concentrates on the socio-economic hurdles faced by Laila in marrying the commoner Ameer.

Attia Hosain also shows how the two communities begin to drift apart, particularly after the reorganization of the Muslim League and the 1937 elections. This is reflected in the gradual hardening of attitudes among some of Laila's cousins and friends. Laila's nationalistic leanings are clear from her school days when she vows to fight for the country's freedom as she had seen the satyagrahis doing. On the other hand one of her cousins Zahid feels that the Muslims need to be united against all dangers and is prepared to die for Islam, but unlike his brother Asad he has no faith in non-violence. One of Laila's friends, Nadira, likewise believes that 'Muslims had to defend their heritage' (125). Another cousin, Saleem's beliefs are influenced by his attachment to Nadira. By the time of the 1937 elections the divisions are fairly clear. In Laila's circle what were once friendly discussions now turn into heated arguments. Saleem, for instance, used to say that the British encouraged Hindu-Muslim quarrels in order to divide and rule. But now he uses the Muslim League's rhetoric to say that the Congress was a Hindu body and that the Muslims in the Congress were being used as 'dupes to give it a secular appearance' (255). As a sign of his new allegiance he throws himself into the election campaign of Nadira's mother, Begum Waheed, who is contesting the elections on a Muslim League ticket. Laila can only despairingly say what has already been quoted above: 'How can we live together as a nation if all the time only the differences between the different communities are being preached?' (245).

Too often Muslim attitudes to Partition are talked of in the singular as though Muslims in India were a unified body, with the same set of interests and a single point of view, and that they all reacted to Partition in only one way. Such a reductive assumption, exemplified by what a refugee from Pakistan says in the novel, 'They are all bloody traitors—every bloody Muslim—deep in their bloody hearts' (302), stands firmly repudiated in the light of what happens in the novel. This dismissive statement involves the issue of loyalty that was far more urgent in the days of Partition and immediately afterwards than it is now. It is to Attia Hosain's credit that she confronts this question unflinchingly by making it a point of discussion in the final family reunion, in the dining room at Ashiana, before the countdown for Partition begins. To whom does one owe one's loyalty: to the country of one's ancestors and of one's birth or to one's religion?

Her nationalistic sympathies, notwithstanding, Attia Hosain gives full utterance to the points of view of people like Saleem and Nadira who see in Pakistan a fulfilment of their ideals and ambitions. Saleem sees Pakistan as a land of opportunities. And his wife Nadira proposes the idea of loyalty to one's faith in opposition to Kemal's idea of loyalty to the country of one's birth: 'Pakistan needs us to build it up as a refuge where all Muslims can be safe and free' (288). Others who opt for Pakistan, include Zahira and her ambitious husband, Naseer, and Waliuddin, who is purely opportunistic.

Here one must pause to remark that this is one of those scenes where the writer achieves a fine unsentimental balance between her characters. When Laila satirically laughs at Nadira and Saleem saying—'Your ideals and Saleem's ambitions harmonize perfectly', Attia Hosain does not let her remark go unchallenged. Nadira at once shoots back: 'You believe in nothing. All you do is to be sarcastic and destructive' (289).

But not everybody chose to ride the Pakistan bandwagon. There are those who, like Uncle Hamid, had landed interests to protect and who saw no difficulty in working together with Hindus on a political and personal level: 'I always found it was possible for Hindus and Muslims to work together on a political level and live together in personal friendship' (234).

Then there are those who are intellectually committed to their native country. The nationalistic viewpoint shared by Laila, Asad and Kemal is vocalized by Kemal for whom the creation of what he facetiously calls the neo-paradise across the border does not mean any real choice: 'A choice presupposes both sides mean the same to me. They don't. This is my country. I belong to it. I love it. That's all' (287). Later he defines the idea of belonging in terms of allegiance to one's past: 'I see my future in my past. I was born here, and generations of my ancestors before me. I am content to die here and be buried with them' (288). This is an idealistic position to take but it is entirely credible because if Partition time was the worst of times in terms of violence, it was also the best of times for ideals and idealism.

Here it is tempting to recall two scenes, one from Rahi Masoom Reza's *Aadha Gaon* and the other from Amitav Ghosh's *The Shadow Lines* that exemplify the idea of belonging. In *Aadha Gaon* an old *hakim* is speaking on his deathbed about going to Pakistan. His son Saddan had come for a short stay and had gone back:

> Saddan was saying why he should send money to Abba. 'Why doesn't he come over to Pakistan?' 'But how can I go? Only yesterday my late father appeared to me saying 'Beta Kabir! Will you also leave me and go to Pakistan?' I said, 'No, Baba, how can you say this? . . . Whether Zamindari remains or goes, whether patients come or don't come, I shall never desert you. I am not Saddan. . . . '[4]

In *The Shadow Lines* similarly there is an old man, Ukil Babu, who continues to stay alone, in his own house in Dhaka, looked after by a Muslim rickshaw puller. Some of the old man's relations go to persuade him to move to Calcutta but he refuses point blank. Here is a snippet of the conversation between the narrator's grandmother and Ukil Babu who is her uncle:

> 'It's not safe for you here', my grandmother said urgently. 'I know these people look after you well, but it's not the same thing. You don't understand.'
>
> 'I understand very well', the old man muttered. 'I know everything. I understand everything. Once you start moving you never stop. That's what I told my sons when they took the trains.' I said: 'I don't believe in this India—shindia. It's all very well, you're going away now, but suppose when you get there they decide to draw another line somewhere? What will you do then?' . . . As for me, *I was born here, and I'll die here.* (italics added)[5]

The issue of belongingness is obviously crucial in Partition fiction. For Attia Hosain it is so important that Laila raises an accusing finger at Zahira—for the first and the only time she does so—for not coming to India to see her ailing mother for fear that frequent visits might jeopardize his (Naseer) chances of promotion: 'She denied the country of her birth with the zeal of a convert' (303).

Attia Hosain's technique of handling painful events needs to be mentioned. It is important to remember that the family reunion scene in the dining room is not recalled by Laila as are the other scenes up to the end of Part III. Part IV opens in 1952, some 14 years after the close of Part III. During this interval many painful events, including the death of her husband, the death of Zahid in communal violence and the splitting up of the family, have taken place. All these incidents are retrieved by Laila through memory as she wanders through the different rooms of Ashiana on a wintry day in 1952. She is now a widow with a 14-year old daughter. The distancing technique used by the writer enables her to review painful events with mature sensitivity and greater compassion. The family reunion scene, in which Saleem and Nadira finally decide to go, is a stormy one. But the storminess is tempered by the realization that Partition is already an accomplished fact and that they have migrated to Pakistan and have also been back for a brief visit. This late retrieval takes the sting out of the memory. Laila has forgotten the ideological quarrel and points up the pathos of the situation created by Partition in which families were split up and brother was separated from brother: 'Less than two months later Saleem and Nadira left for Pakistan and it was easier for them thereafter to visit the whole world than the home which had once been theirs' (289).

Partition enacts yet another more tragic separation, for Asad's younger brother Zahid is killed while travelling on a train to Pakistan. Attia Hosain's treatment of Zahid's death is an even better example of her distancing technique. Instead of giving a close up of the event she soberly, almost unsentimentally, reports the killing.

In raising the problem of split families and divided loyalties the writer raises issues that are important even today. The continuing relevance of split families is reflected in Shyam Benegal's film *Mammo* (1995) and in a recent Pakistani play *Ek Thi Nani* which revolves round the lives of the celebrated theatre artiste Zohra Sehgal and her Pakistani sister.

Attia Hosain also shows a sober awareness of the bitter legacy of Partition in the form of problems of Muslims who stayed on in India. Saleem speaks of these when he tries to dissuade his brother Kemal from staying on. He talks of 'discrimination' and 'suspicion, prejudice, even hatred' (286-7). Later Zahira refers to the 'injustice and prejudice that are destroying . . . Muslim culture and language' (303). But the writer also knows that there are no easy options available. The obvious option for them is to identify themselves completely with their country and join the mainstream. The career graphs of Kemal and Asad suggest that the possibilities did exist.

Explaining the need for literature on Partition, Mushirul Hasan says, 'What political debate will never fully do—and the reason we so badly need literature—is *defeat the urge to lay the blame, which keeps animosity alive*. Only literature truly evokes the sufferings of the innocent, whose pain is more universal and ultimately a vehicle of more honest reconciliation than political discourse' (italics added).[6] *Sunlight on a Broken Column* falls in this category because while it gives the varied motivational drives of Muslims at the time of Partition, it avoids apportioning blame and is, in the ultimate analysis, non-judgemental.

NOTES

1. Attia Hosain, *Sunlight on a Broken Column* (1st edn, 1961, repr., New Delhi, 1992), p. 245. All further references to this text will be indicated by page numbers within parentheses.
2. Rupinderjit Saini, 'From Harmony to Holocaust: A Study of Communal Relations in the Partition Novels', *Studies in Humanities and Social Sciences*, No. 1 (November 1994), p. 111.
3. *The Other Side of Silence: Voices from the Partition of India* (New Delhi, 1998), p. 221.
4. Rahi Masoom Reza, *Aadha Gaon* (in Hindi) (1st edn, 1966, New Delhi, 1998), p. 355.
5. Amitav Ghosh, *The Shadow Lines* (1988), p. 215.
6. Quoted from Mushirul Hasan, 'Memories of a Fragmented Nation: Rewriting the Histories of India's Partition, in this volume.

Partition Revisited: Looking at Ashfaque Ahmed's 'Gadariya'

AMEENA K. ANSARI

When freedom came to India at the stroke of the midnight hour on 14/15 August 1947, the world's greatest empire handed over the reigns of government to its people. With this freedom came Partition, which was born of the mutual distrust of the peoples of the subcontinent and it tore asunder the social fabric of the region. With the formation of India and Pakistan, there followed a frenzied bout of murder and rioting, as masses of humanity migrated to the nation of their choice and carried with them tales of till then unheard horrors perpetrated on migrants. As the dust of this mayhem settled, and the two nations went about the business of governance, there was born a body of literature that gave voice to the traumatic realities of independence and Partition. By creating a special fictional space and by speaking through the voice of their characters, writers of the two nations have given us various perspectives on, and sensitive portrayals of, the occurrences of those days. Even 50 years after these cataclysmic events, such literary pieces shake the core of our being as they highlight, in fictional terms, the shades of communalism, the sense of displacement, the sensibilities of migration and an underlying sense of despair.

One of the Urdu short stories that captures the spirit of Partition is Ashfaque Ahmed's 'Gadariya'. It is the tale of Munshi Chintram, better known as Dauji, who is a dedicated scholar of Islamic cerebration and Persian literature. He stands as the symbol of the *guru-shishya parampara*, or the teacher/taught relationship, which has marked the scholastic traditions of the subcontinent since times immemorial. Finding himself, a Hindu, in the newly created Pakistan and refusing to give up his ancestral village, Dauji has to contend with the harsh realities of Partition.

It is in an undivided India that the story opens. Dauji, the son of a

* Based on Ashfaque Ahmed's 'Gadariya' trans. into English, by Ameena K. Ansari, in Joginder Paul, *Sleepwalkers* (New Delhi, 1998), pp. 137-92.

milkman and a *khatri* by caste, earned his living by drafting petitions at the local court-house but his real vocation lay in his being an avid scholar of Persian. He took a special delight in trying to infuse his enthusiasm for the subject into others, but he found such people lacking. Dauji's wife, Bebe, was a virago who derived perverse pleasure in humiliating her husband, indulging in gossip and supplementing the family income by stitching clothes for the neighbourhood women. Their daughter Qurratulain, nicknamed Bibi, was the apple of her father's eye and this often resulted in Bebe lashing out at her and Dauji both. Their son, Amichand, was a bright pupil who was a classmate of the story's narrator. It is through Amichand that the lives of Dauji and Golu, the narrator, intersect.

Golu's poor performance in the class X examination and his father's violent despair results in Dauji being summoned to tutor the boy. He had earlier tutored Aftab, the narrator's elder brother, but due to some unexplained differences, coldness had crept into the relationship between Dauji and Doctor Sahib, the father. Golu's performance, however, is enough to bring about a thaw in the relationship between the two men. Doctor Sahib hands over his son to Dauji, in the hope that the boy will at least be able to clear the high school examinations, in the second attempt, in the following year. Once Dauji takes him under his wing, the boy becomes the centre of his existence. All his sleeping and waking hours are spent in trying to hone his ward's academic skills. The teacher is extremely confident that his pupil will be able to secure a first division. In fact, the story begins with Dauji shaking his pupil awake on a freezing winter night and asking him to translate a sentence into Persian. Tears and abuses showered on him by his pupil leave Dauji unmoved. Dauji does not budge till Golu has repeated the right answer by rote.

A strange relationship exists between the enthusiastic *guru* and his reluctant *shishya*. There are inexplicable moments of violent dislike, ironic humour and intimate camaraderie between the two as they struggle to achieve their goals. To ensure that his son is given adequate coaching, Doctor Sahib even has his son move into Dauji's house. Golu is adopted as a member of his teacher's household and is also given Amichand's room, when the latter moves to the city to attend college. His playful, non-serious nature interferes constantly with his lessons and even the mild Bibi reports that, instead of studying, he makes toys out of sticks. Dauji's enthusiasm, however, never wanes and, exercizing superhuman patience, he constantly endeavours to bring his ward up to the standards required for passing the coming examinations. Through the maze of algebra, geometry, history, English grammar and comprehension, the pupil and the teacher tediously make their way.

On seeing Dauji one day, surreptitiously enjoying a cup of rich jaggery tea on the court-house premises, away from the oppressive atmosphere of Bebe's presence, Golu is filled with a surge of tenderness for the man who gives so much without desiring anything in return. On another occasion, Dauji, in Bebe's absence, begins to make tea with the connivance and assistance of Bibi and Golu. A gay mood prevails that day in the otherwise discordant marital environment of Dauji's house. It is Bebe's unexpected arrival in the midst of this merrymaking and her verbal and physical violence, that intensifies Dauji's sense of isolation within his own household and sets him thinking about his past. He goes down memory lane, eulogizing his teacher, his *aqa-e-inamdar*, who commands his greatest awe and respect. He remembers his teacher's erudition and his ability to transform an ignoramus into a man of letters. Thanks to his *aqa's* tutelage, Dauji was able to rise from Chintu, the goatherd, to Munshi Chintram, a man of considerable intellectual prowess. He revels in remembering how he carried his physically handicapped teacher on his back, whenever the gentleman needed a change of scene, away from the closed environs of his traditional Muslim household. To him, his *aqa* was the *huma*, a legendary bird, that brought good luck to those upon whom it alighted. Dauji remembers how closely welded their lives were and how he was a very welcome guest in the home of his teacher. When a particularly intricate geometrical problem could not be solved by the combined efforts of the duo, the *aqa-e-inamdar* suggested that his pupil should go to Delhi and seek the assistance of one who was a master in this field. Fearing that his mother would never allow him to go, Dauji left his village without informing either her or his teacher and reached the unfamiliar city of Delhi.

After much difficulty, he was able to reach the home of Hakim Nasir Ali Seestani, the scholar recommended by his *aqa-e-inamdar*. Seestani, too, had a handicap—he was blind but made up for this deficiency through his keen sense of touch. His pupils would draw difficult geometric configurations with their index fingers on his bare back and he would help them find solutions. Dauji remembers staying in Delhi for a year, thirstily expanding the vistas of his knowledge, under the tutelage of Hakim Seestani. When he returned home, his old teacher wept to see him and enjoined that never again in the future should his favourite pupil leave him desolate. Dauji's intense regard, his indebtedness and his humility, whenever he remembers his benefactor, are the high points of the story.

Religious affinities are pushed to the background and are superseded by intellectual and spiritual ones, as Dauji and his *aqa* forge a bond that reiterates the glorious tradition of the *guru/shishya*.

The memory of his teacher spurs Dauji to forge similar links with his students. Dauji is successful in donning the role of the *aqa* only as far as his relationship with Golu is concerned. He evinces a keen interest in all his schoolwork, infuriating his pupil with a barrage of questions that pertain to the on-coming examinations. His gentle responses to Golu's subsequent bouts of wrath succeed in emphasizing that Dauji's true vocation was that of a teacher and his seasonal work at the court-house was only a kind of drudgery, done to keep his household fire burning.

His tragedy is that no one appreciates or values his passion for disseminating knowledge. Bebe is too coarse and ignorant a woman to understand her husband's talent and humane outlook. Bibi, though lovingly tutored by her father in Persian, is looked upon as an aberration by her father-in-law. Golu is only too glad to flee the parental home and join in rightist political activities that contravene his father's secular sensibilities and ideology. He also fails to appreciate either his teacher's scholarship or his humane qualities. Despite his teacher's care and dedication, Golu does not perform as well as he should have in the examination. He misses the first division by a single mark and the irony is that it is his teacher who suffers a greater sense of failure than Golu. Once the results are declared the teacher/pupil bond becomes tenuous. Golu leaves to join college and is impressed by the urbanity of the new surroundings into which he has entered. There is, initially, a desultory correspondence between him and Dauji, but it peters out with time, which marches relentlessly forward as the country's independence and the inevitable Partition draw near.

News of communal rioting spreads to Dauji's town, which till then, had remained a place of sanity and tolerance. It is only when the migrant Muslims arrive and the local Hindus and Sikhs flee, that a thirst for violence overtakes the town's inhabitants. Hearing the tales of butchery and terror told by the incoming migrants, a wave of looting, arson and murder sweeps the town. The peaceful tenor of life is broken as bloodthirsty mobs, bent on revenge, take to the streets and display a sadistic delight in torturing any Hindu they can lay their hands on. For Golu, it is a strange world, as aliens move into those houses from which the non-Muslims have fled. He experiences a pang of betrayal on learning that Dauji's family, too, has vanished. He feels that this silent escape went against Dauji's grain, yet this seems to have inexplicably happened.

The climax of the story occurs when Golu, on seeing a mob swirling around someone, catches a glimpse of Dauji as the object of attention. His pleas to let the old man go fall on deaf ears and Dauji is handed over to Ranu, the town's depraved loafer. Ranu takes perverse pleasure in humiliating Dauji, whom he saw as the cause of his brush with the law, on an earlier occasion after he had made obscene references to Dauji's daughter, Bibi. Ranu uses this seemingly heaven-sent opportunity to get even with a man whom he sees as his enemy. First, he roughly hacks away Dauji's tuft of long hair and then, as a special concession and given the man's age, decides that Dauji's life would be spared. In return, the old man would tend Ranu's goats. Before he leaves to tend his new charges, Dauji is asked to reel off the *kalma*, one of Islam's basic observances. On enquiring which particular one he should recite, Dauji is struck on the head by Ranu for his impertinence. Only Dauji of all the people present there knew the relevance of his question, as there is more than one *kalma*. The illiterate Ranu has not a clue and takes the question to be a challenge to his newly bestowed authority. Swift physical retribution is meted out to the old and helpless Dauji and the story ends with the description of his stoicism, as he faces a life of servility under the likes of Ranu.

Written in a kind of flashback-within-flashback technique, 'Gadariya' is a story that reverberates with strong psycho-political undertones. This perspective is related to what Tomislav Longinovic calls 'the irreducible connection between what apparently is an individual artistic expression in the text and the broader ideological and hegemonic context'.[1] This perspective involves elements that are historical, political as well as psychoanalytical. The culmination of the freedom struggle in the subcontinent saw the transfer of power not to one but to two nations. From the torso of undivided India were born two nations built on particular brands of religious affinities and this resulted in some of the bloodiest massacres in human history. A seemingly peaceful nation was partitioned into a seething cauldron of senseless bloodletting. This is the historical/political backdrop that Ashfaque Ahmed chooses for his story.

The denouement of the story subtly focuses on this tortuous aspect of history, but its impact can be better appreciated through an understanding of the pre-Partition mode of life. This forms a major section of the story and the author's subjective artistic expression takes delight in describing it. Through Dauji's ecstatic memories of his *aqa-e-inamdar*, the reader is given an insight into a relationship that transcended the barriers of religion, caste and status. It was, instead, based on the simple human expedient of a man seeking to quench his thirst for knowledge and it grew, as Ahmed writes, into a bond shared by, what the author considers, a low-caste Hindu and a Muslim scholar. Whenever Dauji ruminates upon his past, he is overwhelmed by a sense of gratitude and indebtedness to his teacher, who raised him from the brute level of life to the level of scholastic endeavour and piety. Their relationship truly symbolizes a composite culture and integration, besides glorifying the teacher/taught tradition of spiritual bondage that goes beyond the confines of the material world.

When Dauji takes on the role of a teacher, he fails to get dedicated students like himself. The narrator is forcibly put under his charge and, apart from a few occasions when he genuinely acknowledges the value of Dauji, he remains a reluctant, at times even an abusive, student. Dauji can only recount the regard he had for his teacher; he could never get the same from his students, who belong to a new generation that is caught up in the race for material prosperity. For these young men, the niceties and conventions that guided Dauji in his interaction with his mentor have no meaning. The teacher is seen, by this generation, as a means for acquiring a socially desirable degree and affluence. The moment of ultimate rejection comes with Ranu's treatment of Dauji. His physical manhandling of the old man, and the severing of his *bodhi* (tuft of hair), symbolically portrays, through the insensitivity of a fictional character, the destruction of a value system that died with Partition.

The author's vision juxtaposes the subjective/internal with the objective/external, thus bringing about a merger of the psychological and the ideological. Artistic expression conceptualized and broadened the historical/political realities in a manner that placed before the reader the dehumanizing and traumatic realities of Partition. From a psychoanalytical view point, Dauji and Ranu, respectively, represent the human and the bestial on different levels. Ranu's brutish behaviour is evidence of a world gone mad, a situation in which sheer physical strength cancels out the finer human emotions of mankind. Dauji's recitation of the *kalma* completes, ritualistically, a conversion to a way of life that is radically different from his past. The occasion emphatically brings out all the pathos and tragedy that were the emotional aftermath of the subcontinent's breakup.

Dauji's faith is not a 'received' one; rather it is, as Joseph Brodsky said, 'a matter of arrival'.[2] The old man seeks to counterbalance his inherited Hinduism with an understanding of Islam, which he arrived at after his interaction with his teacher. This had made him both comfortable and conversant with the Muslim idiom, but Ranu, despite his 'received' faith, is not only ill at ease but also bestial in the scene where he becomes the master and Dauji, the slave. It is with this stark contrast that the powerful ironic twist of the tale is brought out.

The theme of displacement is another aspect of the psycho-political undertones of the story. The mass migration and the displacement of population that occurred in 1947 form an important backdrop, but it is other forms of displacement that give the story, a touch of sensitive realism. In fact, as far as the protagonists are concerned, there is no physical displacement or migration and both are strongly rooted in their respective abodes. Golu is in his ancestral town when the rioting breaks out. At the same time, Dauji prefers to return to his familial dwelling after visiting his relatives. The displacement of both has to do with psyche and spirit. Golu's initial sense of displacement is the result of his academic non-performance, when he is cast out of his family home and is placed under Dauji's tutelage. Dauji's affection and his family's acceptance of the young Muslim boy into their household heals the emotional wrench that he experienced at that time. The adult Golu's sense of displacement has to do with the helpless outrage that he experiences when verbal and physical abuse is being heaped upon Dauji by the scum of his town. In the recesses of his being, he is horrified, even guilty, of mutely witnessing his teacher's degrading humiliation, knowing that it would be compounded by time and that Dauji would never again gain the respectable eminence that he once had as Munshi Chintram.

Dauji's sense of displacement is highlighted in his communication, or the lack of it, within his family. His wife, who looks upon herself as the real financial support of the family, considers him an idler. With his son he shares a relationship that verges on coldness as their rare exchanges are more academic than anything else. His daughter gives him a sympathetic ear but her marriage leaves him desolate. He tries to build emotional bridges with his ward but there, too, he meets with failure, as there is a specific reason and, therefore, a time limit to their relationship. Each of these individuals seeks to displace and exclude Dauji from their inner worlds and he is driven to seek solace in the past, when his *aqa-e-inamdar* gave him the human regard and recognition, that every man craves for.

The tumultuous events of 1947 pushed Dauji to even greater depths of psychological displacement, as he becomes an allegorical victim caught in the tide of historical circumstances that shook the roots of society. He became a stranger in his own home, which had been forcibly inhabited by migrants. He was finally left at the mercy of a crazed mob, which symbolically pronounced a future of death-in-life for him, assigning him to Ranu as a goatherd. The horizons of knowledge that he hankered for, and took delight in, were thus closed to him forever. He was left an abandoned and isolated figure, without books, family or home, grazing Ranu's goats for the rest of his life. At the end of the story, Dauji is an emotionally shattered and spiritually broken man, whose stoic silence only serves to reiterate what he had been throughout his life—the metaphorical outsider, unsung, unwept, chained by, and yet a gem of, the human race.

'The first step in liquidating a people', wrote Milan Kundera, 'is to erase its memory, destroy its books, its culture, its history'.[3] Dauji embodies these words and stands for the composite cultural traditions of the subcontinent, that the Partition tore apart. By taking away his books, his culture and his history, the real Dauji is stamped out of existence by society and in his place is born an unnatural shadow that is physiologically alive but dead in all other respects.

With the resurgence of translation studies, 'Gadariya' is now accessible to many of those who are unfamiliar with the Urdu language and literature. Its special significance lies in the fact that it belongs to a corpus of writing that is now referred to as 'Partition literature'. More than 50 years after the event, 'Gadariya', like many stories of its kind, succeeds in capturing the emotional and historical essence of a particularly gruesome event of history. The recent spate of translations present new perspectives of Partition. Comparative analysis of translations is not the thrust of this article, but there are two aspects of it that shed interesting light on the thematic concerns of the story. One has to do with the translation of the title, the other is concerned with the translation of the last sentence of the story. In terms of absolute equivalence, *gadariya* is a shepherd and this is the title given by Jai Ratan,[4] Alok Bhalla[5] and Umar Memon[6] in their translated versions. This is an example of a pure linguistic translation that narrows and confines the cultural context of the story to a Christian connotational framework of the shepherd/messiah leading his flock/believers. In fact, it is the other way round, as it is the flock, comprising the narrator, Amichand, Bibi, Bebe and society in general, that chooses to abandon the shepherd, Dauji. He is no shepherd, as he has no flock; he is only a goatherd, with no ownership rights over the cattle that belong to Ranu.

Even more interesting are the translated versions of the climactic sentence of the story in which Dauji, in a trance, walks behind the goats as he leads them out to pasture. His stoical demeanour and carriage as he goes to perform this menial task is likened by Jai Ratan, to 'a long-haired jinn';[7] is said to resemble 'an angel with long and flowing hair' by Alok Bhalla;[8]

is described as 'Farida, the one with long flowing hair' by Umar Memon;[9] and is said to be 'like a long-haired Baba Farid', Punjab's Sufi mystic, in my own translation that appears in Joginder Paul's *Sleepwalkers*. The varied versions are reflective of the Eastern bent of mind, that is, in conflict with the Western tradition into which it is rendered.

There is no methodology that can define exactly the extent and ways that translations can be allowed to differ from the original, but a translator should alert the reader so that he/she can understand what is happening to the text, as it transcends linguistic and social boundaries. Culturally bound and homogenous elements of the text can become radically heterogeneous as in this specific instance. In employing generalizing similes for Dauji, the core of the man's stoical Sufi stance is lost, thereby weakening the impact of the story. This makes a very strong case for a productive interaction of the cultural, literary and the linguistic. Translation would be impossible if it is required to be a perfect mirror of the original and so it has to strive and build plausible bridges between the author, the text and the reader as it seeks to create meaning.

Marvin Bell, has said that, 'No translation is ever finished; it is merely abandoned'.[10] Ashfaque Ahmed's 'Gadariya' is living proof of this. It does not moralize or pontificate; rather it aspires to present a version of the historical/individual realities of Partition. The reverberations of its aftermath are felt by the nations of the subcontinent even today as the earlier distrust, intolerance and separatism continue to shake the social fabric more than 50 years after India and Pakistan gained their freedom.

NOTES

1. Tomislav Longinovic, '1989: A Psychopolitical Analysis of the Eastern European Revolution', in Daniel Weissbort and Arvind Krishna Mehrotra, eds, *Periplus: Poetry in Translation* (Delhi, 1993), pp. 164-75.
2. Interview with Joseph Brodsky by Gregory Musial at the University of Iowa, USA, 1989.
3. Milan Kundera, *The Book of Laughter and Forgetting* (New York, 1981), p. 159.
4. Jai Ratan, trans., *Contemporary Urdu Short Stories* (New Delhi, 1991), pp. 87-105.
5. Alok Bhalla, *Stories About the Partition of India* (New Delhi, 1994), pp. 1-48.
6. Muhammad Umar Memon, trans., *An Epic Unwritten: Urdu Stories about Partition* (1998), pp. 30-86.
7. Jai Ratan, op.cit., p. 105.
8. Bhalla, op.cit., p. 40.
9. Memon, op.cit., p. 86.
10. Marvin Bell, Address to American Literary Translators' Association, 1989, in Weissbort and Mehrotra, eds, op. cit., p. 3.

Representing the Holocaust: The Partition in Two Bengali Plays

JAYANTI CHATTOPADHYAY

In the preface to his play *Dalil* (The Deed), 1947,[1] dealing with the Partition and the problems of the refugees, the author Ritwik Kumar Ghatak (1925-76) had commented on the inadequacy of the genre to deal with a theme that was too widespread and too intense. 'The present reality', he had added, 'can only be represented in an epic'. Yet as he had confessed later[2] he could never disassociate himself from the subject. Whether as a playwright or as a film maker, Ghatak had never stopped addressing it, throughout his entire career as a creative artist. Nor could most of the other playwrights (or for that matter many of the other Indian creative writers) of the late 1940s and the 1950s. As described by many, the Partition was the most cataclysmic event in the history of twentieth century India, and its impact was profound on all walks of life, including even literature. But, for the literatures of the language areas that were directly involved in the Partition, the effect was simply overwhelming and all pervasive.

In Bengal, it will be recalled, the nightmares had begun even earlier with the outbreak of the Second World War. As Calcutta became a centre of war activities, swarms of soldiers and officials descended upon the city. As a result, war profiteering and black marketeering flourished, and was accompanied by erosions in human values. On the other hand, Burma, Asia's greatest exporter of rice in the inter-war period, stopped its supply. In 1942, a severe cyclone hit and devastated large areas of south-eastern Bengal and, a year later, a terrible famine gripped the region, killing between one and a half to two million people, many of whom died on the streets of Calcutta, where they had dragged themselves in a vain search for food. The already bitter relations between the Hindus and the Muslims had worsened, in the meantime, and the following few years were scarred with bitter communal violence on an unprecedented scale. The Partition

* Based on Salil Sen, *Natur Ihudi* (The New Jews), 1950, and Tulsidas Lahiri, *Banglar Mati* (The Earth of Bengal), 1953. All translations from the Bengali are mine.

of the province was the final blow. The scalpel of Radcliffe, took away one-third of its area (the rich eastern delta) and the drier and the less fertile west remained in India. But the worst was the uprooting of millions who had been driven away from their homes under conditions of incomparable horror and misery. They had witnessed their near and dear ones being hacked to death, their houses ransacked, looted and set on fire by their neighbours and their womenfolk abducted and, at times, raped before their own eyes.

To make matters worse, unlike in the western sector, the exchange of population on the eastern side was never total and the evacuation here remained a slow and an almost never ending process. It turned the borderlands into a vast territory of destitutes and the metropolis of Calcutta into a vast slum. All the open spaces, railway platforms, the shelters under the flyovers, the pavements and the parks became the home of these refugees, who were haunted constantly by the memories of looting, arson and rape. It was the greatest exodus in the recorded history of man and no Bengali writer worth his name could remain indifferent to or unaffected by it.

Creative writers have described this great catastrophe in various modes and genres. However, in this paper we will be concerned only with some of the plays written in the first decade after independence. For playwrights the task was far from easy. The representation of a theme like the Partition puts a tremendous strain on the genre. The horror and vulnerability that plays depicting such subjects possibly conjure would spill out of the stage and overwhelm the audience. There were other factors as well. Commercial theatres in Calcutta were passing through a bad patch during that period. The soaring prices of essential items as well as the attraction of the cinema (the tickets were comparatively much cheaper), kept the audience away from theatre halls. The managers, quite understandably, were not keen to put up plays on traumatic and agonizing subjects. They felt much safer in staging drawing-room comedies or hackneyed love themes. 'One gets a weird feeling of unreality', writes a historian of Bengali drama, 'when one recollects the plays one saw at the professional theatre those days.'[3]

The members and close associates of the Indian People's Theatre Association (hereafter IPTA), were outside the purview of the commercial theatre and were willing to address the theme directly but they also faced some constraints. With the establishment of this anti-fascist theatre organization in July 1943, a new theatre movement had emerged in Bengal. It promised to enact new and vibrant themes on the stage and build up a rapport with the audience. It had already presented significant and powerful representations of the famine in plays like *Jabanbandi* (The Statement),

1943, and *Nabanna* (The New Rice), 1944. But the association soon showed signs of strain and disintegration. There were rivalries and infighting among the members. Moreover, though the members were indeterminate in their allegiance to Marxist ideas, the government was hostile to the organization. The West Bengal government had banned the Communist Party in February 1948 and tried to revive the infamous Dramatic Performance Act of 1876, which would enable it to stop any performance of the organization if it found a play politically motivated. Slowly, the Bengal unit of the IPTA got splintered and the members shifted away and formed groups of their own that had varying degrees of stability and success.

The writers who wanted to deal with the theme of Partition, had to reckon with the above mentioned factors. How did they negotiate these forces? What effect the process had on the treatment of their themes, the conception of characters and on the climax of their plays? In this short paper, I have attempted to seek answers to these questions. I have chosen to analyse two well-known plays on the theme, that apparently have a few points of similarities. In the process I have attempted to trace the politics of the representation of Partition in them.

II

Salil Sen's *Natun Ihudi* (The New Jews), 1950, is our first play under discussion. The historians of Bengali drama do not tell us much about the author, except that he was closely associated with IPTA and had later joined an amateur theatre group, named Uttarsarathi. *Natun Ihudi*, his maiden play, was initially staged by this group and had a fairly successful stage run.

The play is about the plight of a Hindu family of East Pakistan which wanted to settle down in Calcutta, shortly after the Partition. Manomohan Bhattacharya, mostly referred to as Pandit Mosai (which indicates his caste and profession) in the play, was a Sanskrit teacher in a village school in East Bengal. With the emergence of Pakistan, Sanskrit ceased to be a compulsory subject, in the school curriculum, and Manomohan loses his job. Historians tell us that from the late 1930s there had been a gradual increase in Muslim representation in local and district boards in the Muslim majority district of East Bengal.[4] As the Muslim influence in the school boards increased there was occasional friction between the two communities over various issues. School committees, which were earlier dominated by Hindus were now no longer under Hindu control, and they refused to continue with certain practices that were peculiar to Hindu tradition, like the continuation of Sanskrit, considered to be the 'sacred language' of the Hindus. The play *Natun Ihudi*, does not take up the communal issue in any detail. In fact, the only criticism of the school authorities comes from Mirza, the *maulavi* of the school, a friend and well-wisher of the Bhattacharya family. He questions the morality of the president of the school who:

> Gave contract to his own son to construct the school building. With the money allotted for the purpose, only one storey of the school building was constructed, and the rest of the money was spent on building a two storey house of his own. No shame, *toba toba* you talk about Islam and Behasta, now and then and indulge in blackmarketeering of rice, sugar and kerosene. Was Pakistan born for this? (Scene 1)

The scared Manomohan refuses to comment. He sold his house and migrated to Calcutta with his family, consisting of his wife and three grown up children (two sons and one daughter). One son had died earlier. His dues are not paid by the school committee. The city does not prove to be friendly either and like the quintessential outsider (as the title of the play implies) he alongwith the other 'New Jews' struggle to rehabilitate themselves in an alien and hostile environment. From the second scene onwards, the locale of the play shifts, from one place to another, exposing the inadequate government machinery to handle the rehabilitation of the refugees, the insolent behaviour of the local gentry towards these outsiders and the preponderance of the anti-social elements in the society. At the same time it highlights the strong feeling of solidarity among the lower strata of the society. Thus while Manomohan and his family members are unable to get any support from the educated upper class, Bhiku, a Bihari railway porter, goes out of his way to rehabilitate a low caste couple, also refugees from East Pakistan.

Desperate to get a job, but unable to find one which suits his class and caste, Manomohan accepts the offer to serve as an assistant to the cook in marriage feasts. But the pain and humiliation in doing a job considered degrading for his class (though not for his caste), as also the insolent behaviour of his employers, take their toll on him. He falls sick and eventually dies.

Dukhiya, the slightly retarded and older of the two remaining sons, as well as Pari, the daughter, fall into the clutches of anti-social elements that were becoming an accepted part of the society in those days. Dukhiya turns into a petty criminal and dies as a result of a road accident. A tout in the flesh trade lures Pari to go away with him. Thus, the three deaths (two physical, one social) in quick succession leave the remaining two members of the family—the mother and the younger son, Mohan—stunned and bewildered with shock and grief. When the mother lies unconscious, Mohan cries out in extreme pain and anguish. He had till then not lost courage, had worked as a porter first, resisted the temptation to accept employment in a paint factory, where the workers were on strike, and had ultimately turned into a small time street peddler. But faced with the prospect of losing his mother, he cries in a voice full of anger:

> I do not want to save my mother. I would rather die myself. But before dying I would take revenge on them, I will murder them, set their houses on fire, and then I will die. (Scene XVII)

It is in this darkest hour when his existence is at its nadir that Mahendra, a well wisher of Mohan and a trade union leader, who happens to be there, comforts the latter with strong words. He urges Mohan to leave the path of self-destruction and in its stead join the collective protest. He reminds Mohan that his father and brother are dead and says:

> But the causes that led to their death still persist, and they have left you to demand an explanation. . . . So be one with the oppressed and take a vow that you will punish the selfish and the greedy and those who are playing with the lives of all of you. Take a vow that you will end the exploitation of the cruel oppressors. (ibid.)

For reasons that were obvious, neither Mohan nor Mahendra specify the identity of the oppressors and use only the third person pronoun to refer to them. Mahendra's speech, referred to above, which is the longest and brings the curtain down on the play does just this. It also reminds us of some of the pamphlets[5] issued secretly by the Communist Party, which was preparing for an armed struggle against the government during this period. And the message was more than evident to the contemporary audience. In fact, Sachin Sengupta one of the earliest reviewers of the play, who was also a member of the IPTA, felt a little irked by the dominating presence of Mahendra in the play. *Natun Ihudi*, he thought, had overdone the political message.[6]

However, what Sengupta does not notice or at least does not comment upon, is the second strand of the text, which urges the audience to look into the Partition of Bengal, in 1947, in the light of the first partition of the region by Lord Curzon in 1905. The decision, as we all know, provoked the first mass nationalist agitation in India, the Swadeshi movement, which ultimately had 'unsettled the settled fact', as Surendranath Bannerji said, of dividing Bengal into two regions. *Natun Ihudi,* represents the contemporary political struggle of the Left as the continuation of the Swadeshi movement and in the process it sidetracks many issues, suppresses and bypasses many gaps and contradictions in the theme of the play.

The play opens with the singing of a very well known, patriotic song[7] of D.L. Ray (1863-1913), a poet and dramatist, who had been 'deeply stirred by the nationalistic Swadeshi Movement'.[8] The song is first sung in a chorus and ends in a solitary female voice, with a mime showing the Hindus leaving the country, and Mirza, the *maulavi*, frantically urging them to stay back. As the actual narrative unfolds, we are told in the first scene itself about the deceased eldest son of the family. Actively involved in the Swadeshi movement, he had died as a political prisoner in a British jail, leaving a permanent scar on his mother's heart, who loses consciousness at the very mention of his name and recovers only at the call of her youngest son, Mohan. This occurs a few more times in the narrative, gaining more emphasis with each repetition, and ultimately acquires a symbolic dimension. In the last scene, when Mohan refuses to bring his mother back to consciousness for, according to him, she would wake up to a sorrowful and disgusting reality, Mahendra advises him:

> Wake up your mother take lesson from her, withstanding the grief of losing her eldest son she has brought you all up. Learn the *mantra* of perseverance from her, be a disciple of your elder brother. (ibid.)

As the curtain comes down, the last line of the same song that had been sung at the beginning, is heard in a solo female voice in the background.

The song, too well-known to the audience, alongwith the mime and the words of Mahendra, give a symbolic dimension to the relation between a mother (she has been named Annapurna, meaning the bountiful) and her three sons. The first, who died in the Swadeshi mover .ent symbolizes the past struggle of the country, is linked with the third, who has been assigned the task of leading the future course of the struggle. The second son, retarded as he is, picks up fights with the members of the other community at the slightest pretext and leaves the straight path of law and order, is only an aberration, that was probably best got rid of.

Probably, the strategies adopted by the author, for example, his oblique references to the identity of the oppressors, saved *Natun Ihudi* (though provocative at certain places) from the wrath of the government. But *Banglar Mati* (The Earth of Bengal), 1953, by Tulsidas Lahiri (1896-1959), the second play to be discussed in this paper, was less fortunate on this count. After its first stage performance, on 3 October 1953, the play was banned by the government, and only after deletion of certain lines was it allowed to be staged again.

A veteran actor of the commercial theatre for a fairly long time and member of the IPTA, Lahiri had written three successful plays, *Dukkhir Iman* (The Honesty of the Poor), 1947, *Pathik* (The Traveller), 1948, and *Chenda Tar* (The Broken String), 1950, dealing with the problems and exploitation of the peasants and the factory workers, before he turned to the theme of the Partition in *Banglar Mati.* Like Salil Sen, he also focuses on the Swadeshi movement in various ways in this play. In addition to the title, which has been taken from a famous song, composed by Rabindranath Tagore in 1905, the text refers to other incidents that occurred during this period. The playwright quotes from a number of Swadeshi songs to problematize and resolve (though not very convincingly) the feelings of distrust and hostilities between the two communities, the Hindus and the Muslims. According to the play this animosity was generated after the first partition of the region.

Consisting of four acts, of one scene each, the play starts with the predicament of an upper caste Hindu family of East Pakistan. Kalibabu, a retired government official, had decided to remain in East Pakistan after the Partition. However, within a short period of five years he and his family members, consisting of his widowed daughter-in-law, Kiran Shashi, and the two grown-up grandchildren, Chitra and Latka or Harikinkar, are sceptical of the earlier decision. Because of their minority status in the new nation, which had imposed a number of rules and restrictions on them, Kalibabu and his family feel like strangers in their own homeland. The static locale of the play, which remains confined to the drawing room of the family, from the beginning to the end, seems to symbolize their limited and confined existence. However, of the four members in the family, Kiran Shashi's role, like her presence in the play, remains vague and uncertain. Latka, the 'non-matric' and 'good for nothing' grandson of Kalibabu finds out a novel way of dealing with the changing circumstances. He replaces the photograph of Ramakrishna Paramhansa that was hanging on the drawing room wall with that of Jinnah, deletes the first part of his name Hari (the name of a Hindu god) from Harikinkar, and is happy to sing loudly on the streets of Pakistan in praise of the new nation. But for Kalibabu and his granddaughter Chitra, the situation becomes increasingly suffocating and unbearable. As she says, 'the noose around our necks is getting tighter every day'.

It is not difficult to understand the plight of Kalibabu. An English educated upper caste Hindu, belonging to the urban professional class, Kalibabu must have enjoyed a superior social position for a fairly long time. He is, therefore, bewildered and unable to cope with the changing social circumstances, where the illiterate, lower class Muslim, Garibulla, who had always remained the lowest of the low in society, dares to defy him now. Moreover, both Kalibabu and Chitra are firm believers in a traditional and orthodox social order. They are, therefore, anxious about the loss of orthodox traditions, which would pose a threat to this established order. Latka's acts of transgression irritate and frighten them. For Chitra, in particular, the idea of purity of caste and religion has almost become an obsession to the extent that it seems to have destroyed the finer sensibilities, the feelings of love and kindness in her. She fails to understand how her childhood friend, Anita (now Anowara Khatun), who driven by poverty and other misfortunes has, for sheer survival, got converted into Islam and married a Muslim. Chitra is now determined to go to Calcutta leaving her family members behind, because that seems the only way of survival for her.

Ironically however, in her obsessive desire to achieve her goal, Chitra herself trangresses a social code. She decides to go to Calcutta with a Muslim youth, Nuru Mian, secretly. The couple are intercepted at the station and brought back to their respective homes. But the act generates a lot of commotion in the city. While the Hindus are eager to make it out to be a case of kidnapping of a Hindu girl by a Muslim youth, the Muslim police officers in order to prevent this, want to put pressure and harrass Kalibabu and Chitra, unnecessarily. Salim Mian, the father of Nuru Mian, an active member of the Muslim League, takes this opportunity to express his anger against the predominance of Bengali Hindus in the society. 'You have', he tells Kalibabu, 'brought destruction for the Muslims, by inviting the Britishers to reign on us . . . you have snatched away from the Muslims all valuables' (Act IV). To Sadanandababu, a neighbour and friend of Kalibabu, he uses almost abusive language, 'you are like a dog wagging your tail, you bark, but you do not have the courage to bite' (ibid.).

Abu Mian, the grandfather of Nuru Mian, who is educated and a radical, as well as a lifelong friend of Kalibabu, suggests to Chitra to marry his grandson, not however out of love and concern for the family but as he himself declares, to fulfill his lifelong dream—the unity between the Hindu and the Muslim. Chitra, for whom even the intermarriage between upper caste Hindus is a violation of the traditional code, vehemently opposes the suggestion, which was made in good faith. The incident, however, shakes the already nervous Kalibabu, who till then had no intention of leaving his home and country. But now he becomes very anxious to leave, for he feels that, 'this country will turn us into non-humans from humans' (ibid.).

The preparations for leaving the country go on. Abu Mian, deeply repentant about having made his suggestion, watches helplessly, when suddenly, an act of Latka lifts the two families out of the impasse. The play, it may be remembered, is situated in East Pakistan of 1952, the year when the movement to establish Bengali as the national language had taken a violent and definitive turn and the Ansar Army, which was established primarily to curb the *Bangla bhasa andolan* (Bengali linguistic movement), had on several occasions come down heavily on processions of students. Participating in one such procession, Latka is injured in police action and is arrested, along with Nuru Mian, for disobeying the government. As Nuru Mian and Latka march away, hand in hand, proudly to the police station, Chitra declares her decision to stay back in East Pakistan:

It had become impossible for me to watch unopposed oppression every day. But now I know that there are people to fight back. They will fight and I will be a runaway. No, I would not do that never. . . . (ibid.)

The glaring anomalies in Chitra's thinking have been pointed out by some critics, but there are contradictions in the behaviour of other characters, also, which have not been commented upon. The noble and radical Abu Mian, probably the mouthpiece of the author, chides Kalibabu for his orthodox world view, which treats the Muslims as untouchables. He says 'If you had not been proud of your social customs so much, the country would not have to see these bad days' (Act I). But even he would not identify himself with the rural, illiterate, poor and lower class Muslim, Garibulla. At one point in the play, thinking of the changing times, Kalibabu hesitates to refer to Garibulla as *chotolok* (as opposed to *bhadralok*), Abu Mian almost reprimands him, 'Kalida, why are you afraid to call a *chotolok* a *chotolok*' (ibid).

As the members of the two families, the two mothers of Nuru and Latka, as well as Sadananda and Salim Mian, reunite in the hour of crisis, the misunderstanding between the two lifelong friends, Kalibabu and Abu Mian, also evaporates. They sit on the bench, hand in hand, and sing in duet the title song of the play:

Banglar mati, banglar jal
Banglar bayu, banglar phal
Punya hoyuk, punya hoyuk
Punya hoyuk, he bhagaban.

(Let the earth and the water and the air and the fruits of Bengal be holy, my Lord.)

It reminds the audience of the days of the Swadeshi movement when the unity between the two communities, the Hindus and the Muslims, had become the most important item on the national agenda. Poor Garibulla sits at their feet and looks up at the two élite men, belonging to two communities, perhaps hoping in vain for better days to come.

III

Theatre to IPTA, as repeatedly declared in its journal, *Lokratya*, was part of the mass struggle of the peasants, workers and youth. Both Salil Sen and Tulsidas Lahiri had addressed the issues involving the underprivileged in their plays. We have already mentioned three such plays by Tulsidas Lahiri. *Mouchor* (The Honey Thief), the play Salil Sen was to write after *Natun Ihudi*, deals with the poor landless peasants of Sundarbans, in West Bengal. Yet, in spite of their limited presence, the issue of the underdog never becomes the central concern of the respective authors of *Natun Ihudi* and *Banglar Mati*.

Then again neither of these playwrights address the Hindu Muslim question directly—they do not reflect its complexities and the frenzy that erupted immediately before and after the Partition. Both the plays have chosen instead to represent the Partition as the plight of a group of upper caste Hindus or, to be more precise, the *bhadralok*. The reasons behind such a choice are not difficult to comprehend, once we look back at the past of Bengal and of the history of the *bhadralok*. Though the exact connotations to the term have been discussed and debated by outside scholars, the word *bhadralok* is used widely as well as understood by the native speakers of the Bengali language quite easily to mean upper caste Hindus having landed property. It is, for example, quite interesting to note that nowhere in the play *Banglar Mati*, does the author mention the caste names of Kali or Sadananda. Because the use of the word *babu* was a clear enough indication that they belonged to the upper caste, were educated and, possibly, also had landed property. Though the members of this class were quite different in education and economic status, as Manomohan Bhattacharya and Kalibabu, there were certain common characteristics. For example, this was the class that did not work on the land but lived off the rental income it generated. They also possessed some kind of education, be it vernacular education, like Manomohan, or a Western education, like Kalibabu. Finally, the particular privileges that the *bhadralok* enjoyed were not available to the vast majority of

Bengali Muslims and low caste Hindus, for a variety of historical reasons.

In 1905, when the proposed partition of Bengal was announced by Lord Curzon, which meant that the province was to be divided, it provoked the first mass nationalist agenda—the Swadeshi movement. Probably it was the nationalist imagination of the *bhadralok* that flourished secretly during this movement. The dominant form of the imagined nation in Bengal at the time of the Swadeshi movement was seen to contain 'at one and the same time, an Indian nationalism built around a natural history of Aryan Hindu tradition, a linguistic nationalism valourizing Bengal's cultural unity and a rhetoric of Hindu Muslim unity'.[9] It is interesting to note that such a combination did not pose a problem (at least for a long time) even in the Hindu minority plus Muslim majority places like East Bengal. The nationalist élites of Bengal, predominantly the *bhadralok*, remained comfortably ensconed in their position as leaders of the society as well as the nation that they had imagined into existence till the 1940s. Then came the war, the Famine and lastly the Partition—events that shook the very existence of this class. The following passage, written by Ritwik Kumar Ghatak, is indicative of the general reaction of this class to these calamities:

> We had seen a rich and complete Bengal in our childhood and youth. Rabindranath with his world-winning genius was crowning the Bengali literature, which at the same time was receiving new ideas from the writers of the Kallol group. The youths in schools and colleges were involved with the freedom struggle. The villages of Bengal were vibrating with hopes of new life, they were enjoying festivals and rituals throughout the year. Suddenly came war and famine; the members of the Congress Party and that of Muslim League acquired a divided Independence for the country; the country was flooded with communal riots . . . our dreams were shattered, we were left with a wretched and truncated Bengal.[10]

With disintegration threatening every aspect of their life, the *bhadralok*, as is evident from the passage quoted above, searched for an anchor and this they found in looking back to an apparently more impressive past that had culiminated in the Swadeshi movement—a movement that had energetically and courageously foiled the attempts of Lord Curzon to divide the province into two parts. Reverting to the Swadeshi movement gave the *bhadralok* an opportunity to valourize the cultural unity of Bengal and to propagate the rhetoric of Hindu Muslim unity. The Partition in 1947, in this context, could then be evoked as only an aberration, a mark of loss and failure.

NOTES

1. The play was fist enacted by Anushilan Shakha of the IPTA in 1947. In 1950 it was banned by the government along with 68 plays for three years.
2. Ritwik Kumar Ghatak, 'Amar Chhabi', in *Chalachitra Manus Ebang Avo Kichu* (in Bengali) (Calcutta, 1975), p. 25.
3. Kironmoy Raha, *Bengali Theatre* (New Delhi, 1978), p. 153.
4. Joya Chatterji, *Bengal Divided: Hindu Communalism and Partition 1932-47* (Cambridge, 1995), pp. 203-11.
5. (a) '. . . Set fire to the whole of Calcutta and the whole of Bengal' and (b) 'Labourers, peasants, students and citizens, take revenge on them. . . . Hang those murderers. Destroy the Ministry', V.B. Sinha, *The Red Rebel in India: A Study of Communist Strategy and Tactics* (New Delhi, 1968), p. 60.
6. The review was published in Digindranath Bandyopadhyaya, *Natyalok*, a fortnightly magazine on Bengali drama in 1951. Cited in Sunil Dutta, *Natya Andoloner Tris Bachar* (in Bengali) (Jatya Sahitya Parishad, 1972), p. 50.
7. *Dhana dhanne pusphe bhara amader ei basundhara* . . . (our this earth full of riches, rice and flowers . . .).
8. Kironmoy Raha, op.cit., p. 80.
9. Partha Chatterji, 'The Second Partition of Bengal', in *The Present History of West Bengal, Essays in Political Criticism* (Delhi, 1997), p. 30.
10. Ritwik Kumar Ghatak, op.cit., p. 25.

Fiction as History: Partition Stories

M. ASADUDDIN

The relationship between history and fiction has always been problematic. From Plato's banishment of poets, from the ideal Republic and Sir Philip Sydney's differentiation, between the probable truth of 'poesy' and the particular truth of history, to Frederic Jameson's edict, 'always historicize', one encounters a range of responses that underline the value of literature as a human document and that supplement the historical reconstruction of reality. Instead of trying to draw generalized, magisterial conclusions from isolated events and imposing some arbitrary pattern on them, literature records the writers' endeavours to reconstruct reality in slices and fragments by dramatizing some human situations. An act of remembrance is always partial and fragmentary. With post-modern insights we know that reality in its totality is unknowable, because it is fractured not seamless. We can grasp it only in fragments. These fragments can then be integrated to build a comprehensive picture of the event under study

The Partition of India, a momentous event in Indian history, continues to tantalize historians, haunt the Indian psyche and cast its shadow on our social and political life. It is closely linked with the chronicle of our freedom struggle that made the actual liberation of the country from foreign yoke an experience of violence, slaughter and exile for many. One of the most massive demographic dislocations in history, with its attendant human tragedy, it defies chroniclers to come to grips with it in all its dimensions. Tomes of analysis and exegesis by historians and bureaucrats have not led us anywhere closer to a definitive understanding of the phenomenon, even though the recent works of Bipin Chandra, Ian Talbot, Ayesha Jalal and Mushirul Hasan have brought fresh insights into the field. Historical

* Based on Alok Bhalla, ed., *Stories about the Partition of India*, 3 vols (New Delhi, 1997). All references will be indicated by the number of the volume, followed by the page number within parenthesis.

accounts and official documents, despite their apparent 'transparency' and 'factuality' can tell us only about the statistics—at least one million deaths, ten million refugees, and so on. But the human dimension—broken families, ties and relationships, physical disability and disease, the psychological trauma of torture, amputation, rape, abduction, forced witnessing of atrocities and their consequences, through generations, can never be fully quantified. This is where literature comes in as it gives us insights that enable us to a better understanding of human situations. Tolstoy's *War and Peace* gives us a more holistic and comprehensive understanding of nineteenth century Russia, its people and the effects of the Napoleonic wars, than history. The horror of Auschwitz, Sobibor or Bosnia in all its brutality cannot be conveyed by linear history writing as can be done by literature, a fact which has been demonstrated by holocaust literature, such as Primo Levi's *Survival in Auschwitz.*[1] Some realities need to be fictionalized before human imagination can come to terms with its horrors and unbearable pain. Fiction also provides us with competing versions of truth and multiple points of view and thus leads us to a richer and more nuanced understanding of events and people. Alok Bhalla's three volumes, which stand at the interface of fiction, history and politics, are relevant in this context and have taken a significant place in the growing genre of Partition literature in the Indian subcontinent.

II

Alok Bhalla has selected 63 short stories from different Indian languages, including those by well-known writers and some of their best works. The language-wise break-up of the stories is as follows: Urdu–30, Hindi–14, Bangla–8, Punjabi–3, English–2, Malayalam–2, Sindhi–2, Marathi–1 and Dogri–1. As is obvious, Urdu and Hindi stories predominate. Is it because the impact of the Partition was felt most acutely in the Urdu-Hindi heartland? But the impact on the eastern side was no less violent and devastating. Why then are works of similar depth and urgency not found in Bangla? I am making this statement with full awareness of such writings as Atin Bandopadhyaya's *Nilkantha Pakhir Khonje,* Jyotirmoyi Devi's *Epar Ganga Opar Ganga*, Prafulla Roy's *Keya Patar Nauka* and Samaresh Basu's *Khandita.* Was the Bengali imagination not stirred to its depth by the fact of displacement? On the other hand, the near absence of stories from Bangladesh (erstwhile East Pakistan) is a serious lacuna in a work that claims to represent the whole subcontinent. Then, why is there such a preponderance (28 stories out of a total of 63) of Muslim writers? Does it mean that the Muslims were more affected by Partition? Did the fact of migration and exile touch deeper chords in their hearts, because of the concept of *hijrat*, Prophet Muhammad's departure from Mecca to Medina, that grand narrative of migrancy and exile, which is deeply ingrained in Muslim consciousness? Such questions plague the mind and cry for answers. It is a pity that Bhalla's quite lengthy (28 pages) and weighty 'Introduction' does not address any of these issues. He also does not say anything about his principle of selection, which makes one wonder whether it was purely arbitrary and whether some languages have been privileged over others in terms of representation.

The majority of the stories are anchored in the 'composite' Indian culture and history and are set against the background of the high politics of Partition. Of course, the perception of this history and culture differs from writer to writer. One must have some rudimentary knowledge of Indian history and mythology, the build up of the freedom struggle, the 'separatist' politics of the Muslim League and the revivalist Hindu movements to properly understand the historical context in which they have been placed. These stories recreate a shared past wherein Hindus and Muslims have been living in harmony for centuries. Small strifes occurred as they do in any society, but these did not seriously disturb communal harmony. For the writers, this assimilative strength was one of the primary features of Indian civilization and the cause of its resilience. It was an unbroken continuum, which was violently ruptured by the 'madness' of Partition. The writers are as bewildered as their dramatis personae: they do not have either the courage or the necessary rigour to fix the agency/ agencies that cause or perpetrate the violence; and they do not find anything in the past history of the people that could warrant such descent into bestiality. The only way they explain this is that it was a temporary madness, whose eruption was caused by an uncomprehending mess of events. This, however, is to ignore the history of communalism, in the two decades preceding Partition, and the propaganda and rumours that fuelled it. Ishtiaq Hussain Qureshi[2] has brought out in vivid details how communal relationships rapidly deteriorated and the culture of intolerance developed, particularly in urban areas, as freedom approached. As far as the narrative strategy followed in the stories is concerned, it depends on the all too familiar 'balancing act' between different forms of communal violence.

A small number of the stories offer the contrary view. They dramatize the past as one of distrust and discord. These stories are predicated upon the supposedly essential difference between the Muslims and the Hindus and Sikhs. The endeavours of the writers here are directed towards showing the superiority of their own religion over the others. Then there are stories that look at the violence and barbarity of Partition as a plain and simple descent into the heart of darkness and bestiality that is inherent in man. Here the writers stare violence in the face and are in no need of any rhetorical consolation. However, no such classification can be watertight as the themes intersect and overlap. They defy Bhalla's own classification of the stories into four categories. Further, not all the stories lend themselves easily to the kind of reading that Bhalla has subjected them to, with the Gandhian ideology providing the framework.

III

Among the writers of rupture and loss, Intizar Hussain, the most powerful and prolific Urdu short story writer from Pakistan, is decidedly the best. His preferred mode is the older forms of fabulist narration of the Orient—fables, parables and allegories as found in the *Panchatantra* and the *Jatakas*—alongwith an awareness of the modern and highly self-conscious modes of narration in the West, exemplified in the works of Kafka and Joyce. Memory and myth are the means through which Hussain frames the past and explores its contemporary relevance. The three stories by Hussain included here, 'An Unwritten Epic', 'A Letter from India' and 'The City of Sorrow', deal with the cultural disorientation and psychological trauma of people caught in the vortex of the competitive savagery of Partition.

'An Unwritten Epic', written in the form of a diary, which records the narrator's inner struggle to come to grips with the events of Partition after his migration from India to Pakistan, is written to commemorate the loss and suffering of the people of Qadirpur. He chooses for his hero Pichwa, the village bully, who gets worked up about Pakistan though he does not have the faintest idea about its location and the consequences of such an eventuality. His frenzy has no personal or ideological reasons and he fights Hindus not out of any religious zeal but to prove that he is the best club-wielder. He hangs the flag of the Muslim League from the peepul tree by the side of the temple. Finding that the village he fought for is situated in India after Partition, he leaves for Pakistan with grandiose dreams of prosperity but feels greatly disenchanted to discover that he is a non-entity there. He has lost his status and identity, which was a social construct, and cannot find a place in the new dispensations in Pakistan. Thwarted in his efforts to carve a niche for himself, he feels nostalgic for Qadirpur and comes back only to find that it no longer exists and has been replaced by Jatunagar, the city of the Jats. He is murdered and his head hangs from the peepul tree. The violence in Qadirpur set off by Pichwa reaches its nemesis. The narrator's own struggle to redeem the devastation of Partition, through the recuperative power of writing, goes on conjointly with the struggle of Pichwa and all his efforts to create a hero who could 'fight the wind with a lamp'. The wasteland of his memories becomes a burden and his world gradually becomes barren. There seems to be no possibility of renewal in the future.

'A Letter from India', deals with the altered cultural scenario for Muslims in India after Partition. Though the narrator feels internally diminished because he could not maintain the continuity of the family's cultural tradition, one feels that some of the changes are pregnant with future possibilities. 'The City of Sorrow', written after the partition of Pakistan and the birth of Bangladesh, is a disembodied story, where three unnamed characters, placed in a Kafkaesque limbo, discuss in half-articulated sentences their horrific experiences, when each of them has symbolically 'died'.

'The Shepherd' by Ashfaque Ahmed, recreates the syncretic tradition of the past, through the creation of a powerful character of great nobility and sublime pathos. It tells the story of Chintram, popularly known as Dauji, a Hindu shepherd, who under the tutelage of a Muslim saint—his Hazrat Maulana—became a court scribe from an unlettered goatherd. He had not only learnt Arabic and Persian, but studied the Muslim scriptures and other related literatures, extensively. Thus he integrated himself totally, into the Indo-Persian-Arabic-Muslim ethos and its liberal human tradition, which grew out of a mutual regard for the other's religion and a synthesis of the essentially good, moral and religious elements in each culture and religion. Dauji's Muslim teacher respected the Hindu religion and its rituals and taught him, by example, and not by precepts only, how the notions of morality and religiosity could be given a larger meaning by liberating them from the literal and essentialist interpretations of priests, *granthis* and mullahs. Dauji teaches the children from the narrator's family and is held in respect for his honesty and humility. The boy-narrator and his elder brother stay with the family in the true *guru-shishya parampara.* Several touching events in the story bring home to the readers Dauji's large-hearted notion of cultural synthesis. After his schooling, the narrator goes to college in the town, but keeps on visiting his teacher whenever he comes home. Then there is a chronological leap and the narrator says, 'That year I did not see Dauji during the Dussera vacations, nor during the Christmas celebrations, nor during the Easter break. Soon, I lost all sense of time' (II, 38). The advent of Indian independence has been described in the following way: 'As the day of the country's independence approached, people began to fight each other, and soon there were violent riots all around us' (II, 38-9). When violence breaks out in the *qasba,* Dauji becomes a Gandhian figure in his refusal to escape violence, staying back to counter it with his moral strength. The title of the story also associates him with Christ. Dauji is invested with the humility and compassion of Christ and the presence of such a man in the society is proof enough of the possibility of its redemption.

Variations of the same theme can be found in many other stories. For example, in Maheep Singh's 'The River and the Bridge', people of the entire village of Sarai in Pakistan turn up at the station platform to welcome their neighbours who had left during the Partition and had now come back to Pakistan as pilgrims. There is no doubt about the sincerity of their impassioned plea to their former neighbours to return to their homeland. In Kamaleshwar's 'How Many Pakistans', one can see how the lives of the Muslims and the Hindus were intertwined and how the geo-political Partition divided humanity into a thousand fragments. In Shaikh Ayaz's Sindhi story 'Neighbours', the protagonist 'knew that the lives of the Hindus and the Muslims were so intimately woven together that they were a part of the same cloth' (I, 190), a realization which saves him from ignoble deeds. He could argue sanely: 'If the Hindus in Bihar have killed the Muslims, Pesu Ram's mother has nothing to do with it' (I, 191). If only others like him had applied the same reason, a great deal of retaliatory violence could have been avoided. 'Roots' by Ismat Chughtai is an evocative story where the shared bond between the Muslim and the Hindu families endures, even though there was a temporary rupture. This was because of the efforts of the older generation and also because the communal atmosphere in Marwar was not as vitiated as it was at other places. Yashpal's 'Holy War' offers two perspectives of a situation (as does Vatsayan's 'The Refuge') by counterpoising the views of the father, who believes in the bond of humanity that transcends over parochial communal considerations, with those of the son, who is driven by communal ideology.

Among the stories in the second group, the most significant are—Bhisham Sahni's 'The Train Has Reached Amritsar', Ahmad Nadeem Qasmi's 'Parameshwar Singh' and Krishna Sobti's 'Where is My Mother'? Each of them plays on the stereotypes created by one community against the other, where hatred and prejudice took the place of open-mindedness, and mutual exchange and humanity are divided between 'us' and 'them'.

Sahni's story uses the very familiar motif of a train journey, where the passengers in the coach represent India in microcosm. The train originates from Lahore and proceeds towards Amritsar. The narrator shows how the undercurrent of prejudice and hatred runs through the apparent friendliness and banter. Three Pathans, who lord it over inside the coach, make fun of a Bengali Babu calling him a weakling and advise him either to eat meat and grow strong like them or travel in the ladies' compartment. All the passengers inside the coach, except one old woman, are united in their selfishness in refusing to allow anyone else to enter the coach. When a Hindu family frantically attempts to enter the coach all are vociferous in their protest and one of the Pathans lands a kick on the woman's stomach and she falls down tottering. The Bengali Babu seethes in anger. Then, as the train passes through a burning city, the passengers get jittery and cannot look their neighbours in the eye. When they come to know that the city is the Muslim-dominated Wazirabad, 'the Pathans became less tense, the silence among the Hindus and the Sikhs became more ominous' (I, 152) and the Babu hides on the floor in fear. However, as the train passes the outskirts of Harbanspura and then reaches Amritsar, the tables are turned. The Pathans now look forlorn and nervous, as they hear the Babu calling them filthy names. The Babu then gets off and fetches an iron rod from somewhere to teach a stern lesson to the Pathans who have, in the meantime, relocated themselves. To get even, the Babu brutally kills a Muslim trying to board the train. The temporal division of space in the story into 'our area' and 'their area', found in quite a few other stories as well, becomes symptomatic of the psychological alienation and cultural separateness of people living together, but whose lives do not intersect in any meaningful way.

Qasmi pits the Muslim ethos against the Sikh, in his story 'Parameshwar Singh'. The central character here is a Muslim boy, Akhtar, who gets separated from his folks fleeing from India to Pakistan. Parameshwar brings him home and thinks it would console his bereaved wife for the loss of their son, Kartar Singh. However, the prejudice and hatred against Muslims are so deep-seated in his wife and daughter, that they cannot think of accepting a Muslim boy as their own. The house where they lived formerly belonged to a Muslim and whenever Akhtar says his *namaz* or recites the Koran, they get terribly frightened. As Akhtar's hair grows longer, Parameshwar makes him a Khalsa Sikh and names him Kartar Singh. His wife's hatred gradually subsides. Although Parameshwar Singh protects Akhtar against all odds and showers him with love and affection, he is not able to obliterate Akhtar's hatred for the Sikhs. Eventually Parameshwar is so overwhelmed by the boy's love for his mother that he takes him towards the border so that he can reach her.

As is evident, the above two stories have been structured on the beliefs based on stereotypes. 'You're a Musalla', yell the Sikh boys in 'Parameshwar Singh' and Akhtar retaliates by shouting *sikhra* at them. These are not simple or innocent invectives, hurled by children against each other, but carry with them the baggage of cultural alienation and prejudice accumulated over generations. Just how strong this prejudice could be, has been shown in Krishna Sobti's story, 'Where is My Mother?' The story is about a Pathan, Yunus Khan, who lost his sister in communal violence, as a result of which, he tears along the country driven by an ineluctable force for the establishment of a Muslim state, 'a new Mughal Empire'. In the process he kills Hindus mercilessly. During one of his endlessly frantic journeys he finds a fatally injured Hindu girl by the roadside. Compassion enters his heart and he takes her to the hospital and urges the doctors to cure her by any means. He ministers to her with utmost solicitude and wants to look after her like his own sister, Nooran. When the girl regains consciousness, opens her eyes and finds Yunus Khan sitting next to her, she begins to plead: 'Khan, don't kill me, please don't kill me . . . please.' Yunus Khan is most considerate and reassures her that no one is going to kill her and that he wants to look after her. She is not convinced. She cannot trust the Pathan however kind he may be to her. She gives voice to her hysterical fear of the Muslims: 'No!' the girl shouts with hatred in her voice and begins to strike him with her fists, 'You are a Muslim. . . . You'll kill me' (II, 139).

Khwaja Ahmad Abbas' 'The Death of Shaikh Burhanuddin' and Manto's 'Mozel' also demonstrate the power of a stereotype in vitiating human relationships. Ghulam Abbas in 'Avtar: A Hindu Myth', uses the Hindu myth of Kalki to highlight the debased state of the Hindus as oppressors of innocent Muslims. The story is rather one-dimensional in its depiction of reality in the absolute terms of black and white. The list of crimes accounted for can be attributed not only to the Hindus but to Muslims as well:

> You have raped women; stripped them naked and paraded them through the streets of the city; chopped off their breasts and noses; burnt them alive. You have pierced their children with your spears and flung them in the air. You claimed that you committed these crimes in the name of your religious duty. (II, 204)

The rhetorical questions that the narrator asks of the Hindus are those that any sane person would ask of all perpetrators of violence. The implicit answers and the awareness they display have the power to place a misguided humanity back on the rails:

> What crime had your victims committed? That they believed in a different form of worship than yours? That their style of life was different? Is that such a big crime that they should be exterminated? (ibid.)

N.G. Gore's 'A Mouthful of Water, A Mouthful of Blood' records the complicitous mental attitude of those who, though they did not take part in actual violence, murder or rape, derived vicarious pleasure at seeing the humiliation of the other community and the desecration of its women. The urbane narrator here has a sneaking admiration for the perpetrators of violence belonging to his own community. He witnesses the murder of Anwar, a former acquaintance, and then analyses his own attitude:

> Did I disapprove of these things? No. Honestly, no. I myself did not loot from anyone; didn't shove a knife between anyone's ribs. . . . But what's the point in denying that I felt a sneaky joy in watching these neutering acts committed by others? (III, 227)

The third group of stories include Manto's 'Toba Tek Singh', 'Open It', 'Cold Meat' and two fragments from his *Siyah Hashiye*, Krishan Chander's 'Peshawar Express', Mohan Rakesh's 'The Owner of the Rubble', Ibrahim Jalees' 'A Grave Turned Inside Out' and Satinath Bhaduri's 'A Champion of the People'. These writers are also notable for their use of irony as opposed to the straightforward or sentimental narrative mode employed by most other writers. Manto, by common consent, is the most effective among all the writers in his unblinking and stark gaze at the violence of Partition, his unflinching integrity and the clarity of his vision. The stories and fragments included in the volumes, encapsulate the carnage and brutality of the times in all its ruthless savagery. 'Toba Tek Singh' has become a metaphor for the utter absurdity and mindlessness of Partition. The eponymous story is a devastating indictment of the amateur statesmen and unscrupulous politicians, who draw shadow line boundaries between peoples and countries. Their actions were so insane that even the hard core lunatics of an asylum seem much wiser:

> Where was Pakistan? What were its boundaries? They did not know. For this very reason all the inmates who were altogether mad, found themselves in a quandary; they could not figure out whether they were in Pakistan or India, and if they were in Pakistan, then how was it possible that only a short while ago they had been in India when they had not moved from the asylum at all. (III, 2)

They further surmise 'was there anyone to guarantee that both Pakistan and Hindustan would not disappear some day' (III, 4). One lunatic says with desperate rage, 'I want to live neither in Pakistan nor in Hindustan—I will live on this tree' (III, 2). Bishen Singh, the 'mad' protagonist of the story, contemptuously refutes the verdict of the politicians to be divided between India and Pakistan and prefers to die on the strip of land, which belongs to neither. This is Manto's symbolic rejection of the vivisection of the country and his considered comment on the mindlessness of it.

In Manto's story, 'Open It', Sirajuddin asks eight volunteers of the refugee camp in Pakistan, to find out his daughter, Sakina, left behind in India. They trace her out and, as though her trauma on one side of the border was not enough they, presumably subject her to repeated rape and then abandon her to her fate. She is brought to the doctor's chamber in the camp. When the doctor says 'open the window', Sakina, lying inert on the stretcher, lowers her *salwar* involuntarily. She has become so brutalized and her relationship with language becomes so distorted that henceforth *khol do* (open it), carries just one meaning for her to the exclusion of all others.

The 32 fragments in *Siyah Hashiye* are known for their macabre humour, subversive intent, tongue-in-cheek mode and their brilliant metonymies. The ones chosen here are not as evocative or effective as some others. To me, the finest story is a very brief one, *Mutri* (The Urinal), wherein the whole of undivided India is conceived as a stinking urinal, where politicians are writing obscene graffiti on its wall.

If Krishan Chander's 'Peshawar Express' becomes a 'fitting symbol of liminal spaces and the death of old structural certainties' (I, xxii), Satinath Bhaduri's 'The Champion of the People' shows how Partition became big business for Munim Sahib, the local agent of Johurmal Dokania, and Haji Sahib, the *ijaredar*. They gave the people to understand that they could get an area included in either India or Pakistan, by bribing officials and leaders, and they collected money on that account. Camps are set up—one for India and one for Pakistan—on either side of the river. They raise prices by creating artificial scarcity. But they held tremendous sway over people, who regard them as oracles.

The cavalier and whimsical way in which the Mountbatten Plan and the Radcliffe Award were put into practice is underscored by the fact that for days and weeks after the announcement of Partition, people were uncertain about their actual location in the new dispensation. They kept on wondering whether Lahore, Amritsar, Delhi, etc., in the west or Dacca,

Malda, etc., in the east would be in India or Pakistan. This reviewer comes from an area in Assam, a part of the Sylhet district in undivided India, which was first declared a part of East Pakistan territory, then it was realized that in that case India would be left with no land corridor for Mizoram and Tripura. So, after a few days it once again became a part of India—a truly Toba Tek Singh-like situation, rich with irony! Similar situations have been treated with panache in quite a few stories in the volume. Though both Haji Sahib and Munimji are fertile with ideas about how to exploit the situation to their maximum profit and advantage, Munimji is sharper in business acumen. He sells small flags of India and Pakistan in both the camps. When the final declaration about the division of territories came and people possessing flags of one country find themselves in another, he collects them for free, by warning people that they should not be caught with the wrong flag. Needless to say, he sells the flags over again. The story highlights, as do Upendranath Ashk's 'The Fodder-Cutting Machine' and Narendranath Mitra's 'The Four-Poster Bed', the cupidity of unscrupulous people, which was one of the factors that contributed to violence.

Mohan Rakesh's 'The Owner of the Rubble' shows the greed in Rakkha Pahelwan, who kills his intimate friend and his family just because he wanted to own their house. The house has been reduced to rubble as a result of a conflagration. Nevertheless he guards the rubble jealously as many others who also amass the spoils of Partition. Gani Mian his friend's father comes from Pakistan for a visit and everybody expects a showdown. He confronts Rakkha with unsuspecting love and Rakkha, the dreaded criminal, is rendered speechless and cringes before him. The situation is charged with irony and Mohan Rakesh, true to his genius, wields his pen with utmost dexterity to weave a narrative of compelling power and insight.

Ibrahim Jalees' 'The Grave Turned Inside Out' brings to light the plight of the Biharis who, when they migrated to East Pakistan, faced persecution after the creation of Bangladesh and sought asylum in Karachi, in West Pakistan. For Ayesha, the protagonist, the double migration and exile brought only misery and dehumanization. In Pakistan she seeks refuge inside a hovel in a graveyard, which is, in fact, a Bengali settlement. But two *goondas* masquerading as government officials arrive before long and 'in order to punish Ayesha for illegally grabbing government land, made a grab for the land of her body' (II, 151). The people in the camp are so terrified of the lumpens that when they discover Ayesha's dead body the next morning, they give it out that she has died because of a snake bite. With devastating irony, worthy of a Manto, the narrator says: 'Yes, Ayesha had been bitten by a snake who had left his underwear behind . . . He was a funny snake. . . . ! He wore an underwear' (II, 152).

'I Am Game' by Sultan Jamil Nasim, moves on the same trajectory—Dacca, Kathmandu and then Karachi, where the mother, a hardworking woman of staunch principles, is so bruised and battered by circumstances that she is ready to prostitute herself in order to save her daughter from a similiar fate. Umme Ummara's 'More Sinned Against Than Sinning' tells the story of an emigree Bihari Muslim family, the members of which embrace the Bengali language and culture and are involved in the struggle to liberate East Pakistan from the oppressive rule of West Pakistan. But they still do not find acceptance in that country. Their homestead is burnt down killing several members of the family. What is of special significance about these stories is the fact that here the oppressor and the oppressed belong to the same religion.

IV

There are stories, which figure in all the above groups and outside them as well, which are eloquent in their depiction of the suffering of women. In all internecine warfare and communal violence—be it in Bosnia, Rwanda or Surat—a woman's body becomes the contested site for possession, violence and sexual assault. Since women carry the reproductive burden in their womb, their experience becomes all the more agonistic. Traditional historical writings on Partition have not paid adequate attention to this aspect. In this context, Urvashi Butalia's observations are pertinent:

> Recent research has also begun to uncover an aspect of Partition that historians have paid little attention to: its gendered nature, the experiences of women —not only the thousands who were raped and abducted, but also the equally large numbers who were widowed and had to spend much of their lives dependent on the state, the many who joined 'social service', working with refugees, the many whose lives were disrupted in ways, that, at the time, may not have seemed anything to remark upon, but later acquired a different significance [for example, there were women of 'marriageable age' for whom that moment passed because of the dislocation of Partition, and who have had to spend much of their lives single], the many who were forced to give up their children. But in attempting to recover these histories, researchers have faced a problem: while it may be possible to reconstruct the stories of women from statistics and documents, how can they start to touch the other dimensions of these histories, how can they know what the

women felt, how they rebuilt their lives, how they dealt with that unspoken—and unspeakable—of all things, sexuality.[3]

'Cold Meat' by Manto, is a chilling story about the loss of manhood. Ishar Singh, a lusty young Sikh who enjoys his romps with his voluptuous wife, Kulwant Kaur, gets himself into a rage on hearing tales of Muslim atrocities and rushes out of his home in a mad frenzy, vowing revenge. He returns home in bad shape only to be struck fatally by his jealous wife, when he cannot perform in bed. On her insistence, he gives an account of his 'manly' exploits on that day:

> The house I broke into. . . . There were seven people in it. Six men. . . . I killed them . . . there was a beautiful girl. I could have killed her, but I didn't. . . . I said to myself Ishar Sian, you enjoy Kulwant everyday, taste this delicacy also. (I, 96)

He then carried her on his shoulder and, little realizing that the girl has already died of fright, copulated with the corpse. When he discovered it, the shock was so great that it rendered him impotent. The story vividly depicts man's descent into savagery.

Amrit Rai's 'Filth' conveys an impression of great debauchery in the exchanges between four apparently middle class railway passengers, who share the satisfaction of having taught the Muslims a lesson. The story is built on irony:

> Then Harbans told them softly, in whispers, passionate stories about Muslim women who had been abducted in west Punjab . . . how many had been sent to brothels . . . how the heads of those women who had protested had been separated from their bodies, and how even those who had quietly submitted their youthful bodies had finally been sent to hell. (III, 118)

Jamila Hashmi's 'Exile' and Bedi's 'Lajwanti' highlight the plight of abducted women. A world of great loneliness lay ahead for the unnamed protagonist of 'Exile'. She was picked up by a Sikh, by whom she had two sons and a daughter. She had also endeared herself to her Sikh mother-in-law. But all this cannot take the place of her lost world. Her brother, to whom she was deeply attached, never came from across the border to see her, because she had been 'defiled'. It was truly a 'No Exit' situation for her:

> Where else can I go after so much suffering? Who will accept a woman who has been despoiled? Besides, Munni is now with me. She now stands as an obstacle between me and my relatives on the other side. The distance between *them* and *us* is very great. (emphasis added) (II, 45)

She compares her fate with Sita's abduction and exile. This Hindu myth that Jamila Hashmi takes recourse to (as do many other Muslim writers, like Intizar Hussain, Ashfaque Ahmed and Ghulam Abbas), alongwith the Dussehra celebrations, marking the destruction of Ravana, foregrounds a racial memory and a consciousness in which the tragedy of women cuts across religion and community.

In Bedi's story, Sunderlal whose wife had been lost in the communal upheaval becomes a champion of abducted women and mobilizes people for their rehabilitation. But he feels out of depths, when his own wife turns up one day. He cannot accept her as his wife because he had raised her to a high pedestal and had worshipped her, like a *devi*, which hindered her integration into the family structure and to leading a normal life. Abducted women during Partition were not just victims of violence and rape by 'enemies', but were also made to suffer in their own homes and at the hands of their own people. Thousands of women were rejected by their husbands and families, and had no option but to live out their lives in ashrams and brothels.

An unexpected and pleasant find in the volumes are the two stories by Lalithambika Antarjanam, the Malayalam writer, known for her works on Namboodiri Brahmin women, 'The Mother of Dhirendu Muzumdar' and 'A Leaf in the Storm'. The first, deals with the pangs of a mother, torn between pluralities of attachments and the conflicting demands on her—of her husband, a staunch supporter of the British, and her son, a freedom fighter, close in touch with legendary revolutionaries like Surya Sen and Preetilata Vardhar. In Antarjanam's second story 'A Leaf in the Storm', Jyoti is burdened with an unwanted and forced pregnancy, which she can neither get rid of, nor come to terms with. Her nightmares consist of 'the prison in which she had lain unconscious. An awful lot of men must have come into the cell!' (I, 144). The story, however, ends on a hopeful note, with Jyoti giving birth to a child and accepting it as her own.

Ram Lall's story 'A Visitor from Pakistan' and Vishnu Prabhakar's story 'I Shall Live' tell us about women who, thinking that their husbands were killed in the carnage of Partition, start living with other men. One can imagine the conflict in the mind of Saraswati when, one day, she finds Baldev, her former husband whom she thought to be dead, turn up to claim her from Sunderdas, her present husband, who rescued her and her family and who helped them through dangerous days. Baldev, the visitor from Pakistan, had to return empty-handed. However, in Prabhakar's story, the husband takes his wife back from Pran. The prostitute in Suraiya Qasim's story 'Where Did She Belong?' does not know her actual country. She wondered—'Who lost and who died in the Partition?' because she finds the rich of both the communities ready to pay a high price for her flesh.

Closely linked with the plight of women is the plight of children who were lost, adopted by surrogate or childless parents and then snatched once again when the real parents or their relatives turn up, much against the wishes of the adoptive parents and, sometimes, of the children themselves. Two remarkable stories—'Pali' by Bhisham Sahni and 'Parameshwar Singh' (discussed earlier) by Ahmad Nadeem Qasmi explore, in moving details, the trauma of these children. 'Childishness' by Manik Bandhopadhyaya ironically contrasts the normal childishness of children with the gory 'childishness' of adults. 'The Abandoned Child' by Gurmukh Singh Musafir has two families living together, for the love of a child. 'Post Box' by S.H. Vatsayan 'Agyeya' has a lost child in the camp wanting to send a letter to his father asking him to come and rescue him, but the child does not know where he is after he has left his village, Shekhupura.

Historical documents record statistics in the case of women as well—about 30,000 women recovered, 12,000 Muslim and 18,000 non-Muslim, by the police and social workers, between 1947 and 1952. But, can they fathom or even recount, without the aid of literature, the utter anguish and suffering of these women? I think, not.

V

An issue that needs to be addressed seriously and that I have not seen touched so far in the discussion of these volumes, is the mediatory role of translation through which the stories have reached us—the pan-Indian and the trans-Indian audience. We know that unless the translator is extremely sensitive, circumspect and resourceful, translation can do curious things to the original text and the writer. It can falsify the intent of the original, distort the vision of the writers and can do violence to the context in other ways.

I took up just one story—'Roots' by Ismat Chughtai—and compared it with the original text and was shocked to find some glaring instances of misreading and misrepresentation, which cannot be called mere inadequacies of translation. For example, in the beginning of the story, the state of 'Marwar' has been replaced by 'Mewar'. Well, though the place names, which serve as the locale are important and more so in works which have historical bearings, I thought it might be a case of oversight and let it go. But there were greater lapses also. Earlier the tiffs of the children of the two families, one Hindu and one Muslim, would be dismissed without any pernicious thought entering the mind, but which now took ominous overtones in the communally charged atmosphere. The narrator describes a boy who comes home after fighting with the children of the other family, as a hero: *Par aaj jab Chabba ladkar aaye tau unki aisi aao bhagat hui jaise mard-e-ghazi maidan maarkar aaya hai* (But, today, when Chabba returned after the fight, he was feted as a crusader, having won a battle). The English translation reads as follows: 'But now when Chabba came home after a fight, he was greeted as if *Mahmud Ghazni* has returned house victorious' (emphasis added) (III, 14). Now, the replacement of *mard-e-ghazi* by Mahmud Ghazni, despite their homophonic similarity, is a lapse that seriously distorts the perspective of the writer and predisposes the reader to a certain kind of reading of the text not intended by the original Urdu writer.

Then I took up Ashfaque Ahmed's 'The Shepherd', which is a culturally loaded text and found that the cultural specificity and angularity had been flattened out, in addition to other lapses and inadequacies.[4] The question of translation is obviously important but a fuller discussion requires a separate paper. There is also the ubiquitous problem of transliteration of non-English words, including proper names, which are also misspelt (*appa* for *aapa*, *akka-e-namdar* for *aaqa-e-naamda*, 'Aga' for 'Agha', 'Muzumdar' for 'Mojumdar', 'Yaspal' for 'Yashpal','Gulam Abbas' for 'Ghulam Abbas', and so on).

VI

To conclude, the stories in the three volumes present us, in their vast panoply of images and symbols, irony and narrative points of view, the picture of Partition from different perspectives and angles. The violence perpetrated during Partition was essentially mob violence where the individual merged his identity with the mob and surrendered his sanity to it making it an impersonal and an abstract force. This is a difficult phenomenon for literature to grapple with. Literature, as pointed out in the beginning of this paper, focuses on individuals, private sorrows and particular situations which, nevertheless, acquire a representative value and indicate the general trend of the time. Whereas history merely records events or offers interpretations of them, literature, in the form of these stories goes beyond that and touches human beings at their sensitive and contemplative best. It heals and humanizes through empathy. More than dealing with the external events, it attempts to probe the inner workings of the characters' mind and thus provides a mental map of Partition as well. Jason Francisco observes in this context:

> Only the literature truly evokes the suffering of the innocent, whose pain is more universal, and ultimately a vehicle of more honest reconciliation than political discourse. The literary work on the Partition affirms that the subject of the Partition was first the human being – not the Hindu human being, nor the Muslim, nor the Sikh. In the world of the stories, the experiences of each community distinctly mirror one another, indeed reach out to and clutch at one another. No crime, no despair, no grief in exile belongs uniquely to anyone.[5]

Because literature transcends time, these stories are relevant for us today as they vividly portray the existential absurdity of hatred. Whatever their formal or stylistic blemishes as specimens of literature, they ably seek to negotiate the complexity and liminality of experiences of people caught in the competitive savagery of Partition. In their manifold implications they also voice our civilizational and moral concerns today, when the forces of division and fragmentation are once again raising their ugly head. A few stories in the volumes may seem banal in the advocacy of some ersatz morals but the best among them interface dialectically with history and politics and offer corrective insights into our past, as much as they also illuminate our contemporary situation.

NOTES

1. Primo Levi, *Survival in Auschwitz,* trans. by Stuart Woolf (New York, 1988).
2. Ishtiaq Hussain Qureshi, 'Hindu Muslim Relations 1935-47', in Mushirul Hasan, *India Partitioned: The Other Face of Freedom*, Vol. II (New Delhi, 1997), pp. 172-83.
3. Urvashi Butalia, 'Voices of Women', in *Indian Review of Books,* Vol.V, No. 2 (Delhi, 1996), pp. 4-5.
4. Readers not aquainted with Urdu may turn to Muhammad Umar Memon's translation of the same story in *An Epic Unwritten: Urdu Stories about Partition* (New Delhi, 1998).
5. Jason Francisco, 'In the Heat of Fracticide: The Literature of India's Partition Burning Freshly', in *The Annual of Urdu Studies*, Vol. II (Madison, 1996), pp. 227-50.

The Long Trek of Karamanwali

KAMLESH MOHAN

'Karamanwali represents the agonizing internal journey of that generation of women whose children were left behind, while they migrated to Pakistan or India. Karamanwali is the heroine of my novel but as real as any woman walking in the street,' observed Janab Kashmiri Lal Zakir while explaining to me the relationship between literature and history. As a witness to, and a sufferer in, the horrifying tragedy of the Partition of the Punjab, he articulated his raw anger against barbarity, large-scale violence in all its hideous forms, the disruption of the traditional social harmony and, above all, against the mutilation of cultural processes. A score of his stories, especially 'Teen Cheethre',[1] 'Andhere ki Kokh'[2] and 'Yeh Khandhar Mere Hain',[3] illustrate this mood. His resurgent faith in human nobility finds expression in 'Aane Wala Kal'[4] and 'Ek Naya Mehman'[5]. The short story 'Ek Dari Hui Ladki'[6] captures the long term psychological impact of sexual violence during the Partition on two generations of a mother and her daughter.

His novel *Karamanwali* is the product of 'emotions recollected in tranquillity', to use Wordsworth's description of the creative process. Zakir concedes that cataclysmic events, like the Partition, leave deep scars on collective consciousness and bring irreversible changes in the lives and fortunes of those individuals or nations, who are caught in the crossfire of its communal madness and ethnic cleansing. The wave of religio-political terrorism in Punjab, culminating in the blood-curdling massacre of the Sikhs in various parts of India, in October/November 1984, brought back the memories of the Partition days to his generation. But mercifully, the madness was short-lived. In his view, each creative writer, despite being on the periphery of the political processes and events, responds to them in his/her own distinctive style and perceives interconnections between past and present.

* Based on Kashmiri Lal Zakir, *Karamanwali* (1st pub. in Urdu, 1980). All translations from the original are mine.

Zakir's novel, *Karamanwali*, was first published in Urdu in 1980. Its Hindi version came out in 1987; and its Punjabi version was released in 1994, by Seema Biswas, the heroine, when the novel was adapted and staged as a play by the National School of Drama, Delhi. Her scintillating performance in *Karamanwali* won her the coveted role of Phulan Devi in the film *Bandit Queen*.

The author picked up the central idea of *Karamanwali* from an unusual news report, published in the *Tribune* of 5 March 1980. This story relates to an old Muslim woman, whose almost four decade long obsessive search for her separated son, Khushia, ended on a happy note when she met him, as a married man with a son, in her old home at village Balsandan. The novelist first toyed with the idea of writing a long story or a novelette, on this 'delicate' theme but finally decided to pen a full length novel. The Partition memories of his cousin and other young girls in Jhelum, who managed to escape from their Muslim captors, through the kindness of their attendant, became a part of the narrative. The terrifying experiences of his ten year old maternal cousin and his four year old sister, who had helplessly watched the cold-blooded murder of their parents in Mirpur, had kept fermenting in his imagination and needed an outlet. The novelist's admiration for his mother's beauty and her tinkling laughter suffused the portrayal of the heroine's mother. His own remembrance of his village in West Punjab and his actual visit to Balsandan, flowed into his descriptions and helped situate the novel's surroundings. A rich socio-cultural interaction among Hindus, Muslims and Sikhs is described. But the pangs of the Partition are reflected in the unbearable torture which still scar individual and collective consciousness with equal intensity.

In short, a writer's creative process is multi-dimensional, underpinned by myriad currents of joys and sorrows, mental impressions of day-to-day life and social as well as political developments. Contemporary writers may be swayed by radical or communal ideologies temporarily, but literary writings on events like the Partition do not endorse the inhuman killings by fanatics among the Hindus, Sikhs or Muslims alike. All of them—Sadaat Hasan Manto, Intizar Hussain, K.S. Duggal, Nanak Singh, Kashmiri Lal Zakir, Krishan Chander, Rajinder Singh Bedi, Qurratulain Hyder, Ismat Chugtai, Krishna Sobti, Amrita Pritam and Bhisham Sahni—focus on the themes of futility and tragedy, of demarcating geographical boundaries, the impossibility of dividing hearts and homes and sexual violence in the name of religion, community and male honour. Their requiem for millions of dead men, women and children, for warped emotional bonds between communities, for shared joys and sorrows and for a common cultural heritage, is sincere and moving. It is the white heat of the painful but cathartic process that enabled the creative writers to go beyond their numbing individual experiences of traumatic and multiple dislocation, material loss and brutal murders to capture the broader human significance of the Partition, through their powerful social sensitivity and creative imagination.

Let us return to *Karamanwali*, which has been spun out of a human interest story about separated children and mothers, brothers and sisters and husbands and wives, on both sides of the border. Although, the broad canvas of this novel encompasses the entire gamut of emotions—rupture, anger, protest and healing in the context of the social experience of the Partition, the story is focused upon the process of healing, vibrancy of life and triumph of faith in basic human goodness.

Two stories are interwoven in *Karamanwali*, the biography of an innocent but romantic village girl from her youth to old age and the history of the Indian subcontinent, especially the heroic achievement of national independence, which is marred by the construction of polarized religious identities, through religio-political mobilization, culminating in the partition of boundaries, hearts and homes. Chronologically speaking, these two stories register major landmarks between two points: August 1947 and March 1980. Karamanwali, the chief protagonist of the novel, recounts her happy childhood in the idyllic rural setting of Balsandan in East Punjab, her blissful married life with Faizdin, a small peasant proprietor; and the birth of a son, which fulfils her dream of motherhood. Her son Khushia is barely five years old when the 'red storm' of communal hatred gradually engulfs the villages and towns of East and West Punjab and warps their social fabric. Here the first phase of her life ends.

The second phase of Karamanwali's life is marked by dislocation and uprooting—physical, psychological and cultural. Like millions of Hindu, Sikh and Muslim families, the couple along with their young son, Khushia, shift temporarily to Siswan where Karamanwali's brother Karim Khan lived. Owing to the escalating tension, they can neither return home nor prolong their stay with Karim Khan, who pressurizes them to go to Pakistan. Leaving Khushia in the custody of their sister-in-law, Vakilan, who promises to join them in a few days, Karamanwali and Faizdin join the caravan of refugees heading towards the new homeland, Pakistan. After their arrival at the railway station at Lahore, they are transported to one of the refugee camps in the city. Despite the humiliating experiences as refugees, Karamanwali is touched by the warm welcome they receive in Camp No. 512 where its occupants, Akbar and Noori, develop a bond of affection with the young couple.

Karamanwali's brave efforts to settle down in the refugee camp receives its first blow at hearing the news about the deliberate abandonment of Khushia by Vakilan. The death of Noori, who acted as her surrogate mother, was the second blow. Karamanwali's story reaches a decisive point when the couple is rehabilitated in Chak No. 240 in Lyallpur, later renamed Faislabad. The birth of a daughter accelerates the process of rehabilitation in their new home and her emotional recovery. However, the memory of her son Khushia haunts her constantly.

The third phase of Karamanwali's life can best be described as a *safar* (journey, mental quest or feverish search) for her long lost son, Khushia, left as an orphan in Siswan. The distraught child is found in a deserted lane by Natha Singh, a *granthi*. Adopted as a son by Natha Singh and his wife Jamito, the little boy gets an affectionate home. The devout couple facilitate young Khushia's education, training and growth not only as a fervent Muslim but also as a practitioner of liberal human values. After almost two decades, Natha Singh learns about the identity of Khushia's biological parents and about their village home and lands. The concerted efforts of Natha Singh and Faizdin's old friend, Ram Saran, enable Khushia to get back his parental house and landed property and settle down happily with his wife Fatima and their son Javed.

In the meanwhile, Faizdin's death upsets Karamanwali so much that she becomes a *fakiran* (mendicant). Her subdued longing for her separated son Khushia turns into an obsession. Like a possessed woman, she goes to each place of worship to which *jathas* of Indian pilgrims visit from time to time, hoping to get a clue about her son's whereabouts. At last she is able to correspond with her son, through the sincere efforts of Mehardin of Ropar (East Punjab), who is visiting his relatives in Chak No. 240. In March 1980, she travels to Balsandan to meet her son and his family. After three months of an emotionally satisfying stay with Khushia, his wife Fatima and her grandson Javed, she returns to her home in Pakistan where Faizdin's grave beckons her.

What distinguishes *Karamanwali* from other writings in this genre is the feminist rendering of an aspect of the Partition, written by a male novelist. It is a moving, though not melodramatic, rendering of a mother's single-minded effort to search for her long-lost son, which remains only a mental quest during the period when she is engaged in the mechanics of rehabilitation, the care of her growing daughter and of her aging husband. The writer has not only constructed the entire story from a woman's angle but has also made its heroine the chief protagonist of the novel. The literary technique used for articulating her predicament and agony as an innocent victim of the Partition are her memories of Balsandan, familial relationships and *biradari* networks and her perception of the ordeals of the uprooted and the travails as a refugee and settler in a strange 'homeland'. This way of relating a story may be described as the 'stream of consciousness' method,[7] pioneered by the Irish novelist, James Joyce in *Ulysses* (1922), and effectively used by several modern writers.

We could now analyse *Karamanwali's* rendering of the Partition on three issues/aspects. The first concerns different meanings of the conflicting perceptions of 'Pakistan' by men and women, rich and poor, as well as by the successive generations of citizens of the new nation states. Brought up in a composite cultural environment, Karamanwali as a woman has learnt to value social interaction with her neighbours without any emphasis on narrow religious loyalties. Besides, amity is supposed to be embedded in the anthropological ideal of society in the sense that birth, marriage and death are supreme concerns of women. The customary festivals, for example, Id, Diwali and Holi, which are celebrated by women with a greater sense of involvement than men, are deemed to uphold the ideals of communal amity. In view of the crucial stake of women in social harmony as wives and mothers, Karamanwali's scepticism about the *qurbani* (sacrifice) of thousands of men, women and children, who had neither any share nor knowledge about the political decisions regarding the Partition, is an integral part of the feminist thinking. She raises a valid question:

> My country was now Pakistan. Thousands of innocent human beings laid down their lives in the process of its formation. Included among the majority of these martyrs, were those who had no cause to die for. They were trapped into the orgy of arson, loot and murder. All of them were made martyrs—innocent children hung on spikes, lifeless bodies of naked women scattered all over the fields and the mutilated and bleeding bodies of passengers in railway compartments.

Karamanwali's mind was full of doubts. The futility of carving out Pakistan on the basis of religion is starkly projected when its citizens were confronted with yet another fratricidal war among Muslims, which again resulted in the division of hearts as well as homes when a new country called Bangladesh was born. Karamanwali's memory of the Partition gives her a new insight into the civil war in Pakistan. As in any other man made conflict and power game, women would be subjected to sexual violence and humiliation, by the victorious army. While ruminating about these experiences of two partitions in one generation, she identifies herself with the peace-loving and religious-minded Pakistanis who sought explanation for their displacement and dislocation from their homes from

Jinnah, the architect of Pakistan. But ordinary folk continue to grapple with their ordinary dilemmas. While walking through deserted lanes and fields on their way to Siswan, Faizdin and Karamanwali try to find justification for the mad behaviour of their erstwhile neighbours and friends.

The second aspect of the Partition concerns its consequences for individuals, families and society. For individuals, it may take the form of an identity crisis and other psychological problems, for example, fear-psychosis and cultural alienation. For families, uprooting may mean loss of their ancestral homes, property and regular jobs and means of income. More crucial is the loss of the mutual moral, emotional and material support and protection. Forced migrations in times of civil war or communal riots may lead to separation of parents and children, siblings and close relatives. At the societal level, the Partition meant disruption of the ongoing process of building networks of *biradari* and cultural interaction and adjustment among various communities. Women, are inextricably involved in the organization and activities of families, communities and nations, without being major actors in the process of decision-making. The consequences of the Partition need to be analysed from a female perspective. More so in the case of South Asian women, whose fortunes have been linked with their fathers, brothers and husbands owing to their almost total economic dependence upon the male members of their family.

Karamanwali's reaction to the fast-paced political developments affecting her family, socio-cultural environment and her own identity as a woman, can be understood by her impulsive act of picking up a handful of soil from the extreme boundary of her verdant field and tying it securely to the corner of her veil. Instinctively, she feels that the traditional mutual trust, emotional bonds and amity between Hindus and Muslims have gone for ever and thus their return is at best a remote possibility. The terrifying prospect of irrevocable separation from her roots brings tears to her eyes. A lyrical quality flows into the articulation of her inner feelings and thoughts, as the following extract illustrates:

> The next morning would cut off our personal association with everything in Balsandan, we shall never enjoy the sight of its rising sun, soothing moonlight, gentle breeze and never wander around in its lanes and fields. We have been deprived of our friends, loving relationships and warmth of cultural festivals by a cruel quirk of fate. (pp. 26-7)

It is in this emotional state that Karamanwali finds the *elan vitale* in a handful of soil, which she subsequently mingles with the heap of earth on

Faizdin's grave. This impulsive act enables her to cope with her personal crisis and overcome the feeling of alienation as a refugee. It also becomes a source of strength in the gruelling process of rehabilitation in a strange village officially designated as her 'new home'. The coinhabitants of Camp No. 512, in Lahore, Akbar and Noori, have managed to carry with them most of their household goods and valuables. However, they still find it hard to sustain themselves because there can be no surrogate roots. The illiterate, but sensitive, Karamanwali can understand the predicament of the old couple. This is illustrated from her reaction to the snatches from Akbar's monologue, after he has been persuaded to overcome his grief, on the sudden death of his wife, Noori:

> Nobody transplants grown up trees at another spot. But our leaders have committed the indiscretion of uprooting all trees—young and old, sick and withered—from their native homes and grafted them in a strange and hostile land.

When Faizdin fails to continue the dialogue, Karamanwali intervenes to pacify the irate Akbar:

> The political leaders did not make the slightest effort to protect the roots of the people. You are right. Our own roots have also been bruised in this process of displacement. (p. 84)

Her empathy has calmed Akbar, whose emotional distress often lead to abnormal behaviour.

The third issue arising out of the gendered rendering of the Partition, as presented in this novel, is the acute consciousness of the vulnerability of migrant women owing to their sexuality. In the course of her difficult and terrifying journey to Pakistan, Karamanwali is appalled by the crude display of bestiality by policemen. Unlike thousands of unlucky women, who have been abducted and raped, she is subjected to a subtler form of sexual violence—'visual obscenity'. On her arrival at the Lahore station, lewd and lustful stares of the policemen disgust her and deepen her sense of insecurity. While the policemen gloat over the helplessness of the refugees, crouching near their luggage, these homeless women burn with muted anguish. The male mentality, which regards women as physical commodities for pleasure, is fully reflected in the dialogue between one of the policemen on duty and Faizdin:

> 'In case you don't want to go to the refugee camp, come along.'
> 'We are going to the camp, *havaldarji*', said Faizdin.
> Out of sheer disgust, Karmo felt like spitting on the face of the policeman, but had to swallow it.

'I am making this offer to your sister.'
'She is my wife', said Faiza sharply.
'It does not make any difference to me whether she is your sister or wife.'
(pp. 46-7)

Karamanwali recalls the obscenities, which greeted the homeless and defenceless women like her in their new country. She is confronted with an equally unnerving experience when she arrives at the city railway station for the second time. She watches the exhausted refugees, who await their turn to be transported to their respective destinations for resettlement, being abused and insulted by the guardians of the law.

Karamanwali's consciousness also registered the dehumanizing experiences in the refugee camps. The gender-sensitive approach of the author, enabled him to project his heroine's mental agony as she witnessed the physically and emotionally devastated women in camps, where doles and charity are bartered for female bodies and chastity. She is horrified at the sight of the dehumanized males—fathers, brothers and husbands—sacrificing their sisters, wives and mothers, sometimes for honour, material comforts and riches, but sometimes for bare physical survival. In the refugee camps black marketeers mint money in connivance with bureaucrats, businessmen and policemen. Social workers and rich and highly-placed men and women, too, exploit and use these helpless migrant women by offering them and their families expensive clothes and food. The mental anguish of these sexually exploited women has been captured in all its poignancy in the passage quoted below:

The people only noticed their stony gaze and lustreless faces but they could not see through their festering wounds; their honour was violated in *mandirs* and *masjids* without any compunction. (p. 69)

A gendered reading of *Karamanwali*, with some of the other Partition stories, which depict with equal sensitivity the experiences of women who have survived the Partition holocaust raise a number of pertinent questions: Do women have a country? Are they full fledged citizens of their respective countries? Do they enjoy the right to life and personal dignity? And are they immune to oppression from family, community and state?

While raising these questions we are very well aware that creative writers hold a mirror to society but do not offer solutions. If they let their ideological commitments and biases influence their writings, their creativity may be warped. Zakir does not reflect partiality for narrow religious or cultural nationalism, which has a tendency to impose an idealized notion of womanhood. Although he has not completely shed the cultural notions of a rural-based middle class man about women, yet he is a gender-sensitive writer as *Karamanwali* shows. His fervent faith in human values has enabled him to retain warm friendships across the border without compromising national interests. The Partition experience has made him sad but not cynical. That is why *Karamanwali* ends with the invocation:

'May every home prosper by God's grace!'

NOTES

1. 'Teen Cheethre', in *Shahakar* (monthly) (Lahore, 1950).
2. 'Andhere ki Kokh', in *Sharaha* (quarterly) (Delhi, 1950).
3. 'Yeh Khandar Mere Hain', in *Shahakar,* op.cit.
4. 'Aane Wala Kal', in *Afsana* (monthly) (Allahabad, 1949).
5. 'Ek Naya Mehman', in ibid.
6. 'Ek Dari Hui Ladki', in *Tameer-e-Haryana* (Chandigarh, 1978).
7. It is a literary technique for recording the flow of thoughts, feelings and impressions of a character without regard to either their logical association in terms of chronology or narrative sequence. The writer tries to reflect all the forces affecting the psychology of a character at a single moment. Introduced by the French writer, Edouard Dujardin, *We'll to the Woods No More* (1888), the term 'stream of consciousness' was used by William James in *Principles of Psychology* (1890). Among the famous novelists, who used this technique are Henri Bergson, Marcel Proust, Virginia Woolf and William Faulkner.

Khushwant Singh's Train to Pakistan

SHIKOH MOHSIN MIRZA

There are different and even contradictory versions of the political events that led to the Partition of India in 1947. Literature, on its part, has kept alive the memory of the horrendous human tragedy that unfolded in its wake. Partition was indeed a momentous event and has acquired the status of a watershed in the history of modern India. Whatever historical circumstances precipitated the creation of the two nations and the division of the land and people, political exigencies and public posturing did play a significant role in bringing it about. There were conflicts and vested interests entirely associated with power and authority. In order to have their own power bases, many self-seeking politicians and pressure groups launched upon a concerted Machiavellian exploitation and manipulation of the differences between the two communities. In the end, indescribable grief and misery were inflicted upon the people, and against their own will and aspirations, many of them were swept away in the political turmoil of the period. The brutal and gruesome violence that spread to many parts of India and Pakistan in 1947 benumbed all sensitive minds. Saner voices went unheeded, for everyone was caught up in the frenzy of the times. The manner in which humanity was trampled underfoot and dark and evil forces took control, still defies logical explanation. The nightmare of that tumultous phase in our history still haunts the nation's consciousness and both history and literature have worked together to come to terms with it.

The literature of the time highlights the madness that led to the killing, rape and arson. It did try to mute the voices of revenge and recrimination. Since 1947 we have witnessed the growth of Partition literature recreating the trauma suffered by people collectively, as well as individually. It carries out both introspection and attempts to expurgate the effects of the bewildering experience. Such literature also plays the role of sharing the

*Based on Khushwant Singh, *Train to Pakistan* (New Delhi, 1956). All references to the text are indicated by the page number within parenthesis.

collective guilt with succeeding generations and keeping its memory intact, both as a warning for the future and as an act of expiation. Partition literature has consequently earned a niche for itself in Indian literature produced since independence.

Khushwant Singh's novel, *Train to Pakistan* occupies an important place among the novels on Partition. It describes life in a small village, Mano Majra, situated on the borders of India. The village is gradually transformed into a cauldron of conflicting loyalties as divisive forces get the upper hand. The novel picks up the strands of life in Mano Majra from one night in August 1947, and presents events as they unravel in the weeks following. Only a few important characters are depicted, but these suffice to present a vivid picture of village life. Among these are: Juggut Singh, the hardened criminal,with a police record; Imam Baksh, the muezzin of the mosque; his daughter, Nooran, carrying on a liaison with Juggut Singh; Bhai Meet Singh, the Sikh priest; and Banta Singh, the revenue collector and *lambardar*. Two outsiders enter the closed world of Mano Majra, the first Hukum Chand, is the magistrate and district commissioner, and the second, Iqbal, is sent by his party to the village to spread Communist ideology and to bring about a proletarian revolution.

The villagers carry on with their life as usual in spite of the news about widespread violence, looting and rape, from across the border, trickling in. In this village Hindus, Sikhs and Muslims have lived in mutual tolerance and respect for centuries. The author describes a typical morning in Mano Majra as follows:

> Before daybreak, the mail train rushes through on its way to Lahore, and as it approaches the bridge, the driver invariably blows two long blasts of the whistle. In an instant, all Mano Majra comes awake. . . . The mullah at the mosque knows that it is time for the morning prayer. He has a quick wash, stands facing west towards Mecca and with his fingers in his ears cries in long sonorous notes, 'Allah-ho-Akbar'. The priest at the Sikh temple lies in bed till the mullah has called. Then he too gets up, draws a bucket of water from the well in the temple courtyard, pours it over himself, and intones his prayer in monotonous singsong to the sound of splashing water. (pp. 12-13)

Even though the Muslims in the village were tenants of landowning Sikhs, they enjoyed equal status and got due respect. The peace of the village was disturbed by an occasional crime, like the dacoity on the property of Ram Lal, the Hindu moneylender and his murder. This happened on the night the novel opens. Hukum Chand is then sent to the village to prevent the outbreak of communal violence in the village.

With the arrival of a 'ghost train' from Pakistan at the village station, carrying the bodies of dead Sikhs the whole life of the villagers changes. They are, at first, unaware of this event but suspect foul play from the flurry of furtive activity at the station. A meeting is called. Imam Baksh, as is usual, takes the lead and his opinion is, as always, respected. The meeting is interrupted by the appearance of a policeman, who instructs the villagers to provide wood and oil. Later on, when 'a faint acrid smell of searing flesh' fills the air, the deepest fears of the villagers are confirmed. And then subsequently:

> The village was stilled in a deathly silence. No one asked anyone else what the odour was. They all knew. They had known it all the time. The answer was implicit in the fact that the train had come from Pakistan. (p. 100)

The process of transformation began the same day and the long-standing tradition of brotherhood among the different communities was broken: 'That evening, for the first time in the memory of Mano Majra Imam Baksh's sonorous cry did not rise to the heavens to proclaim the glory of God' (pp. 100-1).

Suspicion and fear soon spread their stranglehold. The sub-inspector, at the behest of the district commissioner, spread the rumour that the murder of the moneylender, Ram Lal, had been committed by the dacoit Sultana and that Iqbal was a member of the Muslim League, sent to create mischief. The commissioner's purpose was to provoke enough resentment among the Sikhs towards their Muslim tenants to create communal animosities, which would facilitate him to evacuate the Muslims before any trouble broke out. He was successful and divisions among the villagers were now formed on an entirely religious basis:

> The head constable's visit had divided Mano Majra into two halves as neatly as a knife cuts through a pat of butter.
>
> Muslims sat and moped in their houses. Rumours of atrocities committed by Sikhs on Muslims in Patiala, Ambala and Kapurthala, which they had heard and dismissed, came back to their mind.... Quite suddenly every Sikh in Mano Majra became a stranger with an evil intent.
>
> The Sikhs were sullen and angry. 'Never trust a Mussulman', they said. The last Guru had warned them that Muslims had no loyalties. He was right. (p. 41)

Not that the villagers were not conscious of the 'other'. Juggut's liaison with the Muslim girl Nooran was viewed with envy because she brought with her the added pleasure of the forbidden:

He [Juggut] turned to the driver again.

'Bholeya, I hear a lot of women are being abducted and sold cheap. You could find a wife for yourself.'

'Why, Sardara, if you can find a Mussulmanki without paying for her, am I impotent that I should have to buy an abducted woman?' replied Bhola. (p. 85)

Despite the religious differences the people of Mano Majra accepted each other as individuals. And at moments of distress, unmindful of their religious beliefs, they went to a common deity:

But there is one object that all Mano Majrans—even Lala Ram Lal—venerate. This is a three-foot slab of sandstone that stands upright under a *keekar* tree beside the pond. It is the local deity, the *deo* to which all the villagers—Hindu, Sikh, Muslim or pseudo-Christian repair secretly whenever they are in special need of blessing. (pp. 10-11)

With the arrival of the second 'ghost train' from Pakistan, the rupture between Sikhs and Muslims begins. Another meeting is called—this time with no Muslim participants. There was suppressed anger against what had been done and Muslims are suddenly perceived as traitors and plunderers and are considered a menace. An impulsive Sikh youth, flares up and, instinctively, tries to divert attention towards the Muslims in Mano Majra:

Our problem is: what are we to do with all these pigs we have with us? They have been eating our salt for generations and see what they have done! We have treated them like our own brothers. They have behaved like snakes.

The temperature of the meeting, on hearing this, went up suddenly and Meet Singh interrupted angrily:

'What have they done to you? Have they ousted you from your lands or occupied your houses? Have they seduced your womenfolk? Tell me, what have they done.'

'Ask the refugees what they have done to them', answered the truculent youth who had started the argument, 'You mean to tell us they are lying when they say that gurudwaras have been burned and people massacred.'

'I was only talking of Mano Majra. What have our tenants done?'

'They are Muslims.' (p. 14)

The scene is an enactment of what must have happened innumerable times in the small villages and towns scattered all over India. The Sikhs of Mano Majra suddenly discover an ambiguity and an ambivalence in their feelings and relationships with the Muslims. The same Sikh youth who had earlier referred to the Muslims as pigs is willing to defend the

Muslims of Mano Majra shortly afterwards: 'We would like to see somebody raise his little finger against our tenants while we live' (p. 145). But anger is soon replaced with hatred and the whole community is immediately vilified and thus in their perception transformed into vile objects. The scene is terrifying, the branded Muslims hardly knowing that they had fallen prey to the foulest instincts of their fellow villagers. But there is no unanimity and this is obvious when the youth who cries for blood and calls the Muslims pigs, is put down with a heavy hand. Yet the harm had been done. The violence implicit in the act of stereotyping the 'other' asserts itself, enabling the villagers from Mano Majra to volunteer for the planned attack, on the train leaving for Pakistan, without any feeling of guilt.

The Sikhs could not muster hatred or anger against the Muslims in their village for they could not find anything offensive in them, as individuals. They, however, ostensibly voiced their concern, that incoming refugees might 'wreak vengeance' on Muslim tenants. They spoke thus:

> The peasants thought about their problem. They could not refuse shelter to refugees; hospitality was not a passtime but a sacred duty when those who sought it were homeless. Could they ask their Muslims to go? Quite emphatically not. Loyalty to a fellow villager was above all other considerations. Despite the words they had used, no one had the nerve to suggest throwing them out, even in a purely Sikh gathering.
>
> The mood of the assembly changed from anger to bewilderment. . . .
>
> 'Yes', added another, 'Kapoora and Gujjoo Matta were evacuated last week. Mano Majra is the only place left where there are Muslims. What I would like to know is how these people asked their fellow villagers to leave. We could never say anything like that to our tenants, any more than we could tell our sons to get out of our homes. Is there anyone here who could say to the Muslims, 'Brothers, you should go away from Mano Majra?' (pp. 145-6)

The villagers kept up appearances, but in their hearts they knew that the decision had already been made and that the evacuation of the Muslims, from their ancestral village, had by then become inevitable. This was evident from the fact that Imam Baksh and the Muslims, who used to voice their concern without fear and on equal terms, were missing, from the crucial congregation, for the first time. And when Imam Baksh and other Muslims finally went to the meeting, to know what had been decided about them, they did so as strangers and intruders. They were advised to leave for the sake of their own security and to return only after the trouble had blown over. No one believed that things would normalize again, but it helped in the self-deceit. Suddenly it was felt that forces and circumstances, not of the villagers' own making, nor under their control, had started dictating the course of life in Mano Majra:

> The lambardar felt a strong sense of guilt and was overcome with emotion. He got up and embraced Imam Baksh and started to cry loudly. Sikh and Muslim villagers fell into each other's arms and wept like children. Imam Baksh gently got out of the lambardar's embrace. 'There is no need to cry', he said between sobs. 'This is the way of the world.' (p. 149)

The Muslims have to leave the homes that their fathers and grandfathers had taken 'hundreds of years to make'. Meanwhile another trainload of corpses arrive in Mano Majra. In that hour of tension and sorrow the villagers are easily incited by a Sikh youth to retaliate. They decide to attack the train leaving for Pakistan the next day. The district commissioner releases Juggut Singh, hoping that he might try to prevent the attack on the train, since it would also be carrying his beloved, Nooran. This is exactly what Juggut does. He cuts the rope which was stretched across the bridge to stop the train, exactly as the train was crossing over the bridge. He himself is shot, while the train passes over, without any mishap.

The *Train to Pakistan* vividly portrays the trauma of a nation and the dilemma faced by its people, individually and collectively. Invariably the destiny of individuals, everywhere, is shaped by political decisions, taken at the higher levels. Despite the sincere desire of the villagers of Mano Majra to shelter the small population of Muslims amongst them, they are compelled to expel them because of the external circumstantial factors, in this case, the rumours and the bloodshed all around.

The dark evils lurked as much within, as without, the characters of the novel. In the distressing and compelling scene, referred to earlier, a Sikh teenager succeeds in whipping up passions in the hearts of the peace loving villagers of Mano Majra. The scene described below is also ominous due to the kind of arguments and rhetoric employed to demonize the 'other' community. In it Bhai Meet Singh resists the arguments put forward by the belligerent group, but the youth's calculated replies finally succeed in manipulating the people's emotions and loyalties:

> 'I was going to say', said Meet Singh haltingly, 'I was going to say', he repeated, 'What have the Muslims done to us for us to kill them in revenge for what Muslims in Pakistan are doing? Only people who have committed crimes should be punished.'
>
> The lad glared angrily at Meet Singh. 'What had the Sikhs and Hindus in Pakistan done that they were butchered? Weren't they innocent?'

'Yes', answered Meet Singh meekly, 'but nobody is asking you to befriend them. Besides, the Guru himself had Muslims in his army.'

'And one of them stabbed him while he slept.'

Meet Singh felt uneasy. 'Yes . . . but there are bad ones and . . .'.

'Show me a good one.' (pp. 171-2)

The *Train to Pakistan,* like the best of Partition literature, explores both humanity under duress, as well as the moral probity and courage of the individual. The book encourages introspection and is very relevant even today. It does not end on a pessimistic or a bleak note. The Sikh youth, who provoked the villagers, has also to present arguments, however specious, to appease his own rational and saner self and that of those present in the gurudwara. The attackers pray in order to calm their conscience. Later, Juggut Singh visits the gurudwara to pray for the first time in his life. And when he asks the meaning of the words recited by the priest on his behalf, Bhai Meet Singh tells him: 'It is just the Guru's word. If you are going to do something good, the Guru will help you; if you are going to do something bad, the Guru will stand in your way.' (p. 199)

Juggut Singh succeeds in his mission, and the train crosses over safely into Pakistan, thus negating the passionate arguments of the frenzied youth. The novel explores and lays bare the mysterious wellsprings of courage, endurance and affection, from which human beings draw inspiration at moments of distress to rebuild their lives and to sustain faith in themselves. The *Train to Pakistan* remains, like all Partition literature, more a warning for the future, than a reminder of the past.

Contributors

KRISHNA KUMAR is a Professor of Education, University of Delhi, and currently a Jawaharlal Nehru Fellow.

R.K. AGNIHOTRI is a Professor of Linguistics, University of Delhi.

SATISH GUJRAL is a painter, muralist, sculptor and architect.

PARTHA CHATTERJEE is a film maker and a film critic.

BADRI NARAIN TIWARI is a Fellow, Indian Institute of Advanced Studies, Shimla.

KESHAV MALIK is a poet and an art critic.

ALOK BHALLA is a Professor of English, Central Institute of English and Foreign Languages, Hyderabad.

MRINAL PANDE is currently Senior Editorial Advisor, Hindi News, New Delhi TV.

URVASHI BUTALIA teaches Book Publishing, College of Vocational Studies, University of Delhi, and is also associated with Kali for Women.

MONMAYEE BASU teaches history, Hans Raj College, University of Delhi.

K.S. DUGGAL is a poet, novelist and a Member of Parliament (Rajya Sabha).

MUSHIRUL HASAN is a Professor of History, Jamia Millia Islamia, New Delhi.

NANDI BHATIA teaches English, University of Western Ontario, Canada.

ANINDITA MUKHOPADHYAY is an Associate Fellow, Centre for the Study of Developing Societies, Delhi.

SUKRITA PAUL KUMAR teaches English, Zakir Husain College, University of Delhi.

TAPATI CHAKRAVARTY teaches Bengali, Department of Modern Indian Languages, Deshbandhu College, University of Delhi.

NARESH JAIN taught English, School of Correspondence Courses, University of Delhi.

AMEENA K. ANSARI teaches English, Department of English and Modern European Languages, Jamia Millia Islamia, New Delhi.

JAYANTI CHATTOPADHYAY is a Professor of Bengali, Department of Modern Indian Languages and Literary Studies, University of Delhi.

M. ASADUDDIN teaches English, Department of English and Modern European Languages, Jamia Millia Islamia, New Delhi.

KAMLESH MOHAN teaches history, Panjab University, Chandigarh.

SHIKOH MOHSIN MIRZA teaches English, Department of English and Modern European Languages, Jamia Millia Islamia, New Delhi.

Index